Creating
Der Rosenkavalier

Creating
Der Rosenkavalier

From Chevalier to Cavalier

Michael Reynolds

THE BOYDELL PRESS

© Michael Reynolds 2016

All Rights Reserved. Except as permitted under current legislation no part of this work may be photocopied, stored in a retrieval system, published, performed in public, adapted, broadcast, transmitted, recorded or reproduced in any form or by any means, without the prior permission of the copyright owner

The right of Michael Reynolds to be identified as the author of this work has been asserted in accordance with sections 77 and 78 of the Copyright, Designs and Patents Act 1988

First published 2016
The Boydell Press, Woodbridge
Paperback edition 2023

ISBN 978 1 78327 049 1 hardback
ISBN 978 1 83765 114 6 paperback

The Boydell Press is an imprint of Boydell & Brewer Ltd
PO Box 9, Woodbridge, Suffolk IP12 3DF, UK
and of Boydell & Brewer Inc.
668 Mt Hope Avenue, Rochester, NY 14620–2731, USA
website: www.boydellandbrewer.com

The publisher has no responsibility for the continued existence or accuracy of URLs for external or third-party internet websites referred to in this book, and does not guarantee that any content on such websites is, or will remain, accurate or appropriate.

A CIP catalogue record for this book is available from the British Library

Contents

List of illustrations vi
Preface x
Acknowledgements xiii
Abbreviations xv

Overture
1

Beginners
On the page ... 7
... and onto the stage 13

Act One
The Young Libertine
21

Act Two
Who Was Harry Kessler?
73

Act Three
in two scenes and an Epilogue
Scene One – devising the scenario
113
Scene Two – characterisation and authorship
154

Epilogue
Two views of the authorship of *Der Rosenkavalier*
195

Creating *Der Rosenkavalier* – A Retrospective
209

Bibliography 217
Index 228

Illustrations

Very grateful thanks are due to those who have assisted with illustrations for this book, especially Christophe Mirambeau, Françoise Feltz, Corinne Jahier, Loïc Métrope, Count Stefan Finck von Finckenstein, Felix Brusberg, Roland Kamzelak, Jürgen May, Sabine Walter, Andreas Wehrheim, Tanja Fengler-Veit, Katja Kaluga, Heather Roberts, Ian Brooke, John Roberts, Julian Royle and Mike Hoban. Unless specified otherwise, private collection refers to works owned by the author.

Plates

Plates appear between pages 128 and 129

1. Harry Kessler painted by Edvard Munch in 1906 (BPK/Nationalgalerie, Staatliche Museen zu Berlin / Jörg P. Anders)
2. Jane Alba as Faublas (Le Théâtre no. 218, January [II] 1908, p. 22: private collection)
3. Costume design for Octavian by Alfred Roller (Private collection)
4. Claude Terrasse and two of his sons, painted by Pierre Bonnard (RMN-Grand palais [musée d'Orsay] / Hervé Lewandowski)
5. L'après-midi bourgeoise, painted by Pierre Bonnard (RMN-Grand Palais [musée d'Orsay] / Hervé Lewandowski)
6. Jeanne Petit as Sophie (Le Théâtre no. 218, January (II) 1908, p. 2: private collection)
7. Arlette Dorgère as the Marquise de Bay (Le Théâtre no. 218, January [II] 1908, cover: private collection)
8. The Hotel Cecil on the Strand, London (Private collection)
9. Gerhart Hauptmann, painted by Emil Orlik (Private collection: Count Stefan Finck von Finckenstein)
10. Harry Kessler painted by Edvard Munch in 1904 (…
11. Design for the Marschallin's bedroom by Alfred Roller (Private collection)
12. Costume design for Baron Ochs by Alfred Roller (Private collection)
13. Costume design for Sophie by Alfred Roller (Private collection)
14. *Marriage à la mode* plate 4 (the Countess's levée) painted by William Hogarth (Getty Images)
15. Nearing the final trio: *Der Rosenkavalier* at the Royal Opera House, Covent Garden in 2009 (Mike Hoban / The Hoban Gravett Archive)

Illustrations vii

Figures

1. Count Harry Kessler in 1909 (Deutsches Literatur Archiv, Marbach – photo by Hugo Erfurth) — xi
2. Richard Strauss conducting in 1910 (Richard-Strauss-Institut Garmisch-Partenkirchen) — 2
3. *Mise en scène* for *L'Ingénu libertin* (Christophe Mirambeau: private collection) — 5
4. Jean-Baptiste Louvet de Couvray (*Les Amours de Faublas*, Paris: Jouaust, 1884: private collection) — 6
5. Sophie de Pontis (*Les Amours de Faublas*, Paris: Jouaust, 1884: private collection) — 9
6. Faublas dressed as a girl (*Les Amours de Faublas*, Paris: Jouaust, 1884: private collection) — 10
7. The Marquis de B***, the Marquise de B***and Faublas (*Les Amours de Faublas*, Paris: Jouaust, 1884: private collection) — 11
8. *Faublas* in 1833 (Société de l'Histoire du Théâtre: private collection) — 15
9. The Marquise de B*** and Rosambert (*Les Amours de Faublas*, Paris: Jouaust, 1884: private collection) — 16
10. Milo de Meyer in Feydeau, 1907 (Le Théâtre no. 200, April (II) 1907, p.11: private collection) — 22
11. Théâtre des Bouffes Parisiens in 1878 (Les Théâtres de Paris, Paris: Deviers, 1878: private collection) — 24
12. Extract from *Le Figaro*, 14 December 1907 (Private collection) — 26
13. Claude Terrasse in 1903 (Le Théâtre no. 106, May (II) 1903, p. 18: private collection) — 28
14. The Terrasse family at home (Mme Françoise Feltz: private collection) — 32
15. The figure of Ubu in *Ubu roi* (Private collection) — 34
16. Claude Terrasse, Robert de Flers and Gaston de Caillavet, 1903 (Le Théâtre no. 106, May (II) 1903, p. 18: private collection) — 35
17. Act 1 of *Les Travaux d'Hercule*, 1901 (Le Théâtre no. 56, April (II) 1901, p. 21: private collection) — 36
18. Louis Artus in 1907 (Le Théâtre no. 213, November (I) 1907, p. 16: private collection) — 39
19. Programme book for *L'Ingénu libertin*, 10 December 1907 (Private collection) — 40
20. Programme for dress rehearsal of *L'Ingénu libertin*, 10 December 1907 (Private collection) — 40
21. Faublas in high society company (*Les Amours de Faublas*, Paris: Jouaust, 1884: private collection) — 43
22. Act 1 of *L'Ingénu libertin* (Le Théâtre no. 218, January (II) 1908, p. 18: private collection) — 46
23. Act 3 of *L'Ingénu libertin* (Le Théâtre no. 218, January (II) 1908, p. 1: private collection) — 48

24 Pierre-Antoine Baudouin, *Le Coucher de la mariée* (RMN-Grand Palais (musée du Louvre)/Michel Urtado)   48
25 Front cover of *Comoedia,* 12 December 1907 (Private collection)   51
26 Portrait of Arlette Dorgère by Jane de Montchenu-Lavirotte (Private collection)   53
27 Claude Terrasse and production team onstage after the dress rehearsal (Françoise Feltz: private collection)   56
28 Interior of the Bouffes Parisiens, 1876 (Corinne Jahier, Théâtre des Bouffes Parisiens: private collection)   59
29 Interior of the Bouffes Parisiens, 1871–2 (Corinne Jahier, Théâtre des Bouffes Parisiens: private collection)   60
30 Manuscript orchestral score – overture to *L'Ingénu libertin* (Christophe Mirambeau: private collection)   61
31 The principals in Act 1 of *L'Ingénu libertin* (Le Théâtre no. 218, January (II) 1908, p. 16: private collection)   63
32 Act 2 of *L'Ingénu libertin* (Le Théâtre no. 218, January (II) 1908, p. 20: private collection)   64
33 Preparing for bed – finale to Act 2 of *L'Ingénu libertin* (Le Théâtre no. 218, January (II) 1908, p. 21: private collection)   66
34 Pierre-Antoine Baudouin, *Le Coucher de la mariée* (RMN-Grand Palais (musée du Louvre)/Michel Urtado)   67
35 Act 3 of *L'Ingénu libertin* (Le Théâtre no. 218, January (II) 1908, p. 1: private collection)   68
36 Alice Kessler's private theatre, 19 Boulevard Montmorency (Felix Brusberg: *La Vie Heureuse* no. 3, 1902: private collection)   76
37 Adolf and Alice Kessler with Countess Marie von Bismarck (Private collection: Count Stefan Finck von Finckenstein)   79
38 Alice, Countess Kessler at home in Paris (Private collection: Count Stefan Finck von Finckenstein)   82
39 Portrait photo of Alice Kessler (Private collection: Count Stefan Finck von Finckenstein)   84
40 Portrait photo of Alice Kessler (Private collection: Count Stefan Finck von Finckenstein)   84
41 Alice Kessler as *La Dame aux Camélias* (Felix Brusberg: *La Vie Heureuse* no. 3, 1902: private collection)   86
42 The young Harry Kessler (Deutsches Literatur Archiv, Marbach)   90
43 Hugo von Hofmannsthal in 1904 (Freies Deutsches Hochstift / Frankfurter Goethe Museum)   107
44 Costume design for Octavian by Alfred Roller (Private collection)   112
45 Richard Strauss in 1907 (Richard-Strauss-Institut Garmisch-Partenkirchen)   120
46 Hugo von Hofmannsthal at the turn of the century (Freies Deutsches Hochstift / Frankfurter Goethe Museum)   122

Illustrations   ix

47 Hugo von Hofmannsthal in 1901 (Freies Deutsches Hochstift / Frankfurter Goethe Museum)   134
48 Harry Kessler with Fip (Deutsches Literatur Archiv, Marbach)   134
49 Manuscript of Kessler's diary for 10 February 1909 (Deutsches Literatur Archiv, Marbach)   143
50 Richard Strauss in 1910 (Richard-Strauss-Institut Garmisch-Partenkirchen)   155
51 Stage layout for *L'Ingénu libertin* and *Der Rosenkavalier* compared (Private collection)   160
52 Ella Shields at the London Palladium in 1910 (Getty Images)   171
53 Elizabeth Harwood as the Marschallin, Glyndebourne 1980 and 1982 (Guy Gravett / The Hoban Gravett Archive)   173
54 Hugo von Hofmannsthal at work in Rodaun (Freies Deutsches Hochstift / Frankfurter Goethe Museum)   175
55 *Der Rosenkavalier* in 1911 – Act Three trio (Lebrecht Collection)   187
56 *Der Rosenkavalier* in 1982 – Act Three trio (Guy Gravett / The Hoban Gravett Archive)   187
57 *Der Rosenkavalier* in 1971 – Act Three trio (Eric Thorburn – Scottish Opera)   192
58 *Der Rosenkavalier* in 1971 – Act Two triangle of a different sort (Eric Thorburn – Scottish Opera)   192
59 Harry Kessler in later life (Deutsches Literatur Archiv, Marbach)   206
60 Richard Strauss in his garden at Garmisch-Partenkirchen in 1910 (Richard-Strauss-Institut Garmisch-Partenkirchen)   209
61 Richard Strauss in 1911, after the premiere of *Der Rosenkavalier* (Richard-Strauss-Institut Garmisch-Partenkirchen)   209
62 The villa in Garmisch-Partenkirchen, where Strauss wrote *Der Rosenkavalier* (Richard-Strauss-Institut Garmisch-Partenkirchen)   210
63 Front cover of Edward Gordon Craig's copy of *The Rose-Bearer* (Craig papers at the BNF: private collection)]   215

Preface

This is a book about creation, authorship and relationships. It is not an analysis of the printed elements and artefacts – words, music, scenic instructions and stage directions – that attach to Strauss's best-loved opera, *Der Rosenkavalier*. Such analyses have been done many times before, and are easily available. Rather, it is an exploration of how the onstage characters who people the opera came to be devised, placed onstage alongside each other, and given theatrical life for the musical portrayal that Strauss was to give them. It considers their performative characteristics and tells their story. It reaches some surprising, original conclusions.

Imagine going to a performance of *Der Rosenkavalier* and finding that there is no orchestra, no conductor, no singers. An announcement is made that the text of the libretto will be spoken, the play will be acted. This is something that Hugo von Hofmannsthal dreamed of in his lifetime. He thought that his libretto was that good, and the reaction that he got (in private homes among friends) when he read aloud his text encouraged him to think that *Der Rosenkavalier* could be made to stand alone, as a play. There were also passages in that play where – in Hofmannsthal's view – the text was literally smothered, obliterated by Strauss's music. Few would agree that this is a valid reason for silencing some of the most beautiful, evocative passages of opera music that Strauss ever wrote, but it has to be borne in mind that *Der Rosenkavalier* is a music theatre construct, in which the elements of theatre and of music sometimes come together, sometimes drift apart. They can be analysed as a *Gesamtkunstwerk*, a total work of art, or as a collection of such elements. This book favours the latter approach.

Creating Der Rosenkavalier is thus a look behind the scenes of what countless operagoers – millions all over the world since the first Dresden performance on 26 January 1911 – have seen played out before them. It starts with the work that can be said to have inspired *Der Rosenkavalier*. It then looks at the man who saw that work, and relayed all its elements to Hugo von Hofmannsthal, who was desperately seeking inspiration for an original libretto that he could present to Strauss and work up as a fully-fledged, original music theatre collaboration. It examines the creative process that brought *Der Rosenkavalier* to fruition. It explores the context of that creative process, and the relationships between the three people who really matter in the *Rosenkavalier* story: Richard Strauss, Hugo von Hofmannsthal and Count Harry Kessler. Strauss and Hofmannsthal already have their places in the annals of opera history: this book makes the case that for *Der Rosenkavalier*, Kessler should have a *place d'honneur* beside them.

Of the three names, Kessler (1868–1937) will be the least well-known to English-language readers, especially in this context. We shall meet him in Act Two – or

1 Harry Kessler in 1909. At this stage of his life Kessler had known Hugo von Hofmannsthal for just over ten years, and was eager to embark on a major theatrical collaboration with him

rather, we shall meet some of him, for he is an extraordinarily difficult subject to pin down: a man who was constantly on the move, constantly changing focus, flitting whether in Berlin, Paris or London from high politics over breakfast to fine art books at lunch to theatre or opera in the evening and louche night clubs in the small hours. He was 'the man who knew everybody' or, in W.H. Auden's words, 'the most cosmopolitan man who ever lived'. In 1895 he had inherited a huge fortune from his father. He had a house in Weimar, a flat in Berlin and permanent suites at the Grand Hotel in Paris and the Hotel Cecil (then Europe's largest hotel) on the Strand in London. He was a major collector of the Impressionists and Modernists, of Rodin, Seurat, Bonnard as well as Renoir, Manet and Monet. He was a friend and sponsor of Edvard Munch (who painted the most famous portrait of Kessler), of Aristide Maillol and of Henri van de Velde, who designed the interiors of his flat in Berlin and of his house in Weimar. Kessler, at that time Director of the Museum of Arts and Crafts in Weimar, brought van de Velde to join him, and the work both men did there together led seamlessly into the Bauhaus movement.

If Kessler was known in England at all as a collaborator of Richard Strauss, it was solely because of his 1914 ballet *The Legend of Joseph*, brought from Paris to the Theatre Royal, Drury Lane by Diaghilev's Ballets Russes in June and July of that year. The crowds who came to the première were emblematic of the unified European High Society in which Kessler operated – leading society hostesses such as Lady Cunard, Lady Ripon and the Duchess of Sutherland, unconditional fans of the Ballets Russes and their daring new repertoire, and other artistic figures as diverse as George Bernard Shaw, Sir Thomas Beecham, Siegfried Sassoon and Osbert Sitwell, all of whom wrote about their respective evenings at this particular ballet in later years.[1] But although it was a major event in the London season, and played to packed houses, *Joseph* was neither daringly new nor a critical success, and within weeks of its London performances, Europe was at war. Kessler, a reserve officer, went on immediately to see active service with his cavalry regiment in the Great War and rode into Belgium – in a bizarre coincidence encountering the Duchess of Sutherland at her field hospital in Namur on 26 August 1914.[2] The overall experience of war went on to change his fundamental outlook on life, turning him into a pacifist and a passionate, Weimar Republic democrat. But all that lies well after the period that Creating *Der Rosenkavalier* seeks to cover, and we have to wind right back. For the heart of this story lies between 1908 and 1910, the creative process that concerns us here starting even before Richard Strauss was to write a single note of music. Creating *Der Rosenkavalier* is all about the factors that inspired him to do so.

---

[1] Josh Levithan has made some interesting connections here, published on the website themillions.com.

[2] Kessler notes the encounter in *Diary V* and the Duchess in her memoir *Six Weeks at the War*: on 19 July 1914, only five weeks previously, they had dined together at Lady Ripon's and discussed ballet and art: Millicent Duchess of Sutherland, *Six Weeks at the War* (Chicago: A.C. McClurg, 1915), p. 42.

Acknowledgements

This book derives from my 2014 Ph.D. thesis, 'The Theatrical Vision of Count Harry Kessler and its Impact on the Strauss–Hofmannsthal Partnership'. In a joint project with Rose Bruford College and Goldsmiths, University of London, I assessed the role played by Kessler both in the creation of *Der Rosenkavalier* and in the ballet *Josephs Legende*. For this book I have concentrated on *Der Rosenkavalier* and done further research, aiming to bring out the extraordinary story of a three-way partnership that has largely been ignored or forgotten in the annals of opera history.

For the Ph.D. I owe a huge debt of thanks to many people: notably to Professor Maria Shevtsova and to Professor John London, both of Goldsmiths, and above all to Dr Jane Schopf of Rose Bruford College, who gave me endless guidance, encouragement and wise counsel. My original interest in Kessler had been awoken in Berlin shortly after the fall of the Wall, over lunch in Borchardt (one of Kessler's favourite restaurants) with Hans-Jürgen Kaack: he has my eternal thanks.

Help and advice subsequently came from many quarters in Germany: from the German Literature Archive in Marbach, particularly Dr Roland Kamzelak; from the Freies Deutsches Hochstift in Frankfurt, especially Dr Joachim Seng and Dr Katja Kaluga; from the Richard Strauss Institute in Garmisch Partenkirchen, especially Dr Jürgen May and Dr Claudia Heine, and from Professor Dirk Hoffmann, now in the United States, who co-edited (with Dr Willi Schuh) the 1986 critical edition of *Der Rosenkavalier* and who took a benevolent, kindly interest in my researches into material that only surfaced long after his distinguished work in the field had been published.

My researches in Paris would not have been possible without the generous and unstinting help of Christophe Mirambeau, who found for me the libretto, *mise en scène* and full orchestral score of *L'Ingénu libertin*; and Professor Philippe Cathé, who shared with me his profound knowledge of Claude Terrasse and introduced me to some of his descendants, in particular Nicole Terrasse and Françoise Feltz, whose family photographs and papers were a treasure trove. Denis and Nicole Jeambar proved to be stimulating interlocutors and sleuths on the world of the Belle Epoque that Terrasse inhabited and Loïc Métrope deployed forensic skills to unearth Kessler family documents in various Paris archives. In addition to the Bibliothèque Nationale de France (Richelieu), the Paris libraries that yielded most original material were the Bibliothèque Historique de la Ville de Paris, the library of the Paris Opéra and the Société de l'Histoire du Théâtre. To those who kindly helped me in all these establishments (and there were many), warm thanks. I must also thank Major Henry Blosse Lynch and his son James, who helped me considerably with the genealogy and history of his distinguished family, researches into Alice Blosse Lynch (Kessler's mother) proving to be fascinating and rewarding.

Discussions with established Strauss scholars proved interesting and enlightening: the late Michael Kennedy shared his expertise and enthusiasm, and was a wonderful, generous sounding board for new ideas. I owe him more than I can express. Dr Joseph Jones and Dr Matthew Werley both gave me encouragement and stimulating help along the way. My editor, Richard Barber, has been unfailingly positive, accommodating and extremely helpful. Thank you to all of them.

My wife Jessamy has been at my side for many productions of *Der Rosenkavalier* and at my side while this book has taken shape. I dedicate it to her in gratitude and endless love.

Abbreviations

Artus   Louis Artus, *L'Ingénu libertin* (Paris: Librairie Théâtrale, 1908)
Bablet   Denis Bablet, *The Theatre of Edward Gordon Craig*, trans. Daphne Woodward (London: Eyre Methuen, 1966)
Barthes   Roland Barthes, 'Death of The Author' (1968), in *Image – Music – Text*, essays selected and trans. Stephen Heath (London: Fontana Press, 1977), pp. 142–8
Barzantny   Tamara Barzantny, *Harry Graf Kessler und das Theater* (Köln: Böhlau Verlag, 2002)
Bate   Jonathan Bate, *The Genius of Shakespeare* (London: Picador, 1997)
Bruyas   Florian Bruyas, *Histoire de l'Opérette en France* (Lyon: Emmanuel Vitte, 1974)
Burger   Hugo von Hofmannsthal, Harry Graf Kessler, *Briefwechsel*, ed. Hilde Burger (Frankfurt: Insel, 1968)
Cat. 43   *Harry Graf Kessler, Tagebuch eines Weltmannes*, ed. Gerhard Schuster & Margot Pehle (Marbach: Marbacher Kataloge 43, 1988)
Cathé   Philippe Cathé, *Claude Terrasse* (Paris: L'Hexaèdre, 2004)
Chronik   Franz Trenner, *Richard Strauss Chronik zu Leben und Werk* (Vienna: R. Strauss Verlag, 2003)
CW (I, II, III) Harry Graf Kessler, *Gesammelte Schriften*, ed. Cornelia Blasberg & Gerhard Schuster (3 vols, Frankfurt: Fischer, 1988)
Diary (I, II, III etc.) Harry Graf Kessler, *Das Tagebuch 1880–1937*, ed. various (9 vols, Stuttgart: Cotta, 2004–)
Duteutre   Benoît Duteutre, *L'Opérette en France* (Paris: Editions du Seuil, 1997)
Easton   Laird Easton, *The Red Count* (Berkeley: University of California Press, 2002)
Fassungen   *Der Rosenkavalier, Fassungen, Filmszenarium, Briefe*, ed. Willi Schuh (Frankfurt: S. Fischer Verlag, 1971)
Fell   Jill Fell, *Alfred Jarry* (London: Reaktion Books, 2010)
Gilliam   Bryan Gilliam, 'The Strauss–Hofmannsthal operas', in *The Cambridge Companion to Richard Strauss*, ed. Charles Youmans (Cambridge: Cambridge University Press, 2010)
Grupp   Peter Grupp, *Harry Graf Kessler 1868–1937: Eine Biographie* (München: C.H. Beck, 1995)

Hamm./Osers	*The Correspondence between Richard Strauss and Hugo von Hofmannsthal*, ed. and trans. Hanns Hammelman & Ewald Osers (London: Collins, 1961)
Jefferson	Alan Jefferson, *Richard Strauss: Der Rosenkavalier* (Cambridge: Cambridge University Press, 1985)
Journey	Laird M. Easton, *Journey to the Abyss. The Diaries of Count Harry Kessler, 1880–1918* (New York: Alfred A. Knopf, 2011)
Kennedy	Michael Kennedy, *Richard Strauss, Man, Musician, Enigma* (Cambridge: Cambridge University Press, 1999)
mise en scène	Louis Artus & Claude Terrasse, *L'Ingénu libertin ou La Marquise et le Marmiton – mise en scène* (Paris: Société d'Editions Musicales, 1907)
New Grove	*The New Grove Dictionary of Music and Musicians, Second Edition*, ed. Stanley Sadie (29 vols, Oxford: Oxford University Press, 2001)
Newman	*The Correspondence of Edward Gordon Craig and Count Harry Kessler*, ed. L.M. Newman (London: W.S. Maney and Son, 1995)
Pahlen	Kurt Pahlen, 'Zur Geschichte der Oper "Der Rosenkavalier"', in *Der Rosenkavalier, Textbuch, Einführung und Kommentar*, ed. Kurt Pahlen (Mainz–München: Piper-Schott, 1980)
Pourceaugnac	*Monsieur de Pourceaugnac*, in Molière, *Oeuvres Complètes* (Oxford: Oxford University Press, 1900), pp. 445–64
Rondel	Collection Rondel, Paris, Bibliothèque Nationale de France
Rothe	Friedrich Rothe, *Harry Graf Kessler* (München: Siedler Verlag, 2008)
Simon	*Eberhard von Bodenhausen und Harry Graf Kessler: Ein Briefwechsel 1894–1918*, ed. Hans-Ulrich Simon (Marbach am Neckar: Marbacher Schriften, 1978)
Stenzel	Burkhard Stenzel, *Harry Graf Kessler: Ein Leben Zwischen Kultur und Politik* (Köln: Böhlau, 1995)
Stoullig	Edmond Stoullig, *Les Annales du Théâtre et de la Musique 1907* (Paris: G. Charpentier, 1908)
Trivium	Willi Schuh, *Die Entstehung des Rosenkavalier* (Zurich: Atlantis Verlag, *Trivium*, Year IX, Vol. 2, 1951)
Une Année	Jean-Baptiste Louvet de Couvray, *Une Année de la Vie du Chevalier de Faublas* (London, Paris: Bureau de la Bonneterie, 1787)
Zum Geleit	Hugo von Hofmannsthal, Preface to *Der Rosenkavalier von Richard Strauss, Musik für Alle* Vol. 1, Nr. 246, ed. W. Hirschberg (Berlin: Ullstein, 1927)

Overture

For a young singing actress, it was a tense and exciting moment. The curtain was still down, the orchestral prelude was reaching its climax and onstage an elegant, elaborate bedroom scene was about to be revealed to a packed house. There had been prior warnings that its sensual nature, the portrayal of the aftermath of a passionate love scene between two women, might provoke controversy. But the Censor had approved the scene, both actresses felt secure in their roles, and were confident in the elegance and poetry of the lines they had been given and had so carefully rehearsed. They were ready to deliver star performances. As the house lights dimmed, the beautiful older woman assumed her position in the outsize ornamental bed, her head nestling against a soft white pillow, her exposed right wrist and hand hanging limply and in full view of the audience against the crumpled silk sheets. Her lover, a mezzo soprano playing the part of a 17 year old youth, composed herself in her unbuttoned white shirt and long underbreeches and took up a kneeling position beside the bed for her opening lines, as the curtain slowly rose. And as it did so, and spontaneous applause for the visually sumptuous décor died away, Jeanne Alba in the role of Faublas sang:

> Ah, how I love your hand
> Like a fragile budding flower
> Your delicate wrist, your rosy palm
> Your fingers with their scarlet nails…

For these words of love were not, as anyone who has ever seen the opera might immediately have surmised, from the opening scene of Act I of *Der Rosenkavalier*, but rather constituted the start of Act III of *L'Ingénu libertin*, a three-act opérette with a libretto by Louis Artus and music by Claude Terrasse. The date was 11 December 1907 and the location of this onstage action was the Théâtre des Bouffes Parisiens – Offenbach's former theatre – in rue Monsigny, Paris. The seductive and glamorous older woman still lying in bed was played by a darling of the French stage during the Belle Epoque, Arlette Dorgère, and both she and Alba were to be joined onstage later in the same act by a third actress, Jeanne Petit, for an all-female trio that was both the highlight and the dramatic resolution of the whole work. In that trio, Dorgère in the role of the Marquise de Bay was to recognise that her young Chevalier, Faublas, actually loved his childhood sweetheart Sophie, and so renounced any claims to the teenage lover, with whom she had just spent a night of passion. The dénouement was straightforward: two youngsters, reunited and looking forward to their wedding day, the older woman, abandoned and hurt but with elegance and dignity intact, blessing their union. Curtain.

From Chevalier to Cavalier – this book will chart a journey. It began on that Wednesday night in December 1907 and led just over three years later to an opera that has subsequently far surpassed *L'Ingénu libertin* in every theatrical and musical dimension, the ever-popular three-act comedy for music *Der Rosenkavalier*, with music by Richard Strauss and a libretto by Hugo von Hofmannsthal. Neither man ever saw *L'Ingénu libertin*, however. The man who did see it, and who became the conduit through which all the essential elements of *L'Ingénu libertin* were to pass, was someone who for many years received no more than an occasional mention in the Strauss–Hofmannsthal story and who, only latterly, has begun to be known as the 'third man' in the *Rosenkavalier* context: Count Harry Clément Ulrich Kessler. This book is really about him. It will explore, as the *Rosenkavalier* project developed, the intricacies of his relationship with Hofmannsthal, and of his separate relationships with Strauss and others, and will assess how the three men were able to assemble all the constituent characters, plot and stage elements to make a piece of music theatre that added considerably to Strauss's fortune

2 Richard Strauss in 1910,
during composition of *Der Rosenkavalier*

and made Hofmannsthal a very rich man. Kessler never made a penny from *Der Rosenkavalier* but since, at the time, he was one of the richest men in Europe, that was not in any way his concern. What became his concern later, as we shall see, was that his role in the creation of *Der Rosenkavalier* should receive appropriate acknowledgement. It has taken a century for this to happen.

Strauss was fascinated throughout his composing life by words and music and the interplay between them – indeed, his very last opera *Capriccio* (1942) is little more than an extended onstage conversation, set to exquisite music, about which is the more important, the music or the text. The composer Flamand and the poet Olivier vie for the attentions of Countess Madeleine, but in the final analysis she cannot decide between them. As an attempt to dramatise the dialectic of words versus music, *Capriccio* has its moments, but it lacks almost all of the ingredients that had endeared *Der Rosenkavalier*, from its very first performances, to audiences all over the world. What are these ingredients? Action, first of all, with vivid, empathetic characters; a clear and simple storyline; a fairytale, visually sumptuous theatrical setting and a narrative that gives satisfaction to audiences whenever it is rehearsed before them: two attractive young lovers outwit the less attractive older man and contrive for him to be sent packing so that they can be together. In other words, it is the dramatic structure and theatrical narrative of *Der Rosenkavalier* that makes it so satisfying and ensures that it works so well onstage. It has that extra third dimension – not merely Hofmannsthal's words and Strauss's music, but a theatrical construct and a cast of characters that engage the operagoer from its opening bars and give pleasure until its third act conclusion. The chapters that follow, in three separate Acts, will assess this in detail and examine how it all came about.

It might be argued that *Der Rosenkavalier* has already been explored so thoroughly and analysed so exhaustively in the hundred and four years (at the time of writing) since its first performance[1] that little new remains to be said. Yet this is not the case. Much has indeed been written, and what has been known for a long time, and assumed by some to have been in effect the creative process surrounding *Der Rosenkavalier*, is the correspondence between Hofmannsthal and Strauss. The two men met relatively infrequently (given their markedly different temperaments, this was probably no bad thing for their artistic collaboration) and so they corresponded. The very first book of letters between them was published in 1926,[2] just three years before Hofmannsthal's death, and the process of adding subsequently discovered letters, and including others thought at an earlier time to be overly personal or indiscreet has gone on ever since.[3] But the exchanges between

---

[1] Königliches Opernhaus, Dresden: 26 January 1911. The première, and subsequent run of performances, were hugely successful and before long *Rosenkavalier* trains, packed with opera fans, were running to Dresden from all over Germany.

[2] Richard Strauss, *Briefwechsel mit Hugo von Hofmannsthal*, ed. Dr Franz Strauss (Berlin: Paul Zsolnay Verlag, 1926).

[3] An expanded volume was published in 1952: this first appeared in English translation in 1961, and further augmented German editions followed in the 1970s and 1980s.

Strauss and Hofmannsthal only chronicle two sides of what was in fact a three-way process, and they omit, for reasons that will become apparent, a crucial aspect of the *Rosenkavalier* story. For it was Harry Kessler who introduced the Chevalier de Faublas to Hofmannsthal, and who helped him – creatively, and with extraordinary theatrical vision – to fashion the character into twentieth-century opera's most famous Cavalier, Octavian. This whole side of the story needs telling too.

The highlighting of *L'Ingénu libertin* as the proximate theatrical model for *Der Rosenkavalier* does not of course mean that there were no other literary, artistic and theatrical influences on the work: there were many, and they have been adduced and assessed countless times. Strauss wanted *Der Rosenkavalier* to be his 'Mozart opera', and the character of Cherubino in *Le Nozze di Figaro* has often been taken as a precursor of Octavian, just as the sadness of Countess Almaviva has its parallels with the wistfulness of the Marschallin. The visual narrative of *Der Rosenkavalier* seems inspired in part by the paintings of Hogarth, the circumstances of Baron Ochs by Molière's Monsieur de Pourceaugnac and his character by Shakespeare's Falstaff, and certain passages in the libretto by Alfred de Musset.[4] The difference between what I shall describe as all these traditional, accepted sources of inspiration for *Der Rosenkavalier* and the narrative that follows is simple: *L'Ingénu libertin*, unlike all the other works mentioned, completely disappeared from view after its one and only run of performances in 1907–8. So although it began to be mentioned in parentheses from 1968 onwards, when the correspondence between Hofmannsthal and Kessler was first published,[5] it has never been examined in detail until now. The story of discovery of first the libretto, then the *mise en scène* and finally the full orchestral score (in a dusty archive at the original printers in Milan) will emerge as this book unfolds. So too will the pivotal role of *L'Ingénu libertin* as the source work on which so much of *Der Rosenkavalier* depends.

There is one other crucial source work that guides and informs this whole story. Kessler's daily *Diary*[6] is an extraordinarily detailed chronicle of his life and times, but for many years it was both incomplete and inaccessible and – for the years covering the creation of *Der Rosenkavalier* – thought to have been lost. But what a diary it is! For fifty-seven years Kessler finished most of his days (days that often ran on into the small hours) by writing, with great fluency and extraordinary detail, an account of everything he had done that day – the people he had met, the places he had visited, the works of art he had seen, the social, cultural and political thoughts that had occurred to him. To the German reader, Kessler's *Diary* has all the qualities of the diaries written in English by Sir Harold Nicolson or by Sir

---

[4] Details of all these well-known attributions, and the authorities for them, will be specified later as they are examined alongside the newly discovered elements from *L'Ingénu libertin*.

[5] Hofmannsthal and Kessler wrote nearly 400 letters to each other between 1898 and 1929: the extracts that follow (as with all other German and French texts quoted in this book, unless stated otherwise) are my own translations.

[6] Nine volumes of the *Diary* are planned: eight have appeared so far, with different editors. A one-volume English edited translation of excerpts, by Kessler's English-language biographer Laird Easton, was published in 2011 (*Journey*).

3 The *mise en scène* instructions for *L'Ingénu libertin*, a detailed, prescriptive account of exactly how the opérette is to be performed on stage

Henry 'Chips' Channon, being just as gossipy, just as incisive, full of fascinating period detail and something more besides. There are gaps in Kessler's composite account of his life and times, but they are negligible when compared with the wealth of contemporary and acute observation that he managed to set down and include in what is now widely acknowledged as his written masterpiece. 'I think that you will write the memoirs of our time,' the poet and playwright Richard Dehmel once wrote to him.[7] So it was that Kessler sat down and wrote his account of everything that he had seen and heard on the night that he attended a performance of *L'Ingénu libertin*. So it is that we can now take this and insert it into the narrative of the creation of *Der Rosenkavalier*.

By way of overture, that is all that needs to be said right now. It is time to assemble the beginners.

---

[7] *Diary III*, p. 435.

4 Jean-Baptiste Louvet de Couvray (1760–97), French writer, politician and author of the *Faublas* sequence of novels. Reprinted countless times throughout the nineteenth century, the *Faublas* narrative was also adapted repeatedly for the Parisian stage

Beginners
On the page ...

In terms of its derivation from literature, the story of *Der Rosenkavalier* begins with an eighteenth-century French bookseller, Jean-Baptiste Louvet de Couvray. Born in Paris in 1760, he authored, in his mid-twenties, a wildly successful licentious novel, *Une Année de la Vie du Chevalier de Faublas* (1787), or *Une Année* for short.[1] This book chronicled the life and early amorous adventures of a young aristocrat – Faublas – let loose in Paris with instructions from his father to learn how to grow up, and have some fun, before embarking on the serious business of marriage. *Une Année*, which can aptly be described as a libertine, confessional and frankly erotic novel, enjoyed such popular success that Louvet promptly wrote two further volumes. *Six Semaines de la Vie du Chevalier de Faublas* was published in 1788, and the third and concluding volume, *Fin des Amours du Chevalier de Faublas*, appeared in 1790. This triptych of novels is sometimes referred to as *Les Amours du Chevalier de Faublas* and sometimes as *Les Aventures du Chevalier de Faublas*. Countless reprints and various editions – some with illustrations, some without – continued until Louvet's death in 1797, the book having meanwhile made him a rich man, and well into the nineteenth century. And the name *Faublas* became as famous in France, and as associated with a libertine lifestyle, as did the name *Fanny Hill* in English literature, the memoirs of a woman of pleasure proving as salaciously attractive to succeeding generations of English-language readers – mostly in privately printed editions – as the amorous and frequently comic escapades of Faublas were to prove to the French.

Libertine literature is specifically a French tradition, its origins customarily ascribed to a work of 1655, *L'Ecole des Filles*, published (and possibly also written) by Jean L'Ange and Michel Millot, who swiftly ran foul of the authorities when most of the original 300 copies of their book were seized. *L'Ecole des Filles* is a discussion about sex and sexual techniques between an older, experienced woman, Susanne, and a naïve young girl, Fanchon. Susanne's role in instructing Fanchon is on behalf of Robinet, who wishes to seduce her: once he has done so, a willing Fanchon and Susanne have a further explicit discussion (Second Dialogue) about sexual techniques and positions more generally. Initiation of a young girl

---

[1] This 1787 edition of the first volume is similar in format and pagination to the Garnier edition that was in Harry Kessler's library in Weimar, lent by Kessler to Hofmannsthal when they first began work on their joint music theatre project.

by an older woman into the mysteries of sex – in this case merely by talking about it – then became a recurring theme in works such as *Vénus dans le Cloître* (Abbé Du Prat, 1682) and *Thérèse philosophe* (Anon, 1748), to name but two of a rapidly established and fast-spreading canon.

The French authorities clearly had little success in attempting to suppress *L'Ecole des Filles*, because this was the volume which Samuel Pepys, in his diary entry for 13 January 1668, came across at his bookseller in London, describing it as 'the most bawdy, lewd book that I ever saw' and thus unsuitable as a work to be given as translation material for his wife! Pepys however returned to the bookseller on 9 February 1668 and bought a copy, arguing to himself that it 'could do no wrong once to read for information sake' – having done so, thoroughly, later that day, Pepys then burned the copy that he had bought, so that it should not be found among his possessions. Thus began – and spread – the tradition of the 'naughty French book' celebrated most recently in a sumptuous illustrated anthology entitled *The Libertine*, running from Beaumarchais and Choderlos de Laclos through Crébillon fils, Rousseau, the Marquis de Sade, Marivaux and Diderot: all exponents of libertine love in a genre of French literature that has become as typical of its homeland as the picaresque novel in England.[2]

The characters brought into the world by Louvet are many and various but only five, from the first sixty pages of *Une Année*, are relevant to the distant origins of *Der Rosenkavalier*. They should be introduced, briefly, at the outset, for it is on them that practically all else subsequently depends. Let us start with the young girl whose name was to remain unchanged throughout, from *Une Année* to *L'Ingénu libertin* and on into *Der Rosenkavalier* – Sophie.

The ingénue heroine from the very start of *Une Année* is Sophie, rising 15 at the outset of the work and a convent friend of Faublas's younger sister, Adelaide. Sophie is described as a young Venus, with pale, fine skin, large dark eyes and long black hair. She is slim, with an elegant figure, rosy lips and an air of innocence – *innocence ingénue*, as Louvet describes it. Faublas meets Sophie the very first time he goes to visit Adelaide in the convent, and experiences the *coup de foudre* moment: it is pure, innocent love at first sight. His first attempted (clumsy) compliment to Sophie, an instinctive attempt to embrace her at their parting, is prevented by her governess but produces the traces of a blush to her translucent white cheeks and a slight smile. Sophie is the first of our five beginners.

Faublas himself is rising 16 at the outset of *Une Année*, and since the work is written in first-person confessional style, descriptions of his person are sparing. But we learn that he is of slight build with an elegant figure, the lightest hint of facial hair covering his aristocratic, finely chiselled cheekbones. His soul is described as noble, and his heart as excellent: he also has a fine singing voice. He takes to Paris enthusiastically and he is keen to explore everything that the city has to offer – including its womenfolk. The key attribute of Faublas, however, is his androgynous

---

[2] *The Libertine – the Art of Love in Eighteenth-Century France*, ed. Michel Delon (New York, London: Abbeville Press, 2014).

5 Sophie embracing Faublas – drawn by Paul Avril and engraved by Louis Monzies for the 1884 Jouaust edition of *Les Amours du Chevalier Faublas*

quality: as soon as he dons women's clothing and has his hair and face made up, he passes in the company of other women as a stunningly beautiful young girl. It is dressed as a girl that Faublas first kisses Sophie, in her convent, full on the lips and the erotic charge is instantaneous – *it was the first kiss of love*, as the narrator describes it, inviting his readers to judge for themselves the pleasures that the young lovers thus tasted. It is also dressed as a girl that Faublas enters the company of, and embarks on his erotic affairs with, a succession of aristocratic ladies, who allow him into their beds before 'discovering' the delightful truth – that the charming, adorable young lady whom they have been cosseting is in fact a virile male adolescent eager to be initiated in the arts of lovemaking. Faublas is the second of our beginners, and is finally transformed into Octavian in *Der Rosenkavalier*.

The third beginner is the slightly older, aristocratic lady: for reasons of discretion (and to pique the prurient curiosity of the reader) called the Marquise de B*** by Louvet de Couvray. The Marquise is not merely beautiful and elegant: she is

6 Faublas being dressed – and undressed – as a lady, a constant theme of the *Faublas* narrative (Avril/Monzies). The screen, table and ornamental bed all found their way into *L'Ingénu libertin* and, from there, into *Der Rosenkavalier*

very beautiful and supremely elegant. Heads turn as she passes. Louvet gives us her age – 25 – and characterises her as quick-witted, high-spirited and in control of the situations in which she finds herself. She is the first of Faublas's many bedroom conquests and his teacher in the arts of love: in bed together for the first time, she scolds him like a child (*you little libertine!*) and he pleads for forgiveness from his *dear mamma*. She does indeed forgive him – remarkably quickly – and he receives from her, *with as much astonishment as pleasure, a charming lesson that I went on to repeat more than once*. In other words, she seduces and initiates Faublas, rather than he seducing her, and Louvet makes it clear that she has recognised the adolescent boy cross-dressed in feminine attire long before they find themselves alone, together, in her bedroom. So her indignation at his female impersonation is both feigned and short-lived, and having instructed Faublas in the techniques of lovemaking, she embarks on her affair with him. The Marquise eventually becomes the

Marschallin in *Der Rosenkavalier*, and the Marquise–Faublas relationship the start of the Marschallin–Octavian affair, the end of which *Der Rosenkavalier* chronicles so movingly in its final act.

Our last two beginners, from the pages of *Une Année*, are separate characters with distinct narrative and plot functions in Louvet, but they are blended into one – the biggest single role in *Der Rosenkavalier* – when their attributes and foibles are used to turn them into a composite character, Baron Ochs auf Lerchenau. As beginners they are the Marquis de B***, the young, foppish husband of the Marquise, and the Comte de Rosambert, a young officer friend of Faublas's father, who takes Faublas in hand as he begins to explore the attractions of Paris. The Marquis, who is proud of his expertise in physiognomy, is an incorrigible flirt where ladies are concerned and falls immediately, and heavily, for the charms of the cross-dressed Faublas as soon as the two meet. Thereafter the Marquis pesters Faublas

7 The Marquise de B*** repulsing the Marquis, whose designs are on Faublas, the charming young 'lady' sharing his wife's bed for the night – a construct leading directly to the Ochs/Mariandel sub-plot in *Der Rosenkavalier* (Avril/Monzies)

for little intimacies as the action moves from a ballroom to his own dining table and finally to his wife's bedroom. The Marquis has his own reasons for wanting Faublas to spend the night in the bed of the Marquise (and creeps into the room during the night to make love to Faublas, only to find the Marquise ready and waiting for him: he is scolded and sent out of the room). He is completely fooled by the feminine persona of Faublas, whereas his wife is not: an ironic aspect of the narrative is thus that his own lecherous designs on Faublas are factors that actually help to propel a young (male) lover into the arms of his wife, the Marquise.

The same irony attaches however to the fifth and final beginner, the Comte de Rosambert. Rosambert, a dashing young officer, has already seduced the Marquise at the start of *Une Année* and is six weeks into his affair with her. But to spice up their liaison, and to provoke a lover's jealousy, he persuades Faublas to cross-dress and become the beautiful young girl on his arm at a ball that he, the Marquis and the Marquise are due to attend. Rosambert instructs Faublas in the art of flirtation: his intention is to provoke the Marquise, to augment her passion for him. As the evening progresses, and Rosambert sees that the Marquise and Faublas are getting on only too well, becoming progressively more and more intimate with each other, Rosambert tries to call a halt to his little masquerade and tells the Marquise that Faublas is, after all, a young man *en travesti*. But she refuses (or rather – chooses to refuse) to believe him – and the evening takes its inevitable course towards her bed, with young Faublas in her arms.

These five literary characters – Sophie, Faublas, Marquise, Marquis and Rosambert – are the literary precursors of the four main dramatic characters in *Der Rosenkavalier*. Their transition from page to stage, however, was long and tortuous before they were finally brought to Hofmannsthal's attention – by Kessler – as protagonists in the first original opera libretto he badly wanted to write for Strauss. We turn now to their page-to-stage odyssey, which started even before Louvet de Couvray had published the third and final volume of his *Faublas* trilogy. It testifies to a rich stage history of characters who must have seemed like familiar, much-loved figures to the French public in 1907, who finally saw them incarnated, to such telling effect, by Artus and Terrasse in *L'Ingénu libertin*.

... and onto the stage

1789 – Le Chevalier de Faublas

This first known adaptation of *Faublas* for the stage was by François-Jean Willemain d'Abancourt, who also wrote under the name Léonard Gobemouche (1745–1803). The play, a one-act verse comedy, premièred at the Théâtre de Monsieur, located in the north wing of the Palais des Tuileries, on 3 February 1789. With a clear nod to what the public might have been expecting – even hoping for – the stage adaptation to portray, Abancourt wrote the following somewhat enigmatic words in his own introduction to the piece:

> I have taken the subject of this bagatelle from a novel that is so well-known that it needs no further praise from me: I know that I have not dramatised the most amusing part; but I had a purpose that circumstances external to the work have not permitted me to fulfil. Given the title of the piece, the public might have imagined, I cannot think why, that they would see the Chevalier de Faublas disguised as a woman in the home of the Marquis de B***; I admit that this would have been more intriguing;[1] but my only response is to repeat what I have already said a few lines earlier.[2]

This adaptation hinges on the relationship between Faublas and his father Baron Faublas, who at the outset is determined to marry off Sophie (his ward) to someone else, and to obtain for Faublas a regimental commission. There are several onstage imbroglios involving Sophie and the Comtesse de Rosambert (dressed in a ball gown): they both hide in an ante-room adjacent to Faublas's quarters, exchange dresses so that Sophie can escape (in the ball gown) from under the eyes of Baron Faublas, and after further sub-plots involving Faublas's tutor and his valet, all is resolved when Sophie and Faublas throw themselves on the mercy of the Baron, admit they have behaved immaturely and foolishly, and ask for his permission to marry – which he grants. The verse is moralistic in tone, but light and amusing, with no real attempt by the author to play to the gallery. There is thus no indication in the text of Faublas being, or becoming, a young libertine, –and the Baron's expressed objection to his son being allowed to marry Sophie at the outset is simply that she is too rich for him, and that his son must make his way in the

---

[1] 'Piquant' is the French word used here.
[2] Willemain d'Abancourt, *Le Chevalier de Faublas* (Paris: Chez Brunet, Libraire, 1789).

world before contemplating marriage. *Le Chevalier de Faublas* ran for sixteen performances between its February première and its last performance on 3 June 1789.³

1818 – Une Aventure de Faublas

On 19 February 1818 a one-act vaudeville comedy, *Une Aventure de Faublas* or *Le Lendemain d'un Bal Masqué*, by Thomas Sauvage and N. Lecouturier, premièred at the Théâtre du Vaudeville.⁴ The authors made a number of changes to the names of the principal characters, turning the Marquis and Marquise de B***. into the Marquis and Marquise de Senneville, and turning Faublas's beloved Sophie into a heroine called Clara (who never actually appears onstage). On the cast page there is a stipulation: 'The role of Faublas can only be played by a woman.' Although Faublas cross-dresses as Mademoiselle du Portail and spends time alone onstage with the Marquise de Senneville in this disguise, before revealing his masculine identity and changing back into military uniform, there is no seduction and no love affair between them: the main driver of the plot is an extended, somewhat laboured scene in which Faublas is interrogated (over an accusation of theft) by a pedantic, comic police commissioner, summoned to the house of Madame de Senneville. When Faublas's uncle, Baron Faublas is also summoned to vouch for his nephew's honour, the proceedings are wound up swiftly with general agreement that Faublas can after all now marry Clara. The solo songs and ensemble numbers are set to melodies by several composers, including the conductor of the Vaudeville orchestra in 1818, Joseph Denis Doche, and the work is therefore a true vaudeville. *Une Aventure de Faublas* was revived four years later at the Gymnase Dramatique, this time with music by Douai, but the première on 20 February 1822 was interrupted and booed offstage before it could finish.⁵

1833 – Faublas

In 1833, a much more elaborate, large-scale stage adaptation appeared at the Théâtre Nationale du Vaudeville. *Faublas*, by Messrs Dupeuty, Brunswick and Lhérie, is described as a 'comedy in five acts, interspersed with songs'.⁶ The authors take a considerably broader sweep through Louvet de Couvray's narrative, starting in Act I with a coming-out ball, given for Faublas by his father; and moving in Act II to the boudoir of the Marquise de B. (where Faublas, cross-dressed as Mademoiselle Duportail, is persuaded to spend the night). Act III portrays the subsequent

---

³ http://www.cesar.org.uk/cesar2/titles/titles.php?fct=edit&script_UOID=125891.
⁴ http://books.google.co.uk/books?id=3XlLAAAAcAAJ&printsec=frontcover&source= gbs_ge_summary_r&cad=0#v=onepage&q&f=false.
⁵ http://www.artlyriquefr.fr/dicos/operas%20-%20U.html.
⁶ Charles Dupeuty, Léon-Lévy Brunswick and Victor Lhérie, *Faublas* (Paris: J.N. Barba, Delloye, Bezou, 1836). Léon-Lévy Lhérie and Victor Lhérie were brothers and frequent collaborators: the former habitually used the name Brunswick, and under this name collaborated with Adolphe Adam to create *Le Postillon de Lonjumeau* in 1836.

8 Cover page of *Faublas,* an elaborate five-act musical play of 1833 first staged at the Théâtre Nationale du Vaudeville, Paris

seduction by Faublas – this time cross-dressed as Mademoiselle Brumont – of the Comtesse de Lignolle in her country home. Rosambert and the Marquise de B. both arrive at the Lignolle house and play an elaborate game that threatens to reveal who Mademoiselle Brumont really is: the Marquise then gets rid of Rosambert by marrying him off to an heiress, whose fortune he can use to buy himself a regiment. Act IV sees Rosambert established with his regiment near Metz: he and Faublas talk themselves into fighting a duel over the Marquise de B. but another challenger to Rosambert intervenes and in a duel with pistols, he is lightly wounded (the challenger is the Marquise de B., disguised as a man). Act V reunites all the principals in the apartment of Faublas in his father's house in Paris: neither the Marquis de B. (expert in physiognomy) nor the Comte de Lignolle ever come to realise that Faublas (as Mlle Duportail/Brumont) has seduced their respective wives under their very noses: a final onstage charade, a play within a play, is then interrupted by an announcement

9 Cross-dressing is a constant theme in *Faublas,* with the Marquise de B*** here disguised as a man and fighting a duel with Count Rosambert (Avril/Monzies). In *L'Ingénu libertin* it is Sophie who disguises herself as a boy waiter to infiltrate the Marquise's salon

that the Baron and his daughter Sophie have just arrived for the latter's marriage to Faublas. Faublas then watches the Marquise and the Comtesse make ready to rejoin their husbands and depart: with a muttered: 'Eléonore! ... Julie! ... what a shame', Faublas prepares to meet his beloved Sophie and settle down with her. Neither Sophie nor her father ever actually appear onstage however: the final chorus is all about the mixed emotions felt by the other characters, led by Rosambert, whose final cynical comment to Faublas is: 'You are going to get married? Good luck!'

The musical numbers in *Faublas* are new couplets written to existing, and quite well-known melodies. The opening chorus, for example, has an attribution in brackets, 'Léocadie'. This is the title of a three-act opera, described as a 'drame lyrique', by Auber and Scribe,[7] first performed at the Opéra Comique on 4 November 1824. Other musical numbers are described as having airs or tunes by Doche. The

[7] http://data.bnf.fr/16304770/daniel-francois-esprit_auber_leocadie__awv_12_/.

libretto does not make it clear whether the composer of these was Joseph Denis Doche, conductor of the Théâtre de Vaudeville Orchestra from 1810 to 1823, or his son Alexandre Doche, who conducted the same orchestra from 1828 to 1848.[8] At all events, the musical numbers are relatively brief, with choruses being used to end four of the five acts, and with background orchestral accompaniments being used to add atmosphere at key moments, in true melodrama fashion. A waltz is featured as the climax to the ball in Act I, to a tune by Doche.

The dramaturgy reveals a piece that has been co-written by, in this case, three librettists. It does not obey the Unities, and the action can, perhaps, best be described as episodic. The characters of both the Marquis de B. and of the Comte de Lignolle are too similar – they are both dupes and cuckolds – and the feminine, seductive interest is transferred, rather clumsily, from the Marquise de B. in the first two acts, to the Comtesse de Lignolle, who becomes the mature lady who really holds Faublas's interest – and emotional attachment – to the end of the piece. The stage directions indicate a lavish production, however, with onstage musicians, servants bearing lit torches, and five contrasting, elaborate sets. No evidence of the contemporary reception of this piece has been found in any of the theatrical collections still held by the relevant libraries – notably the Bibliothèque Nationale de France, the Paris Opéra Library, the Bibliothèque Historique de la Ville de Paris and the Société de l'Histoire du Théâtre.

1835 – Les Amours de Faublas

It is reasonable, however, to assume a certain success for the piece, from the fact that a ballet pantomime, *Les Amours de Faublas*, with a libretto ascribed to Lockroy,[9] the pseudonym of Joseph-Philippe Simon, and Léon-Lévy Lhérie (Brunswick), and with music by Alexandre Piccini, premièred at the Théâtre de la Porte Saint Martin on 12 June 1835.[10] The libretto reveals an obvious debt to *Faublas*, with Brunswick reworking the basic outlines of the script he had co-authored two years before. There is however an effective visual addition to the narrative, in the form of a medallion, enclosing a portrait of Sophie, that Faublas carries with him as he embarks on his amorous adventures with, firstly the Marquise de B., and subsequently with the Comtesse de Lignolle. In the first scene of Act II, the boudoir of the Marquise de B., her husband inserts a surreptitious note into Faublas's pocket and finds the medallion there, which he purloins: this visual reminder of the Sophie who is Faublas's true love then forms a balletic sub-plot of its own, as it falls into different hands throughout the piece. As with *Faublas*, however, there is no stage role for Sophie herself – and it should always be remembered that in the pages of *Une Année*, Sophie never sets foot outside her convent walls. She is confined to the one fixed location where Faublas can always find her.

---

[8] *New Grove*, vol. 7, p. 416.
[9] http://data.bnf.fr/13009774/lockroy/#rdt470-13009774.
[10] http://search.ugent.be/meercat/x/bkt01?q=900000017974.

1881 – Faublas

The only other surviving evidence of a stage adaptation of the novel dates from 1881. On 25 October 1881 Edouard Cadol and Georges Duval premièred their *Faublas* at the Théâtre Cluny, with music by Alexandre Luigini, describing it as an opéra comique in three acts.[11] It was a complete flop and lasted for three performances, disappearing as completely as the theatre itself eventually did:

> Pauline Luigini, the director's wife, Mary Albert and Pierre Mesmacker appeared firstly in a revival of Offenbach's *Les Braconniers,* and then in *Faublas* (25 October), [...] which was a failure.[12]

In his subsequent review of the piece, Edmond Stoullig revealed that the authors had in fact withdrawn their names from the playbill at the last moment and went on:

> Pleasant scenery and pretty costumes, with nothing lacking, and whatever Messrs Cadol and Duval may think of it (these authors are never happy), M. Taillefer has arranged things to his own satisfaction, since he is working for his father-in-law, François [sic] Luigini, composer of the Italianate and too often banal music for *Faublas*, and for his wife Pauline Luigini, who acts with spirit and sings the role of the naughty titular hero with a pleasant albeit very tremulous vocal timbre. You cannot hear a single word said by Mme Luigini. You can understand Mlle Clary better: this explains the success of her verses in the third act, a success that a mocking audience had fun in exaggerating with purely ironic calls for a third encore. Dull libretto and poor music.[13]

Withdrawal of the authors' names from the playbill must have caused Stoullig to misremember the name of the composer when he came to write his annual review, for Alexandre Luigini was making a considerable name for himself by 1881, having studied violin at the Paris Conservatoire (second prize) and having gone on to become, firstly, leader and then conductor of the Lyon Opéra orchestra.[14] Luigini subsequently became a conductor at the Opéra Comique in Paris (1897) and composed a number of music theatre pieces, particularly ballets. Of particular interest in the *Faublas* context, and what was to follow, it was Luigini who had first auditioned Claude Terrasse (whom we shall meet in Act One) for a place at the Lyon Conservatoire, in 1880:

> His father then decided to get an opinion from Alexandre Luigini, conductor of the Grand-Théâtre Orchestra and professor of harmony at the Conservatoire. Claude entered a magnificent salon and placed his cornet on a fine table. But when the professor seized his instrument and put it by the piano legs, he suddenly lost confidence

---

[11] Bruyas, p. 309.
[12] Philippe Chauveau, *Les Théâtres Parisiens Disparus* (Paris: Editions de l'Amandier, 1999), p. 169.
[13] Stoullig, 1881, p. 415.
[14] *New Grove*, vol. 15, p. 288.

and played badly. Luckily, Luigini wanted more. He asked him to sight read some scores. Terrasse recovered his aplomb and sight read very well. When he left with his father, he was reassured. The professor had discerned in him some solid musical qualities and had advised him to study the piano and the cornet.[15]

Terrasse subsequently entered Luigini's classes in harmony and composition in the autumn of 1881, just at the time that *Faublas* was about to première at the Théâtre Cluny. Music professors have long enjoyed discussing the finer points of their own compositions with their pupils, but, however tempting a speculation, there is no evidence that Luigini and Terrasse discussed a subject that the latter was to set to music twenty-six years later.

A century of Faublas

This brief exploration of *Faublas* in literature and on the French stage makes clear that the basic construct – innocent love between Sophie and Faublas that leads eventually to marriage, after libertine adventures between Faublas and older women have seen unworthy male rivals ousted and outwitted – was never far removed from the minds of French readers and theatre audiences of the late eighteenth to the early twentieth centuries. And just as succeeding generations read and re-read Louvet de Couvray, so succeeding generations of theatregoers were able to enjoy – or at least to witness – dramatic and music theatre adaptations of the same material on Parisian stages. A century or more of the exploits of Faublas, in print and on stage, made him a national icon. And when played onstage by a woman, with the added frisson of gender-swapping and cross-dressing, Faublas undoubtedly will have cut an alluring and equivocal figure.

Thus to middle-aged and older audience members in the midst of the Belle Epoque, in 1907, it must have seemed both familiar and predictable that a French opérette composer, at the height of his powers, should have joined forces with a noted critic and playwright to produce yet another version of the *Faublas* story. It was high time for it to be retold onstage, twenty-five years after the last attempt, and the atmosphere of Belle Epoque Paris suited the morally ambiguous fable of *Faublas* to perfection. Claude Terrasse and Louis Artus were both well-known in their respective fields, but had not previously worked together. It is now time to meet them, and to assess the context in which they went on to produce what Florian Bruyas has described as one of Terrasse's true opérette masterpieces, and an incarnation of the Belle Epoque itself – *L'Ingénu libertin*.[16]

---

[15] Cathé, p. 15. This book is the only biography of Terrasse and provides an admirably comprehensive, well-written account of his life and works.
[16] Bruyas, p. 360.

Act One

The Young Libertine

The tale of a young libertine, or *L'Ingénu libertin*, clearly took the world of Paris music theatre by storm at the end of 1907 – the glowing press reports and the extra performances that were swiftly laid on attest to that. But it was a storm that passed relatively quickly and left few permanent traces of its own. The original production was never revived, and if Harry Kessler had not been among the 60,000 or so spectators who attended one of the performances between 11 December 1907 and 2 February 1908, it is entirely possible – in fact it is highly likely – that *Der Rosenkavalier* would never have been written. But Kessler did attend, as we shall see, and noted inwardly every detail of what he saw and heard, including the characterisation and the musico-dramatic portrayal of the five characters whom we have already met under 'Beginners'. His ability to do this, and to capture the essence and the theatrical detail of *L'Ingénu libertin* as the canvas on which he, Hofmannsthal and Strauss were later to paint their much grander, more ambitious work, is truly astonishing. For it is to Kessler as a man of the theatre that we owe some of the key features of *Der Rosenkavalier* that delight audiences to this day.

Based on his attendance at a single performance of *L'Ingénu libertin*, Kessler proved able to map the journey from Chevalier to Cavalier. It is time to consider the work itself, the men and women who created it and the context in which their creation was born. And to attempt to recreate *L'Ingénu libertin* as it came across the footlights, to Kessler, as he sat and delighted in a piece of music theatre steeped in Gallic wit, visual elegance, a charming, waltz-dominated score and a familiar literary tale, cleverly and sympathetically refreshed to match the mood of the Belle Epoque at its height.

A major event

The production of *L'Ingénu libertin* was a major – perhaps *the* major – event in the 1907–8 Paris opérette season.[1] It had both resonance and symbolic significance in the theatre world, being a work specially commissioned to return the Théâtre des Bouffes Parisiens to the world of opérette, its original vocation. It had three lavish sets, designed by one of France's leading scenic designers, Eugène-Louis

---

[1] For works in this genre on the French stage, the term 'opérette' will be used throughout this book, to distinguish them from Viennese (and other) operettas.

Carpézat (a pupil of Charles Cambon and his successor in 1876 as chief of design at the Paris Opéra), and built by his close associates and long-term partners, Jean-Baptiste and Antoine Lavastre of Atelier Lavastre.[2] It had costumes designed and made by Maison Landolff, one of the leading couture houses in Paris of the day. It also had three star performers: in pride of place, the versatile and highly striking singing actress, Arlette Dorgère, playing the leading role of the Marquise de Bay. Opposite her, the well-known and popular Milo de Meyer, who had stepped straight into the role of the Marquis de Bay from playing Carlos in the original run of Georges Feydeau's *La Puce à l'Oreille (A Flea in her Ear)* at the Théâtre des Variétés. And holding the whole show together, and giving it musical distinction, the gifted young conductor Philippe Moreau, who conducted without a score and who had rehearsed a small orchestra to an unusual degree of polish and precision, revealing the period charm in Terrasse's delicate and subtle orchestration. All these factors were top quality, and combined to make *L'Ingénu libertin* a huge,

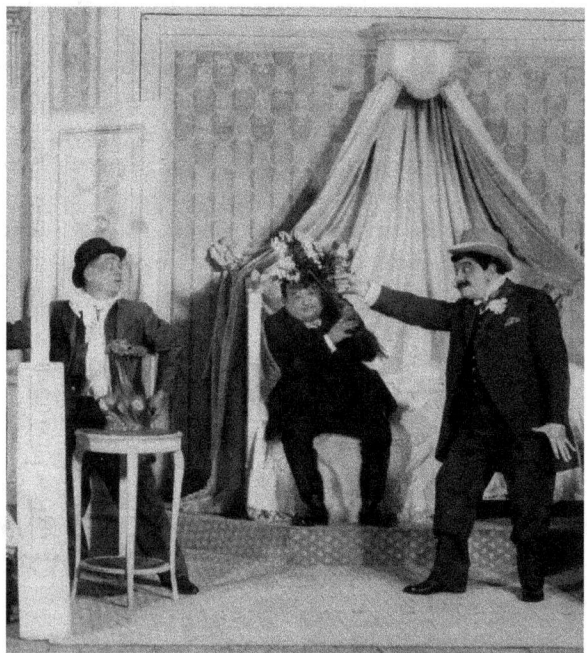

10 Milo de Meyer as Carlos Homenides de Histangua in Act Two of *La Puce à l'Oreille (A Flea in her Ear)* by Georges Feydeau. Meyer was the first Marquis de Bay and thus a prototype for the first Baron Ochs auf Lerchenau

[2] Robin Thurlow Lacy, *A Biographical Dictionary of Scenographers* (New York: Greenwood Press, 1990), respective entries Carpézat, Lavastre. Carpézat designed Chabrier's *L'Etoile* for the Paris Opéra in 1886 and Puccini's *Tosca* for the Opéra Comique in 1905, among many others: his regular partner Jean-Baptiste Lavastre is described as 'one of the great scene painters in the tradition of Pierre Ciceri'. The settings for *L'Ingénu libertin* are sumptuous and visually striking, as described in greater detail later.

immediate, critical and popular musical theatre success, achieving a run of sixty-six consecutive performances and breaking the Bouffes Parisiens box office record that year with its house takings on 24 December 1907.

Part of this success may have been relative, for the 1907–8 Paris opérette season was not particularly distinguished. Hopes had been raised by the première on 5 June 1907 of André Messager's *Fortunio* at the Opéra Comique (libretto by Robert de Flers and Gaston de Caillavet, twenty-seven performances in 1907), but the autumn and winter season consisted largely of revivals, with only a handful of new, original music theatre works.[3] Of these, *Le Chemineau (The Vagabond),* with music by Xavier Leroux to Jean Richepin's own adaptation of his 1897 verse drama of the same name, was hailed as promising, and achieved eighteen performances at the Opéra Comique, but other offerings at the Gaité, Chatelet and Porte Saint Martin seem to have been run of the mill.[4]

L'Ingénu libertin had a sub-title, *La Marquise et le Marmiton* (The Marquise and the Kitchen Boy), and was described as a *Conte galant en trois actes*. It turned out to be the only piece that Terrasse and Artus wrote together. Its dramatic scenario had some subtle, and some major differences from the narrative of *Une Année* and also from all the preceding stage adaptations of *Une Année* already described, the principal innovations being the role given to Sophie, as described later, and the concluding trio for its three leading ladies, one of whom was playing the male role of Faublas *en travesti*. Its dramatic scenario thus has many striking theatrical features in common with *Der Rosenkavalier*, although the narrative flow of the later work was once again to be skilfully reworked, by Kessler, Hofmannsthal and by Strauss. What is crucial for the transition from Chevalier to Cavalier, and for opera history, however, is this: Kessler saw this onstage re-creation of an eighteenth-century aristocratic and erotic tale, noted the effect of its décor, elaborate costumes and stage action on the audience, thought about its literary and philosophical associations and was able, twelve months later, to deconstruct it and reassemble its main elements – with additions and embellishments both from himself and from Hofmannsthal (and later on in the process from Strauss) – into the first full scenario of *Der Rosenkavalier* as we now know the piece. Both Kessler and Hofmannsthal, moreover, hid their tracks very successfully in the work that they went on to do – there is nothing in the contemporary reception of *Der Rosenkavalier* to suggest that any critic, commentator or committed operagoer had any idea that *L'Ingénu libertin* in Paris had yielded so much stage context and content for its much more ambitious reworking three years later in Dresden. Even in an age when there was no effective copyright on ideas and concepts, it must be a possibility that both Kessler and Hofmannsthal were aware of, and anxious to avoid,

---

[3] Stoullig, 1907. Edmond Stoullig, in his cumulative *Les Annales du Théâtre et de la Musique*, lists and comments on all works presented in the major Paris theatres year by year, from 1875 to 1914.

[4] Stoullig, 1907, pp. 135–8. Stoullig records *L'Attaque du Moulin* at the Gaité, *La Princesse sans Gêne* at the Chatelet and *Chevalier d'Eon* at the Théâtre de la Porte Saint Martin, none of which seem to have had any wider resonance at the time or subsequently.

11 Exterior of the Théâtre des Bouffes Parisiens around 1878, from Paul Loiseau-Rousseau: *Les Théâtres de Paris Eaux Fortes* (Paris, Deviers, 1878)

accusations that they had copied so many of the elements of a successful stage work by others, or even of outright plagiarism, but this question, for the moment, cannot be answered with certainty.

The context

Context, as always, is important. After many months of closure for complete refurbishment by its new owners, the Théâtre des Bouffes Parisiens reopened on Wednesday 11 December 1907 – in effect a gala reopening – with a brand new, specially commissioned opérette by Artus and Terrasse.[5] The title of the piece, *L'Ingénu Libertin ou La Marquise et le Marmiton*, gives the tone but is a slight tease – an *ingénu libertin* must refer to a male and in context is probably a young aristocrat, but a *Marquise* and *Marmiton* do not really go together (think *Lady and the Tramp*): what relationship can there be between a titled lady and a kitchen

---

[5] Nozière (Fernand Weyl), *Le Théâtre*, *Gil Blas*, 12 December 1907.

boy – unless the *marmiton* is also the *ingénu libertin*? But that would be faintly shocking for the time, with disruptive social class overtones, and as will be seen later, the sub-title *La Marquise et le Marmiton* was thought to be less elegant and inviting than the definitive *L'Ingénu libertin*. The piece was an instant success, both with critics and public. An unnamed reviewer in *Le Temps* on 13 December 1907 expressed concisely the views of many fellow critics with an opening paragraph that ran:

> Opérette has returned to the Bouffes Parisiens, its true home; let us hope that it never leaves it. The reception given last night to the piece by Messrs Louis Artus and Claude Terrasse gives grounds for hope.[6]

The Théâtre des Bouffes Parisiens, Offenbach's former theatre, was an iconic venue for lovers of French opérette, and contemporary reception of this production is noteworthy in two respects: there is a tangible wave of goodwill towards the theatre's reversion to type, and there are almost daily press headlines chronicling the crowds who flocked to see the show. In the former respect, one of many such articles ran:

> Fans of opérette, a genre that is so delightful, so witty, so artistic when composed by a first-rate musician such as Offenbach, Hervé, Lecocq are thus delighted, and rightly so, on learning that Messrs Deval and Richemond have set themselves the task of repatriating opérette to its very cradle: and they are all the more confident of success on learning that the musician entrusted with the task of writing the opening work is in the group of those 'young artists' totally and undeniably cut out to continue the tradition of the 'old masters', having triumphed already, as it happens in this very theatre in Rue Monsigny, with *Les Travaux d'Hercule*.[7]

In the latter respect, *Le Figaro* was quick to prognosticate:

> *L'Ingénu libertin* looks like being one of the big successes of the season. The house is crowded out each night, applauding the charming fable devised by Louis Artus and the music so perfectly composed for it by Claude Terrasse. Foreign VIPs visiting Paris, and the whole of Parisian high society are making for the Bouffes Parisiens and advance bookings permit one to say that the entire boulevard is back at this delightful theatre – unjustly neglected as it has been for a while.[8]

Given the stir created by *L'Ingénu libertin* and the reports of Parisian high society and VIPs from abroad flocking to it, the spectacle must have attracted Kessler's attention and been on his list of things to do. He was in Paris between 24

---

[6] Unsigned, *Le Temps*, 13 December 1907.

[7] B. de Lomagne, *Les Premières* in *Le Temps*, 12 December 1907. *Les Travaux de Hercule (The Labours of Hercules)* was the first huge popular opérette success for Terrasse, and Kessler most likely saw it at the Bouffes Parisiens in early April 1901 (there are no *Diary* entries for his time in Paris between 29 March and 13 April). It is discussed later in this chapter.

[8] Unsigned, *Le Figaro*, 14 December 1907, p. 5.

> *L'Ingénu libertin* s'annonce comme un des gros succès de la saison. Il y a foule, chaque soir, pour applaudir le charmant Conte imaginé par M. Louis Artus et la musique si parfaitement appropriée de M. Claude Terrasse. Les plus hautes personnalités étrangères, de passage à Paris, la plus brillante société de la capitale se donnent rendez-vous aux Bouffes-Parisiens, et la location déjà réalisée permet de dire que tout le boulevard réapprend le chemin de cet aimable théâtre, — si injustement oublié un instant.

12 *Le Figaro* carried regular reports of the success of *L'Ingénu libertin* throughout December 1907 and January 1908

December 1907 and 2 January 1908, staying as he always stayed at the Grand Hotel on rue Scribe (which is within short walking distance of the Bouffes Parisiens in rue Monsigny). Kessler moreover had a personal potential link to Claude Terrasse through the latter's brother-in-law, Pierre Bonnard, from whom he regularly bought paintings, so that relationship might additionally have alerted him to the nature of *L'Ingénu libertin* and to the success of the piece. So it is slightly surprising – and uncharacteristic of Kessler – that he did not actually see *L'Ingénu libertin* until 18 January 1908, six weeks into its run. The *Diary* does not explain this lacuna, for Kessler was normally to be found at premières, often in a prominent box and in VIP company. Moreover, he had seen Bonnard on 28 December 1907 – when extra performances of *L'Ingénu libertin* were being announced in the newspapers, to accommodate the demand for seats – and the *Diary* records a lengthy and lively, gossipy dinner party in the famous cellar of Vollard,[9] with a group of artistic guests, who must also have been aware of the Bonnard–Terrasse connection and of the theatrical success the latter was again enjoying with *L'Ingénu libertin*.[10] When Kessler did finally see the piece, however, following his return to Paris on 16 January 1908 (and a further meeting with Bonnard in the latter's studio on 17 January), it made its mark on him. Although he frequently noted in his diary no more than the title of a work he had seen or the place of its performance, in this case the work prompted some serious reflections:

---

[9] Ambroise Vollard (1866–1939) was a well-known art dealer and writer, with a cellar for dinners and receptions under his gallery on rue Laffitte: Maillol's first solo exhibition had taken place there in 1902.

[10] *Diary IV*, pp. 393–5.

Act One: The Young Libertine

In the evening an opérette after Faublas: *L'Ingénu libertin*. Dorgère was acting, whom poor Conder[11] liked so much. 18th century libertinage as the pendant to 'sentiment'. Crébillon fils and Rousseau are twins, just like Lovelace and Clarissa. They are inseparable, because both are growing from the same hyper-individual root. You have to illuminate Faublas with Rousseau and Rousseau with Faublas in order to see them both in the right relief. Union in Heine.[12]

These thoughts will be explored and analysed later. It must be remembered, however, that the opérette, which made such a vivid and powerful impression on him – sufficient for him to be able to recount it in every detail to Hofmannsthal over a year later – did not come from nowhere. It was the creation of two men who understood the genre and whose previous work for the stage, working with others, had equipped them for what the reopened Bouffes Parisiens required: a sumptuous spectacle, a witty and slightly erotic plot and libretto, and a take on the libertinage of eighteenth-century Paris that remained just on the right side of good taste, and the Censor. Those two men were Claude Terrasse and Louis Artus.

Who was Claude Terrasse?

Terrasse and his works are not well known today, but in his heyday, the early years of the twentieth century when he had just turned 30, Terrasse was a major musical figure in a popular musical genre in France. A classically trained orchestral player and organist (Conservatoire de Lyon and Ecole Niedermeyer in Paris), he began to write for the stage and, as his entry in *New Grove* puts it: 'He now found his métier in opéra bouffe; his works formed a conspicuous part of the renaissance of this genre which followed the last examples by Audran and Strauss, and was contemporary with Lecocq's last pieces.'[13] It is now as part of this lineage that Terrasse appears in most of the standard works of musical reference. Take Grout, for example:

> The line of French light opera, established in the nineteenth century by Auber, Adam and Offenbach, was continued after 1870 by Alexandre Charles Lecocq (*La Fille de Madame Angot*, 1872), Robert Planquette (whose sentimental, fantastically successful *Cloches de Corneville* came out in 1877), Edmond Audran (*La Mascotte*, 1880), and Louis Varney (*Les Mousquetaires au Couvent*, 1880). Somewhat later began the long and popular series of opérettes by André Messager (1853–1929), distinguished conductor and facile composer in a straightforward, attractively melodious vein (*La Basoche*, 1890; *Les P'tites Michu*, 1897; *Monsieur Beaucaire*, 1919). At the beginning of

---

[11] Charles Conder (1868–1909) was a painter, member of a bohemian artist set in Paris around 1890 and friend of Toulouse-Lautrec: he subsequently moved to London, where Kessler saw him regularly on his frequent visits.
[12] *Diary IV*, p. 400.
[13] *New Grove*, vol. 25, p. 303. The reference to Strauss here is clearly to Johann, not Richard.

13 Claude Terrasse at the height of his success in 1903 with *Le Sire de Vergy*

the twentieth century appeared the opérettes of Claude Terrasse (1867–1923); *Le Sire de Vergy*, 1903; *Monsieur de la Palisse*, 1904).[14]

This placing of Terrasse in a Lecocq–Audran–Messager line of descent does not do full justice to the originality of a musician who, when still in his twenties, was at the heart of the theatrical scandal that was Alfred Jarry's *Ubu roi* at the Théâtre de l'Oeuvre in 1896, but who thereafter rapidly and seamlessly became known throughout France as 'the Offenbach of our times'[15] for the whole series of boulevard opérettes that he created on Parisian stages during the Belle Epoque. It is thus perhaps the facility with which Terrasse can be associated with the opérette genre, and his shorthand identification as a modern-day Offenbach, that have resulted in

---

[14] Donald Jay Grout, *A Short History of Opera* (New York and London: Columbia University Press, 1947), p. 434.
[15] Cathé, p. 70.

serious critical neglect of his music in its own right, even though his period in the opérette limelight lasted well over twenty years, right up until his death in 1923. It may also be, given the importance of the spoken word in both opérette and opéra comique, that the musical status of Terrasse and of his oeuvre has been overshadowed by some of his literary collaborators. His entry in *New Grove* includes:

> The appeal of Terrasse's works in over 30 years came partly from the distinction of his librettists, who were active contributors in a vintage period of French light comedy; they included De Flers and De Caillavet, Tristan Bernard and Franc-Nohain. Jarry himself was a co-librettist.[16]

There are undoubtedly certain features in Terrasse's music that make him worthy of his Offenbach sobriquet. The first is his melodic invention: his tunes are many and various, easy to assimilate on first hearing, and relatively easy to perform – Terrasse having learned quickly that the polyphonic musical style of his first real stage success, *La Petite Femme de Loth* written to a libretto by Tristan Bernard in 1900, was technically too difficult for the average opérette cast, and thus had to be rewritten in simpler vein.[17] The second is his rhythmic verve and musical wit: his scores abound with patter songs, bright, fast choruses, musical numbers and musical jokes that provoke smiles if not outright laughter on the part of audiences. Terrasse was very preoccupied by these aspects of composition: summarising the genius of Offenbach, he himself wrote:

> But his irresistible lever for galvanising an audience is powerful rhythm, persistent rhythm, constant, bold, plunging entire scenes into vertiginous movement. Offenbach is a marvel, an inexhaustible inventor of rhythms. If you want to quote another musician as aware as he was of the virtue of rhythm couched as gesture and of rhythmical insistence, Beethoven is the name that springs to mind. This may seem paradoxical but there is a true parallel.[18]

The third is his skill at orchestration: the orchestral accompaniments to his strophic airs and ballads are constantly varied from verse to verse, the voice being doubled now by an oboe, now a flute, the melody passing from one instrument to another in kaleidoscopic fashion, words being pointed up by tiny (and sometimes ironic) interjections by trombones and other lower wind instruments. Some of these features of the score of *L'Ingénu libertin* in particular are explored in the last section of this chapter, which considers Kessler's reactions to the musical side of the opérette that he heard.

Given this musical distinction in a popular and commercially successful genre, it is surprising that the only full-length biography of Terrasse, written by a professor

---

[16] *New Grove*, vol. 25, p. 303.
[17] Cathé, p. 71.
[18] Claude Terrasse, *L'Oeuvre de Jacques Offenbach* in *Musica* (1908), reprinted in *Ecrits non musicaux* (Paris: Editions du Fourneau, 1997), p. 41.

of musicology at the Sorbonne, Philippe Cathé, did not appear until 2004.[19] This book gives a readable and lively account of his life and achievements. It makes clear, as do other more general writers on this period, that the slight but distinct revival of the French opérette that Terrasse and his collaborators introduced, especially between 1900 and 1914, ran counter to the prevailing tide and fashion of the Viennese operetta, which began to conquer French theatres from the première of Lehár's *The Merry Widow* (1905) onwards.[20] But it still cannot really explain why it was that Terrasse, who had such a run of initially scandalous and then of popular successes, and who worked with such an exalted circle of literary and artistic figures, should have fallen into relative obscurity nowadays. 'Treated roughly by posterity, Terrasse does not occupy the position that seems due to him. A not inconsiderable factor in this comes from the problems arising from his small-scale publishing house.'[21] Duteutre goes further: 'It seems unjust that Terrasse's opérettes should have been totally forgotten.'[22]

Cathé sees Messager and Reynaldo Hahn as the only real rivals of Terrasse in the light opera genre during his lifetime but suggests that of the three, it was solely Terrasse who had the originality to introduce expanded tonality as an almost constant feature of his opérette scores. He attributes this to Terrasse's training at France's leading organ school, the Ecole Niedermeyer, which allowed him to escape the 'tyranny of the degrees in tonal scales', and he suggests:

> In the keys with minor thirds, he uses harmonic progressions for his melodies that are uncommon in the genre, and these abound throughout all his scores. In the major keys, he enlarges his harmonic palette with various substituted chords, like Gabriel Fauré. This quiet and unassuming challenging of conventional tonality takes him much further than one might think. Terrasse is the only opérette musician to go down the same road as Debussy, Dukas, d'Indy and their other illustrious contemporaries and he can be seen as the man who adapts the most important elements of the musical language of the early twentieth century to the particular genre of opérette.[23]

This is praise indeed for the musical qualities of a composer specialising in the lighter and more popular end of the music theatre of his time. In fact however the tuneful score of *L'Ingénu libertin* is mainly diatonic, with only occasional chromatic interludes, and is reminiscent more of Lecocq or of Messager than of Debussy. This is undoubtedly because Terrasse was trying to capture the essence of eighteenth-century musical style in *L'Ingénu libertin*, with conventional harmonic progressions and a small orchestra that included a harpsichord in the pit,

---

[19] The book derives from his own doctoral thesis: Philippe Cathé, 'Claude Terrasse (1867–1923), thèse de nouveau régime' (Paris-IV, 2001), 2 vols, 993 pp. All my quotations from Cathé are from his book, not from the thesis.
[20] Duteutre, p. 100.
[21] Cathé, p. 198.
[22] Duteutre, p. 95.
[23] Cathé, p. 166.

as described later. However, the overall musical strengths of Terrasse's scores have been demonstrated to a new public in a handful of Terrasse revivals in the twenty-first century (*Chonchette, Aux Temps des Croisades* and, most recently, *La Botte Secrète* have all been played in Paris and elsewhere in France on tour by a small and versatile company called Les Brigands).[24] They contain 'musical passages that are simultaneously very precise and very light, almost airborne, that pose the same difficulties as the operas of Mozart. But also a sense of faultless prosody, reminiscent of Offenbach, with the harmonic fluidity of his own era, sometimes echoing Debussy.' This was the verdict of Christophe Grapperon, musical director of the 2009 revival of *Aux Temps des Croisades*, when asked to comment on Terrasse's music.[25]

From Lyon to Paris

Terrasse was born at Arbresle, near Lyon, in 1867 and was of humble origins. Both his parents were in domestic service, although his father subsequently entered the silk trade and was promoted to a senior managerial position with the firm of Mancardi. Aged 7, Terrasse was sent away to boarding school (just as his parents separated – and perhaps because of that) and at 13, having shown distinct signs of musical aptitude, entered the Lyon Conservatoire, with the cornet as his main instrument. In his teenage years he played the cornet in several orchestras, including that of the Lyon Grand-Théâtre, and became a Conservatoire prize-winner in musical theory. After four years in Lyon, he won a place to study with one of France's leading organists, Eugène Gigout, at the prestigious Ecole Niedermeyer in Paris, but in 1887 Terrasse was conscripted into military service. Terrasse and Gigout had swiftly become personal friends, however, and Terrasse continued as a private pupil even after Gigout left the Niedermeyer following a dispute: Terrasse also worked on a jobbing basis as organist and choirmaster in a neighbouring parish at this time.[26]

Terrasse's period of military service is noteworthy for one personal connection he made. Fellow conscript Charles Bonnard, whose family lived near Grenoble, became a close friend and invited Terrasse to spend leave days with him at the family home. Terrasse thus got to know Charles Bonnard's siblings Andrée, whom he went on to marry in 1890, and Pierre, who became a celebrated painter and a member of the modernist group known as the Nabis, or prophets.[27] The family were clearly cultivated and artistic: Andrée was an accomplished pianist and

---

[24] http://www.lesbrigands.fr/v2/?page_id=998. In Paris, Les Brigands have established a close relationship with the Athénée Théâtre Louis Jouvet.
[25] Christophe Grapperon, *Et la musique?* In http://www.lefigaro.fr/musique/2009/12/16/03006-200 91216ARTFIG00028-les-brigandsau-temps-des-croisades-.php.
[26] Cathé, p. 18.
[27] *The Oxford Companion to Art*, ed. Harold Osborne (Oxford: Oxford University Press, 1970), pp. 761–2.

helped her husband to organise seventy or more chamber concerts in the first few years of their married life spent at Arcachon. It was during this period that Terrasse played a hymn of his own composition to the visiting Charles Gounod, who is alleged to have exclaimed: 'But this is opérette, my dear chap! You should try the genre, it would suit you very well!'[28] As for Pierre Bonnard, he illustrated the children's musical textbooks that Terrasse began to write in his Arcachon years (now collectors' items selling for high prices) and later, when both men were in Paris, acted as a prolific source of introductions to the literary and artistic avant-garde comprising and surrounding his fellow Nabis: radical disciples of Gaugin, their number included Paul Sérusier, Maurice Denis, Edouard Vuillard, Ker-Xavier Roussel and Félix Valloton, while others associated with the group included Toulouse-Lautrec, Aristide Maillol, Claude Debussy and the brothers Alexandre and Thadée Natanson (of the *Revue Blanche*). Perhaps inevitably, Kessler was also involved with nearly all the members of this group during his frequent visits to Paris, buying their works and promoting them to the best of his ability in France and elsewhere. And of the members of the Nabis, Bonnard, Sérusier, Vuillard, Roussel and Toulouse-Lautrec were all involved in scenery painting in 1897 for an infamous theatrical première.

14 The children of Claude and Andrée Terrasse in the garden of their home, to be immortalised in Pierre Bonnard's painting *L'après-midi bourgeoise* (see colour plates)

[28] Fanély Révoil, 'Claude Terrasse, compositeur de la Belle Epoque', *Les Annales*, 176 (June 1965), 23, and quoted in Cathé, p. 32. José Bruyr quotes this slightly differently: 'Gounod – No! What a good *buffo* refrain that would make! Give opérette a try.' José Bruyr, *L'Opérette* (Paris: Presses Universitaires de France, 1974), p. 53.

Act One: The Young Libertine

First librettist – Alfred Jarry and *Ubu roi*

Claude and Andrée Terrasse had arrived in Paris from Arcachon in 1896 for Claude to take up a post as second organist at the church of La Trinité. The position was well paid and gave him scope for outside musical activities. Through Pierre Bonnard he quickly met Aurélien Lugné-Poe, who was running the symbolist and avant-garde Théâtre de l'Oeuvre, and through Lugné-Poe he met – and instantly befriended – the latter's new secretary and assistant, Alfred Jarry.[29] When Terrasse learned that a production was planned by Lugné-Poe of Jarry's *Ubu roi*, he offered to compose the incidental music. The infamous first performance, with Claude and Andrée Terrasse in the wings playing between them piano, percussion and almost certainly a cornet, took place on 10 December 1896. Terrasse had scored his music for a whole variety of fairground, and somewhat obscure, instruments but they could not be assembled in time: in his introductory speech, Jarry remarked: 'It was very important that, in order to be serious about being marionettes, we should have had fairground music. We have not had time to get together the brass, gongs and marine trumpets, between which the orchestration should have been divided.'[30] So piano and percussion (and cornet) had to suffice. There is, to this day, uncertainty over the details because the retrospective accounts of those who were – or who claimed to have been – there, at the dress rehearsal and the sole première performance, all differ substantially.[31] What is, however, certain is that Terrasse's musicality, and his ability both to compose original music and to improvise in the theatre, dated from this time and was to become part of his future working practice.

The seminal influence of *Ubu roi* on French Surrealism and its status as the founder-play of avant-garde theatre have been well documented.[32] Less attention has been paid to the originality of Terrasse's music, which Cathé describes as minimalist in the extreme: 'a major step has been taken from the ten minutes of *L'Après-midi d'un faune* to the ten second aphorisms of Claude Terrasse',[33] but an extensive recent study by Peter Lamothe has highlighted and analysed the 'parallel world of absurdity' that Terrasse created in music in response to Jarry's text.[34] What is clear

---

[29] Cathé, p. 44.
[30] Alfred Jarry, *Oeuvres complètes en trois volumes*, ed. Arrivé and others (Paris: Pléiade, 1972–88), vol. 1, p. 400.
[31] Alistair Brotchie, *Alfred Jarry A Pataphysical Life* (Cambridge, MA and London, 2011), p. 159. Brotchie quotes Lugné-Poe as saying that the uproar [at the première] was so loud that Terrasse could not follow the action and struck the cymbals at random 'like a dog catching flies' (p. 164). Fell says that the accompaniment had to be restricted 'to the piano, which he played himself, and the drum' (Fell, p. 82).
[32] Phyllis Hartnoll, ed., *The Oxford Companion to the Theatre, Fourth Edition* (Oxford: Oxford University Press, 1983), p. 436.
[33] Cathé, p. 46.
[34] Peter Lamothe, 'The Music of *Ubu roi*: Terrasse's Parallel World of Absurdity', chapter in 'Theater Music in France, 1864–1914' (diss., University of North Carolina, Chapel Hill, 2008), pp. 169–206.

15 The iconic figure of Alfred Jarry's Ubu,
with a fragment of Terrasse's accompanying music

from the score and from its only extant recording[35] is that Terrasse matched his snatches of music to the fragmented nature of Jarry's text: and was not afraid to break traditional musical conventions – quoting and parodying national anthems, inserting modal and atonal passages and refusing to resolve his final cadences, thus leaving the audience in a state of musical suspense to match the equivocal nature of the dramatic narrative.[36]

The theatrical and musical anarchy of *Ubu roi* did not bring Terrasse to wide public attention (there was only one full public performance, ending in disorder, preceded by a dress rehearsal for friends and initiates).[37] What it did do was to commend him to a small circle of up-and-coming writers (such as Tristan Bernard and Franc-Nohain) who realised that Terrasse would be capable of setting their texts imaginatively and sympathetically to music. It was thus the group of theatrical contacts made from the experience of *Ubu roi* that propelled Terrasse towards his true vocation as a composer of comic operas and opérettes – exactly as Gounod had predicted.

---

[35] http://www.ubu.com/film/jarry_ubu-averty.html. This 1965 film of *Ubu roi* uses all Terrasse's music in reorchestrated form and gives a good impression of just how avant-garde the play and its music must have seemed in 1896.
[36] Cathé, p. 47.
[37] Fell, p. 89.

Success with de Flers and de Caillavet – *Les Travaux d'Hercule* (1901) and *Le Sire de Vergy* (1903)

In the two years immediately following *Ubu roi*, Terrasse, Jarry, Franc-Nohain, Bonnard and others devoted themselves to a small puppet theatre – Théâtre des Pantins – which put on musical revues and entertainments, including a reprise of *Ubu roi* performed solely by marionettes.[38] Terrasse composed the music for the three new shows performed here, one of which, *Vive la France!*, was immediately banned by the Censor for its satirical treatment of a Jew wishing to become French – just in the wake of the Dreyfus affair. But success for Terrasse on the main stages of Paris was not long in coming, and after setting *La petite femme de Loth* to a text by Tristan Bernard, which transferred in 1900 to the Théâtre des Mathurins, was toured elsewhere in France and returned to the Mathurins for a second successful run in 1901, Terrasse found himself the object of career – and life-changing attention. The rich and successful playwriting partners Robert de Flers and Gaston de Caillavet needed a composer for their new opérette, *Les Travaux d'Hercule,* the libretto for which was already written. After protracted financial negotiations, Terrasse found himself with less than a month to compose and fully orchestrate a three-act work: he began the task on 26 January 1901 and completed the full score thirty-one days later on 25 February.[39]

16 Claude Terrasse, Robert de Flers and Gaston de Caillavet – the composer and his celebrated librettists – in 1903

Les Travaux d'Hercule opened at the Bouffes Parisiens on 7 March 1901. It was an immediate critical and popular success and ran for eighty-six performances.

---

[38] Fell, pp. 116–19.
[39] Cathé, p. 74.

Duteutre situates the work in a direct line running from *La belle Hélène* and *Geneviève de Brabant*,[40] the joke in this case being that Hercules is not really a hero at all, in fact a weak and useless cuckold, incapable of performing his famous labours, but happy to take the credit when others accomplish them for him. Terrasse's music has rhythmic verve and élan, some memorable and instantly popular melodies, and some well-developed 'slow waltz' numbers.

17 A scene from Act One of *Les Travaux d'Hercule* at the Bouffes Parisiens – the first, major national success for Terrasse as a composer of opérettes

Two years later the same team had even greater success with *Le Sire de Vergy* at the Théâtre des Variétés, in a production that was to enjoy a run of 110 performances. In a variation of the Hercules joke, the Sire in question pretends to have been away at the Crusades when in fact he has been living a debauched life in Paris. To make his return to Vergy seem more authentic, he persuades his Parisian cronies (including his latest mistress) to impersonate his 'captives' from the Holy Land. His wife however, and her Vergy friends, have been living an equally

---

[40] Duteutre, p. 94.

unchaste existence during his 'crusade': the ensuing imbroglio on his return is farcical comedy couched in conventional opérette form.

In terms of orchestration, Terrasse made major strides in the two years between *Les Travaux d'Hercule* and *Le Sire de Vergy*. The former work is set in conventional four-part harmony and is easy to assimilate, even on first hearing, but there is little specific orchestral colour or timbre to its various characters and dramatic situations: and while admiring the speed at which it had been written, fellow composer Maurice Emmanuel suggested in a contemporary article that Terrasse could have done better if he had been given more time.[41] *Le Sire de Vergy*, on the other hand, is full of obvious and, sometimes, more subtle orchestral effects: from the chromatic horn calls that announce the hunt, to delicate interplay between woodwind and strings in the strophic ballads, to the distinctive oriental sound and colour that Terrasse manages to impart to the song sung by the 'captives' who are led on in Act Two. The geographical setting of Vergy is near Avignon, and Terrasse uses a device that is later to occur in *L'Ingénu libertin*, namely the incorporation of a well-known popular French melody into some of the through-composed passages. In *Le Sire de Vergy* the melodic outlines of *Sur le pont d'Avignon* are worked – with variations – into the extended opening sequences of the first two acts, with highly effective orchestral colouring, whereas in *L'Ingénu libertin* it is the main melody of the Marseillaise that accompanies the heroine, Sophie and her faithful servant boy La Jeunesse, as they describe the risks and perils facing them on the darkened streets of Paris, all alone and late at night.[42]

It was Claude Debussy, reviewing *Le Sire de Vergy* in 1903, who first praised Terrasse's musical invention and orchestration.[43] What he wrote more fully was:

> Offenbach was a terrible orchestrator, C. Terrasse is a fine orchestrator; there too I shall permit myself to tell him that in the way unexpected timbres might be linked, there would be an untapped vein of humour. He certainly knows this better than me, and the car horn that announces the return of the 'crusaders' from the Holy Land in *Le Sire de Vergy* is an undeniable invention.[44]

Two further aspects of *Le Sire de Vergy* should be noted. The first is that the role of the pageboy Fridolin (the trouser role) was played by a striking young actress called Arlette Dorgère, who four years later was to assume the leading role of the Marquise de Bay in *L'Ingénu libertin*. The second is that the critic for *La Presse*, Louis Artus, was in a minority of two in finding fault with *Le Sire de Vergy* in the national press, in effect damning it with faint praise. In an elegant and ironic

---

[41] Cathé, p. 75.
[42] *La Marquise et le Marmiton ou L'Ingénu libertin*, Eschig, undated, private copy of manuscript full orchestral score, 7 p. 23. Eschig took over Terrasse's own publishing house, the Société d'Editions Musicales, and the manuscript full score was stored in Milan (now Casa Ricordi) until 13 November 2009, when it was located by, and made available to the author. It does not appear ever to have been printed.
[43] *New Grove*, vol. 25, p. 303.
[44] Duteutre, p. 94.

put-down of the *La Presse* review that had been written by Artus, published in *Le Figaro* a week after the first night, Gaston de Caillavet highlighted in an interview the factual errors made by Artus in his description of the plot and suggested that as a man of the world who dined late, he clearly had not had the time to see the first act.[45] Whether he accepted the reproach or not, Artus continued to combine his activities as a dramatic critic with a great deal of writing for the stage, and it was he who in 1907 was to approach Terrasse and ask him to set to music a libretto he was in the process of writing – that of *L'Ingénu libertin*. He thus succeeded Jarry, de Flers and de Caillavet as librettist to an opérette composer by now at the height of his powers, and enjoying huge commercial and critical success.

Exemplary collaboration with Louis Artus

The author and critic Louis Artus was born in Paris in 1870. His early education and life have not been documented in any detail – 'A Parisian from Paris, where he was brought up and received all his education' is the laconic biographical note in the programme book for *L'Ingénu libertin*[46] – but by his early twenties he was already making a name for himself as a stage dramatist and as a critic. The Collection Rondel at the Bibliothèque Nationale de France lists stage plays by Artus as first appearing in 1892 (*Clématite, comédie en vers* and *La Duchesse Potiphar, farce romantique*) and includes further comedies and vaudevilles being staged in major theatres such as the Vaudeville, Palais Royal and Cluny until big productions of *Coeur de Moineau* (1905) and *La Ponelle* (1906), both at the Théâtre de l'Athénée.[47] This venue is significant because it brought Artus to the personal attention of impresario Abel Deval, who was running the Théâtre de l'Athénée at the time. When Deval joined forces with Jean Richemond two years later to take over the Théâtre des Bouffes Parisiens and to restore it to its former glory as a home for French opérette, Artus had a ready-made entrée and a favourable reputation. His offer to write what became *L'Ingénu libertin* was readily accepted.

Although clearly a prolific and successful stage author, particularly with comedies (*Coeur de moineau* ran for more than 1,000 performances in all, and reopened at the Théâtre de l'Athénée on 25 December 1907, in direct competition with *L'Ingénu libertin*), Artus remained a regular theatre critic. His biography in the programme book lists him as an increasingly important theatre critic for *La Presse*, then for *L'Intransigeant* and finally (in 1907) as successor to the late Léon Kerst for the *Petit Journal*, a widely read publication. These two functions – critic and stage dramatist – seem to have made Artus sufficiently well-known in theatrical circles

---

[45] Cathé, p. 92.
[46] Rondel côte 50.353. Programme book dated 10 December 1907, printed by Landais and Legay, Paris, Bibliothèque Nationale de France, Richelieu, Arts du Spectacle. The Collection Rondel comprises more than 10,000 theatrical artefacts – programmes, news clippings, photographs and miscellanea.
[47] Rondel, côte 50.353.

Act One: The Young Libertine 39

18 Louis Artus in 1907, already a nationally-acclaimed playwright following an earlier career as a theatre critic

for Nozière, in his Preface to Stoullig's *Annales* for 1907, to include the name of Artus alongside a select group (including Robert de Flers and Gaston de Caillavet) as masters of their art: 'The world of French theatre belongs to a few men who, undoubtedly, have a great deal of talent.'[48] A few years later however, from 1913 onwards Artus moved away from the theatre and became a novelist, his trilogy *La Maison du Fou, La Maison du Sage* and *Le Vin de ta Vigne* establishing his reputation as a prose writer and – as described on the jacket of his biblical novel of 1941 set in Palestine – as a 'catholic moralist'.[49]

L'Ingénu libertin (1907)

An iconic venue

The Bouffes Parisiens (briefly located in Salle Lacaze and since 1856 in Salle Choiseul, rue Monsigny, not far from Palais Garnier), had half a century of history as an

---

[48] Stoullig. 1907, p. xvi.
[49] Louis Artus, *La Plus Belle Histoire d'Amour Du Monde* (Paris: Editions Denoel, 1945).

 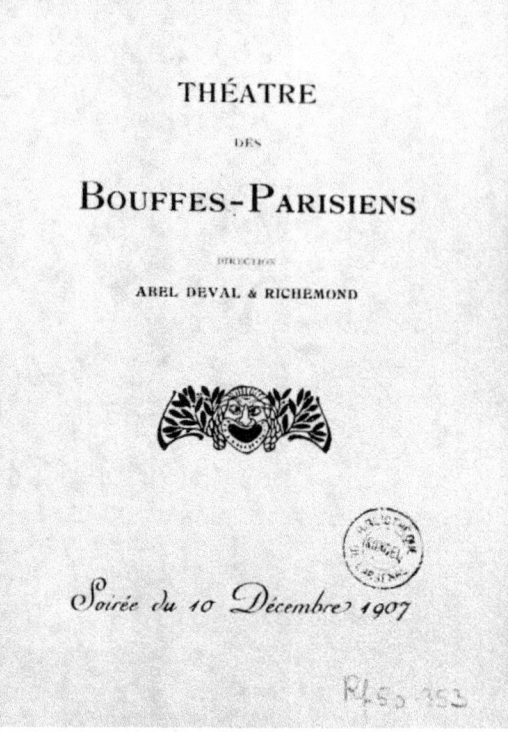

19 Outer cover of the original programme for *L'Ingénu libertin*

20 Programme cover for the dress rehearsal of *L'Ingénu libertin*

opérette theatre by 1900, notably because of its close association with its founder Offenbach and with his works. It had been licensed initially as a theatre for works with fewer than five performers, but Offenbach himself had led the attempt to expand its repertoire and to 'position the Bouffes Parisiens and its emergent genre of *opérette* squarely within the tradition of international comic opera of the past'.[50] Yet by the early years of the twentieth century, with the gradual decline in popularity of French opérette, the Bouffes Parisiens had turned to straight plays, mainly vaudeville comedies, farces and theatrical revues to keep itself going, to general critical disapproval. It was thus a widely welcome and exciting development in the spring of 1907 when two highly successful Parisian theatrical impresarios, Abel Deval and Jean Richemond, announced their intention of closing the theatre for its complete refurbishment and reopening it as an opérette theatre. The archives

[50] Mark Everist, 'Jacques Offenbach – The Music of the Past and the Image of the Present', in *Music, Theater and Cultural Transfer, Paris 1830–1914*, ed. Annegret Fauser and Mark Everist (Chicago: University of Chicago Press, 2009), p. 74.

of the Paris Opéra at Palais Garnier record the event thus: '1907. Reopening of the Bouffes Parisiens on 29 November 1907, thus returning the house to its true vocation, under the presidency of Messrs Devel [sic] and Richemond : Victor Silvestre, director, Chs Samson manager.'[51]

In an interview shortly before opening night with journalist Max Heller, Terrasse made very clear the bespoke nature of the opérette that was going to reopen the theatre:

> When Artus, Claude Terrasse tells me, was told that Deval and Richemond were thinking of taking over the *Bouffes*, he told them of his intention to write an opérette libretto. Since he has long been 'one of the team', especially since his great successes with *Coeur de Moineau* and *La Ponelle*, the two directors told him: 'write your opérette and bring it to us – we shall be delighted to put it on'. Artus took them up on this immediately; and then he offered me the chance to collaborate with him. As you can imagine, I accepted this flattering proposition immediately.[52]

In the same interview, Terrasse detailed the close collaboration that ensued between him and Artus as the text and score took shape:

> I composed most of my score this summer, at Deauville, at the property of my dear friend Mr Louis Mors, who was kind enough to make available an isolated little house for me. I was only a few kilometres away from Louis Artus, and it was an easy journey, because he was staying at Cabourg… And I finished the score, as I always do, in the theatre, having ideas, making changes, fixing things according to the capabilities and dramatic qualities of my cast.[53]

This comment by Terrasse, 'as I always do', confirms once again his credentials as a man of the theatre: he clearly needed to assess the musical and dramatic qualities of the cast who had been assembled to perform his score, before finalising the details in a way that worked convincingly on the stage. We are reminded of Terrasse in the wings of *Ubu roi* a decade earlier, improvising from his score to the chaotic scenes onstage as the play developed.

In a separate open letter to Serge Basset (the pseudonym of playwright and theatre critic Paul Ribon, who wrote for *Le Figaro* and later for the *Petit Parisien*), Terrasse described the evolution of *L'Ingénu libertin* in more detail:

> When Louis Artus read me his play last spring, it was purely an elegant and refined comedy with a fairly well developed comic side to it. All he wanted was for me to add some stage music and the odd couplet here and there. I accepted because it was such a delightful read. While I was working on it, each day he brought me a new piece, a duet here, a couplet there, then some ensembles, a finale, and finally we had

---

[51] Paris Opera library, Palais Garnier: Microfilmed record entitled *Bouffes Parisiens*, réserve pièce no. 39.
[52] Rondel, côte 50.353.
[53] Rondel, côte 50.353.

a proper full score which I tried to keep in eighteenth century character as befitted the subject.[54]

This comment illuminates the elegant, eighteenth-century musical style of the piece alluded to earlier. However, a stage comedy, with some incidental music, would not have fitted the proclaimed ambition of Deval and Richemond to restore the Bouffes Parisiens to its former days of opérette glory with a specially commissioned work. So there may well have been an element of deliberate understatement in Terrasse's open letter to Basset. It emerges clearly nevertheless, both from the letter and from the interview with Heller, that *L'Ingénu libertin* was a truly collaborative effort between librettist and composer, an attempt to match literary and musical style to the nature and period of the dramatic scenario, and an attempt by Terrasse to set the musical numbers in accordance with the vocal and histrionic strengths of the performers at his disposal. Opera and comic opera composers throughout history, including notably Mozart and Verdi, have proceeded in exactly the same way.

Evoking Louvet de Couvray

As if the audience needed reminding, both the programme book and the open letter from Terrasse to Basset give very precise accounts of the derivation of *L'Ingénu libertin*. In the letter, Terrasse writes:

My friend and collaborator was inspired for his play by an episode in the famous novel by Louvet de Couvray, a member of the Convention, *Les Amours du Chevalier de Faublas*. The episode runs from pages 38 to 50 of volume 1 of the fine Garnier edition. It is used for some of the first act and for the main scene of the second act. Artus has made up all the rest. He has also used the same names as those in the eighteenth century novel but he has changed their natures, reckoning that such liberties can be taken with the stuff of legend.[55]

'Artus has made up all the rest.' This is a highly significant comment by Terrasse, for it means, *inter alia*, that Artus has made up the crucial dénouement scene in Act III of *L'Ingénu libertin,* in which the Marquise de Bay and Sophie vie with each other for the love of Faublas (in their all-female trio) until Faublas decides that his true love is Sophie; and the Marquise, with resigned dignity, blesses the union of the two young lovers. There is no such scene with these three characters in Louvet de Couvray. The equivalent scene in Act III of *Der Rosenkavalier*, in which the Marschallin allows Octavian and Sophie to find true love together as a couple, and resignedly blesses their union, can only therefore derive from Artus – and not, as Strauss–Hofmannsthal scholars have traditionally surmised, from Louvet

---

[54] Rondel, côte 50.353.
[55] Rondel, côte 50.353.

21 Faublas setting foot in Parisian society, the charms of which constantly distract him from his one true love – Sophie de Pontis

de Couvray.[56] This, in turn, brings us back to Kessler. For it is inconceivable that he would – or could – have gone on to narrate to Hofmannsthal the full story of *L'Ingénu libertin*, and its effect in performance, without describing its musical and dramatic highlight and resolution in Act III: the love duet between Faublas and Sophie, the all-female trio in which Faublas opts for Sophie rather than the Marquise, and the abrupt dismissal by the latter of Rosambert. The whole course

---

[56] Critical studies of the Richard Strauss operas that pre-date publication of the Hofmannsthal–Kessler correspondence do not mention Artus: Norman Del Mar (1962), William Mann (1964) and Ernst Krause (1964), for example: and even Alan Jefferson, in the Cambridge Opera Handbook on *Der Rosenkavalier* (1985) only mentions Louvet de Couvray, not Artus. One of the earliest articles on *Rosenkavalier* sources was written by Felix Poppenberg in 1911, in *Literarisches Echo 14*, pp. 1254–9, pointing all who read him subsequently towards Louvet de Couvray.

of *Der Rosenkavalier* leads up to this. And this is precisely what Kessler had seen onstage in *L'Ingénu libertin*.

In 'Beginners' we met the five characters from the pages of Louvet de Couvray who found their way, six or more times, from page to stage throughout the nineteenth century. It is time now to look in detail at the specific episode used by Artus as the basis for *L'Ingénu libertin*, which runs as follows in *Une Année*.

An older male friend of Faublas's family, the Comte de Rosambert, who is charged with introducing Faublas to the ways of the world in Paris, is six weeks into his affair with the Marquise de B***. To spice up his budding relationship with the Marquise, Rosambert persuades Faublas to dress up as a young girl and accompany him to a ball, where the Marquise de B*** will see them, imagine that Faublas is Rosambert's new young mistress, and be piqued with jealousy. Faublas is kitted out in a suitable female costume, and in a trial run visits Adelaide in her convent and manages to kiss his beloved Sophie full on the lips. He then sets off to the ball with Rosambert: the Marquis and Marquise de B*** duly meet Rosambert there with his young 'mistress' and both are highly taken by 'her'. The Marquise insists that they all return to her house for supper. The hour grows late and the Marquise insists that 'she' stay the night and do her the honour of sharing her bed. Rosambert makes increasingly desperate attempts to end the fiction and to reveal that his 'mistress' is a young man in disguise, but the Marquise refuses to hear anything of this: Rosambert is dismissed and the Marquise and Faublas go to bed. The Marquise discovers the truth, feigns a degree of indignation but embarks on a night of lovemaking with Faublas anyway (he thus loses his virginity). In a quiet moment during the night the Marquis enters the bedroom intent on his own dalliance with the intriguing young creature: the Marquise and Faublas change places in bed, however, and the Marquise sends her husband packing. The following morning, Faublas dons his dress and is taken back to his lodgings by the Marquis and Marquise: his true identity is protected by his guardian, and his own affair with the Marquise (which will provoke revenge by Rosambert as it develops) is under way. All this is narrated in the first 57 pages of *Une Année*, and a detail to note is that Louvet de Couvray always refers to his mature, female, aristocratic seducer of Faublas as the Marquise de B***. This (not uncommon) literary device undoubtedly provided contemporary readers with the added frisson of a real person possibly being lightly disguised in the fictional narrative: leaving open the intriguing question of who the Marquise de B*** might really be.

Throughout this episode, Sophie is an entirely passive character, innocently in love with Faublas, living in her convent, unaware of anything that is going on in the world outside. Having slept with an older, sophisticated society lady, Faublas promptly visits Sophie in her convent, inwardly swears undying love to her, and promises himself that he will try harder to resist the temptations of the flesh … only to embark immediately on his second escapade with the Marquise the following night. And so the pattern is repeated; not only with the Marquise, but also with her servant, Justine, with other aristocratic ladies whom he meets such as the Comtesse de Lignolle, and with delightful stage creatures such as *les filles de l'Opéra*.

Treatment by Artus

Taking the above narrative episode as the framework for his dramatic scenario, and ignoring the various intervening stage adaptations, Artus made a number of changes to the disposition of the main characters and to the milieu in which they meet. Since he was creating an individual, delicate and complex stage character, and the female role that was to carry the entire plot forward from the moment of her entrance in Act I, Artus renamed the Marquise de B*** as the Marquise de Bay. Apart from the obvious onomatopoeia, he was on relatively safe ground with his choice of name: there had once been a real Marquis de Bay, in the form of Alexandre, Maître de Bay, who had been elevated by King Philip V of Spain to the rank and title of Marquis de Bay in 1704, but by the nineteenth century the family title subsisted only in the form of Marquis de Maître, and use of de Bay seems to have died out – moreover, they were certainly never a socially active, prominent Parisian aristocratic family who could have been taken as the inspiration for Artus's stage creations.[57] The much more important change made by Artus however was to the character and role of Sophie. Instead of leaving her passively in her convent, awaiting periodic visits from Faublas, Artus decided to bring her in Act I on to the streets of Paris, at carnival time, accompanied by her duenna, Mademoiselle Sauce and by her comic, country lad servant boy, La Jeunesse. The Sophie created by Artus is a modern, twentieth-century spirited girl, determined to have a bit of fun. Since she thus becomes her own free agent, Sophie is in a position to observe the cross-dressed Faublas (whom she recognises) being presented to the Marquise. She thereafter takes matters into her own hands and becomes, to some extent, the real heroine and mover of the piece – she goes for, and gets her man.

To structure his plot, Artus moves from a street scene and public open air ball (the *Jardins d'Armide*) in Act I, to an extended supper scene in the grand reception room of the Marquise de Bay in Act II, to the bedroom of the Marquise de Bay in Act III. The first act is thus a significant change of milieu from Louvet de Couvray: whereas the latter sets the initial encounters between Faublas and the Marquise as aristocratic, high-society, indoor social occasions with invited guests only, the opening stage picture in *L'Ingénu libertin* is that of a popular street party, with all social classes represented. The stage directions make this clear: *As the curtain rises, a lively crowd is seen onstage: grisettes, soldiers, masked ladies, servants, clergymen. A joyous throng of people on carnival night.*[58] The choice of *Les Jardins d'Armide* as the name and setting for the public open air ball at which the Marquise de Bay and Faublas will first become attracted to each other will also have had particular

---

[57] Jean-Baptiste Pierre Courcelles, *Dictionnaire universel de la noblesse de France*, digitised as http://books.google.co.uk/books?id=Tops_B93JPgC&pg=PA428&redir_esc=y#v=onepage&q&f=false.
[58] Artus, p. 5.

22 Outside the inn at carnival time – the setting for Act One of *L'Ingénu libertin* (and a pre-echo of the inn scene in Act Three of *Der Rosenkavalier*).

resonance for enlightened members of the audience such as Kessler: as Noémie Courtès puts it, in her 2004 essay on *Les Jardins d'Armide*:

> Thus Armide, the most emblematic sorceress of the XVIIth century, the creature who is the very incarnation of the ambivalent powers of charm – feminine seduction and magical powers – is inextricably linked to her magical gardens, to the extent that the phrase 'jardin(s) d'Armide' became a popular reference [...][59]

By 1907 there had been twenty-six operas written on the story of Armide, notably by Lully, Gluck, Haydn, Rossini and Dvorak,[60] and in November 1907 the Fokine–Benois ballet *Le Pavillon d'Armide* had premièred in St Petersburg, with the 18 year old Vaslav Nijinsky dancing the role of Armida's slave. This timing is no

---

[59] Noémie Courtès, 'Les Jardins d'Armide – du topos classique au mythe moderne', in *Les mythologies du jardin de l'antiquité à la fin du XIXe siècle*, ed. Gérard Peylet (Bordeaux: Presses Universitaires de Bordeaux, 2004), p. 101.

[60] John Warrack and Ewan West, *The Oxford Dictionary of Opera* (Oxford: Oxford University Press, 1992), p. 31.

more than coincidental (Artus having finished his work by then), but the Bouffes Parisiens decorative setting for the *Jardins d'Armide* – stage right and into the rear stage distance, behind an avenue of plane trees – will undoubtedly have had symbolic meaning as a place of enchantment and feminine seduction. Moreover, when Kessler saw the Ballets Russes dance *Le Pavillon d'Armide* in Paris in June 1909, he immediately made the seductive, feminine connection, and went on to make a number of visual and decorative suggestions to Hofmannsthal for the look and atmosphere of the nascent *Der Rosenkavalier*.

The dramatic structure adopted by Artus is as follows. In Act I, after the opening chorus in which strangers flirt with and kiss each other as part of the carnival atmosphere, Rosambert (baritone) and Faublas (mezzo soprano) meet by chance in the street. Rosambert persuades Faublas to cross-dress for his planned encounter with the Marquise (soprano), whom he intends to seduce. They soon all meet up, watched by an unseen Sophie (soprano), and the Marquise invites everyone to supper. Observing and overhearing that a traiteur will be supplying the supper and staff to wait at table, Sophie cross-dresses in the tunic of a kitchen boy and becomes a member of the traiteur's staff. The cast in procession then moves to the house of the Marquise.

In Act II, both the Marquis (tenor) and the Marquise flirt at table with the disguised Faublas, both Rosambert and the disguised Sophie become increasingly uncomfortable with the way things are developing (the meal at table includes comic business by Sophie as a maladroit waiter as she witnesses the flirtation between Faublas and the Marquise), and when the Marquise and Faublas make preparations for bed, Rosambert storms off swearing revenge, and Sophie despairs of her true love. The climax of the act is the arrival of the vice squad, or *police des moeurs*, prompted by Rosambert and the Marquis, with orders to search the house for the Chevalier de Faublas disguised as a woman and bent on immoral behaviour. To save Faublas, Sophie removes her kitchen boy tunic, dons his discarded Act 1 dress instead and gives herself up to the police, pretending to be Faublas in disguise (one cross-dressed girl thus substituting for another). Faublas and the Marquise are thus left alone, in bed, for the night.

In Act III, as morning breaks in the sumptuously furnished bedroom of the Marquise de Bay, the Marquise and Faublas awake after a night of passionate lovemaking and sing an endearing duet; they regret that it is day already. They learn that it was Sophie who was arrested and taken away in the night. Faublas is troubled: the Marquise recognises the object of his young love and sends discreet word by letter to her friend, the chief of police, who owes her a favour. Prompted by the Marquise, and since the dress he wore the previous evening has been appropriated by Sophie, Faublas now dons the kitchen boy tunic that Sophie had previously worn. Shortly thereafter Sophie is released and arrives back at the house. She tells Faublas that she now hates him for the way he has behaved. The Marquise, Faublas and Sophie have an extended scene together: Sophie firstly recalls a romantic air that Faublas once wrote for her, and sang in the garden beneath her convent window: she and Faublas then sing the air as a simple duet, and this leads directly to the all-female

23 The trio – a leitmotif running from *L'Ingénu libertin* to the final, moving pages of *Der Rosenkavalier*. Here the Marquise blindfolds Faublas and invites him to let his senses choose between her and his childhood love, Sophie

24 *Le coucher de la mariée* by Pierre-Antoine Baudouin (1723–69). Part of the Rothschild Collection at the Louvre, this original print shows clearly how detailed and accurate a copy was made of the room and bed in question for Act Three of *L'Ingénu libertin*

trio that is the longest number in the piece, and its musical and dramatic highlight. The Marquise blindfolds Faublas with her scarf and asks him to follow his heart, not his eyes: in an amorous form of blind man's buff, Faublas moves instinctively between the two ladies, relives the delights of his night with the Marquise, but decides finally that it is Sophie whom he really loves and has done all along. The Marquise blesses their union, tells Sophie that she is the more deserving of Faublas's love, hands him over to her younger rival and sheds a wistful tear. The rest of the cast then enter and a final rousing chorus points up the moral of the piece.

The theatrical and visual effectiveness of *L'Ingénu libertin* must have been striking, both for the sumptuousness of the costumes and for the ingenuity of the cross-dressing: hardly a new feature of opérette and comic opera, but exploited here by Artus to an unusually sophisticated degree. With his keen eye for visual detail, Kessler cannot fail to have noticed the progression and swapping of roles: first seeing Faublas in his elegant chevalier costume, in knee-high boots, dark red silk taffeta trousers and jacket, with green and white silk-embroidered waistcoat; then cross-dressed in a cream-coloured silk shepherdess outfit; and finally dressed again as a young man in the kitchen boy tunic (white satin jacket, culotte and beret) discarded by Sophie. For her, the progression is reversed: from her lavender-coloured

Act One: The Young Libertine

dress in Act I, to the kitchen boy tunic in Act II, to Faublas's discarded shepherdess outfit in Act III.[61] The two young lovers, at the end of the piece, are thus in each other's costumes as they swear undying love to each other, and both are played by women anyway: the sexual frisson in many productions of both the opening and the closing scenes of *Der Rosenkavalier* is foreshadowed here.

In schematic form, the changes made by Artus to the Louvet de Couvray narrative are shown in the following chart. It should be noted at this stage that between February and July 1909 Hofmannsthal only had Kessler's oral account of the Artus scenario and libretto, plus whatever Kessler saw fit (and was able) to relate about Terrasse's musical treatment of the piece, to work on: it was not until 28 July 1909 that Hofmannsthal wrote to Kessler saying that he had just obtained from Paris a copy of the libretto of *L'Ingénu libertin*, which he found 'very charming'.[62] But by that time Strauss was already in possession of nearly complete versions of Acts I and II, had completed what he described as the musical 'rough sketch' of the first act, and was well ahead with his musical inspiration for the whole piece.[63]

Louvet de Couvray	Artus
Faublas meets Sophie when he visits his sister Adelaide in the latter's convent, and falls instantly for her.	Faublas and Sophie are already childhood sweethearts before the play starts.
Sophie remains in her convent with Adelaide while Faublas explores Paris.	Sophie has escaped from her convent to enjoy a street party in Paris.
Faublas visits the convent dressed as a girl to get close to Sophie and give her a first kiss on the lips.	No equivalent incident.
Rosambert has embarked on his affair with the Marquise de B and wants a disguised Faublas to give added piquancy to their liaison.	Rosambert wants Faublas disguised as a girl to excite the Marquise's jealousy and provoke her into embarking on an affair with him.
Rosambert has no interest in Sophie.	Rosambert tells Faublas he will soon marry Sophie but wants to enjoy his affair with the Marquise de Bay first.
Sophie knows nothing of the encounter between Faublas and the Marquise de B.	Sophie cross-dresses as a kitchen boy to enter the Marquise de Bay's home and to observe her and Faublas.

---

[61] *Comoedia*, 12 December 1907, pp. 1–2. This fully illustrated account of the piece and its first night reception includes articles by Edmond Diet, Louis Schneider and Pierre Souvestre, with detailed descriptions of the *mise en scène*, décors and costumes.
[62] Burger, p. 253.
[63] Hamm./Osers, p. 33.

The Marquis de B is a comic dupe, 'expert" in physiognomy. He tries to creep into bed with the disguised Faublas: the Marquise sees him off.	The Marquis de Bay is a comic dupe, 'expert' in physiognomy, and flirts with the cross-dressed Faublas at table: he also insists on a goodnight kiss from the Marquise and from Faublas.
Sophie remains in her convent throughout.	Sophie saves Faublas from the vice squad by impersonating him and by allowing herself to be arrested.
After his night of passion with the Marquise, Faublas is taken by her and the Marquis back to his guardian: his adventures continue.	After his night of passion with the Marquise, Faublas has to choose between her and Sophie: he chooses the latter. The Marquise de Bay gives way to the young lovers and blesses their union.
Justine, clever and resourceful maid to the Marquise, acts as go-between to Faublas and is seduced by him.	Justine, clever and resourceful maid to the Marquise, has her own love interest and sub-plot.

Reception

L'Ingénu libertin opened to near universal critical approval. As indicated at the start of this chapter, there was a chorus of goodwill for the return of opérette to its spiritual home, the Bouffes Parisiens. Yet the musical and dramatic qualities of *L'Ingénu libertin* drew widespread critical plaudits in their own right.

The veteran poet and playwright Catulle Mendès had nothing but praise for the work. 'It is utterly charming. The libretto? The music? Equally fine. Thoughtful, amusing, scintillating, sparkling, enchanting'.[64] Paul Reboux wrote:

> The music by Claude Terrasse was applauded as enthusiastically as the delicious comedy by M. Artus. The composer has managed to recreate the style of the age without reverting to pastiche. Maybe his melodies are not that memorable and do not stay indelibly with you after it is all over, but they are all graceful, accented, original and tender: and all his orchestral accompaniments are distinguished by masterful originality.[65]

Nozière, who had himself just made a stage version of *Les Liaisons Dangereuses*, which played outside Paris at the château of Le Comte de Clermont Tonnerre in Maisons Laffitte in December 1907, concentrated initially on the stage adaptation:

> M. Louis Artus has inspired me to read all the adventures of this irresistible Chevalier. Onstage at the Bouffes Parisiens we can watch a lady giving first lessons to this adolescent, this Cherubino, this Fortunio. It is a very enjoyable show with a delicious

---

[64] Catulle Mendès, *Le Journal*, 12 December 1907. Catulle Mendès, born 1841, was to die just over a year later, in 1909.

[65] Paul Reboux, *L'Intransigeant*, 13 December 1907.

Act One: The Young Libertine

25 The title page of *Comoedia* on 12 December 1907. Details of *L'Ingénu libertin* costumes, sets, principals and performances occupied half this issue. *Comoedia* provided a daily record of the arts, especially music and theatre, from October 1907 until August 1914

frisson to it. M. Louis Artus knows how to maintain the exquisite tone of the eighteenth century, he has almost entirely avoided words that shock us, he lets us see some daring scenes, but they are always elegant. Claude Terrasse's music is a fitting accompaniment to this play and is nearly always of great distinction.[66]

Nozière's reference to the adolescent Faublas as a Cherubino has been echoed many times by scholars attempting to examine the literary, stage and operatic forerunners of Octavian in *Der Rosenkavalier*: an extended essay on precisely this topic by Juliane Vogel forms part of an anthology of writings on the women in the Strauss–Hofmannsthal operatic canon.[67] But Vogel looks no further than Cherubino for Octavian's operatic ancestor and role model. More interestingly, Nozière

---

[66] Nozière, *Gil Blas*, 12 December 1907.
[67] *Richard Strauss, Hugo von Hofmannsthal Frauenbilder*, ed. Ilja Dürhammer and Pia Janke (Vienna: Edition Praesens, 2001), pp. 97–107.

also refers to Fortunio in the Faublas context: the première of Messager's opérette *Fortunio* had taken place at the Opéra Comique a mere five months previously, and onstage seduction of an adolescent boy was still clearly a topic worth mentioning, although Messager had deliberately set the part of Fortunio for a lyric tenor, thus avoiding the sexual ambiguities of a girl, cross-dressed as a boy, being seduced by an older woman.

Writing in *Le Soir* on 13 December 1907, B. de Lomagne assessed the work thus:

> For this fine libretto M. Claude Terrasse has written a full and brilliant score, in keeping with the subject, without trying to be archaic and with many numbers that were warmly applauded. In particular: in Act I the 'physiognomy' song, the duet for the Marquise and Faublas, the chorus for the kitchen boys; in Act II, the air for Justine, a touching soubrette, the buffo duet, the drinking song; in Act III the awakening duet, the ensemble for the Marquise's levée (a fascinating reconstruction of the famous Baudoin painting called 'le coucher de la mariée' etc.[68]

In *Libre Parole*, Jean Drault wrote:

> M. Terrasse has also taken care over his orchestration. This is perhaps the first time in opérette that we can hear certain sonorities that have been the province of modern symphony orchestras until now. The composer also had a personal success playing the harpsichord to accompany the sad refrain of the heroine who thinks that the Marquise has trapped the man she loves. In brief, it's a success.[69]

Robert de Flers was even more fulsome in *Liberté*:

> Last night M. Claude Terrasse, to whom we owe *Les Travaux d'Hercule*, *Le Sire de Vergy* and *Monsieur de la Palisse*, which I cannot manage to put completely out of mind, proved himself to be the Marivaux of the opérette.[70] In so doing he found a variety of rhythms and melodies that bear witness to the flexibility of his inspiration and the finesse of his art. The trio in the last act is the very best in opéra-comique, and of the utmost delicacy. The duet between the soubrette and La Jeunesse in the second act is the most joyful type of *opéra bouffe* and I could quote twenty more numbers, the tunes of which you would remember more readily than their names.[71]

In terms of the cast, contemporary reception of *L'Ingénu libertin* makes clear that the star feature of the piece was the role of the Marquise, played by Arlette Dorgère. She was 27 at the time and had already appeared in the *travesti* role in Terrasse's *Le Sire de Vergy* four years previously. Raoul Aubry encapsulated the views of many critics when he wrote of her:

---

[68] B. de Lomagne, *Le Soir*, 13 December 1907. The Baudoin painting and its inspiration for the opening scene of *Der Rosenkavalier* will be addressed later.

[69] Jean Drault, *Libre Parole*, 12 December 1907.

[70] Pierre Marivaux (1688–1763) was a master of the playful, sometimes erotic eighteenth-century style onstage, to which Artus and Terrasse aspired.

[71] Robert de Flers, *Liberté*, 12 December 1907.

Arlette Dorgère, rosy under her blonde hair, and flirtatious, and elegant, and sly, could have settled for being adorably pretty. But just imagine, she decides to sing, to act, and she sings enchantingly, in a voice with a natural, delicious timbre, and she acts to the manner born, with mischievous grace that is absolutely eighteenth century![72]

26 Arlette Dorgère by Jane de Montchenu-Lavirotte (1857–1924), exhibited at the Salon des femmes peintres, an annual exhibition of the works of women artists

Other adjectives used of her performance include 'exquisite', 'adorable', 'seductive', with unanimous praise for her singing and acting abilities and comments on her beauty onstage: 'Mlle Arlette Dorgère is a ravishing Marquise de Bay, as well dressed in Act I as undressed in Act III.'[73] And the part clearly marked a sort

[72] Raoul Aubry, *Soirée Parisienne* (undated).
[73] Mondor, *La Presse*, 13 December 1907.

of coming of age for her: in an interview dated 10 May 1910, after Dorgère had abandoned the opérette stage to launch her career as a serious actress, she recalled:

> But it was lucky chance that made me accept a job with the Bouffes to create a new character in *L'Ingénu libertin*, a cautionary tale, delicate and spiritual, and I was filled with such intense joy at getting into every minute aspect of the role I had to play that I immediately decided to focus all my efforts on acting.[74]

In the role of Faublas, Jeanne Alba had good, but slightly more mixed reviews. Nozière praised her 'clear diction, warm voice and natural movement' but added that 'she does not yet have that star quality, that mastery that unleashes an audience's enthusiasm'.[75] The *Libre Parole* reviewer, Drault, seeing in the part qualities that Alba did not possess, wrote, 'What this role should have had was a Déjazet or a Granier!'[76] He and others questioned the effectiveness of having a woman dressed as a man who disguises herself as a woman for much of the play – ignoring perhaps the musical opportunities this gave Terrasse for contrasting and occasionally harmonising three very different female voices, and the long stage history of precisely that *travesti* construct, exemplified by Déjazet on the nineteenth-century French stage, and in the opera houses of Europe for even longer.

The Sophie of Jeanne Petit was praised for her delicacy and artistry but the minor role that elicited real enthusiasm from the critics – and clearly from the audience – was that of the soubrette Justine, played by Andrée Divonne. Robert Dieudonné went as far as to say:

> Finally, the greatest triumph of the evening, be it said, was that of Andrée Divonne who enchanted the whole audience with her small soubrette part. It is impossible to act more gaily, more charmingly, more adroitly and let me assure you that looking at her onstage doubles the pleasure you get in hearing her sing.[77]

General critical opinion of the male roles was less favourable, with Jean Coizeau being found too lightweight (and with too small a baritone voice) in the role of Rosambert, and Milo de Meyer being accused of somewhat gross overacting in the role of the Marquis de Bay (an accusation that many a Baron Ochs has faced in the hundred years of *Der Rosenkavalier*). But unanimous and high praise was given to the chorus and orchestra, conducted from memory – as several critics noted – by a young conductor making his debut, Philippe Moreau, who was studying composition with Xavier Leroux at the Paris Conservatoire at the time.[78] Moreau's

---

[74] Arlette Dorgère, microfiche in the Collection Rondel, BNF, Paris.
[75] Nozière, *Gil Blas*, 12 December 1907.
[76] Virginie Déjazet (1798–1875) and Jeanne Granier (1852–1939) were among the leading French actresses of their day, often playing young male roles *en travesti*.
[77] Robert Dieudonné, untitled and undated press cutting, from *Le Courrier de la Presse*, presumed December 1907.
[78] Leroux himself had studied with Jules Massenet and went on to compose many operas: his works were played at the Promenade concerts in London until the 1920s.

father, Emile, had collaborated with Victorien Sardou on the hugely successful play *Madame Sans Gêne*.

Thus in contemporary review after review – around thirty in total – the same adjectives to describe the libretto, music and cast keep recurring: delicate, charming, inspired, witty, gracious, refined, joyful, brilliant; while the only mildly critical remarks refer to the suggestive nature of the erotic theme itself ('disturbingly equivocal') and the difficulty for Jeanne Alba, the mezzo playing Faublas, to convey the complexities of a woman playing a young man who cross-dresses as a woman. But the overwhelming critical consensus is that the work is cleverly and delicately written, and set to music by Terrasse in entirely appropriate fashion. The anonymous critic 'Intérim' summed up many other reviews in *Echo* when he wrote:

> The score by M. Claude Terrasse envelops this light-hearted libretto in an atmosphere full of finesse and charm. It is as light and airy as the characters but also has lots more verve. All the verses received ovations; and several were encored, including a delicious romance of an archaic nature, which the composer himself accompanied at the harpsichord. This is one of the best and most refined scores that M. Claude Terrasse has ever written.[79]

Likewise Edmond Diet in *Comoedia*, whose overall summing up ran as follows:

> A full and sonorous orchestra, with two trumpets improving on the traditional two cornets, brought out charming instrumental details, under the decisive and authoritative baton of M. Philippe Moreau, an astonishing 'capellmeister', who conducted entirely from memory without a single lapse. At last we have the Bouffes back on its original course, which it never should have abandoned. Experience shows that one cannot run a theatre profitably if you change its genre.

This overall favourable critical consensus subsequently found its way into the standard companion guide to French opérette, *Histoire de l'Opérette en France* by Florian Bruyas. Bruyas writes:

> But near the end of the year, the Bouffes Parisiens were to be applauded for a fine piece of work. This was the 'galante' opérette by Louis Artus originally called *La Marquise et le Marmiton* but finally and more invitingly called *L'Ingénu libertin*. Claude Terrasse himself had written the score. On the very stage where *Les Travaux d'Hercule* had been performed with such success, he put on the most charming and delightful light-hearted tale, in the manner of the eighteenth century, that you could possibly imagine. His score was elegant and gracious. It proved that the young master was capable of reinventing himself, and that even if his normal style was Offenbach buffoonery, he was capable of writing refined scores with the Lecocq style much in evidence. *L'Ingénu libertin* was a big success ... with *L'Ingénu libertin* Claude Terrasse

---

[79] Intérim, *Echo*, 13 December 1907.

had given proof that he was just as capable of writing refined and sentimental music as he was of writing buffo or parody scores.[80]

27 Claude Terrasse (on the bed) and members of the production team on 10 December 1907, at the end of the (public) dress rehearsal of *L'Ingénu libertin*

This, then, was the subsequent received critical opinion of the work. Its immediate success, and the raft of favourable contemporary reviews (to which Kessler had ready access, during the twenty-eight days that he spent on and off in Paris during its run) must have been among those factors that inspired Kessler, just over one year later, to suggest it to Hofmannsthal as a matrix for the new comedy to be set to music by Strauss. There is, however, one unexplained aspect to its reception and stage history. On 19 January 1908 (the day after Kessler saw the piece), a column on page 5 of *Le Figaro* announced that its fiftieth performance would be on 20 January and wrote:

> The first stage towards great success: and this first stage will not be the only one, to judge by the large sums currently coming in via the box office and the unanimous cheers of the audience, night after night.

Fifty performances of a new piece in an original run were regarded as a success on the Paris stages of the time: a hundred performances were celebrated, even more, as a great success. In exactly the same vein, *Le Petit Parisien* made the

[80] Bruyas, pp. 354–5.

same announcement (that the fiftieth performance of *L'Ingénu libertin* would take place the following day) and added: 'And this is still only the beginning of its stage career.'[81] However, on 28 January the same newspaper reported that rehearsals were at an advanced stage for a new revue at the Bouffes Parisiens, and that Deval and Richemond were therefore announcing the final performances of *L'Ingénu libertin*.[82] A clue as to what might have happened came with a report, elsewhere in the press, on the same day:

> Tomorrow Miss Arlette Dorgère will resume the role in *L'Ingénu libertin* of the Marquise de Bay, which is such a remarkable creation of hers. During her absence she has been replaced by Mademoiselle Brieux: a charming artist who has stood in for her brilliant colleague very skillfully.[83]

Arlette Dorgère therefore came back for the last six performances only, as subsequently reported in *Le Figaro* on 1 February: 'Tonight and tomorrow (matinée and evening) the last three performances of *L'Ingénu libertin*, which will be taken off in the midst of its success.' There was, however, no report as to where Dorgère might have been, nor of what might have happened to her, either in *Le Figaro* or elsewhere in the press. As it happens, the Marquise de Bay was to be the last opérette role taken by Dorgère for some time, but the reasons for her sudden disappearance (and reappearance for the last few performances) are unexplained. It might be that she quarrelled with the management, or made financial demands on them that could not be met, or there may have been some mundane reason such as illness that kept her offstage at a key moment in the developing commercial success of the piece. Of possible significance is that the revue, which came out of nowhere to replace *L'Ingénu libertin*, had in its cast four of the main performers from that work: Jeanne Alba (Faublas), Milo de Meyer (Marquis de Bay), Hasti (La Jeunesse) and Andrée Divonne (Justine) and some of the supporting performers too. Their presence, and the absence of Dorgère, seems to indicate that personal factors relating to her, of one sort or another, were at work. The net outcome, for whatever reasons, was that *L'Ingénu libertin* enjoyed twenty-five performances in 1907 and forty-one in 1908, a grand (and perfectly respectable) total of sixty-six performances in all.

So this huge commercial and critical success for the Bouffes Parisiens, which put the theatre firmly back on the map, came to a somewhat abrupt and surprising end. The reception of *L'Ingénu libertin* speaks for itself, however. And before we leave it, the work needs to be recreated as a piece of music theatre, its musico-dramatic and performative elements described, and its impact – particularly and specifically on Kessler as he sat and took in the work – assessed, for what was to follow. I can only attempt this because of the generous help I was given in the course of my researches, as follows. When I first came across references to *L'Ingénu*

---

[81] Unsigned, *Le Petit Parisien*, 19 January 1908, p. 4.
[82] *Le Petit Parisien*, 28 January 1908, p. 4.
[83] *Le Figaro*, 28 January 1908, pp. 4–5.

libertin, I tried – in vain – to track it down. The BNF in Paris claimed to have both libretto and score, but repeated attempts to locate these items failed – and I was told that 'for technical reasons' they were 'unavailable' (ie presumed lost). But working through friends in Paris, and friends of friends, I came across the incredibly knowledgeable and helpful Christophe Mirambeau, who made it his business to locate and to try and obtain everything I wanted. First, he found me a secondhand copy of the libretto. Then, with more difficulty, a copy of the *mise en scène* – that truly valuable document (called *Regiebuch* by the Germans) that itemises every aspect of the piece as it is to be performed: where props and costume changes are to be left around the stage, where each character stands onstage, how every musical and visual clue is to be picked up and timed in performance. And finally he found for me, through the good offices of French Universal, the original, autograph pages of the full orchestral score, languishing in a drawer on the premises of the original printers in Milan, who had printed a Vocal Score for Terrasse's own company, the Société d'Editions Musicales in 1907, but never – apparently – a full orchestral score. The search took a year, but at the end of it I had everything necessary for a thorough analysis of both the music and the theatre in this music theatre piece. Without it, none of what follows could have been written.

L'Ingénu libertin in performance

Let us take a seat alongside Kessler, and try to recreate what he saw and heard as he entered and took his place in the Bouffes Parisiens, waiting for the 8.45 p.m. performance on Saturday 18 January to start. When we meet Kessler the man and explore his passion for all forms of theatre – a passion that developed from a young age and was with him throughout his life – we shall understand better how he was able to absorb all the salient features of a single performance of *L'Ingénu libertin*, and to rearrange those performative elements into the nascent *Der Rosenkavalier*. But what did he actually experience that Saturday night?

The theatre first of all – it had been re-carpeted, re-curtained, re-lit and the red plush velvet seats renewed. Money had been spent on a complete makeover, the chandeliers sparkled and there was a distinct buzz from the expectant, capacity house. The Bouffes had originally been intended (and licensed) as an intimate, small-scale performance venue but the building – Salle Choiseul – was remodelled several times and in December 1907 the auditorium had 1,100 seats. (It was reduced to its present size of 600 seats in the last rebuild of 1913.) Despite its overall size, the orchestra pit, as in Offenbach's day, was still small and shallow, just seven and a half metres wide and two and a third metres deep.[84] This gave comfortable

---

[84] These dimensions were provided in person by the current stage management staff, during two visits to the theatre on 5 and 8 March 2012, after careful measurement and some further research. The historical records of the period were removed and either lost or destroyed during the period of ownership (1986–2007) of the Bouffes Parisiens by Jean-Claude Brialy (1933–2007): very few have found their way to the BNF or to the BHVP.

Act One: The Young Libertine 59

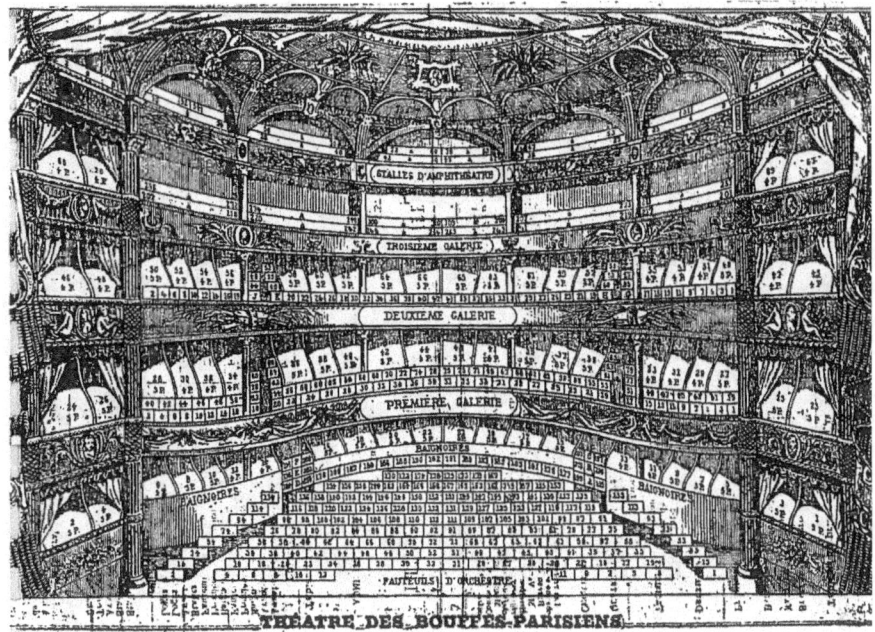

28 Interior of the Théâtre des Bouffes Parisiens in 1876

playing space to an orchestra of eighteen to twenty musicians, with possible space for up to twenty-five: however, for *L'Ingénu libertin* there was also a harpsichord in the pit, played by Terrasse himself each night that he attended a performance, which points to around twenty players in all (the programme does not list the orchestra).

The work is scored for the standard string section (first and second violins, viola, cello and double bass), timpani, trombone, two trumpets, two horns, bassoon, two clarinets, oboe, piccolo and flute, again implying an orchestra of twenty. For the size of auditorium and acoustic of the Bouffes Parisiens, this orchestra will have been more than adequate, and as already noted, with a generous prior rehearsal period under the talented young conductor Philippe Moreau, who had learned the score by heart and conducted it from memory, the musical results were clearly impressive.

The lights dim and the overture begins – bright and rousing, in D major (two trumpets) and 2/4 time, and immediately more interesting than standard opérette fare, with a suggestion of Bach counterpoint in the strings and an eighteenth-century, classical feel to the modulatory passages: Kessler moreover will have heard almost at once that the work is to be full of waltz melodies. For after the opening arpeggio flourishes, for full orchestra, the music softens to play Sophie's solo *Romance* from Act II, an *Andantino* in waltz time, firstly just played by strings and then gradually with flute, oboe and clarinet lending colour to the plaintive melodic

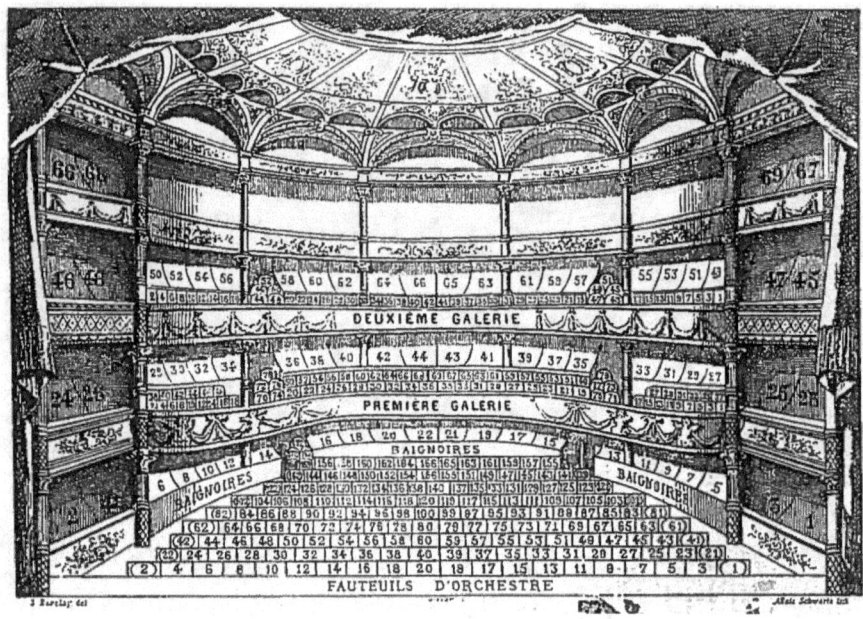

29 Théâtre des Bouffes Parisiens in 1871–2, before its enlargement

line. After another brief modulation, the orchestra then takes up the refrain of the first extended number in Act I between the Marquise de Bay and Faublas: *Duo et Valse des Questions Amoureuses*, a waltz tune that is to recur as a motif (in different keys) throughout the piece, and to be used as the finale to the whole work in Act III, sung by the Marquise and Faublas, this time over full chorus, and in the home key of D major. (In its B flat major incarnation in Act I, this number has some interesting and subtle orchestration, with a high solo violin accompanying and embellishing the melodic line of the Marquise as the voice is sustained by the lower strings, violas and celli.) The overture then has a lively passage in A major, anticipating both the full chorus of servants and kitchen boys in the finale to Act I, and the duet for Sophie and her servant La Jeunesse as they arrive in the home of the Marquise de Bay in Act II, before reverting to an orchestral flourish in D major in its final bars.

Curtain up. Full chorus, singing of the joys of carnival, swirling movement, gaiety onstage. The stage picture is a well-built, beautifully designed and constructed outdoor street and park scene with a riot of vivid colours and bright lights – the *mise en scène* specifies Venetian lanterns forming garlands of light among the branches and leaves of the plane trees, with the entrance to the public ball area (*Les Jardins d'Armide*) brilliantly lit. The stage is crowded and the action lively from the outset, in an atmosphere of 'anything goes', with entrances, exits and a constant procession by members of the chorus in contrasting carnival costumes – a clergyman *en travesti*, a Harlequin and a Columbine, some of the men in military

Act One: The Young Libertine 61

30 Overture to *L'Ingénu libertin* in full orchestral score (manuscript).
A determined search with the help of Christophe Mirambeau of Universal Music
France led to discovery of this delightful music in a store cupboard in Milan

uniform, many of the ladies masked. And emerging from the chorus, as they sing in two-part harmony of the naughtiness of the goings-on at carnival time, the audience is introduced to the resourceful Justine, chambermaid to the Marquise (*pace* Susanna to the Countess in *Le Nozze di Figaro*), then to Faublas, the elegant principal boy, and then to Rosambert. Justine sings of servants and masters, all masked, all mingling at the ball and doing what they want – until midnight strikes – and then, as Faublas and Rosambert meet by chance and catch up with each other, Faublas develops his own musical introduction (his E minor/major Air in slow waltz time being one of the leitmotifs of the work), telling Rosambert that this is the little song that he has often sung outside the convent walls, like a troubadour, to the girl whom he loves and who has been confined within the convent by her father. Faublas does not give her name, and Rosambert does not ask, but the audience know immediately that Sophie is the girl he means – and loves.

The first act is constructed symmetrically, starting and ending with full chorus and onstage action, the intervening numbers being the solo Air for Faublas, introductory solos and a duet for Sophie and La Jeunesse, an extended quartet for the Marquis, Marquise, Faublas and Rosambert, a patter song for the Marquis (*Couplets de la Physiognomie*), a duet for Sophie and La Jeunesse, and a duet for the Marquise and Faublas – nine numbers in total in the space of under forty minutes – with all the principals being allowed to establish their character, interrelationships and plot functions. For Kessler, who knew *Une Année*, the biggest surprise will have been the spirited and independent figure of Sophie: clearly an original take on the *Faublas* narrative canon. And knowing what was going to develop between Faublas and the Marquise later in the piece, the plot question in Kessler's head must have been: how is Artus going to sustain this love triangle dramatically until it can be resolved? If Sophie is on the loose, and is clearly a spirited and independent young lady, how can he keep these characters apart until they have to come together at the end?

Meanwhile however he will have enjoyed the effectiveness and the pantomime of an opening number where a great deal is going on in a party atmosphere onstage. The little masquerades, with protagonists in disguise, with nobody necessarily being whom they seem or purport to be: the action moving swiftly from a table outside the inn where Rosambert and Faublas have their preliminary drink together to the circular wooden seat surrounding one of the decorated plane trees where Sophie and La Jeunesse, when they make their entrance, exchange their own thoughts and observations on the action elsewhere onstage and make their plans. He will have noted the deftness of the dialogue, in which Rosambert (rather coarsely) boasts to Faublas of his forthcoming marriage to Sophie and of his plan to seduce the Marquise first, while Faublas reveals to the audience (but not to Rosambert) that Sophie is the girl whom he already adores. And following our own introduction to Sophie – determined to join in the street party and escape the confines of her convent for just one night – and 'protected' by her duenna Mademoiselle Sauce and her faithful servant from childhood, La Jeunesse, Kessler will have noted the neat progression of parallel stage narratives: Faublas (already disguised as a girl) being introduced by Rosambert to the Marquis and Marquise de Bay and getting to know them, Sophie and La Jeunesse observing and overhearing all the action unseen, and finally disguising themselves as kitchen staff for the traiteur who is to supply the Marquis de Bay with his planned midnight feast. So in addition to being visually and theatrically attractive from the outset, and pantomimic in its broad outlines, Act I provides all the features of the well-made play in opérette form: clear, vivid (and contrasting) characters, a simple storyline, expert and delicate orchestration and a rousing finale, with all the cast preparing themselves to move off to the Hotel du Marquis de Bay (hampers being stacked on stage, torches and a torch-lit procession at the ready – just like the ending of the first act in Rostand's *Cyrano de Bergerac*, when the cast decamp with loud cries and huge enthusiasm to the Porte de Nesle). The effect must have been as fresh theatrically as enjoyable musically – an expert piece of music theatre.

The visual impact of Act II must have been equally striking. The grand drawing room, or boudoir of the Marquise de Bay is described in the *mise en scène* as a *salon riche, style Louis XV*. Pastoral pictures in the style of Watteau hang from the solid, silver-grey walls, an open fire burning in the central fireplace, with four sets of double doors leading to the other rooms of the house – including the Marquise's bedroom. The effect is highly decorative, the stage furniture sumptuous. We have now moved into the private sphere, and the act opens with another solo for

Act One: The Young Libertine 63

31 Four of the principals in Act One of *L'Ingénu libertin*. Milo de Meyer as the
Marquis de Bay is struck by the feminine attractions of Faublas
(as will be Baron Ochs by the allure of Mariandel)

Justine, back from the street party, singing of the equality of masters and servants at carnival time – but ready to spring into action with the return of the Marquise, Faublas, Rosambert and the Marquis leading their torch-lit retinue, just ahead of the traiteur's staff bringing in supper.

Kessler will have noted, just as in Act I, the alternation of each strand in the plot and narrative development of the piece. Sophie and La Jeunesse are interlopers in the Marquise's house but they meet Justine – who turns out to have known La Jeunesse in childhood, and the two have an amusing 'reminiscence' duet. Here, as throughout, the orchestration is painted with a fine brush, especially when words in the libretto are to be pointed up: and as Justine and La Jeunesse reminisce (but disagree on which particular animals they used to see in the countryside fields around them), Kessler cannot fail to have heard horns and bassoon making little interjections to depict the cows and the sheep they summon up in their respective imaginations – a feature of the score noted subsequently by several of the music critics who had attended the première, and typical of Terrasse's musical wit.

Act II is fast-moving (a minority of the critics declaring it to be the best in the piece). Rosambert tries to persuade Faublas to call off the masquerade, but Faublas declines – he is enjoying himself, and requires supper. As a table is laid in the boudoir, centre stage, and places taken, the Marquis and Marquise sit either side of Faublas and both try to cosy up to him (he rebuffs the former but not the latter). As matters progress, Rosambert becomes increasingly exasperated, Sophie increasingly anxious at the relationship developing between Faublas and the Marquise, and stage business is given free rein: Faublas fending off the Marquis (who is surprised that a young girl should be so feisty and strong-handed), and Sophie spilling food and drink as her dismay gets the better of her rudimentary waiting skills at table. Kessler will have noted the distinct elements of farcical comedy here: the situation is not quite identical, but the attempted seduction of Mariandel by Baron Ochs at the private table of the inn in Act III of *Der Rosenkavalier* owes much to the stage business between Faublas and the Marquis. The Marquis asks the 'ladies' to entertain the company with a song, and the Marquise obliges with her *Chanson du Joli Jardin*, a deceptively simple strophic song in which Faublas and Rosambert gradually participate too: the words are witty and slightly *risqué*, the moral being that for a Marquise's garden to flourish, she needs the right gardener. The stage for seduction is being set in words and music.

The Marquise now acts decisively – it is late, and time for her to take Rosambert's charming young lady companion to bed. Rosambert again tries to abandon his little deception and tells the Marquise that she has been exchanging intimacies not with a young lady but with the chevalier de Faublas, but the Marquise flatly refuses to believe him: she and Rosambert exchange heated words and the orchestra introduces a cleverly written septet. The Marquise and the Marquis sing goodnight to Rosambert, he sings of his rage and his desire to take revenge on Faublas,

32 Act Two of *L'Ingénu libertin* nearing its climax, with an anxious Sophie centre stage (dressed as a male waiter) anticipating the seduction of Faublas that is about to happen under the nose of the Marquis de Bay

the latter reminds Rosambert that the whole situation is his doing anyway, while Sophie, La Jeunesse and Justine echo the words and sentiments of their employers. As the seven principals sing their respective melodic lines, a distinct musical warning around Rosambert's name can be heard in the orchestra, in the form of a woodwind *appoggiatura* playing recurring minor seconds, as the Marquise tries to get rid of him and he sings of his anger about what is happening. And as the number progresses further, high flutes play little mocking phrases as Rosambert realises he has been outwitted: the orchestration and musical characterisation are witty and vivid here. So, as he and the Marquis are ushered outside the room, bassoon, clarinets and horns darken the orchestral sound to indicate that bedtime is approaching; Sophie, La Jeunesse and Justine are dismissed by the Marquise (not without resistance from Sophie, who fears what is going to happen) and finally the Marquise's four maidservants enter to the strains of a graceful minuet, as they arrive to undress 'the ladies' for bed. That too gives rise to comedy, Faublas being as keen that the girls should not unlace his costume and see him as he is (or is supposed to be), as they are to do their young guest a customary service. And so they too are dismissed, with the Marquise and Faublas left alone onstage, for a charming and romantic solo by the Marquise, the *Couplets de la Petite Maman*. The melody is wistful, the orchestration delicate and the couple ever more physically intimate in a large easy chair in which the Marquise has made space for Faublas to sit beside her as she sings. They snuggle up together in a tender moment.

There must of course be a further interruption. The Marquis bangs on the salon door, asking if he can watch his wife going to bed: the Marquise refuses, then she and Faublas quickly hide behind separate screens, nightdresses in their hands, as the Marquis forces the door open and demands a forfeit from each lady for leaving them in peace. Each of them kisses him on the cheek in turn and he leaves. It is now the turn of Faublas for a solo, the *Couplets de la Déclaration*, in which he sings of his nascent desires, his mounting passion, until he distractedly seizes the bare foot of the Marquise and kisses it ardently, just above the ankle. 'Good heavens! It is a man!' she exclaims at last, feigning indignation at something she has known for some time, and after chiding Faublas and debating aloud the delicate situation in which she now finds herself, the Marquise takes a decision and explains herself both to him and to the audience:

Faublas: Oh, please forgive me, dear *maman*.
Marquise: Yes, your dear *maman*. You really care about your dear *maman*, you little libertine! (*Pause, and then finally giving in*:) Faublas, you know the Marquis; I was married off, I had no say in it, I was sacrificed. What woman will ever be forgiven if I am judged severely?
Faublas: Oh madame! Do you forgive me then?
Marquise: My dear Faublas! My friend! Come with me. (*In a tender embrace they both enter the Marquise's bedroom.*)

Did Kessler ever think back to this exchange when, a year later, he and Hofmannsthal were starting to characterise the Marschallin in *Der Rosenkavalier* and provide her back story, the young girl fresh from her convent who was married off to the Field Marshall with no say in the matter? It can only be a matter of conjecture, of course, but the parallels are striking. However, Act II is not yet over. Sophie and La Jeunesse are still in the house and they re-enter the salon. Sophie now has her own song of despair, a *Romance* in G major in which she laments the infidelity of Faublas, the man she loved and who once made her happy. She asks a somewhat tipsy La Jeunesse what he makes of the situation, but he has urgent and alarming news of his own – Rosambert has alerted the police that there are imposters in the house, and they are all about to be discovered and undone. As the rousing finale to Act II then gets under way and a posse of police enters the house, Sophie finds the dress discarded by Faublas, swaps it for her kitchen boy outfit and decides to save his name and reputation by pretending to be him: the stage is then crowded with police officers, servants, the Marquis in his nightshirt, all bent on searching the house from top to bottom. They have no need to do so: Sophie steps forward, says she is the Chevalier de Faublas and is led away to prison for the night. The Marquise and Faublas are briefly disturbed by all the commotion, and both emerge from the bedroom in somewhat crumpled nightdresses (*dans un aimable désordre*, as the stage directions put it), but the Marquis takes charge and insists they return to the Marquise's bedroom. And as they do so, the music fades into ¾ time for the

33 Faublas and the Marquise de Bay being undressed for bed by the Marquise's maidservants. Faublas cannot of course allow them to undress him fully and see him as he (supposedly) is, so takes refuge behind a screen at the crucial moment

repeated waltz melody that is the motif of the whole work. The music theatre here is both effective and suggestive, with the principals now all making their way to their respective bedrooms, candles in hand, to an orchestral *decrescendo*, and a stage direction that says: *In the wings we hear a great wave of voluptuous murmuring, encouraging the lovemaking between Faublas and the Marquise.* In other words, there is musical (and in this case choral) depiction of the sexual act(s) that take place between the Marquise and young Faublas behind the closed stage curtain, a construct that was also used by Strauss when he went on to compose the passionate, sensual prelude to Act I of *Der Rosenkavalier* before the curtain first rises.

Acts I and II, in their different ways, must have persuaded Kessler that he was seeing a clever and original piece of music theatre, an operétte with distinct erotic overtones, more ingenious than most and remarkably faithful to the canonical style of the literature from which it was derived. And both sets had provided spectacular settings for the onstage action. But neither act necessarily prepared him for the stage picture as the curtain rose on the third and final act: the bedroom of the Marquise. The libretto describes it laconically:

> The décor is the famous picture by Baudoin, *Le Coucher de la Mariée*. Upstage a huge bed, richly decorated in Louis XV style. Upstage left, a door behind a screen. Downstage right, another door. Chairs, dressing table, various pieces of furniture exactly in the right style.[85]

34 Detail from Baudouin's *Le Coucher de la mariée*.

[85] Artus, p. 125.

The *mise en scène* is even more specific:

> A bedroom in *petite maîtresse* Pompadour style, with Boucher decorations. An excessively coquettish bed with rich curtains hanging from an overhead ceiling frame decorated with little roses intertwined with hearts. A deerskin acting as a bed runner. Very elegant décor.[86]

35 Detail from the Carpézat set for Act Three of *L'Ingénu libertin*, showing the Baudouin setting in its onstage incarnation

The act opens with a tender duet for Faublas and the Marquise. They have had their night of passion and the stage atmosphere is one of post-coital tristesse, as they sing sweet nothings to each other in a waltz time duet in F major. But daylight means that the action is about to restart: Justine enters and tells of Sophie's arrest during the night – to the dismay of Faublas. The Marquise notices his reaction, reads the situation correctly and writes a letter to the chief of police, who owes her a favour, for Justine to deliver. The Marquis now enters, followed by Rosambert: their initial satisfaction that the police made an arrest during the night and took away Faublas is followed by a dawning realisation on Rosambert's part that his plan has misfired, that the police took away the wrong person, and that Faublas has enjoyed his night of passion with the Marquise after all. But he and the Marquis are then dismissed, for the Marquise to begin her levée.

The elaborate pantomime that follows is described in the libretto, and in the solo now sung by Faublas along with a chorus of the Marquise's four maidservants,

---

[86] *mise en* scène, p. 34.

Act One: The Young Libertine

as a re-enactment of Baudoin's famous picture *Le Coucher de la Mariée*. The *mise en scène* gives very precise directions:

> Faublas, having given his hand to the Marquise to help her to get out of bed, crosses downstage left to sing the two verses of his song, while two of the maidservants and Justine go centre stage, to the right of the Marquise. First maidservant holds the fur-lined cape of the Marquise. Third maidservant, left of the Marquise, bends down to put on her shoes, while second maidservant holds her blouse. Justine steadies the Marquise with her right arm. Fourth maidservant, right behind the armchair, holds a small hand mirror and then passes it to third maidservant for the latter to hold it in front of the Marquise, who looks at it and tidies her hair, once Justine has passed her the blouse from the second maidservant. Then the fur-lined cape, which the Marquise does up, helped by Justine. This whole scene makes a tableau reminiscent of Baudoin's painting *Le Coucher de la Mariée*.[87]

The sight of a beautiful woman being dressed onstage by her maid, Justine, and four maidservants, while her lover Faublas sings the two verses of a strophic song downstage, may once again have come to Kessler as he and Hofmannsthal worked on the levée scene in Act I of *Der Rosenkavalier* – the theatrical construct, and the effect on audiences, is very similar. The Marquise now leaves the stage however, to finish her toilette, while Sophie and La Jeunesse are returned to the house from their prison cells: the letter from the Marquise to the Chief of Police has had its effect. Faublas sees them: overhears their conversation for a few moments, then steps forward to attempt to make his peace with Sophie.

The scene that follows must have been remarkably modern for 1907 audiences. Sophie reproaches Faublas for having been unfaithful to her, for having slept in the Marquise's bed. Faublas tries to assure her that for a man to sleep with someone else is a matter of little importance – soldiers bunk up with each other, and other people, all the time – things happen. Sophie counters that the Marquise de Bay is hardly a soldier: each of the principals, Faublas, Sophie and La Jeunesse then sing one verse apiece in a strophic song about what it means to share a bed, and how one behaves under the bedclothes. Sophie tells Faublas that she now hates him: he pleads for forgiveness and throws himself at her feet, kissing her hands as he does so. At the height of their quarrel, with a tearful and repentant Faublas clinging to an angry Sophie, the Marquise makes a dignified entrance through the door, stage left, takes stock of the situation and advances towards the young couple, Faublas centre stage, Sophie stage right. They form a tableau.

The Marquise wants to know whom Faublas has been deceiving: is she Faublas's victim, or is it Sophie. Faublas hesitates between the two beautiful women either side of him and again asks Sophie to forgive him: Sophie then reminds him of the love song he used to sing from outside the walls of the convent. The Marquise is intrigued and asks to hear the song, so Sophie (after Faublas tries to stop her)

---

[87] *mise en scène*, p. 38.

reprises the E minor/major Air in slow waltz time that Faublas first sang in Act I to Rosambert, with Faublas finally joining in to sing the last four lines in simple harmony. The Marquise is moved, and tells Faublas that the time has come for him to decide. She makes him kneel by the bed, and blindfolds him with a silk handkerchief. The musical trio then starts, the most elaborate (and longest) single number in the work. The Marquise takes the blindfolded Faublas by the hands and the two circle the stage, singing. As the chorus is repeated, the Marquise hands over to Sophie, so the latter and Faublas now hold hands and circle the stage, while the Marquise moves slowly upstage right. After hesitating, almost unable to choose between the charms and attractions of both women, Faublas reaches his decision: it is Sophie that he loves, and he begs the Marquise for forgiveness. She graciously grants his request. At a sign from the Marquise, Sophie (downstage left) unties the blindfold from behind, and Faublas looks upstage right towards the Marquise, but she smiles, and gestures towards Sophie, to whom Faublas now turns, holding out his arms and enveloping Sophie in his embrace.

The gesture and pantomime of three women in a passionate trio, set in the elaborate bedroom scene evoked by Baudoin's *Coucher de la Mariée*, exchanging places onstage and revolving in statuesque fashion around Faublas as he finally reaches his decision on the girl he loves, must have made a particularly vivid and powerful impression on Kessler. In visual (and musical) terms, it completely eclipses the wholly conventional finale that follows: the whole cast come on stage, Sophie's forthcoming wedding to Faublas is announced, and the final chorus delivers the moral of the piece (colloquial, not literal translation):

The Marquis	So in our dénouement all ends in clover
	The Marquis is happy, with no fear of a lover
[...]	
Sophie	Sophie is happy as she so desired
	She's marrying Faublas – inspired!
[...]	
Faublas	Faublas fares better than in the well-known story
	Where his dealings with a lady
	Were rather shady
The Marquise	Will you accept this *conte galant*?
	As you see it, have the authors
	Depicted a Marquise
	Who was conquered with too much ease?[88]

The stage picture is colourful once again, the music is bright and jolly in the home key of D major, so the audience leaves the theatre with a satisfied feeling that the story has come to a happy end and that most of the characters (with, perhaps, the exception of Rosambert) have enjoyed themselves along the way. The 'take'

---

[88] Artus, p. 165.

on *Une Année* has been witty, clever and sophisticated, with music to match the elegance of the characterisation and staging. All this may have been in Kessler's mind as he made his short return journey to the Grand Hotel. And the names that came to him as he made his diary entry that night – Crébillon fils, Rousseau, Richardson, Heine – must all have been evoked by the two hours of stage characters, constructs and music theatre in which he had been immersed.

But the big question is how and why Harry Kessler reacted to *L'Ingénu libertin* in the way that he did, and how he was able to reconstruct all of its theatrical, visual and emotional elements in a way that proved such a prolific source of inspiration for Hofmannsthal and, through him, for Strauss over a year later. Let us find out.

Act Two

Who was Harry Kessler?

Harry Kessler was an extraordinary man, with achievements in several different fields. Yet until relatively recently, his name was not really well known internationally or remembered outside certain specialist circles (lovers of fine books, for example, who have long collected the fine art editions published by Kessler's Cranach Press). Viewed chronologically, one can divide interest in Kessler and critical appreciation of his achievements into several distinct periods: relative neglect from his death in 1937 until the 1960s; increasing (critical and general public) interest in his Weimar Republic activities following publication in 1961 of his *Diary* for the 1918–37 period,[1] and much greater interest in the earlier aspects of Kessler's life and activities following publication in 1968 of his correspondence with Hofmannsthal[2] and in 1978 with Bodenhausen.[3] This interest was largely confined to the German-speaking world, however, since neither of the latter two volumes has been translated into English.

But after the discovery in 1983 of the *Diary* pages covering the last major gap in Kessler's recorded life, 1902–14, greater critical attention began to be paid to the whole of his life and works. The 1988 exhibition at the German Literature Archive in Marbach, designed in the main to celebrate acquisition of this long-missing link, was accompanied by an illustrated 536-page catalogue,[4] which has since run to three editions, and several general biographies of Kessler have followed.

The first was a 1991 dissertation (in English) by American scholar Laird Easton.[5] This circulated quite widely and aroused sufficient interest to be published as a book eleven years later.[6] For the English reader, *The Red Count* is an admirable and comprehensive introduction to nearly all things Kessler, and the text enjoyed

---

[1] Harry Graf Kessler, *Tagebücher 1918–1937*, ed. Wolfgang Pfeiffer-Belli (Frankfurt am Main: Insel Verlag, 1961). The period, and Kessler's slant on it, were of sufficient interest to English readers for extracts, translated by Sarah Gainham, to be published in *Encounter* (XXIX, 1, July 1967) and for a full translation to follow four years later: Count Harry Kessler, *The Diaries of a Cosmopolitan 1918–1937*, trans. and ed. Charles Kessler (London: Weidenfeld & Nicolson, 1971).
[2] Burger.
[3] Simon.
[4] *Cat.* 43.
[5] Laird Easton, 'The Red Count: The Life and Times of Harry Kessler' (Ph.D diss. Stanford University, 1991).
[6] Easton.

the subsequent accolade of being translated into, and published in German.[7] More recently, Easton has translated into English substantial extracts from Kessler's *Diary* for the years 1880–1918.[8] In the meantime, two German-language biographies of Kessler had appeared, both in 1995, one by German foreign policy historian Peter Grupp covering all aspects of Kessler's life,[9] and one by Weimar-based literary historian Burkhard Stenzel, concentrating on Kessler's cultural and culture promotional activities.[10] The only other full biography of Kessler followed in 2008, its author Friedrich Rothe taking a more thematic, impressionistic approach to the various ages and stages of Kessler's development.[11] But if the approach taken by each of Kessler's recent biographers has been different, the one aspect on which they have all agreed is the difficulty they have faced in pinning down the real Kessler. The 'who was Kessler' question thus remains valid and needs to be addressed, even though extracts from his *Diary* are now starting to crop up ever more frequently in works that deal with the turn of the twentieth century in Europe – *The Vertigo Years* by Philipp Blom starts with a Kessler quote, for example[12] – and he crops up at intervals thereafter: likewise he makes frequent appearances in the recent impressionistic chronicle by Florian Illies of the year 1913,[13] and in Charles Emmerson's book with the same title.[14] And since 2013 there has been a Kessler Society – the Harry-Graf-Kessler Gesellschaft e.V – based in Berlin and with a mission to promote and honour the memory of 'the man who knew everybody', as one of his epithets runs. Knowledge of Kessler – or at least, awareness of his multi-faceted interests and trajectory in life – can thus be said to be growing.

Kessler's earliest years

Lives can have multiple narratives, and the life of Harry Clément Ulrich Kessler, born in Paris on 23 May 1868 to a German father, Adolf Kessler, and an Anglo-Irish mother (Alice Harriet Blosse Lynch, born in Bombay), had far more than most. Looking back on his life, there is no recognisable career to be outlined, but he was in his time, and sometimes with overlaps, a printer and publisher, writer, modern art collector and propagandist, curator, artists' patron, soldier, unofficial German Foreign Office emissary, secret agent, ambassador, political orator, and – above all else – a diarist of his times. He was also, in all of these fields, an inveterate traveller and a consummate behind-the-scenes intermediary, door-opener and impresario.

Interspersed with all his activities, and of most relevance to the team role

---

[7] Laird M. Easton, *Der Rote Graf: Harry Graf Kessler und seine Zeit* (Stuttgart: Klett-Cotta, 2005).
[8] *Journey*.
[9] Grupp.
[10] Stenzel.
[11] Rothe.
[12] Philipp Blom, *The Vertigo Years: Change and Culture in the West 1900–1914* (London: Weidenfeld & Nicolson, 2008).
[13] Florian Illies, *1913 Der Sommer des Jahrhunderts* (Frankfurt am Main: S. Fischer, 2012).
[14] Charles Emmerson, *1913 The World before the Great War* (London: The Bodley Head, 2013).

he played in creating *Der Rosenkavalier*, Kessler lived and breathed theatre and opera, in Europe and in North America (and even in Japan) from his teenage years onwards. He was also friend, confidant and sponsor to some of the major European theatrical figures of his adult life, in particular from the 1890s to the outbreak of the First World War in 1914. Two books have dealt with some of these aspects of Kessler's life: Lindsay Newman on Kessler and Edward Gordon Craig,[15] and Tamara Barzantny on Kessler's involvement with theatre more generally.[16] But neither author – nor Kessler's more general biographers – have ever looked specifically and in detail at the creative use he made of the now-forgotten French opérette, which is at the heart of this book and has already been explored in detail in Act One, to help fashion *Der Rosenkavalier*.

Kessler's receptivity to what he was to see and hear onstage in his formative years was conditioned by his cosmopolitan, international upbringing. His own laconic account of his earliest years made up his *Diary* entry on his thirteenth birthday, 23 May 1881 (written in English in the original) and the circumstances he describes gave rise to the epithet often used of Kessler, and the title of the first chapter of Rothe's biography – *Sohn dreier Vaterländer*, or the 'son of three fatherlands'. His birth certificate incidentally (entry no. 754 of 25 May 1868 in the register of the 1st arrondissement of Paris) reflects those three countries perfectly: his first names are given as Harry (English, or Anglo-Irish), Clément (French) and Ulrich (German):

> It was my birthday today. I was born in Paris at the corner of the rue de Luxembourg and the rue du Mont Thabor at the 3 étage in 1868 but soon after went to Hamburg. When 4 I went to America and stopped there till I was five then I came to England and Mamma and Papa soon after (about 2 years after) settled in Paris where I was during the remarkably cold winter of 1879–1880 in which the cold amounted to 24 degrees Cent. I saw the Seine frozen.[17]

What this bald account of a childhood spent moving from France to Germany to America to England and back to France does not include is any reference to the rapidly growing prosperity of Kessler's family as a result of his father's success as banker and capitalist entrepreneur. The substantial wealth that he acquired relatively quickly saw his family rise in Paris society inexorably towards the top. They moved from a modest flat (5 rue de Luxembourg, later renamed rue Cambon) to a much larger, luxurious flat (89 Boulevard Malesherbes) and then to a palais or fully representative town house, an *hôtel particulier* at 30, Cours la Reine (between the Champs Elysées and the Seine). This property provided a stage on which both Harry Kessler's parents could shine in high society: and when the family made their final move in Paris in 1890, to a house at 19 Boulevard Montmorency, Kessler's mother commissioned a fully equipped professional theatre in a pavilion in the

---

[15] Newman.
[16] Barzantny.
[17] *Cat. 43*, pp. 23–5.

garden. The stage she had constructed in that building was reportedly as large as that of the Théâtre du Gymnase, and the auditorium had an audience capacity of 250.[18] Two contemporary accounts of the Kessler family's way of life in Harry's formative years make clear the sort of atmosphere in which he, particularly as he approached adulthood, was brought up:

36 Alice Kessler's private theatre at 19 boulevard Montmorency in Paris. His mother's appearances onstage – both as actress and singer – were deeply formative experiences for the young Harry Kessler

After dinner cigars and coffee and fragrant Turkish cigarettes in an inner salon, where I talked long to Monsieur de Lesseps on things of Panama, and of the Court of Berlin and the German Empress, who is French at heart. Also of champagne and winegrowing with connoisseurs who praised the Count of Kessler's cellar and smacked their lips remembering the pleasure that was past. Also of journalism with M. Magnard of

---

[18] *La Vie Heureuse*, an illustrated fortnightly magazine, devoted six pages to Alice Kessler's theatre and its productions in its issue no. 3 of 15 December 1902.

the *Figaro*, who asked me many things and told me much, of theatres and actresses with Monsieur Koning, who rules the Gymnase and is Jane Hading's husband. Meanwhile the Comtesse's reception had begun, and swarms of charming girls had filled the bright salons, and elegant cavaliers… It was worth looking on to see the perfect tact and hostess-ship of Madame de Kessler and the Count's bonhomie and kindly hospitality. An excellent host, the Count of Kessler, ever alert and all attentive. I am glad I dined at the beautiful hotel in the Cours la Reine. Vedi Napoli – No, dine chez Madame la Comtesse de Kessler, e poi Muorir – Yes, gladly.[19]

Ferdinand de Lesseps was clearly a frequent visitor to the Kessler salon, and likewise the Editor of *Le Figaro*, François Magnard, as a similar atmospheric, insider account by the English writer and prolific biographer of Oscar Wilde, Robert Harborough Sherard, makes clear:

> A week or two later I dined one night at the house of Count Kessler on the Cours-la-Reine. The Count was married to an Irish lady of remarkable beauty and the greatest charm. Their house – they entertained very largely – was one of the very best houses in Paris. One met everybody there. The countess's little dinners had a European reputation. Kessler was the kindest of men and an admirable host. His death a few years ago left a great gap in Parisian society.
>
> That night there were many very distinguished people among the guests who were assembled in the drawing room. There was a superfluous king, there was an American railway magnate, there was the needy Princess Pierre Bonaparte and her millionaire son Roland, there was a French Minister of State, there was the editor of the *Figaro*, and a number of other people of note and distinction. Standing with his back to the fire was the grand Français Ferdinand de Lesseps. He was talking to the superfluous king and the railway magnate, and a bevy of adoring women were standing around the group. I was very pleased to see a man there whom I respected, but it never occurred to me that he would remember me, nor did I expect him to take any notice of a person whose intrinsic insignificance was heightened by the splendour of the company in which he found himself.
>
> Shortly before dinner was announced, Kessler came up to me and said, 'Oh, I want to introduce you to Magnard, the editor of the *Figaro*. He's a man you ought to know in Paris, and he might be useful to you. Come along.'[20]

Grand occasions, with exotic guests, were therefore routine occurrences in the household, calling no doubt on all members of the host family for the ability to perform: as instigators of conversation and contact, as charming entertainers, as creators of splendid social events. So prominent was the Kessler family, that a

---

[19] Maître Friand, 'Chez Madame la Comtesse de Kessler', *The Table*, 28 January 1888, requoted in *Cat. 43*, p. 21.

[20] Robert Harborough Sherard, *Twenty Years in Paris* (London: Hutchinson & Co., 1905), p. 131.

report on the front page of *Le Figaro* on 5 June 1884 (when Harry Kessler was 16) made gala events sound almost like regular household occurrences:

> Grand dinner and evening entertainment last night at the home of the Count and Countess Kessler, in honour of Count Beust who was visiting Paris. [...] The reception that followed the dinner was a brilliant occasion. There was dancing and music: Countess Kessler sang one of Count Beust's melodies, *Farewell to Vienna*. Impossible to list who was there, we would have to name everyone in Parisian aristocratic and bourgeois high society.[21]

So Harry Kessler can hardly have failed to absorb the theatricality of what was going on around him, to play his part in proceedings, and to notice the following qualities in his father:

> Adolf Wilhelm Kessler, a brilliant businessman, enjoyed representative functions, and loved being in society. He had a tenor voice to make anyone proud. At soirées he loved to sing Verdi duets with his wife, who had been trained as a mezzo soprano at the Paris Conservatoire. He loved showing her off to best advantage in whatever way possible and making her the centre of society.[22]

It is worth digressing for a moment on Adolf Wilhelm Kessler, who by any standards had a spectacularly successful banking and business career. His own mother was a member of the Hamburg merchant and banking Auffmordt family and, at a young age, he had joined the family firm. His rise within the Auffmordt ranks was rapid: he headed their financial operations in Paris, moved to their London bank whenever Franco-German tensions became too close for comfort (after 1870, for example), crossed the Atlantic to spearhead major Auffmordt commercial operations and acquisitions in the USA and Canada, and diversified his own commercial interests in daring and remarkably modern ways. In New York Adolf Kessler became the lead investor in the Eden Musée, founded in 1884 near Madison Park as a much more elaborate version of Madame Tussaud's, with entertainment acts, bars and restaurants, a winter garden and even an early cinema: the music being supplied by Prince Paul Esterhazy's Hungarian Orchestra. But Adolf Kessler both traded with North America and invested in it: at one stage his forestry holdings along the St Maurice River in Canada covered an area the size of Bavaria in Germany! In today's terms, he could almost be regarded as a minor oligarch – his commercial operations extended from Germany, France and England to North and South America, but also to Switzerland and Persia. So the huge fortune that he left on his early death (from throat cancer) aged 57 saw his widow, son and daughter able to live in remarkable luxury for many years to come. If Harry Kessler had decided to go into business, or banking, and to try to succeed like his father, he would have found Adolf Kessler an incredibly hard act to follow. That may of course be, in part, why Harry Kessler's life took such a different course.

---

[21] *Le Figaro*, 5 June 1884, p. 6.
[22] Rothe, p. 24. He and others are wrong about the Paris Conservatoire – see below.

Act Two: Who Was Harry Kessler?

37 Countess Marie von Bismarck (only daughter of Otto von Bismarck), Adolf and Allice Kessler, photographed in Bad Kissingen in 1874, the year that the Bismarck and Kessler families became friends – when Harry Kessler was six years old

Even more than the example set by his father, however, the earliest and strongest lasting theatrical imprint on Harry Kessler undoubtedly came from his mother, and this influence will now be explored.

Alice Harriet Kessler, née Blosse Lynch

The beautiful and exotic Alice Harriet Blosse Lynch cultivated a slight air of mystery about herself, and this has confused biographers of Kessler ever since. Some accept and repeat her claim to have been born in 1852 (that would have made her 14 when she was married and 16 when Harry was born in 1868!), and some describe her as a Baroness, or otherwise as a lady of noble birth. Alice was neither, although she was born into an interesting and distinguished family. Her birth and her story are as follows.

The Lynch family is one of Ireland's oldest, Lynch being one of the original 'Tribes of Galway'. Some have suggested that they came originally from Linz (in

Austria) and some that the name derives from Anglo-Norman *de Lench*. Whatever their distant origins, Sir Henry Lynch, became 1st Baronet in 1622, and over a century later the 6th Baronet, Sir Robert Lynch assumed the additional surname of Blosse as a condition of his marriage to Elizabeth Barker of Belstead, Suffolk (heir to one Tobias Blosse). The family seat was at Athavallie House in County Mayo and the Lynch-Blosse Baronetcy (although not the house) survives to this day.

A separate and junior branch of the family, based since 1667 at Partry House, Ballinrobe, County Mayo, followed the Lynch-Blosses' example by adopting the additional courtesy name of Blosse, for reasons of kinship. Thus Henry Blosse Lynch (unhyphenated) was born at Partry in 1807, the third of eleven sons. At the age of 16, and like several of his brothers, he went to India, enlisting as a midshipman in the East India Company Navy in 1823.

In *Soldier Sahibs*, Charles Allen has described young men like Henry Blosse Lynch to perfection:

> However, it is worth bearing in mind that these officers were all gentlemen and, even if they called themselves Englishmen, mostly Scots, Scots-Irish or Anglo-Irish: in the main, younger sons of small country squires, lairds and vicars who lacked the means to set them up at home. The Queen's Army, the Navy, the clergy – and India: these were the classic outlets that might, if fortune (and patronage) smiled, bring advancement and 'genteel enrichment' sufficient to retire on at fifty. [...] As a group, these poor gentry were well-educated, hardy and ambitious.[23]

The real education of Henry Blosse Lynch came in East India Company service: employed for several years surveying the Persian Gulf, he studied Persian and Arabic sufficiently well to become Persian and Arabic interpreter to the Gulf squadron until 1832. He also served as second in command to the 1836–7 expedition led by Sir Francis Chesney to explore the Tigris and Euphrates rivers as alternative passages to India. Henry Blosse Lynch and two of his younger brothers, Thomas and Stephen, then founded firstly a commercial shipping office in Baghdad in 1841 (Lynch Brothers) and much later the Euphrates and Tigris Steam Navigation Company, incorporated in England on 25 April 1861. His commercial ventures thus went some way beyond the 'advancement and genteel enrichment' described by Allen.

The British Minister in Baghdad at this time was the legendary Colonel Robert Taylor, who during his earlier travels in Mesopotamia had eloped with and married a well-born Armenian girl called Rose, aged around 12 and reputedly a member of the Persian royal family. Taylor and his wife subsequently had two daughters, Caroline Anne (born 1817) and Harriet (born 1822). During their frequent visits to Baghdad, both Henry Blosse Lynch and his younger brother Thomas Kerr Blosse Lynch became regular guests at Taylor's Residence, getting to know and then marrying the two Taylor daughters. Henry Blosse Lynch married Caroline Anne in

---

[23] Charles Allen, *Soldier Sahibs* (London: John Murray, 2000), pp. 10–11.

1840 and Thomas married Harriet a few years later. Henry and Caroline Anne had four children: Rose born in 1841, Alice Harriet (to become Kessler's mother) born in 1844, Caroline Jane Mary in 1848 and Quested Finnis in 1850. At the time of Alice's birth in 1844 the family were living in comfortable circumstances in Bombay, in the latter stages of East India Company rule that was to be ended by the Government of India Act of 1858.

Alice had a talented, ambitious, hard-working and prosperous father. Promoted finally to the rank of Captain in 1847, his last service distinction was the award of Companion of the Bath (CB) at the conclusion of the Second Anglo-Burmese War in 1853, following which he retired from Indian service and established himself in Paris, where he took a flat at 6 rue Royale in the Faubourg St Honoré. At this time Alice was 12.

Alice was thus a daughter of Empire and a child of the Raj. As a teenager she seems to have moved with her family between Partry, the family seat in Ireland, and Paris, but details of her education are not recorded. What is recorded is that she met Adolf Kessler in Parisian society and, after a whirlwind courtship, married him in Paris on 24 September 1866, giving birth to her only son Harry nearly two years later on 23 May 1868. Soon after her wedding, she became a rising star in Parisian society. Her particular beauty was clearly fascinating and striking, and as Easton puts it: 'The remarkable and exotic family background of his mother fascinated Kessler. Its spell must have been doubly strong on the young boy.'[24] The lines of Armenian and of Anglo-Irish descent that ran through her into Harry Kessler's personality were undoubtedly complicating factors in his makeup, and in the sometimes idiosyncratic views he formed of the societies in which he operated.

Kessler only completed and saw through to publication the first of a planned three-volume memoir of his life: it was published in German by Fischer in 1935[25] and in French, with revisions and added passages, by Librairie Plon in 1936.[26] The German text (and the added passages in French in an Appendix) was finally republished in 1988 as part of a three-volume edition of Kessler's complete writings.[27] In prior negotiation with an alternative possible publisher, Heinrich Simon, Kessler had made it clear that his memoir would start with a whole chapter on his mother, in an effort to disprove once and for all the rumour that had dogged him all his life – that he was in fact the illegitimate son of Wilhelm I, who had become infatuated with Alice Kessler from a meeting in 1870 in Bad Ems onwards.[28] But the 106 pages that he finally devoted to Mémé, as Alice was called by the family, are much more to do with her social and theatrical appearances and accomplishments

---

[24] Easton, p. 15.
[25] Harry Graf Kessler, *Gesichter und Zeiten – Erinnerungen: Erster Band Völker und Vaterländer* (Berlin: S. Fischer Verlag, 1935).
[26] Harry Graf Kessler, *Souvenirs d'un Européen I: de Bismarck à Nietzsche, traduit de l'Allemand par Blaise Briod* (Paris: Librairie Plon, 1936).
[27] *CW (I, II, III)*.
[28] *Diary IX*, p. 396.

– the admiration of son for mother shining through – than with the circumstances of his own birth. Much of it, too, is taken from Alice Kessler's own unfinished, and unpublished personal memoirs. This narrative mixture of passages by mother and by son is emblematic in itself of the close personal bond between them. As Kessler writes early on, 'I remember my youthful pleasure, mixed with childish pride, when people along the promenade at Ems would climb onto tables and chairs to watch her drive or stroll past.'[29] Elsewhere he made a specific theatrical parallel: 'I believe this special way she had of greeting and smiling contributed greatly to my falling fatally in love, when I was eight, with the beautiful Hortense Schneider in Offenbach's *Belle Helène*, because I recognised in her the same, familiar greeting

38 Alice Kessler in a characteristically coquettish pose

---

[29] *CW I*, p. 13.

and smiling expression.'[30] Kessler was eight in 1876, by which time Schneider, a great star and creator of roles in Offenbach's operettas at the Théâtre des Bouffes Parisiens, was 43 and nearing the end of her career.[31] In the light of Kessler's subsequent theatrical alchemy with a Bouffes Parisiens opérette over thirty years later, it is significant that he saw, so young, aspects of his mother in the alluring stage creature that was La Sneyder, as Hortense was popularly known.

The 1870 meeting between Alice Kessler and Wilhelm I was very public and well-documented: if, as has largely been accepted, it was their first ever meeting then Wilhelm I could not possibly have been father to Harry, born on 23 May 1868. But Wilhelm I had spent long periods in the summer of 1867 in Paris, visiting the World Fair, and for at least one distinguished German writer, it was in the summer of 1867 that he and Alice had first met:

> If only I had known who he was, everything that he had experienced, oh I would have begged to be allowed to visit him and ask him questions until his patience ran out. Kessler, legally the son of a banker from an old St Gallen family, was actually – this is very highly likely – the son of the Kaiser Wilhelm I. The Kaiser, or the King as he then was, must have been 70 when he produced him, probably in the margins of the 1867 Paris World Fair, because Kessler was born the following year in Paris. Later Wilhelm made him a Count, or more precisely he asked a Fürst zur Lippe to do it for him, undoubtedly the only time in the history of German nobility that a mere Fürst has created a Graf. Obviously the rank only applied to the bastard son.[32]

Golo Mann quotes no source for his assertions and they may be based on little more than supposition and gossip. And a number of suppositions about Alice Kessler are inaccurate. Her enrolment and training at the Paris Conservatoire, for example – first mentioned in Kessler's memoirs[33] and requoted by Kessler's biographers – is not confirmed by the written records of the Conservatoire, now held at the French National Archives at Saint Denis. There is no trace of Alice Harriet Blosse Lynch in any of the relevant files. What seems more likely is that a teacher, with a connection to the Conservatoire, came to her home and gave her private lessons. A second supposition – and this even appears in each volume of the *Diary* – is that Alice married Adolf Kessler on 10 August 1867.[34] In fact she had married him a whole year earlier, on 24 September 1866, with the marriage contract being registered (entry 690 of 29 September 1866) at the town hall of the 1st arrondissement in Paris. Harry Kessler was therefore born some twenty months after the wedding of his parents, not the bare nine months that has often been supposed.

---

[30] *CW I*, pp. 13–14.
[31] *Dictionnaire Encyclopédique Larousse*, ed. Claude Dubois (Paris: Librairie Larousse, 1979), p. 1280.
[32] Golo Mann, *Erinnerungen und Gedanken: Eine Jugend in Deutschland* (Frankfurt: S. Fischer, 1986), pp. 255–6. A Fürst is a Prince and a Graf a Count: furthermore it was Heinrich XIV of the cadet line of Reuss who actually ennobled Kessler's father (with the title of Graf, or Count, passing to Harry Kessler on the death of his father in 1895).
[33] *CW I*, p. 20.
[34] *Diary II*, p. 641 and all subsequent volumes quote this date. It is almost a year out.

Nevertheless, the gossip was fed by the fact that Wilhelm I kept a photograph of Alice Kessler on his desk in Berlin, was later to become godfather to Harry Kessler's younger sister (Wilhelmina, or Wilma as she came to be known) and did indeed persuade Heinrich XIV of Reuss to fast-track the ennoblement of Adolf Kessler in an unprecedented manner. The justification given – 'services to the German community in Paris' – was generally regarded as an extraordinarily weak reason for enabling Adolf Kessler to skip all the customary stages in the German procedure for ennoblement. But skip them he did, and the result was that Alice became Countess Kessler, and an even more distinguished member of the Parisian society in which she had begun to shine.

39 Portrait photograph of Alice Kessler

40 Portrait photograph of Alice Kessler. Kaiser Wilhelm I had a photograph of Alice permanently on his desk at his palace in Berlin

It is instructive to consider the various ways in which Alice Kessler might have transmitted a sense of the theatrical to her young son. Firstly, her very existence as a salon hostess, among the Parisian and international (notably German) social elite of the 1870s and 1880s, placed her centre stage metaphorically and often literally. Rothe summarises her position neatly:

Adolf Wilhelm and Alice Kessler, with or without the title of Count bestowed by [the Principality of] Reuss, lived extravagantly and ran a household in which economic prosperity was transformed into refined Parisian salon culture. Their salon, where Alice received on Monday afternoons, gave an erotic atmosphere to the wealth of the banker that increased by leaps and bounds, and this was further enhanced by musical and theatrical performances. The lady of the house was also to be found now and then among the real virtuosi. Her huge success in the leading role of Maupassant's sentimental play *Musotte* made her particularly proud, her appearance as a Parisian model eliciting from the famous author the words 'just like a budding wild rose'.[35]

In Alice Kessler's own account of Guy de Maupassant's reaction to her incarnation of the Musotte role, she says that a few days after her performance, Maupassant sent her a copy of the text with the dedication: 'To Countess Kessler to commemorate her unforgettable Musotte – the eighteen year old grisette I had dreamed of'.[36] Yet she shone also in a very different genre of play, taking the part of Nora in Ibsen's *A Doll's House*, and acting with sufficient verve and passion (particularly in her tarantella dance in the final act) that Ibsen himself was given a full description of her thespian talents, by a society hostess and salon friend, Madame Nérisaie de Lalande, who visited Christiana (Oslo) for the specific purpose of inviting Ibsen privately to one of her performances.[37] It has, incidentally, often been assumed that Ibsen accepted this invitation, but the memoirs do not confirm this specifically. It was at Nérisaie de Lalande's private theatre that Alice Kessler had started her amateur acting career in Paris, but once the family had moved to Cours la Reine, and then finally to Boulevard Montmorency, her ambitions increased: with her own theatre in the garden she was able to assemble her own troupe. Hereafter the standard of what was performed seems to have been of a rather high, albeit still notionally amateur standard. Kessler describes the daily pre-production routine, with a 9.00 a.m. start every morning to rehearsals: the director arriving first, then the prompter and then the cast, and he names prominent members of the audiences for his mother's plays as Tommaso Salvini, Ermete Novelli and Eleonore Duse.[38] Easton also names Duse as one of her salon guests but adds Guy de Maupassant, Sarah Bernhardt, Henrik Ibsen and Auguste Rodin to the list, saying that the actors and actresses among these guests performed alongside her.[39] The inescapable conclusion is that Kessler, as he was growing up, was surrounded when at home with his parents by theatrical and musical figures of note and distinction: and that the atmosphere of theatrical creation was all around him.

---

[35] Rothe, p. 24.
[36] *CW I*, p. 84.
[37] *CW I*, pp. 85–6.
[38] *CW I*, pp. 83–4.
[39] *Journey*, p. xix.

41 Alice Kessler in the title role of *La Dame aux Camélias*, performed in her private theatre at 19 Boulevard Montmorency

Exposure to theatre and growing dramatic awareness

If part of Kessler's privileged upbringing consisted of the material things in life that his family's wealth and social status brought him, the greater privilege undoubtedly came from the opportunities he was given, from a young age, to immerse himself in the theatrical and musical performance culture of three countries: France, Germany and England. The most detailed record of where he went, what he saw, and what he thought of works (often premières) and their performance, is to be found in the first four volumes of his *Diary*, but his subsequent memoirs, although not always strictly in accordance with his contemporaneous diary entries, also shed light on Kessler's own development as a culturally aware, and in certain fields expert, critic and practitioner.

The memoirs portray a lonely child (Kessler was an only child until the birth of his sister Wilma in 1877, when he was nine) and, as is not uncommon in lonely children, an imaginative one, seeking refuge where he could find it. What is striking from this early age is Kessler's preoccupation with the visual aspects of everything that interested him, and of everything in which he became involved:

> In bed in the evenings, half-asleep but not yet dreaming, I built onto palaces for my princesses and fairies, rows and rows of labyrinthine courts and halls, sparkling with jewels and swimming in wonderful light, although, for reasons I no longer remember, I seem to recall they were underground. Making no distinction between the people I had met that day and those I had heard of in nursery rhymes, I then led them through this splendour. Sometimes I worked every night for weeks on end planning and decorating one and the same fairy-tale castle, rebuilding it and making it lovelier; until it seemed to me to be worthy of the illustrious society figures whom I was considering inviting.[40]

There are also early signs of what can only be described as infatuation with his mother, with her voice being described as 'a light alloy of silver and flexible steel', which was capable, when Alice spoke to her son, of 'casting me in a magic circle, which cut us off from the rest of the world'.[41] Kessler likewise became aware of the power of performance in his early years, once again centred on his mother:

> She seemed to me to be a combination of all the perfect features that I detected in other women. Merely her voice moved me in a special way, rivalled only by the voices, later, of the greatest singers. She had a somewhat low, very soft and full mezzo soprano, and sang Italian music above all, Rossini and Verdi, the mad scene from Donizetti's *Lucia* and the role of Zerlina from *Don Giovanni*. I have never been able to listen to 'Una voce poco fa' or the last act of *Traviata* without hearing inside me, in addition to the singer's voice, a second deeply-moving voice coming from the earliest days of my childhood.[42]

Towards the end of the first section of his memoirs, the extended passage in the book that Kessler had intended originally to be a rebuttal of rumours concerning his parentage, he asks a rhetorical question about the real quality of his mother's theatrical and performative talents, and answers that question in a way that came to stand for Kessler's lifelong attitude to the essence of performance and theatrical techniques:

> Today, if I ask myself whether and how my mother's talent went beyond the amateur, the basic element that I perceive, in addition to her beauty and gracefulness in performance, is the mimic quality, the strongly expressive combination of her dark eyes, her tenderly-flared nostrils and her finely curved mouth, which seemed to sculpt every word and to give it a wonderfully-formed body. Her theatrical artistry was different to that of the word-based traditional French style, it was visual rather

---

[40] *CW I*, p. 19.
[41] *CW I*, p. 20.
[42] *CW I*, p. 20.

than audible, plastic rather than musical. When she floated around on her little feet, and her gentle face expressed with truthful conviction every nuance of a particular feeling, whether joy or pain, expectation or anger, this was not salon art, it was art pure and simple.[43]

This early realisation by Kessler of the importance of appearance onstage, the effectiveness of pantomime and mimic expression as part of the visual world created in the theatre, was to play a major part in his life a few years later, both when he became convinced of the importance of Edward Gordon Craig's stage designs and new aesthetics of the theatre, and when he became an occasional but important friend and adviser to Hofmannsthal, as the latter began to make the theatre a major outlet for his writing skills. In both cases, Kessler proved to be a man of theatrical vision.

Kessler did not, however, spend all his childhood at home. Aged 12, he was sent away to England to board at St George's School, Ascot (for two years) and aged 14, he was transferred to a well-known *Gymnasium*, the Johanneum in Hamburg (his father's old school), where he was to lodge with the family of a middle-class Pastor for the next six years, until he began his university career. These formative teenage years, 1880–8, were marked by Kessler's immersion in the Classics (Latin, but above all, Greek), in English literature and in the art of becoming a gentleman while at St George's: and by his gradual realisation of his deeper, spiritual German roots, as he became more absorbed by classical German literature, and of the German attitude to education.[44] As he observed to himself: 'German education was, in principle, generalised and was supposed to prepare one for everything.'[45] This realisation of his essential and spiritual German-ness began while he was still in Hamburg at the Johanneum, and continued through his university years at Bonn (1888–9) and then at Leipzig (1889–91). It was not, however, until 5 January 1891, at the outset of Kessler's last year in Leipzig, that he finally made the switch from English to German as the language in which his *Diary* was written (although regular, and sometimes lengthy, excursions into both French and English were to be a hallmark of the *Diary* until its final entry of all, on 30 September 1937).

Kessler recalled later, with affection, his experiences of theatre at St George's:

At thirteen we translated at sight Caesar and Livy, Sophocles and Aristophanes, omitting the choruses. We even performed 'The Clouds' by Aristophanes in the original and I played Pheidippides. English history and literature were taught thoroughly and interestingly, not in a dry or dusty way. Shakespeare, Byron, Walter Scott, Dickens entered our imaginations. We all took roles and read aloud the 'Merry Wives', 'As You Like It' and 'The Merchant of Venice'; and we also acted out those scenes that were particularly funny. [...] Readings or role-playing often took place on lesson-free days, in the late afternoon, when after sports and a shower we chosen ones, specially

---

[43] *CW I*, p. 87.
[44] Kessler uses the word *Bildung* and comments on what it did, and did not, embrace at his school.
[45] *CW I*, p. 128.

invited and in our monkey jackets that were the boys' version of tailcoats, appeared in the salon and sat at Mr Kinnersley's feet on floor cushions, while Mrs Kinnersley handed out tea and cakes.[46]

The *Diary*, moreover, records the theatre and opera visits that Kessler began to make, in London, in Paris, and then in various German cities, from 1881 onwards. The bare statistics mount up gradually but quite impressively: from eight theatre and opera visits in 1881 and sixteen in 1882, by 1889 Kessler is recording twenty-eight such visits, and then forty-nine in 1890: giving a total of 149 plays and operas seen by Kessler by the time he was 22.[47] More important than the numbers, however, are the works that Kessler saw onstage and the major houses in which he saw them: his first *Tannhäuser* in Berlin (21 March 1883), his first *Parsifal* in Hamburg (26 April 1886) and his first *Tristan und Isolde* in Hamburg (19 May 1887). Of the performance of *Parsifal* he wrote:

> After breakfast went to hear *Parsifal*. Magnificent music, especially the Communion scene and the Good Fridays [sic] miracle are really superb. I do not think I have ever heard anything so majestically grand as the Communion scene, with the bells clanging, the impressive choruses of the knights and the sweet choruses of the boys behind the scenes. I was so excited by the music that I could not get to sleep tonight till very late (26 April 1886).

His experience of *Tristan* was recorded in similar terms: 'Gorgeous music: the love scene in the second act is one of the most sublime things I have ever heard' (19 May 1887). In parallel with this early exposure to the Wagner canon, Kessler was also seeing boulevard theatre and operetta. He saw Gilbert and Sullivan's *Patience* at the Savoy Theatre in 1881, noting next day in his *Diary*: 'I am utterly consummately intense wearing sun flowers and poppies and dahlias in my button hole' (16 October 1881), and he saw *La Mascotte,* Edmond Audran's major opérette success, both at its 400th performance at the Théâtre des Bouffes Parisiens (14 January 1882) and at the Strand Theatre in London five months later (14 June 1882). This gave rise to Kessler's first mild attempt at comparative criticism: of the Paris performance he noted: 'There are some pretty airs in it' (14 January 1882), whereas, after the Strand Theatre production, he wrote: 'I liked the music better this time than when I saw it in Paris although the acting in London cannot be compared to the acting in Paris' (14 June 1882).

Kessler's exposure to different productions, in different theatres and opera houses, of the same piece, was undoubtedly an early factor in what came to be his well-stocked theatrical mind, however unformed and unsophisticated his *Diary* comments in the early years clearly were. His first ever *Das Rheingold* in Hamburg

---

[46] *CW I*, p. 105.
[47] All references to Kessler's theatrical experiences prior to 1892, which is when *Diary II* starts, are taken from the raw text contained on the first CD-ROM issued to subscribers to the entire edition, and are identified by the appropriate date; this is by kind permission of Dr Roland Kamzelak of the DLA, Marbach. The edited print edition of *Diary I* is still awaited (November 2015).

42 Portrait photograph of the twenty year old Harry Kessler, taken in Hamburg, 1888

he liked 'very middlingly' (23 May 1888), but when he saw it again, in Leipzig, he noted: 'I liked it much better than the first time, some parts are magnificent' (5 June 1890); he went on to see it again in Berlin on 8 September 1894[48] and then yet again, on his first visit for a complete *Ring* cycle in Bayreuth conducted by Hans Richter on 19 July 1896.[49] On that visit, Kessler found the décor for the second and third acts of *Siegfried* to be 'a revelation' and noted that Lili Lehmann as Brünnhilde in *Götterdämmerung* left him completely cold, in marked contrast to the Sieglinde of Rosa Sucher in Act One of *Die Walküre*, who had 'torn people from their seats'.[50] Kessler's previous visits to Bayreuth had been in 1889, the year he had

[48] *Diary II*, p. 278.
[49] *Diary II*, p. 459.
[50] *Diary II*, p. 460.

joined the Wagner Society, when he saw *Die Meistersinger von Nürnberg* and *Parsifal*, and in 1891, when he had seen *Parsifal* and *Tannhäuser*. His 1889 experience of *Parsifal* had been close to mystical: 'No words can describe my sensations: it far, far surpassed my expectations. I am too excited to form any definite opinion' (18 August 1889). It was the second production of *Parsifal* he had seen in three years, and he was to see it for a third time, always at Bayreuth, in 1891. This compares with the seven productions of *Meistersinger* that he saw, in Hamburg, Cologne, Bayreuth, Leipzig, Potsdam and Berlin (twice), the last eliciting the comment: 'One is always amazed at the daemonic power of woman over man.'[51] On previous occasions he had been taken by the 'gorgeous music' (25 April 1888), thereafter noting: 'The opera pleased me more than ever' (24 November 1888) and: 'Magnificent, especially the choruses and orchestra' (17 August 1889).

Bearing in mind the associations with Mozart (especially *Le Nozze di Figaro*, and, to a lesser extent, *Die Zauberflöte*) and with Wagner (especially *Meistersinger*) that were later to be made with *Der Rosenkavalier*, it is worth noting Kessler's early reactions to the performances of these works that he saw. His comments on *Meistersinger* have been given above: in 1890, however, he saw both Mozart operas a few months apart. His reaction to *Figaro* in Leipzig was:

> Heard Mozart's *Figaro*; a never ceasing stream of purest melody, flowing like a clear crystal brook; such combined grace, and sweetness, and abundance of imagination no other composition has ever attained (7 February 1890).

Kessler was similarly struck by Mozart's last opera, and clearly also by the circumstances of its creation:

> Then to hear the *Zauberflöte*; few operas have ever pleased me so; Mozart certainly resembled Raphael in many points, the same exquisite grace, the same even flow of beauty, the same sweetness and purity of style; it is almost incredible that a man so unhappy as Mozart could have written works so perfectly serene and lovely (26 October 1890).

Yet, even more than Kessler's specific reactions to some of the works (both routine and of genius) that he encountered in the theatres and opera houses during this formative period, the outcome of his activities at this time was the rapid development of his thinking on theatre, arising from sheer exposure to all aspects of performance, theatricality, popular and classical music and – importantly – dance. Indeed, Kessler recorded some fascinating thoughts – in view of what was to come over twenty years later with his ballet for Diaghilev, *Josephs Legende* – when he took his friend Alfred von Nostitz to the opera house in Leipzig:

> Theatre in the evening with Nostitz: Mehul *Joseph in Egypt*. Then a new ballet: *Light*. If the ballerinas were to abandon their nasty gauze skirts and their graceless hopping around, ballet could be turned into a high form of art, possibly the most perfect

[51] *Diary II*, p. 416.

expression and demonstration of grace and beauty in human form, vibrant and harmonious splendour in colours, beauty of décor combined with the power of music: there would, however, have to be a very great painter and a very great musician combined in one person for this (12 October 1891).[52]

Comments like this perhaps account for the following assessment by Grupp in his 1995 biography:

> Kessler felt himself drawn to dance and ballet from an early age. [...] Dance and ballet seemed to him to be the almost ideal realisation of a desired synthesis of body and soul, intellect and sensuality, and simultaneously as an augmentation and bringing to life of sculpture.[53]

To summarise, if one takes an arbitrary cut-off date of 11 May 1898, the day that Kessler and Hofmannsthal were to meet for the first time, just twelve days before Kessler's thirtieth birthday, the *Diary* records until then a total of around 350 theatrical spectacles seen by Kessler all over the world. He had visited regularly, in Paris, the Opéra, Opéra Comique, Comédie Française, Théâtre du Châtelet, Odéon, and many of the boulevard theatres including the Théâtre des Bouffes Parisiens. In Berlin he was a regular visitor to the Opera, Kroll Opera, Deutsches Theater, Berliner Theater, Freie Bühne, Neues Theater, Lessing Theater and other major houses. He had been to the Metropolitan Opera in New York, to theatres in Tokyo and Shanghai, to West End theatres in London and to the opera houses of Cologne, Hamburg, Leipzig, Munich and, repeatedly, Bayreuth. He had also, in Paris and elsewhere, attended music halls and revues, the commercial and popular end of public places of entertainment attracting his interest alongside his exposure to Mozart, Wagner and to the living composers of his time whose premières he frequently attended. This extraordinarily wide range of theatrical experiences also helped Kessler to develop his critical appreciation of the works he saw. From mere description of the earliest performances of Wagner and other operas that he attended, Kessler had begun to develop critical insight and a mind of his own by the time he saw the 1897 *Ring* cycle in Bayreuth:

> The *Walküre*. A performance that for the first time gave me even in reality an approximate picture of music drama; no longer operatic, a real echo of ancient Greek tragedy. It could convert one to the views in *The Birth of Tragedy*. And yet, interest in the trilogy is always merely episodic, centred on what is actually happening onstage at that moment, without being lifted in any way by what came before or what comes after. Wagner has not succeeded in turning the thread that is supposed to

---

[52] 'Das Licht', music by Joseph Hellmesberger junior (1855–1907), choreography by Jean Golinelli, was a ballet in six scenes that premièred at the Neues Theater, Leipzig the night that Kessler saw it. The roles of Amor and Psyche were danced by Ms Sperling and Ms Hruby, and the Sun (prima ballerina) was Ms Fiebig. I am grateful to Melanie Hahn of the Stadtarchiv, Leipzig for researching Theaterzettel 1.3.5.23.2 for 21.10.1891.

[53] Grupp, p. 146.

hold everything together, the metaphysical-philosophical thread, into art, or to make it artistically effective. This means that the very scenes that are vital for the whole, for example the scene between Fricka and Wotan, come across as long, superfluous passages that could be cut without harming the artistic effect, despite the fact that if one looks at the *Ring* as a dramatic whole, they are the climaxes of the plot. This is an artistic objection that nothing can refute.[54]

As he immersed himself ever more in the theatre and opera of the major European houses, Kessler came to regard his own ability to discern, plan and order dramatic structure as greatly superior to Hofmannsthal's abilities in this area. But even the earlier *Diary* entries, such as the one above, show that Kessler began to consider dramatic structure and its effectiveness for stage narrative from a relatively early age.

Three months later (in October 1897) Kessler was beginning to consider his own attitude to drama and theatre, recording his thoughts while on a train journey from Amiens to London. His vague project was to write a play called *Der Einsame* ('The Lonely One') but his interest was in the loneliness stemming from an individual's own nature, and not in mere ideas about loneliness such as he had found in Hauptmann's *Einsame Menschen* ('Lonely People'); in other words, what concerned Kessler was cause, not effect:

> Mama is urging me to try to write drama. But basically my conceptual form of drama is undramatic; a born dramatist sees plot, circumstances, events, not characters; and if he has talent or genius, he drills down from the plot into the fundamentals; he goes from an event that he has found interesting or exciting back into the characters, who would come together to make that event plausible, convincing, from the flower into the roots, and the deeper he goes, the more his work stands the test of time (Shakspeare) [sic]. On the other hand there can also be masterpieces (Goethe); but nothing that is necessarily and actually dramatic, i.e. that demands to be performed on the stage in order to be realised in full.[55]

Kessler had recently seen *Mutter Erde* ('Mother Earth') by Max Halbe[56] in Berlin, three days after its première, describing it as: 'Almost a masterpiece; what it lacks is power of conviction for the preconditions on which the conflict is based.'[57] This had given rise to his own thoughts about characterisation in the theatre:

> If one looks at drama as drama, i.e. as a work for the stage, then characterisation is always merely the means to an end; the purpose it serves is to make what has happened seem necessary, i.e. to remove any doubts in the audience's mind as to the

---

[54] *Diary III*, p. 72.
[55] *Diary III*, p. 92.
[56] Max Halbe (1865–1944) was an author and playwright and a member of the supervisory board of *Pan*. Kessler had particular admiration for his authorship of female roles onstage.
[57] *Diary III*, p. 81.

veracity of what takes place before their eyes; in this respect, it is a sort of continuation and amplification of the exposition.[58]

Yet Kessler was in no doubt as to the fundamental theatrical importance of effective characterisation, concluding the same entry with:

> But on the other hand it is precisely the fact that characterisation in drama is a necessity, whereas in all other forms of art it is either an incidental luxury or can be substituted by other means, that has resulted in drama doing more than all the other arts in penetrating and portraying the human soul. In itself this penetration is not art, i.e. not a stimulant of the soul, but rather science, a broadening of understanding, a quenching of the thirst for knowledge and understanding.[59]

Although his thoughts on stage characterisation were evolving in this period, much influenced by the sheer variety of what he was experiencing in the theatre in the 1890s, Kessler seems to have seen quite clearly his own strengths and weaknesses in this area. It is significant, therefore, that when he and Hofmannsthal began to work together on *Der Rosenkavalier*, Kessler was in no doubt that his main responsibility would be for the dramatic structure, and that he would be able to rely on Hofmannsthal to make the characters come alive through their language and stage dialogue.

Kessler and theatre, 1892–1908

Exploration of Kessler's private thread of thought on theatre and drama, as confided to his *Diary*, has left aside until now the way in which this fitted into his more general development. He had been schooled in France, England and Germany, and had studied law at the universities of Bonn and Leipzig, as a prelude to a career in government service, preferably the German Diplomatic Service. His hopes of such an appointment were to last until April 1902, when he was finally informed that 'too many people are against it'.[60] Kessler's real interests while in Leipzig, however, had been art and culture, in particular the art history lectures of Anton Springer that he regularly attended,[61] and the psychology classes of Wilhelm Wundt, the latter informing Kessler's rapidly growing interest in Friedrich Nietzsche.[62] Kessler's subsequent involvement with the art world, the leading French, English and German neo-impressionists he came to know, and his passionate engagement with Nietzsche and his friendship with the philosopher's sister Elisabeth Förster-Nietzsche, precisely around the turn of the twentieth century and thereafter, are

---

[58] *Diary III*, p. 82.
[59] *Diary III*, p. 82.
[60] *Diary III*, p. 487.
[61] Easton, pp. 36–9.
[62] Easton, pp. 39–44.

substantial chapters of his life in themselves, and have been well covered already by his biographers.[63]

After leaving Leipzig he had made a slightly truncated world tour (December 1891–July 1892), and had completed his compulsory year of military service with his cavalry regiment of choice, the Third Guard Lancers based in Potsdam (September 1892–September 1893). It was during this year that he had enjoyed his first fully fledged homosexual affair with a fellow officer, Otto von Dungern, confirming the homosexual feelings he had started to feel while still at the Hamburg Johanneum.[64] Kessler then began work in October 1893 at the District Court in Spandau, Berlin, while continuing to work on his doctoral dissertation. His *Diary* is almost silent on his legal work for the next few years, but eloquent on the glittering social life he began to lead, and on the artistic and theatrical friends and acquaintances he started to make. His immersion into the world of Berlin theatre had already begun, however, from late 1892 onwards, when he and regimental colleagues often made the short journey from Potsdam to partake of the bigger city's cultural life. Kessler's heavy involvement in this cultural life was to last over a decade, until he moved to Weimar in 1903, and even after this move, he returned to Berlin regularly and continued his close involvement with some of its leading theatrical and artistic figures.

This pre-*Der Rosenkavalier* period in Kessler's adult life, taking him from 24 to 40, divides quite neatly into three: his ten years in Berlin, meeting most of the significant figures in the overlapping worlds of art, theatre, literature and politics, and absorbing everything that he experienced there; his three subsequent years of official but unpaid appointment in Weimar as Curator of the Grand-Ducal Museum of Arts and Crafts (1903–6), which were marked by his constant efforts to bring the artistic avant-garde from Berlin, and from abroad, to a conservative city and court whose officials resisted and obstructed many of his efforts, until they secured his (enforced) resignation; and his three years thereafter, when he had no official position, but continued to dream of a new Weimar, which he could help to flourish in cultural terms, while continuing with his incessant schedule of European travel. Two and a half years into his Weimar curatorship, on 15 November 1905, Kessler had already reflected in his *Diary* on what he thought his connections and activities really signified at this stage in his life:

> I have thought about my means of achieving things in Germany: the German Artists' Association, my position in Weimar including its prestige, despite the idiocy of the Grand Duke, my connections with Reinhardt's theatre, my intimate links with the Nietzsche Archive, my close links with Dehmel, Liliencron, Klinger, Liebermann, Ansorge, Gerhard (sic) Hauptmann, and with the two influential magazines *Zukunft* and *Neue Rundschau*, and completely on the other hand Berlin society, the Harrachs, Richters, Sascha Schlippenbach, the regiment, and finally my personal prestige. The

---

[63] Rothe, in particular pp. 114–32, summarises both aspects.
[64] Easton, pp. 53–5.

outcome is surprising, and undoubtedly unique. Nobody else in Germany has such a strong position that radiates in so many directions. To make use of this in the service of a renewal of German culture: mirage or real possibility? Someone with these resources could undoubtedly be Princeps Juventutis. Is it worth it?[65]

This self-assessment was, however, wide of the mark: in particular, it ignored the opposition that was building, in conservative circles in Weimar, to much of what Kessler was attempting to achieve. For all that Kessler could attract to Weimar illustrious personalities from every artistic field – as visits by Hofmannsthal, Hauptmann, Richard Dehmel, Auguste Rodin, André Gide, Aristide Maillol and many others were to prove – he failed to gauge realistically the effect he was having on small-minded, traditional officialdom in and around the Court there, and he neglected to make the case, locally, for his attempted radical renewal of all art forms in Weimar. His personal vision of a new Weimar as a crucible of cultural modernism thus came to an early, perhaps inevitable end.

Although Kessler only ever completed the first volume of his memoirs, in 1934–5 he sketched out the sequence of chapters that were to follow, and these indicate the developments in his life that, retrospectively, he himself regarded as important. After a chapter on Berlin court society, the emergence of banking and industrial magnates and traditional artist circles in the city, his planned sequence continued:

> VII. *First combative years* from around 1892–3 on. Growth of naturalism. Gerhart Hauptmann, 'Die Weber', première of 'Florian Geyer'. Max Liebermann. Establishment of *Pan*. Meier-Graefe, Otto Julius Bierbaum, Bode, Eberhard Bodenhausen, Richard Dehmel. Bohemians: Stanislaw Przybyszewski, Duscha, Edvard Munch etc. Visit to Nietzsche on his sickbed in Naumburg. Hofmannsthal. – Rainer Maria Rilke.[66]

A planned chapter on developments in Paris is then followed by Berlin at the turn of the century, including: 'Art and theatre in Berlin. The beginnings of Max Reinhardt. The Secession' and later, most intriguingly of all, by:

> XII. *In the shadows of the coming catastrophe 1911–1914*. The fever of European society, wanting to live it up. Berlin – Paris – London. The Russian ballet. Diaghilev. Nijinsky. [Ida] Rubinstein. Richard Strauss. Hofmannsthal. *Der Rosenkavalier. Josephs Legende*. The last London season. Height of the euphoria.[67]

Kessler had his *Diary*, for these years, with him in Mallorca as he contemplated writing his own retrospective account of his relationships with all those he named. One can only speculate on what he might have said. Even with the raw materials, the *Diary* text and the extant letters now available and easily accessible, it is hard

---

[65] *Diary III*, pp. 812–13.
[66] *CW I*, p. 310.
[67] *CW I*, p. 311.

to find real coherence in the plethora of activities, in quick succession, that such a highly mobile young man undertook. Stenzel describes Kessler as constantly going to museums, exhibitions and theatres in his spare time from 1892–3 onwards and associates him with the so-called Friedrichshagen Group:

> The best-known bohemian group in Berlin was the 'Friedrichshagen Group'. Among those attending meetings in the Berlin suburb of Friedrichshagen were the Naturalists Arno Holz, the Hart brothers, Gerhart Hauptmann, Max Halbe, Bruno Wille, Richard Dehmel, the Scandinavians Knut Hamsun, August Strindberg and the Polish writer Stanislaw Przybyszewski.[68]

Of these names, the foremost German exponent of naturalism in the theatre, Hauptmann, and his developing relationship with Kessler, is one factor in parallel with several others that governed the development of Kessler's theatrical understanding and vision, which proved so vital when the *Rosenkavalier* project came to be taken forward. And given that Kessler's feeling for effective theatre was almost certainly greater than Hofmannsthal's when the two men sat down to work up *Der Rosenkavalier* together, we should look briefly at four very different theatrical influences on Kessler before coming to his initial, pre-*Der Rosenkavalier* relationship with Hugo von Hofmannsthal.

Kessler and Hauptmann

Kessler saw *Die Weber* ('The Weavers') on 5 March 1893, a week after it had begun a run of private performances for members of the Freie Bühne. The *Diary* records his fascination with the contrast between the luxurious new theatre and its elegant, refined audience, and the stark misery depicted onstage: 'The main characters in the great drama that was enacted were the public and the thrust of the play, and this drama was perhaps almost world historical.'[69] He was to take a very similar view when he also attended the first ever public performance of *Die Weber* eighteen months later, wondering how bejewelled high society could applaud the play so warmly given its subject matter, but concluding that man's inner duality of spirit explained things:

> In this case the applause is only for aesthetic pleasure, nervous stimulation as it were, and it by no means indicates that those applauding will find their oysters at Dressel any less tasty just because they have seen the Baumert family eating dog meat for dinner.[70]

In 1893 he had also seen *Der Biberpelz* ('The Beaver Coat') on 23 September and *Hanneles Himmelfahrt* ('Hannele's Ascension') on 23 November, which enchanted him: he was to see it twice more in 1894 and 1896. By December 1895 Kessler was

---

[68] Stenzel, p. 44.
[69] *Diary II*, p. 208.
[70] *Diary II*, p. 282.

comparing Hauptmann and Wagner, as onstage master dramatists of group psychology, with Mozart, as a master of individual psychology.[71] Then, on 4 January 1896, after the tumultuous and highly contested première of *Florian Geyer* at the Deutsches Theater, Kessler found himself in a minority of one, defending the play against the negative opinions of a whole group of his friends.[72] Kessler regarded *Florian Geyer* as an advance on *Die Weber*, and having obtained and then read the text at least twice in the following days, came to a striking judgement on Hauptmann's skill as a dramatist:

> In Germany we have not had as grandiose a characterisation as Florian since Goethe; the dry humour, the resignation that flows from comparison between the nothingness of reality and the lustre of his own imagination, in other words the poetic resignation which is so deeply Germanic (cf. Bismarck in Nikolsburg), the splendid and suggestive language, all of this makes *Geyer* as a work of art in a class of its own amongst today's productions. I only know one living author who could create something similar: Ibsen. But the simplicity of the means that Hauptmann uses to achieve his main effects puts him, in my eyes, in the capital scenes, <u>over and above</u> everything of Ibsen that I know, even above *Rosmersholm*.[73]

By this time, Kessler was moving in artistic and literary circles in Berlin that were bound, sooner or later, to bring him into personal contact with Hauptmann. His association with the group of friends who launched the seminal German arts and letters journal, *Pan*, dated from its earliest planning stages in 1894, although he was not elected to the supervisory board of *Pan* until late 1895: from that date, until the journal ceased publication in 1900, Kessler was both a contributor to *Pan* (two major articles) and a tireless, unpaid worker on its behalf. He sat on the editorial committee, commissioned work for the journal from authors and artists in Germany, France and England and was even invited (by Bodenhausen, chairman of the supervisory board, in August 1895) to take over 'the direction of *Pan*' – he declined.[74] The sheer quality of *Pan* – its layout, expensive paper, elegant design and modernist content[75] – gave Kessler added prestige as one of its leading figures and also gave focus to his exploration of the worlds of art, literature and theatre that was under way already: as Easton puts it:

> One of the benefits Kessler drew from his experience with *Pan* was a growing acquaintance with modern French art and literature. Given his family connections

---

[71] *Diary II*, p. 417.
[72] *Diary II*, p. 421.
[73] *Diary II*, p. 426.
[74] Simon, p. 121.
[75] *Pan* in its entirety has now been digitised by the University of Heidelberg and is available online at: http://www.ub.uni-heidelberg.de/Englisch/helios/fachinfo/www/kunst/digilit/artjournals/pan.html.

and his interests, he of course would have encountered French modernism anyway, but the missions he undertook on behalf of *Pan* accelerated the process.[76]

One such mission saw Kessler dining for the first time with Hauptmann, and the latter's future (second) wife Margarete, on 14 December 1899:

> Hauptmann quiet at table, afterwards we talked for quite a long time. When he speaks he struggles with the words, creases his forehead into deep wrinkles and lowers his head; this way of speaking gives more weight to what he says than its content. We discussed Zacconi, Rittner and new theatrical style; he thinks for the moment it does not apply to Shakspeare; but he thinks we shall live to experience the creation of a new, intimate Shakspeare style. Talk then turned to a Dehmel poem set to music by Strauss ('Du wirst nicht weinen' ('You will not cry')), which Hofmann did not like, but I then read it aloud, whereupon both Hauptmann and Hofmann said it was very wonderful.[77]

This first meeting was to lead, in time, to a friendship between both men that saw Hauptmann dedicate his 1908 book *Griechischer Frühling* ('Greek Spring') to Kessler, and Kessler to reply in print with his 1909 essay with the same title.[78] The *Diary* records an entire Sunday spent with Hauptmann in Berlin in December 1904 – 'deeply sympathetic impression of Hauptmann'[79] – an excursion to Leipzig with him in April 1905, meetings in Berlin in October 1905[80] and for the rest of that year, culminating in a stay by Hauptmann with Kessler at the latter's house in Weimar on 10/11 December: the social highlight was a small dinner in honour of the Grand Duke (Wilhelm Ernst) on the first night, the theatrical highlight a reading by Hauptmann of his new play *Und Pippa Tanzt* ('And Pippa Dances') to a small, invited audience on the second day.[81] By this stage the *Diary* records regular meetings with Hauptmann, but only occasional details of exactly what the two men discussed: there are, however, intriguing glimpses such as a meal with Hauptmann and the dancer Ruth St Denis,[82] after a matinée performance by the latter in Berlin in November 1906, of which the *Diary* notes difficulties over a language in common (Kessler clearly acting as interpreter) and continues:

---

[76] Easton, p. 70.
[77] *Diary III*, p. 287. Ludwig von Hofmann, graphic artist and a leading member of *Pan*, was a friend of both men.
[78] *CW II*, pp. 147–79.
[79] *Diary III*, p. 768.
[80] *Diary III*, pp. 809–10.
[81] *Diary III*, p. 820.
[82] Ruth St Denis (1877–1968) was an American dancer who became a sensation in Europe: Kessler first wrote about her to Hofmannsthal on 26 October 1906, saying he must see her if possible, and again on 29 October, saying that Hofmannsthal absolutely *must* see her: 'I have seen her again in one of her major numbers which made the greatest impression that the art of dance has ever made on me' (Burger, p. 130).

> But the mood was good throughout, as both Hauptmann and St. Denis are in essence simple and naïve people and thus not at all bothered by being silent while others talk. The heart of the conversation was naturally dance and pantomime. Half-joking, I told Hauptmann across the table: you have your Pippa now. – Even if not exactly that, he said, he had an idea for a sort of pantomime which would be suitable for St. Denis [...][83]

This encounter, and exchange, gave rise a short time later to a conversation between Hauptmann and Kessler that goes to the heart of the way that Kessler saw and understood theatre, the principles that were to inform his input to the *Rosenkavalier* project three years later. For just as Kessler looked at art works and analysed their composition, seeing (particularly in Hogarth) the use of light, form and rhythm to portray strong narrative values,[84] so he approached theatre first and foremost from its visual aspects. This emphasis on the visual also explains Kessler's fascination with dance, and his enthusiastic championing of Ruth St Denis and, later, of Nijinsky and the Ballets Russes. The *Diary* records his exchange with Hauptmann thus:

> After the meal all the others sat in a circle around St. Denis; I sat alone with Hauptmann by the fire. Once again he went into great detail on the question of pantomime in drama. "You know, maybe, that originally I wanted to be a sculptor. Actually, I regret to this day that I did not pursue this". I said: "A drama too is actually nothing more than plastic in motion, enacted in words. – He said: "Yes, undoubtedly, you are absolutely right there. I have already often thought that you should actually through-compose a play with your eyes, and only then start to write it. An entire situation can be expressed in a single word; but then the pantomime has to be there too, so that the word has its effect in the right place and at the right moment. Maybe you will not remember this; but I have a scene just like this in *Friedensfest*. Right from the start I have tried to get my actors to move. Earlier on, I had long discussions about this with Kainz. Nowadays he does so and often even overdoes it; but then he was not easy to convince. In those days actors stood still beside each other and merely declaimed. This is why Antoine was so interesting. He was the first to walk about, to move, to give us the pantomime (*Ghosts*)".[85]

Kessler's close involvement with Hauptmann, and the thoughts that the two men exchanged, were, however, just one strand in the web of theatrical connections made by Kessler in the pre-*Der Rosenkavalier* period. Of equal importance were the relationships he developed at the same time with the director and theatre manager Max Reinhardt, with the playwright Frank Wedekind (whose plays were first performed in Reinhardt's theatres) and with the artist, designer and director Edward Gordon Craig. Of these, Wedekind has received perhaps the least

---

[83] *Diary IV*, p. 205.
[84] *Diary IV*, pp. 139–41 provides a striking example of this.
[85] *Diary IV*, pp. 206–7.

attention, but his approach to theatre intrigued Kessler, and their relationship should be noted.

Kessler and Frank Wedekind

As in the case of Hauptmann, Kessler moved slowly and steadily towards him, firstly seeing his work in the theatre: *Erdgeist* ('Earth Spirit') in January 1903 and *Der Kammersänger* ('The Chamber Singer'), in a double bill with Wilde's *Salome*, in October 1903. The latter elicited no comment, but Kessler was intrigued by *Erdgeist*: 'Some of the scenes are irresistibly funny, despite murder and suicide,'[86] and he found Punch and Judy elements in Wedekind's treatment of the narrative, concluding:

> The possibilities that are in Wedekind's drama are undeveloped. It is still 100 years before Shakspeare. It is, as it were, pre-Raphaelite, with latent power like a bud. The perfect dramatic form would have been for Lulu's love affairs to have been written into her <u>last</u> adventure, performed for us as elements of this final conflict, not recounted one after the other.[87]

The *Diary* records subsequent discussions on Wedekind with Hauptmann[88] and with Hofmannsthal,[89] the latter admitting to Kessler that he found Wedekind a master of style, and was studying his dramatic writings because of that. Then, on 17 December 1905 Kessler saw Wedekind onstage in a production of *Der Marquis von Keith* ('The Marquis of Keith') and noted: 'A great deal of wit, a great deal of Dumas and one brilliant comedy scene: the one between Wildenfels and Scholz at the end of Act IV.'[90] Kessler added however that much of the play remained intellectual, more so than Shaw, whose female characters, he thought, had more life to them.

Shortly thereafter, on 2 February 1906, Kessler met Wedekind properly for the first time, at a dinner arranged by Max Reinhardt following the première of Hofmannsthal's *Oedipus*. The *Diary* records Wedekind's highly negative opinion of the piece and an admission: 'Speaking of his own plays, Wedekind said that they were actually only a collection of aphorisms. They were not dramatic at all.'[91] A month later Kessler and Wedekind met at another dinner arranged by Reinhardt, this time in honour of the visiting Maxim Gorki. Thereafter, they began to see more of each other, especially towards the end of 1906: after a supper given by Walter Rathenau[92] that included Reinhardt, Kessler and Wedekind, the party broke up

---

[86] *Diary III*, p. 532.
[87] *Diary III*, p. 532.
[88] *Diary III*, p. 810.
[89] *Diary III*, p. 816.
[90] *Diary III*, p. 823.
[91] *Diary IV*, p. 93.
[92] Walther Rathenau (1867–1922) was an industrialist – rising to become head of AEG, the conglomerate originally founded by his father – who then entered government service and politics,

around 1.30 a.m. and Kessler recorded walking 'home with Wedekind as far as the bridge' without, however, noting their subjects of discussion.[93] Yet what Kessler undoubtedly got from his relationship with Wedekind was exposure to dramatic and theatrical narrative of an entirely different – and not always successful – kind, a complete contrast to the naturalism of Hauptmann, but a bold and valid attempt to structure drama in a new and original way. Wedekind was a further enrichment of Kessler's developing theatrical understanding and vision as the prospect of his creative collaboration with Hofmannsthal approached.

Kessler and Max Reinhardt

If Kessler was interested in, and involved with, the naturalist Hauptmann and the precursor of Expressionism and Symbolism Wedekind, as theatrical authors whose works were constantly being developed and first performed at this time, he was equally fascinated by theatre projects and by the business of theatre, always looking for ways that his network of international connections could be brought together and put to good use in an artistic cause. He had taken a strong interest in the work of Max Reinhardt since the latter's early days as a director in Berlin from 1902 onwards: he was to become ever closer to Reinhardt in succeeding years through projects – many of them unrealised – involving Hofmannsthal, Craig and the Belgian architect and designer Henry van de Velde, who was a particular protégé of Kessler's.[94] The value to Kessler of his association with Reinhardt was the frequent, easy and informal access he enjoyed, afforded by their friendship, to the creative theatrical team around the man who revolutionised the Berlin theatre scene from the 1890s onwards, first with the Kleines Theater and the Neues Theater and then – from 1905 – with the Deutsches Theater, whose *Kuratorium* or board of governors Kessler joined in 1905. Moreover, Reinhardt's strikingly new stage pictures, and production values, chimed with Kessler's own emphasis on the importance of the visual elements onstage. Conversely, the value of Kessler to Reinhardt was the stream of ideas, suggestions and contacts that he constantly put forward, from Berlin high society circles whom Kessler managed to interest in Reinhardt's work[95] to the planned creative association with Craig that ultimately

---

eventually being assassinated by right-wing extremists while serving as Foreign Minister. Kessler knew Rathenau from the mid-1890s onwards, both being associated with *Pan*: Kessler's acclaimed biography of Rathenau was published in 1928.

[93] *Diary IV*, p. 187.

[94] Henry van de Velde (1863–1957) played an important part in Kessler's life, and vice versa. He designed Kessler's flat in Berlin and his house in Weimar: in 1900 he moved to Berlin and with Kessler's help was appointed head of Arts and Crafts at the Court of Weimar in December 1901. Kessler followed Van de Velde to Weimar just over a year later and tried, over a long period, to obtain commercial commissions for Van de Velde's theatre designs.

[95] Kessler's *Diary* for 4 December 1905 records: 'Reinhardt came in the evening. Discussed *Oedipus* with him, also how to interest Berlin society in him and his theatre, so as to break through at last into the predominance of high finance governing art' (*Diary III*, p. 817).

failed to prosper. Barzantny provides a good summary of Kessler's relationship with Reinhardt, concluding with an apposite quote from a 21 March 1911 telegram sent by the latter to Kessler: 'Thank you so much for your very interesting letter which once again, as so often, proves to me the great importance for our theatre that regular consultation with you would provide.'[96] Likewise a *Diary* entry for 18 October 1905 records an exchange in the early hours between both men, following Kessler's private tour of the renovated Deutsches Theater, the night before it was due to reopen:

> Reinhardt mentioned his theatre school. I told him that in my view the most important aspect, in addition to diction, was that the body be brought into play again, to add enchantment, such as is solely the case nowadays with Kainz, or with Moissi at a pinch. The best way of achieving this would be to take children and to get them used to acting, dancing and acrobatics <u>completely naked</u>. Since that would provoke a scandal, given our prudery, then to give them as little clothing as possible. Reinhardt agreed. He added that in Germany, gesture always followed the word, whereas in real life and with good actors it preceded the word; all the word actually did was to explain the gesture.[97]

Kessler's interest in, and engagement with Reinhardt was because he recognised the sheer theatrical quality and innovation of what was being achieved. On 20 November 1905 Kessler saw *The Merchant of Venice* at the Garrick Theatre in London and commented: 'After this performance in one of the leading [London] theatres I now have a much higher opinion of Reinhardt.'[98] Kessler's high opinion of Reinhardt's work was by no means uncritical, however, as shown by his reaction to a later production of *Twelfth Night*:

> In the evening to *Twelfth Night* with Musch Richter, in Schroeder's translation. Reinhardt's effects with the revolving stage. He links successive scenes by leaving the stage open while the turntable operates, and by showing the actors and extras getting ready for the next location from scene to scene. He thus creates very pretty living pictures. The costumes are also particularly pretty this time. But he has no feel for tempi and above all for the contrasting tempi in Shakspeare. He allows the clown scenes to be played just as *adagio* as the lyrical scenes. The effect is like playing all the movements of a symphony in one and the same tempo. Shakspeare's dynamics elude him; and this is unforgivable in this case, because you can feel them with Schroeder's translation.[99]

Kessler's involvement and friendship with Reinhardt was to continue for many years, however, and in 1911 it was Reinhardt who was to step in as director of the

---

[96] Barzantny, pp. 139–44.
[97] *Diary III*, pp. 808–9.
[98] *Diary III*, p. 813.
[99] *Diary IV*, p. 364.

first-ever Dresden production of *Der Rosenkavalier* when the local director, Georg Toller, proved to be inadequate for the task.

Kessler and Edward Gordon Craig

Four years previously, Kessler had found theatrical enchantment of a different sort in a London production by Craig, at the Imperial Theatre, of Ibsen's *The Vikings*. Kessler noted:

> A highly remarkable attempt to reform the stage. Main changes: that he gets rid of footlights completely, and the scenery almost completely; all he uses is overhead lighting and props. All around the stage are drapes that are almost invisible under changing lighting effects and coloured lighting gauzes. You have the impression that you are looking into infinite space.[100]

Kessler found this approach, and Craig's basic ideas of ridding the stage of all artificial elements, ground-breaking and very valuable, and seized his first opportunity to meet Craig in person: they were introduced by Will Rothenstein at the Café Royal in London on 29 September 1903. In the meantime, Kessler had seen Craig's production of *Much Ado About Nothing*, with Craig's mother Ellen Terry playing Beatrice in May, and three open-air productions (not directed by Craig) in the Botanic Gardens in July – *Comus* by Milton and *Hue and Cry after Cupid* by Ben Jonson on 1 July, *The Faithful Shepherdess* by John Fletcher on 11 July.[101] Kessler's visual imagination was stimulated in particular by *Comus*: 'It was a wonderful night, moonlit and mild, and the performance truly fairylike; artistic pleasure such as I have never previously experienced as purely and without anything extraneous.'[102] This led to Kessler, at their first meeting, to propose that Craig direct an open-air production, in the park of Schloss Belvedere in Weimar, of a masque or entertainment to be written by Hofmannsthal: Craig, however, immediately declared his antipathy to open-air theatre, and the project proved abortive, although Kessler's correspondence with Hofmannsthal continued on the matter for some time.

Kessler's subsequent, passionate advocacy of Craig in Germany, and the committed efforts he made over many years to see the work of a uniquely important – albeit more theoretical than practical – theatrical reformer staged in German houses, has already been covered thoroughly by various authors and requires summary restatement only.[103] Kessler launched Craig into potential working rela-

---

[100] *Diary IV*, pp. 556–7.
[101] *Diary III*, p. 586.
[102] *Diary III*, p. 584.
[103] Bablet. His book provides a good general introduction to Craig and Kessler (pp. 68–74) but was written before Kessler's *Diary* for the period came to light and is thus incomplete. Newman, first published in 1995, rectifies that omission and provides the best overall account of the relationship between Craig and Kessler. Barzantny provides a useful, concise summary with several insights of her own (pp. 125–39).

tionships with Otto Brahm, with Hofmannsthal, with Reinhardt and even with Diaghilev but, in every case, Craig's insistence on absolute control over every aspect of production – coupled with his high financial demands – led either to only partial realisation of each project (Brahm – two scenes in *Das Gerettete Venedig*, Hofmannsthal's reworking of Thomas Otway's *Venice Preserved*) or to a breaking off of negotiations. The impact this was to have at the height of the *Rosenkavalier* creative process in 1910, when Craig failed to come to terms with Reinhardt and Hofmannsthal over a planned production of the latter's *Oedipus*, was considerable.

Kessler's theatrical vision had been broad enough, and eclectic enough, to embrace Craig's ideas from the moment he first saw Craig's work in the theatre (*The Vikings*), but even before that, Kessler had been very impressed by Craig's artistry with bookplates: 'Ex Libris exhibition. The best and most original were those by Gordon Craig, simple, very powerfully and distinctively formed characters in the style of old trade names; absolutely right for an Ex Libris.'[104] This gave Kessler the idea of arranging and sponsoring an exhibition of Craig's work in Germany: it duly opened on 3 December 1904 at Friedmann and Weber's Gallery in Berlin:

> It comprised sixty items, including designs for *Acis and Galatea*, *The Masque of London*, *Much Ado About Nothing*, *Henry V*, *The Vikings*, *The Masque of Love*, etc., some English landscape sketches, and a number of portraits and illustrations. The very important introduction to the catalogue is signed 'Harry Graf Kessler'.[105]

This 'very important introduction' became better known when it was reprinted as the introduction to Craig's seminal work *The Art of the Theatre*[106] in its German translation, *Die Kunst des Theaters*, which actually appeared in print before the English text was published.[107] Since this text is Kessler's attempt, in his own words, to introduce to a German public the theatrical ideas and vision of Craig for the first time, the essential concepts adumbrated by Kessler reveal much of the latter's own thinking at this stage of his life. Kessler started to write this essay on his journey from Weimar to Paris on 22 November 1904.[108] He finished it while in Paris, and sent it to Craig six days later, on 28 November.

Kessler's introduction, reprinted in his collected writings, starts by listing the disappointments and deficiencies of most theatrical productions being seen by the public at the time, and then offers a ray of hope:

---

[104] *Diary III*, p. 555.
[105] Bablet, p. 73.
[106] Edward Gordon Craig, *The Art of the Theatre* (Edinburgh and London: Foulis, 1905).
[107] Edward Gordon Craig, *Die Kunst des Theaters*, ed. and trans. Maurice Magnus with an introduction by Harry Graf Kessler (Berlin and Leipzig: Seeman, 1905). As Lorenzo Mango has pointed out in his detailed analysis of the manuscripts, the German edition was published in June 1905 and was followed later that summer by the English: see http://www.actingarchives.unior.it/Public/Articoli/e277a742-fd1b-4547-9e20-91b9eee30dc4/Allegati/Lorenzo%20Mango_The%20Manuscripts%20of%20The%20Art%20of%20the%20Theatre.pdf.
[108] *Diary III*, p. 763.

A few, whose plays seem like rare flowers in the barren forest of modern stage productions, have repeatedly given hope for this desire: Hauptmann, Hofmannsthal, Maeterlinck. They have offered the soul what it desires: art once again, not artifice. But the poetry ought to inspire a stage picture of equal value, not leaving a great actor alone as a mere fragment of the artistic imagery that is required; only then would we have an art of the theatre.[109]

He goes on to argue in favour of the all-powerful stage director, not someone who is subject to the whims of theatre managers and the troupe of actors, and not reliant on conventional scenery painters, but someone capable of directing and inspiring every aspect of theatrical production, a 'creative artist with a fine, sure sense of proportion, line, colour, so that he can design for himself every visual image in each play'.[110] Characteristically for Kessler, he evokes the dancing of Loie Fuller and Sada Yacco as having, almost by chance, 'revealed to us this dream, these possibilities of imaginative art on the stage'. Kessler then comments on what Craig has tried to achieve with his stage designs to date, and concludes:

> Craig anticipates a further development, however. The stage artist could himself become a creator. Craig believes that a stage work does not have to be created on old lines, three parts of writing and one part painting and music. On the contrary: if there is a single onstage element that is more important than all the others, it is not the word but the movement, gesture.
>
> So Craig would like to link up with ancient pantomime and, even further back, with dance, out of which Greek tragedy emerged. He has composed a work on these lines: *Hunger*. Craig definitely predicts a completely different role for the theatre in the next century. He does not despise the writer, but he protests against the way that theatre people, directors, actors, stage painters, rely on the writer. He wants to return to the theatre its own form of art. He has clearly recognised the conditions for this pure art of the theatre that is desired by so many, and he has realised them, it would seem, in his own person. The *Gesamtkunstwerk* (total work of art), that Wagner attempted with music and poetry, may now once again be realised by him, or its realisation stimulated by him, by painting, dance and gesture.[111]

Kessler must have found this introduction to Craig's ideas on theatre easy to write: as stated, he finished it in a few days, and the ideas expressed by Craig coincide so closely with Kessler's own vision of theatre, with the overriding importance of gesture, visual elements, pantomime and dance, that Kessler's enthusiasm for his new protégé – and the chance to get his work shown on German stages – is easy to understand. Although the latter aim was largely unfulfilled, Craig was to remain for ever in Kessler's debt:

---

[109] *CW II*, p. 92.
[110] *CW II*, p. 93.
[111] *CW II*, pp. 94–5.

Kessler, the mentor of taste at Weimar and 'one of the men who has done most for the German theatre'[5], was now to do more than anyone else to make Craig's work known in Germany and help him carry out and propagate his ideas. Craig always remained deeply grateful to the man of whom he gives the following description: 'My friend was immensely energetic. All the time he went unceasingly here and there, placing sums of money in one branch of art after another. Wood-engraving – Painting – the Stage – Publishing – Printing – Type-cutting – Paper-making – Literature – Sculpture – Music – there was nothing in the Arts that he missed'.[112]

In 1910, however, it was Kessler's passionate advocacy of Craig that was to lead to a serious rift in Kessler's relationship with the last theatrical influence to be examined here, that of Hofmannsthal.

Getting to know Hofmannsthal

43 Hugo von Hofmannsthal in 1904,
photographed by Felix Salten

Kessler's relationship with Hugo von Hofmannsthal began in 1898, developed rapidly and became particularly intense during Kessler's years in Weimar, leading up to their eventual decision to collaborate on the *Rosenkavalier* project. The dynamic of that collaboration included the potential that Kessler saw in Hofmannsthal's

---

[112] Bablet, p. 69. He attributes his quote [5] to *On the Art of the Theatre*, facing p. 136 and adds: 'Not in the Mercury Books edition'.

pen early on, in the turn of the century period when Kessler's exposure to all forms of theatre was enabling him to develop a theatrical vision of his own.

Kessler clearly did not think that highly of Hofmannsthal's first theatrical excursions: there is little or no comment in the *Diary* about the earliest performances of Hofmannsthal plays that he saw in Berlin in 1898 and 1899: and it was not until the première of *Elektra* on 30 October 1903 that he regarded Hofmannsthal as having had real theatrical success and having reached a turning point in his development as a dramatist. This had not, however, prevented Kessler from considering, and discussing with Hofmannsthal, the possibility that the latter should follow Kessler to Weimar and take over the Court Theatre there: the *Diary* records on 26 August 1903: 'Afterwards I discussed with Hofmannsthal whether he would like to become [the theatre] *Intendant* here. He did not say yes, but he did not seem to reject the idea.'[113] The following day, Hofmannsthal gave Kessler a preview of the way *Elektra* would be staged, and spoke of his longing to have a theatrical success that would bring him real money: 'He was in such straightened circumstances. He thought that a financial success would be a huge boost for his productivity.'[114] The first extant letter from Kessler to Hofmannsthal, after this discussion in Weimar, evokes the mooted open-air production in the gardens of Schloss Belvedere and records Hofmannsthal's decision to play a part in Weimar. In his reply to Kessler, Hofmannsthal writes of his own excitement at the project, and the possible collaboration with Craig:

> Now I reach the main topic: Gordon Craig. That is the most important thing in the world. I cannot tell you how happy and grateful I was at your telegram. The fact that you involve me, without being asked, in something that is precisely what I need, how lovely, how beneficial! Moreover, I do not think you really know *totally* how important it is to me. I thought continually: this festival production in the park is *only possible* as something special if I get the right stage designer for it, whether it is Appia, or Fortuny, or Gordon Craig, one of the three in Europe who are trying to realise the same ends.[115]

Hofmannsthal's stated commitment to do something in Weimar that involved Kessler – apart from after-dinner readings from his works, to small assembled audiences, that became a regular feature during his stays with his host – was to last for some time. On a visit in November 1905, when Kessler's increasingly precarious relationship with his employer had already become apparent, Hofmannsthal asked Kessler if he thought he would survive in Weimar. Kessler's reply was that he would stay on in Weimar and work for its cultural renewal, regardless of whether

---

[113] *Diary III*, p. 592.
[114] *Diary III*, p. 593.
[115] Burger, p. 55. Newman adds that Hofmannsthal considered the three leading stage-designers in Europe to be Appia, Fortuny and Craig, but adds: '[...] but to Kessler the figure of a visionary creator, intoxicated by his dream, suggested only Craig' (Newman, p. 6).

he continued to be employed in an official position, and the *Diary* records his exchange with Hofmannsthal in the following terms:

> All we have to do is to stick together, strengthen our relationships and make new ones in all directions, do all in our power to support each and every one of us, and increasingly take as our centre Weimar, which because of its past and its name is better as a centre than any other place in Germany, the Court being basically an irrelevance. Hofmannsthal agreed and promised to come here ever more frequently and for longer periods, maybe even taking a small flat here. It would be important to bind in Gerhard Hauptmann with Weimar and with us in similar fashion.[116]

This stated determination to work together found even more passionate expression the following year, after Kessler had resigned as Curator and had begun to consider what he should do next. In his first letter to Hofmannsthal, informing him of the latest developments, Kessler repeated: '[…] what is truly important is to stick together. The circle that we constitute, not the relationship with a Weimar Grand Duke who is insignificant anyway.'[117] Kessler repeated the same thoughts, with variations, in several follow-up letters, enthusing about Hofmannsthal's own writings and adding on 17 July 1906:

> We have to create new forms of living, *between ourselves* through our friendship; *to the outside world* through our works, and these could be immeasurably important if we really are that which we have considered ourselves to be so far.[118]

Stressing the need to stay closely in touch and to plan exactly how they would work together, Kessler finally gave Hofmannsthal the clearest possible indication of what he was envisaging: in his letter of 26 January 1906, he promised Hofmannsthal that he would always be the one to provide whatever help he could possibly give him, and continued:

> I should also like, in my modest way, to produce something myself. I have neglected this aspect far too much, and would like to, and will, catch up now. For me personally, for at least the next few years, *this direct production* must be the main purpose of my life. For my spiritual health, I need a work under my belt. It may say a lot or very little to others, but this is indispensible as the basis for my life.[119]

With a vast range of theatrical experiences and contacts behind him at this point, Kessler must have seemed to Hofmannsthal to be an almost ideal resource: someone who would produce interesting and original ideas, keep him up to date with the wider European theatrical scene and act as his advocate in leading theatrical circles. Their relationship, as it actually developed in the period immediately preceding *Der Rosenkavalier*, is precisely on these lines: Hofmannsthal was one

---

[116] *Diary III*, p. 815.
[117] Burger, p. 118.
[118] Burger, p. 123.
[119] Burger, pp. 126–7.

of several significant contacts in Kessler's involvement with theatrical life around the turn of the twentieth century, while Kessler – increasingly – began to discern for himself a way of playing a part in Hofmannsthal's theatrical output, seeing faults in his playwriting that he, Kessler, could begin to address. This too – a role in Hofmannsthal's creative process – became part of Kessler's internal theatrical vision at the time.

The making and shaping of Kessler's theatrical vision, and the close theatrical contacts he made in the years either side of 1900, illustrate the journey that he undertook from small child, born into a highly theatrical and socially representative family, to well-informed advocate for the radical new concepts of theatrical staging that Craig espoused – and tried, with Kessler's help, to see implemented in Germany. As Kessler saw more and more theatre and opera in Germany, France and England, as he grew up and developed his understanding of the art form, there developed a recurring theme in Kessler's conversations with Hauptmann, with Reinhardt, with Craig – the overriding importance to him of the visual elements of theatre, the pantomime, gesture of the actors, and the aesthetic impact of dance. Kessler's exposure to, and understanding of painting and sculpture, and the extraordinary circle of artist friends he developed (and in some cases supported financially) from the 1890s onwards, fed into his feeling for theatre and for the artistic values that he thought it should exemplify: but Auguste Rodin, Aristide Maillol, Pierre Bonnard, Edvard Munch, Maurice Denis, Max Liebermann, Augustus John, Will Rothenstein and many others would all require substantial chapters of their own if Kessler's overlapping interests in the art world of his time were to be assessed thoroughly. For the run-up to the creation of *Der Rosenkavalier*, what needs to be borne in mind is that Kessler approached all theatre with its visual, gestural and pantomime aspects firmly to the fore. His creative input to *Der Rosenkavalier* was to demonstrate precisely that within a year of his exposure to, and critical enjoyment of, *L'Ingénu libertin* in Paris. We turn now to how exactly that came about.

44 The Rose Cavalier – costume design by Alfred Roller for Octavian's appearance in Act Two of *Der Rosenkavalier*

Act Three
in two scenes and an Epilogue

Scene One – devising the scenario

Between 18 January 1908, when he recorded various thoughts about the work he had seen that evening at the Théâtre des Bouffes Parisiens, and 9 February 1909, when he enthused Hugo von Hofmannsthal with the notion, there is no evidence that Kessler gave any serious thought to adapting or to reworking *L'Ingénu libertin* as a new piece for the stage. There is no further mention of the work in the *Diary*, nor in his regular correspondence with Hofmannsthal. The *Diary* does, however, illuminate why Kessler may have refrained from putting forward a completely new theatrical suggestion to Hofmannsthal for so long. Following his week in Paris (16–22 January 1908) when he saw *L'Ingénu libertin*, Kessler went to London and spent several days looking at art, in particular at two exhibitions of pictures by Hogarth. He then returned to Paris for the rest of February, before moving on to Berlin and spending much of the second half of March in the city in Hofmannsthal's company. The *Diary* records that on 13 March 1908, Hofmannsthal gave Kessler a full account of the Casanova scenario that he intended to write as an opera for Strauss. From Kessler's written description, it appears that Hofmannsthal had planned the opera in some detail, right down to the ending:

> When the curtain rises again, Casanova is still seated at the table in the dawn light; suddenly his friend descends the stairs alone, Casanova jumps up, goes for his dagger, but his friend rushes joyfully to Casanova, embraces him, and thanks him for the happiness that he has bestowed, from above you hear the girl's voice lovingly calling the friend's name. Curtain. Hofmannsthal: in this opera Casanova is a sort of counter-figure to Figaro: someone who moves things along simply by virtue of his affirmation of life, his temperament. Kainz had told him this story from Casanova, actually exactly as he now saw it.[1]

Kessler may well have thought, from this thorough and enthusiastic description, that Hofmannsthal had the project well planned and would see it through to

---

[1] *Diary IV*, p. 433.

completion. He may have continued to think that too during his extensive travels in Greece, Italy and France before his return to Germany in December that year. But then, in February 1909, the Hofmannsthals came to stay with him in Weimar. On 8 February, in a long and agonised evening conversation, Hofmannsthal told Kessler that he could not see any way of salvaging the Casanova play that he had been writing for so long (the work that was to become *Cristinas Heimreise* (*Cristina's Homecoming*)), the scenario that Strauss had been urging him for over a year to turn into an opera collaboration. So he was going to abandon it. Kessler however made various practical suggestions for changing the relative attributes of the main characters, prompting this credo from Hofmannsthal:

> But you understand, the aesthetic problem was so attractive, introducing the Carlo character whom I needed later, in this unforced and unepisodic way as early as the second act; this was precisely the whole charm of the play for me. If that is omitted, if I have to turn this one character into two, then the material loses all its attraction for me. What I want is something very particular. **Namely: just as the warp and the weft knit together in a woven fabric, I want to weave well-made French scenarios into something that is inside me**, whether you call it my temperament or my ideal or whatever. And this is precisely what this scene gave me.[2]

In their further lengthy conversation that evening, Kessler drew Hofmannsthal's attention to Falstaff, to Greek ship's captains of old, to characters who acted naturally, spontaneously and instinctively, and finished by suggesting Tristan Bernard[3] as a role model for the sea captain in *Cristina's Homecoming*. The *Diary* records Hofmannsthal's immediate take-up of the suggestion: 'H: yes, I don't think anyone could give me so much for my play as absolutely as Tristan Bernard. Look, I now feel there is a possibility once again of saving my piece.'[4]

Hofmannsthal's doubts and difficulties over the Casanova material for Strauss, and his reference to the 'well-made French scenario', may well have set Kessler's creative imagination into motion. However, the specific trigger for their joint endeavour that was to see, within two weeks of intensive collaboration, a complete and basically stageworthy scenario for a three-act comic opera to be set to music by Strauss, came from Hofmannsthal's request to Kessler, made in the afternoon of 9 February during a walk in Tiefurt Park in Weimar, to tell him about Terrasse's *Les Travaux d'Hercule*. Having done so, and while he was still in Terrasse vein, Kessler spontaneously went on to narrate and to describe *L'Ingénu libertin* in detail, to Hofmannsthal's immediate and obvious excitement: 'Hofmannsthal delighted. This was exactly the sort of thing he wanted to do for Strauss; he would get out *Faublas* again immediately and see if it yielded material. If it worked, he

---

[2] *Diary IV*, p. 555 – my emphasis added.
[3] The larger than life figure of French writer Tristan Bernard, drawn notably by Toulouse-Lautrec, was well-known to both men: Bernard had also supplied the libretto for *La Petite Femme de Loth*, set to music by Terrasse in 1900.
[4] *Diary IV*, p. 557.

would be made financially for years.'[5] Kessler, naturally, had a copy of *Une Année* in his well-stocked library in Weimar, and Hofmannsthal must have made a beeline for it as soon as the two men returned home from their walk. From Kessler's house in Cranachstrasse to Tiefurt Park is a leisurely and attractive stroll of some 40 minutes along the banks of the River Ilm.

Kessler and Hofmannsthal were now to spend the next fourteen days – Tuesday 9 February 1909 in Weimar until Monday 22 February 1909 in Berlin – inventing, crafting and polishing the scenario for *Der Rosenkavalier*. But to get the project off the ground, they needed agreement by Strauss to compose the music. The task of persuading him was undertaken by Hofmannsthal.

Strauss and Hofmannsthal in 1909

Modern critical assessment of the Strauss–Hofmannsthal partnership has been determined largely by the body of work, as a whole, that the two men went on to achieve in a working partnership that spanned twenty-three years (1906–29). It is thus largely retrospective in nature. *Der Rosenkavalier* has been seen as a natural (and spectacularly successful) link in the chain that ran from *Elektra* to the unfinished *Arabella*, so much so that a recent judgement by one of the doyens of Strauss scholarship, Bryan Gilliam, is emblematic of much of the received wisdom since the death of Strauss in 1949: 'The collaboration between Richard Strauss and Hugo von Hofmannsthal was one of the greatest composer-librettist relationships of all time. [...] It was an artistic association at the level of Verdi–Boito or Mozart–Da Ponte...'.[6] Kurt Pahlen, in the Piper-Schott edition of *Der Rosenkavalier*, makes a very similar claim in his extensive commentary on the work: 'In the history of music theatre there is hardly another instance of a poet and a composer of the first rank working so purposefully and insistently on their creations together.'[7] But these and all similar judgements, entirely valid as they may be from today's perspective, are made with the benefit of hindsight, and fail to take a considered view of how things actually were in 1909. Instead, if one looks at the creation of *Der Rosenkavalier* solely in the light of the prior social and artistic relationship between Strauss and Hofmannsthal – in other words, as things stood between them when they embarked on this particular venture – a rather different picture emerges.

Various sources, including the Fischer paperback edition of Hofmannsthal's *Collected Works* in ten volumes,[8] suggest that the two men first met in 1898, but this seems to be a full year out: they actually met for the first time in March 1899

---

[5] *Diary IV*, pp. 557–8.
[6] Gilliam, p. 119.
[7] Pahlen, p. 293.
[8] Hugo von Hofmannsthal, *Gesammelte Werke*, ed. Bernd Schoeller and Rudolf Hirsch (Frankfurt am Main: Fischer Taschenbuch Verlag, 1979). The date 1898 appears in the *Lebensdaten* at the end of each volume: in volume 4 this is on page 572.

in Berlin at a gathering hosted by the writer Richard Dehmel. Had they met in 1898 it is almost certain to have been recorded in the Richard Strauss *Chronik*, but there is no such mention. It is equally almost certain that Hofmannsthal would have mentioned the fact of a meeting with Strauss in his 1898 letters to his parents (again, no such mention) and it is highly likely that such a meeting would have been flagged in the Hofmannsthal–Kessler correspondence for 1898 – but it is not. There are two authoritative accounts of the first meeting, the first by Willi Schuh:

> On 23 March 1899 Hugo von Hofmannsthal lunched with Count Harry Kessler, and then the two drove to visit Dehmel in the Berlin suburb of Pankow, where they also met Richard and Pauline Strauss, Paul Scheerbart and Wilhelm Schäfer. The date is important, because it was probably Strauss's first meeting with Dehmel, and certainly his first with Hofmannsthal.[9]

The date is indeed important and 23 March is also given in the *Chronik*, but it is almost certainly a case of a handwritten '8' being mistaken for a '3'. For the best evidence of all, from Kessler's continuous and handwritten daily *Diary*, suggests that they in fact first met on 28 March 1899 at Dehmel's house in Pankow as a result of an introduction by Kessler. Kessler had known Dehmel since 1894, had worked with him subsequently on the board of *Pan* and had spent considerable time and effort in 1898 arranging the publication in *Pan* of various writings by Hofmannsthal.[10] Kessler's entry for 28 March 1899 states:

> Hofmannsthal ate with me in the morning.[11] I then took him to the Dehmels out in Pankow. Those still there were Richard Strauss and his wife, Scheerbart and Schäfer. Hofmannsthal is beginning to irk me; it is partly because of his vanity that it never occurs to him that he might have outstayed his welcome.[12]

By contrast the entry for 23 March 1899 merely states: 'Hofmannsthal ate with me in the morning.'[13] Kessler himself had first encountered Strauss in 1894 and by 1899, because of the Dehmel connection to both men and because of his own considerable public profile, was undoubtedly known to Strauss, although the *Diary* does not record any other face-to-face meetings with the composer in the intervening period.

Hofmannsthal subsequently spent 13 February to 2 May 1900 in Paris, living in a student room at 192 Boulevard Haussmann, working intensively on various literary projects and networking through the good offices of the Austrian and

---

[9] Willi Schuh, trans. Mary Whittall, *Richard Strauss: A Chronicle of the Early Years 1864–1898* (New York: Cambridge University Press, 1982) p. 442. Likewise Kennedy, p. 126: he also gives the date as 23 March 1899, whereas it was 28 March.

[10] *Donna Dianora*, the first version of *Die Frau im Fenster*, was published in *Pan* in 1898, for example.

[11] In his *Diary*, Kessler uses the word *gefrühstückt*, nowadays 'breakfasted' but in Kessler's time used for any morning meal, including lunch.

[12] *Diary III*, p. 231.

[13] *Diary III*, p. 230.

German embassies.[14] During this stay, on 6 March 1900 he met socially with Strauss and had a conversation about ballet. On 17 and again on 30 November 1900 Hofmannsthal wrote to Strauss, recalling their conversation in Paris and inviting Strauss to compose the music for his newly written ballet libretto *Der Triumph der Zeit*.[15] Strauss declined the offer.

There is then a five-year gap, both men working on their own projects, until Strauss saw Hofmannsthal's stage play *Elektra* during its revival run at the Deutsches Theater in Berlin in October/November 1905. Strauss was immediately struck by the operatic possibilities in Hofmannsthal's reworking of Sophocles, in particular by the power and by what has been aptly called the 'crescendo of action' in the treatment,[16] and recontacted Hofmannsthal, seeking permission to use a version of his text as an opera libretto. They met in Berlin on 22 February 1906 and Hofmannsthal gave Strauss permission to go ahead.

The Strauss–Hofmannsthal correspondence in 1906–7 (there are only nineteen letters in all, mostly rather formal in tone) documents how this particular collaborative relationship worked in practice. Strauss took Hofmannsthal's play text, cut it down substantially, made musical annotations in the margin and began to compose the first scene in earnest in June 1906.[17] At the same time he began to voice doubts as to whether or not he really wanted to set material so similar to that of *Salome* (in which Hofmannsthal had played no part). From his perspective, Hofmannsthal stressed the differences between *Salome* and *Elektra* – with evident concern that his embryonic association with the illustrious composer might come to nothing – and prevailed to the extent that Strauss continued work. But a constant theme in the correspondence, articulated by Strauss as early as in his letter of 11 March 1906, is his desire to get Hofmannsthal started on a new, original and quite different opera libretto. As the letter says:

> That is why anyway I should be glad to know if you've got anything else in stock for me, and if I might perhaps have a go at some other subject from your pen, farther removed from *Salome*, before doing *Elektra*. Apart from *Semiramis*, which I am extremely anxious to see, you mentioned some other work that you had in hand: perhaps I could see something of it soon? [...] Have you got an entertaining renaissance subject for me? A really wild *Cesare Borgia* or *Savanarola* would be the answer to my prayers.[18]

Hofmannsthal, at this time as throughout his life, did indeed have other works in hand – 'fragmentary scenarios and sketches' as he was to describe them to Strauss two years later – but he held out little prospect to the composer that they would or could be produced before work on *Elektra* had progressed further, despite Strauss's

[14] Burger, pp. 463–4.
[15] Hamm./Osers, pp. 1–2.
[16] Gilliam, p. 121.
[17] Hamm./Osers, p. 7.
[18] Hamm./Osers, p. 3.

mentions of Saul and David, of *Dantons Tod* by Büchner, of *Thermidor* by Sardou, and despite Strauss's repeated pleas to see something of *Semiramis*. Thus some of Strauss's frustration clearly showed when he next met Hofmannsthal (in Kessler's company) on 10 December 1906, for the Kessler *Diary* entry for that day runs:

> Then with Hofmannsthal to an appointment with Richard Strauss at Töpfer's. Schillings, the African, Max Schillings's brother happened to be there and joined us to hear what Strauss thought of the *Moloch* [three-act tragic opera by Max von Schillings that had just premièred] and the impression it made in Dresden. Strauss was really negative. All that was onstage were ideas, no real people. If an opera were to be effective, it had to say something to the ordinary lad in the gallery. […] [Strauss:] 'As for my "goal", I don't know what it is. I just do what amuses me at the time. What do I care about some goal or other that is behind it all? We all have only one goal, death. I do what I have to do, not because I have any goal. And I can't even always do that, even if I want to. Take *Elektra* for instance. About one third is completed. But I've got stuck in Clytemnestra's conversation with Elektra. My imagination has let me down. I have no ideas. Maybe I should take a break and write a light, comic work before continuing. I have been thinking of *Tartuffe*. It may be that *Elektra* is too similar to *Salome*; my imagination needs a rest in this area.' Hofmannsthal was rather dismayed by this statement. He tried to persuade Strauss how perfect *Elektra* was for him, because of the rapid urgency towards the end and because of events inside the house, which could only be revealed by the orchestra. Strauss said yes, yes, he would compose it to the end but he could not say when. Hofmannsthal then left and Strauss and I sat down with the Schirachs and with other musical people, and Strauss asked me about my conflict in Weimar.[19]

This is a fascinating and revealing passage, which does not yet seem to have found its way into the main body of Strauss–Hofmannsthal scholarship. It shows that Strauss was happy to voice in public, in front of Kessler and others, the thoughts that he had vouchsafed privately in his letter to Hofmannsthal nine months previously. It shows that Kessler knew directly from Strauss's own mouth, as early as December 1906, of the composer's desire to write a light, comic opera that would appeal to the gallery, *Tartuffe* being a possible subject. It shows that Hofmannsthal was hurt by Strauss's remarks – as Kessler noticed – and left the gathering early. In the light of the subsequent working relationship between Hofmannsthal and Kessler on *Der Rosenkavalier*, it is a significant piece of evidence.

Work on *Elektra* continued however, at Strauss's pace, and as the musical tapestry thickened in 1908, Hofmannsthal was asked by Strauss to supply some new words to be set: 'eight, sixteen, twenty lines, as many as you can, rising all the time towards a climax'.[20] This rather limited further input by Hofmannsthal to the opera that was taking shape has led to the widely held, and correct judgement that 'it was not technically a collaboration […] the libretto is strictly Strauss's work, a

---

[19] *Diary IV*, p. 219.
[20] Hamm./Osers, p. 16.

skilful reduction of the play',[21] and: '*Elektra* was not really a collaboration, for [...] Strauss received permission from a delighted Hofmannsthal to use his text as he saw fit'.[22] Even musical reference books suggest the same: 'By the time the piece [*Elektra*] was performed, he was already working on his **first real collaboration** with Hofmannsthal [...].'[23] Strauss moreover was finding himself perplexed by a crucial part of Hofmannsthal's original *Elektra* scenario:

> One more thing: I still don't understand the scenic action at the end. Surely, Orestes is *in* the house. Surely, the front door in the middle is shut. Chrysothemis and the serving maids hurried off on page 88 *into the house on the left*. On page 91 they are 'rushing out madly'. Out of where? The left or through the middle? Page 93: Chrysothemis comes running out. Out which way? Through the courtyard gate on the right? What for? Surely, Orestes is in the centre of the house! Why is she at the end beating at the front door? Surely because it is barred? Do please answer these questions of mine in detail. I have never been quite clear about the scenario since reading it through.[24]

This very direct – brusque almost – catalogue of questions was perhaps prompted by an admission by Hofmannsthal, in his letter to Strauss of 4 June 1908 that preceded it. Moreover, this admission goes to the heart of the case that on his own, even by 1909, Hofmannsthal was not technically or psychologically equipped to devise and execute the 'full and entirely original scenario for an opera'[25] that was to presage *Der Rosenkavalier* and that, as argued below, must be regarded as one of the most misleading letters in opera history. For in his previous letter (the one of 4 June 1908), Hofmannsthal had said:

> But now allow me to discuss at once your main point, and please set my mind at rest by an immediate reply. You understand, don't you – and have never counted on anything else – that I shall have the comedy [*Cristinas Heimreise*], just as it comes from my pen, performed first on the ordinary stage. There is, I think, in any case no other alternative, for what attracts me as an artist to the subject and what I aim at (now that I have got this good, slim scenario) is to round out the characters as much as possible and to produce as natural and varied a dialogue as I can. Quite conceivably you may be able to make direct use of this dialogue, after extensive cuts, as you did in the case of *Salome*. If so, all the better. But it is equally possible that you may wish me to transpose the whole thing into a simpler and more lyrical key, while preserving the scenario entire, an operation such as Da Ponte carried out on the text of the comedy *Le Mariage de Figaro*. This I would willingly undertake, **but never could I attempt to formulate the text from the outset in this lyrical manner which leaves most of the characterization to the composer.** To do this would make me lose all

---

[21] Kennedy, p. 155.
[22] Gilliam, p. 121.
[23] *New Grove*, vol. 24, p. 501 – my added emphasis.
[24] Hamm./Osers, p. 16.
[25] Hamm./Osers, p. 27.

certainty of touch and so produce something that falls between two stools. On the other hand, once the comedy is done and has succeeded on the stage, and once each character has gained, so to speak, something of an independent existence, then it is possible to summon up the necessary effrontery to treat it all, if need be, very much *en raccourci*.[26]

This perceived inability on the poet's part to invent new and original characters for the stage and to construct plausible scenarios around them was very much a feature of Hofmannsthal's thinking at this time. With adaptations from antiquity, with Sophocles as the model for his undoubtedly powerful and exciting *Elektra*, Hofmannsthal felt more secure, and the modern psychological insights he brought to the characters made the play come alive and resonate with early twentieth-century audiences. But with what Strauss really wanted from him at this time – a new, colourful, comic work (that in Strauss's mind would extend the *opera buffa* lineage

45 Richard Strauss in 1907

[26] Hamm./Osers, p. 15 – my added emphasis.

through the comic operas of Mozart and da Ponte and Wagner's *Die Meistersinger*) – Hofmannsthal felt a decided lack of confidence. It is true that he had come through the crisis of language that in 1902 had found eloquent expression in his sensational *Chandos-Brief*,[27] but it is not true that he was ready, or knew how, to plunge into a new, collaborative opera partnership with Strauss using an original plot or scenario of his own. The persistent tenor of Hofmannsthal's contribution to the Strauss-Hofmannsthal correspondence of this period (1900-8) is that of a gifted, lyrical, poetic wordsmith becoming more and more hassled by a practical but impatient composer keen on original libretti that he can set to music – and having to explain why he feels unable to comply.

The prior relationship between Hofmannsthal and Strauss (in other words, their pre-*Der Rosenkavalier* relationship) can thus be characterised objectively as embryonic and rather distant. Strauss was already famous as a composer and conductor, Hofmannsthal was making his name as a writer and lyric poet, who possessed an extraordinary facility in the German language. His stage works – with the exception of *Elektra* – were attracting lukewarm critical appreciation and very limited success with the public. With the adaptation of *Elektra* from stage play to opera, it was Strauss who fashioned the libretto, just as he had done previously with *Salome*, and it was Strauss who dictated exactly what he wanted to see on the stage. In the light of all this, one can only imagine Strauss's astonishment when he read in Hofmannsthal's letter of 11 February 1909:

> Now something which is (as I hope) of far greater importance to the two of us. I have spent three quiet afternoons here drafting the full and entirely original scenario for an opera, full of burlesque situations and characters, with lively action, pellucid almost like a pantomime. There are opportunities in it for lyrical passages, for fun and humour, even for a small ballet. I find the scenario enchanting and Count Kessler with whom I discussed it is delighted with it. It contains two big parts, one for baritone and another for a graceful girl dressed up as a man, à la Farrar or Mary Garden. Period: the old Vienna under the Empress Maria Theresa.[28]

This news came from the man who, eight months earlier, had written: 'never could I attempt to formulate the text from the outset in this lyrical manner which leaves most of the characterization to the composer'. So something had clearly changed in the interim. That 'something' can only be ascribed to the third man named (so misleadingly) in the letter, Harry Kessler.

---

[27] *Ein Brief* was a fictitious letter from Philip, Lord Chandos to Francis Bacon published in *Der Tag* in October 1902: it bemoans the author's loss of coherent thinking and speech and has generally been regarded as autobiographical, although the noted Hofmannsthal scholar Rudolf Hirsch has argued convincingly that this is not entirely so: Rudolf Hirsch, *Ein Brief des Lord Chandos* in *Beiträge zum Verständnis Hugo von Hofmannsthals* (Frankfurt am Main: S. Fischer Verlag, 1995), pp. 45–51.

[28] Hamm./Osers, p. 27.

Kessler and Hofmannsthal in 1909

There is much more documentary evidence of the pre-*Der Rosenkavalier* relationship between Kessler and Hofmannsthal than is the case for Strauss and Hofmannsthal. There is the Kessler *Diary*, chronicling his activities, encounters and innermost thoughts day by day throughout this period.[29] There are letters about Kessler (and about Hofmannsthal) that were exchanged between their large circle of mutual friends – Eberhard von Bodenhausen, Richard Dehmel, Ottonie Degenfeld, Helene von Nostitz and many others. And there is the Hofmannsthal–Kessler

46 Hugo von Hofmannsthal at the turn of the century

[29] The handwritten pages of the *Diary*, written continuously and in close script, can be inspected at the German Literature Archive in Marbach, and that body has confirmed in the published volumes to date that, although there are corrections and insertions (and clear signs that Kessler reread and marked certain passages for inclusion in his planned three-volume memoirs in 1934–5) there are very few instances of entries being altered or inserted at much later dates: the *Diary* text can thus be regarded as a contemporaneous record.

correspondence, running to almost 400 letters in the period 1898–1929, and to 300 in the pre-*Der Rosenkavalier* period alone. The quality and the texture of Hofmannsthal's ever-changing relationship with Kessler, who was his sponsor, practical helper, adviser and (at least until 1910) intimate friend can thus be analysed in great detail.

The precocious flowering of a new German language literary talent, the teenage Hugo von Hofmannsthal having chosen to publish under the pseudonym Loris, was guaranteed rapidly to come to the attention of Kessler, who by the mid to late 1890s, and with the fortune he had inherited from his father in 1895, was starting as we have seen to collect friends and influential contacts in every branch of the arts – painters, sculptors, designers, printers and musicians. Indeed, the second volume of *Pan* in 1895 saw the publication of *Terzinen* by Loris, a collection of *terza rima* poems that enchanted Kessler, who promptly tried to find out more about the author.[30] He evidently contacted Princess Cantacuzène,[31] for in an unpublished letter of 8 May 1896 from her to Kessler she says: 'Since you are interested in Loris and since I promised you, I am enclosing a letter and two poems by him.'[32] The following year Eberhard von Bodenhausen wrote to Hofmannsthal on 25 September 1897 and said: 'You must read the letters that I have just sent to Kessler and Flaischlein about your wonderful, wonderful poem.'[33] So the ground was being prepared by intermediaries. However, the first actual meeting between the two did not take place until 11 May 1898, in Berlin, and was recorded thus by Kessler in his *Diary*:

> In the afternoon Hofmannsthal visited me; he is a small, jolly Viennese who speaks in a high, resonant voice, but thoroughly sympathetic and natural (? or rather affectedly natural) in his manner.[34]

Kessler was nearly 30, Hofmannsthal six years his junior at 24.

Hofmannsthal had come to Berlin for the first-ever performance in the theatre (a matinée) of one of his plays. *Die Frau im Fenster (The Woman in the Window)* was directed by Otto Brahm, who was later to be linked with Kessler, at the *Freie Bühne* or small experimental stage attached to the Deutsches Theater. Kessler attended the performance on 15 May 1898 but (as is frequently the case for his entries on works that made no particularly good or bad impression on him) made no comment about it in his *Diary*. He wrote to Hofmannsthal on 11 July 1898 however, saying that the play had impressed him much more on subsequent reading than it had done in the theatre, and asking for permission to reinstate certain passages, cut by Hofmannsthal, for the version that Kessler wished to have printed in

---

[30] Burger, p. 433.
[31] Princess Cantacuzène's father, Frederick Dent Grant, had been appointed US Minister to the Austro-Hungarian Empire in 1889 and she was at the centre of social life in Vienna in the 1890s.
[32] Burger, p. 453.
[33] Burger, p. 453.
[34] *Diary III*, p. 143.

Pan.³⁵ Kessler's lack of inhibition in criticising – and in praising – Hofmannsthal's work is evident even at this very early stage of their relationship.

The May 1898 visit to Berlin was evidently not an unqualified success and Kessler's mixed feelings about Hofmannsthal as a person are recorded. Whereas on 14 May 1898 he wrote: 'He improves greatly on further acquaintance,'³⁶ two days later, the two men having been in each other's company daily, he came to a somewhat harsher judgement:

> Above all he is vain and socially ambitious; he is still in danger of ending up like Heyse or Bourget, as a tea party poet and boudoir philosopher; his temperament is completely unrevolutionary, and over time one's thoughts usually adjust to one's temperament. In addition it is clear that he regards the poet as a very particular creature, with a gulf separating him from everyone else.³⁷

However, the ties that began to bind them were stronger than the character traits that irked, and their tone in correspondence between 1898 and 1908 is one of growing mutual admiration, on Kessler's part for Hofmannsthal's extraordinary lyrical writing talent and on Hofmannsthal's part for Kessler's wide knowledge, astute critical judgement and extremely useful circle of friends. By February 1899 Kessler was writing: 'Dear Herr von Hofmannsthal! There is no question of my having a problem with the *Pan* Committee over your work; on the contrary, I find it very flattering to serve as your sponsor.'³⁸ Then, in March 1899, Hofmannsthal came to Berlin for an extended stay (he spent time with Kessler on numerous occasions between 11 and 30 March)³⁹ in an attempt to gauge his literary effect on those he described as 'real Germans', outside Viennese literary circles. The *Diary* records some creative interaction. On 12 March for example: 'We must get Hofmannsthal used to cutting out the chatter in his verses.'⁴⁰ On 18 March Kessler made a slightly fuller entry: 'Première of Hofmannsthal's *Sobeide* and *Abenteurer*.⁴¹ In *Abenteurer* Kainz was so brilliant that it is hard to judge the play as a whole. In the interval Dehmel was horrified by *Sobeide*.'⁴² The most significant entry during this stay however, in terms of the theatrical collaboration that was to follow between Kessler and Hofmannsthal, is that of 22 March:

> Ate with Hofmannsthal, who had just arrived back from Hauptmann; Hauptmann had read him 'The Shepherd's Song'. Hofmannsthal complained that **he could never**

---

³⁵ Burger, p. 6.
³⁶ *Diary III*, p. 144.
³⁷ *Diary III*, p. 145.
³⁸ Burger, p. 16.
³⁹ The *Diary* records time spent by Kessler with Hofmannsthal on 11, 18, 22, 23, 24, 25, 27, 28, 29 and 30 March 1899.
⁴⁰ *Diary III*, p. 229.
⁴¹ Hofmannsthal's two short plays *Die Hochzeit der Sobeide* (*The Sobeide Wedding*) and *Der Abenteurer und die Sängerin* (*The Adventurer and the Singer*) premièred simultaneously on 18 March 1899 at the Deutsches Theater in Berlin and at the Burgtheater in Vienna.
⁴² *Diary III*, p. 230.

think of subjects for plays; please would I look out for some in memoirs and the like, and convey them to him.[43]

This admission by the rapidly up-and-coming Hofmannsthal that he lacked the imagination to think up, independently, suitable plots and scenarios for his stage plays was to lead Kessler into providing a constant stream of suggestions in years to come. The role of mentor, stimulator and general guardian of Hofmannsthal's imaginative and creative development was clearly one that appealed to him. Likewise, Kessler's persona and aura undoubtedly appealed almost immediately, and equally strongly, to Hofmannsthal: on 18 November 1899 the latter wrote to him:

> The sympathetic interest you showed in me during my stay in Berlin, which I can hardly explain to myself, is among my dearest and I should add most mysterious memories. Probably for the first time in my life I was confronted by someone who combined personal superiority allied to true culture. This letter is becoming ever more impossible to write.[44]

The scale, and range of Kessler's theatrical experiences and his undoubted ability to discuss artistic, theatrical and dramaturgical matters, as detailed in Act Two, may have prompted Hofmannsthal's reference to 'personal superiority allied to true culture'. Kessler had in fact ventured some mild criticism of Hofmannsthal's sentimentality in his double bill, and Hofmannsthal had admitted to being wounded by it: 'I was no less than personally hurt – I understood immediately that you were completely right [...],'[45] but these exchanges served further to establish and clarify the dynamics of the relationship that was beginning to form between them. Kessler took up Hofmannsthal's claim to have been hurt in his own letter in reply of 22 November 1899:

> I don't regret in the slightest having irritated you in Berlin by criticism that may have been incorrect. Your verses are such "charmeurs" that you probably never get to hear the unwelcome comments that talent needs; and what you can create is of such value to me that I am prepared to accept any amount of temporary cooling-off in our relationship if I stand a chance of challenging your talent into creating ever more fruitful and delightful work. So you can be certain that if you continue to give me the opportunity, I shall never refrain from saying something that you may not want to hear about any of your writings.[46]

These ground rules established, the two men began to explore, through frequent correspondence and occasional meetings, the various ways in which they could be of service to each other. The correspondence reveals lively exchanges of view on matters social, political and above all artistic. It also reveals a deepening

---

[43] *Diary III*, p. 230 – my added emphasis.
[44] Burger, p. 19.
[45] Burger, p. 18.
[46] Burger, pp. 19–20.

of the emotional attachment they both began to feel and, sometimes, quite openly to express to each other. In marked contrast to the Strauss–Hofmannsthal correspondence, which remained for many years at the formal 'You' (German: *Sie*) level and in which Strauss normally opened 'Dear Herr von Hofmannsthal' and Hofmannsthal 'Dear Dr. Strauss', the Hofmannsthal–Kessler correspondence has three clearly defined stages. Between 1898 and 1902 they are formal with each other, using full names and the *Sie* form. A friendlier and more informal tone emerges between 1903 and 1905, with Kessler writing '*Mein lieber Hofmannsthal*' and Hofmannsthal '*Mein lieber Graf*' or '*Mein lieber Kessler*'. Then, from February 1905 onwards, they switch to the informal '*Du*' form and salutations become '*Lieber Hugo*' or simply '*Lieber*' or '*Mein lieber*'. In other words, their form of address towards the end of the pre-*Rosenkavalier* period indicates close and informal friendship and affection, almost intimacy, a state of grace that Hofmannsthal was never to achieve with Strauss.

Exegesis of the 1898–1908 Hofmannsthal–Kessler correspondence is important for the light it casts on a question not posed at all hitherto in Strauss–Hofmannsthal scholarship – why was Hofmannsthal prepared to take from Kessler a complete scenario for a major opera, incorporate some ideas of his own, work on it with him for a few days in Weimar and then present the entire proposition confidently to Strauss in Berlin as the subject for their first proper opera collaboration? As outlined above, Hofmannsthal had resisted every such entreaty from Strauss to that date. He had said that he absolutely had to see onstage any characters that he had authored, so that he could then assess and decide how to turn their spoken words into a libretto for musical setting by the composer. He had insisted, moreover, that he could not produce lyrical passages of spoken text that depended on the composer's own musical characterisation. So he must have had complete faith in Kessler's artistic judgement. He must also have accepted Kessler's assurances that a reworked, rewritten *L'Ingénu libertin* would succeed on the stage. A fuller answer to the question can only come, however, from a closer look at the Hofmannsthal–Kessler correspondence when read against Kessler's *Diary*. The editor of the Hofmannsthal–Kessler correspondence, Hilde Burger, completed her work in 1968, some fifteen years before the missing volumes of *Diary* were discovered in Mallorca. So some of the judgements she reached at the time require amending in the light of Kessler's incredibly detailed, personal and private comments on the issues explored in his letters with Hofmannsthal.

The letters themselves reveal respect, admiration and growing affection. The best way to situate the thoughts and ideas expressed by the correspondence in the creative consciousness of Kessler, as outlined in the *Diary*, is to elide the relevant passages. In what follows, all quotes are from the Burger edition of the Hofmannsthal–Kessler correspondence with relevant page numbers in brackets, and all emphases in bold are my own. The specific references to the joint work being undertaken on *Der Rosenkavalier* are preceded by [RK].

Act Three: Scene One – devising the scenario

Hofmannsthal to Kessler

May I say in this context that I feel from your presence such enrichment and encouragement for me, my view of the world and my work, **it is as if you were a very strong and incomparable artist.** Even as I write it down, this *modus irrealis* seems nonsensical to me – and yet it would be very difficult to characterise what you really are […] (p. 29).

I have not had the good fortune to live contemporaneously with many artists whose work would increase my feeling for existence time and again, like flashes out of the foggy grey: **but I anticipate something like this from an appearance such as yours – and I know that I am right** (p. 46).

I sometimes have this strange feeling of distress and fear, more strongly with you than with anyone else, if I don't hear from you, don't know where you are, what you are doing. And it is then so lovely to hear that you have been reading something of mine, that you did not dislike it, **that it has forced you to think of me for periods of time, to think with me** (p. 80).

The desire to ally myself **and my spiritual existence – not only my artistic one – to you** – and to van de Velde as far as this is possible – is becoming ever more passionate inside me […] (p. 94).

[…] **I may not have been able to work, without seeing you first** (p. 103).

In addition *Jedermann* is seething inside me, and a wonderful *Semiramis*, **with which you must help me, help me such a lot** […] (p. 109).

Harry, just don't say that you will be here for less than 3–4 days. **I absolutely have to talk things through with you** […]. We keep saying to each other: Harry is going to come through this door! Harry is going to sit in this armchair! (p. 148).

How often and how vividly I have to think of you while I am working. It is sometimes as if you are standing among my characters: the more they reveal of themselves, the more clearly I see you too. […] You are possibly the only person who will not be surprised, but hopefully amused, by this transformation, this greater realism, new tone, the prose switching between high German and Austrian dialect, and the dialect in turn coloured by respective rank, tailored to the Baron, the servant, the major-domo, the innkeeper. […] **I could never have realised that one could be so much in debt to such a degree and in so many ways as I am to you** […] (pp. 157–8).

How good and how wonderful that you have promised me and yourself never to leave me in the lurch like Hauptmann's friends have abandoned him, just when they could do so much for him by being open with him and critical. **You will always see all my work well in advance, Harry** (pp. 174–5).

How wonderful that you are linked to the best of me, to my work, through your boundless goodwill, your incomparable care and attention (p. 176).

*

[RK] A thousand thanks for your second lovely letter. I am thrilled that on the whole you are pleased by **execution of our joint scenario**. (p. 230).[47]

[RK] I am endlessly grateful to you for your sharp and lively critical comments (p. 234).

[RK] I am still very happy **about your participation** (p. 235).

Kessler to Hofmannsthal

It would be an absolute joy for me if **some of my thoughts could be transformed** into the golden forms of your art (pp. 29–30).

You have such a wonderful, new and rich attitude to the world [...] (p. 52).

I cannot think of anything that could give me greater joy than **my having played a part** in the realisation of a great artist or poet or person (p. 66).

[...] it is obvious that **I always have to be the one who helps you,** as long as it is in my power to do so, and you may only divert your energies to my projects in exceptional cases (p. 126)

For my spiritual wellbeing **I need a work under my belt** (p. 127).

All I know is that I do not deserve the happiness **of being part of this poetic life**, and I enjoy it secretly (p. 159).

First, I am so glad that you are writing. **In my thoughts I am going through your play scene by scene, which I can envisage quite clearly** after your narration[48] (p. 184).

[RK] I am burning for the [*Rosenkavalier*] libretto. So please send me Act I as soon as it is written (p. 217).[49]

The tone that runs through Hofmannsthal's comments is slightly needier, slightly more emotional, in many cases more demanding of psychological help and support: and the exchanges that Kessler had with Hofmannsthal's wife Gerty at the end of 1908, when Hofmannsthal went through one of his periodic nervous, depressive crises, show how finely tuned Kessler was to the emotional needs of his friend and protégé. However, it is the Kessler *Diary* that reveals his innermost thoughts about the man and poet who so interested him, about Hofmannsthal's productive and artistic capabilities, and about the possibility of a practical creative partnership between them.

---

[47] This and the following two quotes post-date the intensive working-up of the *Der Rosenkavalier* scenario in Weimar and subsequently in Berlin.

[48] Hofmannsthal was working on an early version of *Cristina's Homecoming*.

[49] At this stage, 30 March 1909, both men were still clearly committed to a full-scale collaboration.

Plate 1 Harry Graf Kessler by Edvard Munch (1863–1944). Kessler had discovered the impoverished Munch in Berlin and had bought some of his works: for this, the most famous portrait of Kessler, Munch came to Weimar and finished the portrait in three days (9–11 July 1906). Kessler had just submitted his resignation as curator of Arts and Crafts at the Weimar Court

Plate 2 Jane Alba as Faublas in *L'Ingénu libertin*. Critics were divided as to how well she made the girl-boy-girl transition in the piece, but all agreed that she cut a striking and elegant figure as the Chevalier

Plate 3 Act One costume design for Octavian by Alfred Roller. The similarities with the Faublas costume are striking

Plate 4 Claude Terrasse with his sons Jean and Charles, painted by Pierre Bonnard (1867–1923). Terrasse was Bonnard's brother-in-law and theatrical collaborator and Bonnard illustrated Terrasse's text books on music. The painting now hangs in the Musée d'Orsay

Plate 5 *L'après-midi bourgeoise*, painted by Pierre Bonnard and also known as *La famille Terrasse*. Apart from Claude and Andrée Terrasse, the children shown are Jean, Charles, Vivette (Eugénie), Robert and Renée (also shown in the photograph on page 51). The painting now hangs in the Musée d'Orsay

Plate 6 Jeanne Petit as Sophie in Act One of *L'Ingénu libertin*. The role given to Sophie in this piece, with its cross-dressing, feisty behaviour and ample scope for comedy, easily outclasses the rather passive and pallid Sophie of *Der Rosenkavalier*

Plate 7 Arlette Dorgère as the Marquise de Bay in *L'Ingénu libertin*, on the front cover of issue 218 of *Le Théâtre* in January 1908. Dorgère was both a poster girl (Jules Cheret) and pin-up for countless male admirers during the Belle Epoque

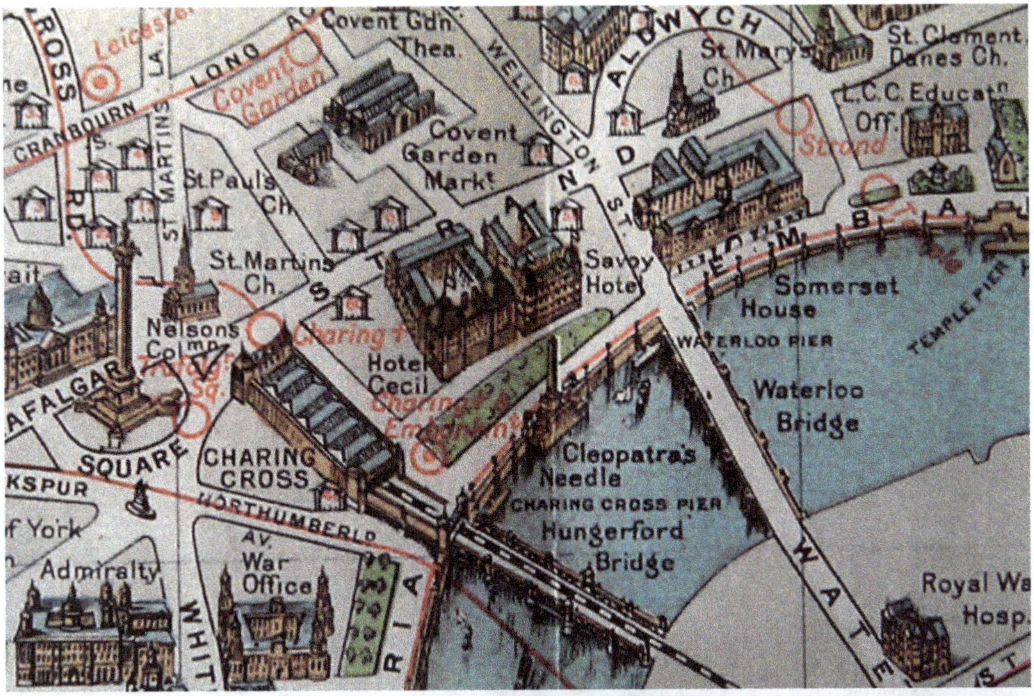

Plate 8 The Hotel Cecil on the Strand in London was even larger than the Savoy, as shown on an early twentieth century street map: Kessler maintained a permanent suite at the Cecil and entertained lavishly, both there and at the Savoy next door

Plate 9 Portrait of Gerhart Hauptmann by Emil Orlik (1870–1932). The plays of Hauptmann and his sense of the theatrical made a profound impression on Kessler and a close and enduring friendship ensued

Plate 10 An earlier portrait of Harry Kessler, painted by Edvard Munch in 1904.

Plate 11 Design by Alfred Roller for Act One of *Der Rosenkavalier* – the Marschallin's bedroom. The visual evocation of Vienna in the 1740s has distinct pre-echoes of the Parisian décor of the 1770s for *L'Ingénu libertin*

Plate 12 Costume design by Alfred Roller for Baron Ochs auf Lerchenau – shown here in a characteristically forceful pose

Plate 13 Costume design by Alfred Roller for Sophie, making her first appearance in Act Two of *Der Rosenkavalier*

Plate 14 The Countess's levée – Plate 4 from *Marriage à la mode* by William Hogarth (1697–1764). The influences on Act One of *Der Rosenkavalier* are immediately apparent. Kessler had studied Hogarth's works intensively between 1906 and 1908 and he and Hofmannsthal readily agreed on the pictorial elements that could be incorporated in a stage comedy for music

Plate 15 All human life is here… Baron Ochs auf Lerchenau is beaten (but unbowed), Octavian will wed Sophie and the Marschallin will have to choose another toyboy lover. Sophie Koch, Peter Rose, Lucy Crowe and Soile Isokowski in the 2009 revival of the classic Schlesinger/Björnson/Dudley production of *Der Rosenkavalier* at Covent Garden

Kessler on Hofmannsthal

During and after a seven-day stay with Kessler in Weimar and Berlin in 1903, Hofmannsthal clearly irked his host on a number of occasions, his frequent bad moods being matched only by the quantities of milk that he drank and ham that he ate: 'Hofmannsthal carries on being ill and eating ham; and eating alarmingly large quantities in general.'[50] Later, after losing an overcoat during a carriage ride: 'Hofmannsthal said the little things in life annoyed him so much that he could never get to the happy medium between enjoyment and irritation.'[51] Then Kessler came to an overall summing-up:

> I particularly noticed Hofmannsthal's curious concern about money. He kept coming back to his wish to earn money, and to his longing to have money, and he seems to think about this all the time. In addition he is rather too preoccupied with the higher levels of Austrian aristocracy. [...] Through this preoccupation with money and aristocracy his conversation is similar to that of the Schwabachs, Bleichroeders and co. A pity.[52]

Kessler's wealth may, of course, have been one of the factors that kept Hofmannsthal close to him. The theme reoccurred later in 1906 after Kessler had advised Hofmannsthal not to write pot-boiler articles on culture for a popular monthly magazine, with Hofmannsthal complaining bitterly:

> 'So what is a man supposed to do when he is forbidden to do the very things that would bring in money? He simply has to earn another 5 to 10,000 M more a year on top of the 30,000 or so that he has. Otherwise he cannot write. The feeling of not being free is exactly what stops him being productive. Once he has paid another 10,000 M into the bank, he will get back his appetite for writing.' I advised him to do some lectures, like those in the five o'clock series. H is the richest of all my artist friends and the only one who goes on and on talking and complaining about money; clearly a strange residue of his Jewishness.[53]

Nevertheless, Kessler's ability to distinguish the man, with his annoying traits, and the artist, emerges clearly from his diary entries at the time of the *Elektra* première – the play, not the opera – in October 1903. On 30 October he wrote: 'The piece reminds me of Marlowe, with its mixture of refined and beautiful speech and exaggerated cruelty. This will be a turning point in H's development.'[54] Then, by 1 November he had added to the portrait: 'He is a curious mixture of businessman, snob, poet and ingratiating oriental rent boy; naïve and laughably egotistical.'[55] However a productive working relationship was starting to emerge. From being

---

[50] *Diary III*, p. 593.
[51] *Diary III*, p. 595.
[52] *Diary III*, p. 596.
[53] *Diary IV*, p. 214.
[54] *Diary III*, p. 616.
[55] *Diary III*, p. 617.

someone who regularly sent Hofmannsthal esoteric books that he had possibly never encountered, thoughts on the classics that both men had read, ideas for his projects and writings, Kessler by 1905 was able to note: 'In the evening he read out the first scene of Act II and then the first half of the second scene of Act II [of *Oedipus*]. We cut out a lot together.'[56] Two days later, even more substantially:

> Spent the morning with Hofmannsthal on the third scene of Act II. I recommended a few <u>additions</u> to the words of the "people", so that it is even clearer that the people are demanding of Tiresias <u>something other</u> than Antiope and Creon. The three different demands have to be differentiated just like three different *values*.[57] So I recommended that as soon as Tiresias appears, the very first words should be stormy cries by the people for a saviour to be designated, with the three demands then being spoken strictly symmetrically one after the other. – In the evening Reinhardt came.[58]

Oedipus was premièred in February 1906 and was a success, despite criticism of its length (5 hours) and of its Wagnerian, operatic qualities.[59] However, Kessler (characteristically) was not sparing in his private criticism of Hofmannsthal's dramatic characterisation and noted:

> Talked to Hofmannsthal about *Oedipus* again. I told him he had made a bad error: the flaw in the character of Oedipus in Act I. [...] Anyone would have acted in the same way as Oedipus here, whereas what we had to feel was that it was only he who would have acted in this way, only he driven as he was by this terrible bloodlust. Hofmannsthal seemed to be very affected by my remarks. He said, I was absolutely right. He now felt that he would only be able to write the third part, *Oedipus der Magier*, once he had rewritten this first act along the lines I had outlined.[60]

By this stage in their relationship (nearly ten years since they had first met), both men seem to have known, and been comfortable with, each other's capabilities and limits. When Hofmannsthal was asked in late 1907 by Max Reinhardt for advice on a forthcoming production of *Lysistrata* for example, he turned to Kessler for advice:

> Hofmannsthal asked me to read through *Lysistrata* so that I could help him to advise Reinhardt: 'Look, I've had this idea that you read through the piece and mark up those passages where you think there are particularly strong *values*; and also those passages where there is a particularly strong contrast in tone with another passage,

---

[56] *Diary III*, p. 816.
[57] A characteristic and frequently used word in Kessler's *Diary* – which he wrote in English from 1880 to 1891 and in German thereafter (although always with passages in French and, indeed, seamlessly in all three languages when it suited him) – is *valeurs*, translated throughout as 'values'. Kessler always scrutinised works of art for their *valeurs* and often commented on them.
[58] *Diary III*, p. 817.
[59] Franz Wedekind was one such critic, Max Liebermann another, as noted by Kessler on 2 and 4 February 1906 (*Diary IV*, p. 93).
[60] *Diary IV*, p. 99.

eg lyrical as opposed to the smutty sections and that sort of thing. This will give us a sort of schematic, which will absolutely have to be observed in performance, whatever else'.[61]

Three months later, when Kessler suggested to Hofmannsthal that his earlier play *The Sobeide Wedding* could be improved by cutting out the third scene, Hofmannsthal told Kessler that the scene had been added in by [Otto] Brahm (the director) and added spontaneously, 'I feel an incredible urge to rewrite it as you suggest right now! Go on, shall we do it?'[62] Then, shortly afterwards, on 13 March 1908, Hofmannsthal told Kessler all about the opera libretto that he wanted to write for Strauss, the work that eventually (with Kessler's help) became the play *Cristina's Homecoming*. In the *Diary*, Kessler noted down very full details of the scenario, act by act, and then recorded Hofmannsthal's doubts about the venture as vouchsafed to him on 19 March 1908:

> He then reverted to his opera libretto. 'If only one could be as relaxed and light-hearted about it as in the 18th century, like Crébillon. It always seems to me that authors in those days bore no burdens at all. But if you tried to do that nowadays, it would simply be unethical; it would be *Kitsch*. I could very easily do *Kitsch* of this sort. But it would have no value at all'.[63]

Crébillon fils was the very author whose name had popped into Kessler's mind when he had seen *L'Ingénu libertin* in Paris seven weeks previously. It is entirely plausible that he noted inwardly this comment by Hofmannsthal, and began to put things together in his own mind. The *Diary* is silent on this, however, overtaken as it was by the tragic-comedy and fiasco of a long-planned trip to Greece, undertaken by Hofmannsthal in the company of Kessler and of Aristide Maillol, the French sculptor[64] in the spring of 1908, on which Kessler has much to say. Since this trip exposed both men to the limits of what they found acceptable in each other, and led to an interim summary judgement by Kessler on Hofmannsthal, it is worth a very brief recapitulation of the salient features.

Hofmannsthal had told Kessler repeatedly of his dislike of travel in general, and of his feeling that if ever travel were to become palatable to him, it could only be with Kessler as company. The latter – perhaps misguidedly seeing himself as the sponsor of two completely different protégés who would flower in his company on a trip to Greece – conceived of a holiday threesome: his protégé, the earthy, monoglot French sculptor Maillol, the moody, refined and elegant Hofmannsthal and himself as epicentre of the triangle. The three men met up in Athens on 1 May 1908.

---

[61] *Diary IV*, p. 374.
[62] *Diary IV*, p. 424.
[63] *Diary IV*, p. 435.
[64] Kessler got to know Maillol in 1904 and became not only his sponsor but a major collector of his work. Maillol eventually provided the woodcuts for Kessler's Cranach Press edition of Virgil's *Eclogues*.

In *The Red Count*, Laird Easton gives a succinct and accurate account of what transpired.[65] Yet the *Diary* entries need to be read in full to experience the growing scorn and contempt Kessler felt for Hofmannsthal, who from the moment of his arrival had started to complain that he did not like Greece and wanted to go home. His (somewhat incoherently expressed) problem was that he did not feel any attachment to a country whose language he did not speak, and he resented anyway that Kessler and Maillol always spoke French with each other, thus cutting him out (although Hofmannsthal was perfectly fluent in French). The threesome began to break up, Kessler and Maillol doing one thing and Hofmannsthal another, until the entry for 7 May records:

> On the way back, half an hour from Delphi, Hofmannsthal met us; and there followed the most unpleasant thing that has ever happened between us so far. Hofmannsthal told me, clearly not thinking anything of it, that during my absence he had gone through my travel case looking for a book; he had found a sealed package and had opened it, to find two brochures: both were not worth anything incidentally. As he spoke it was as if someone were slapping me round the ears, for allowing someone to get so close to me who is far from being a gentleman. I told him 'I am astonished' and went ahead to join Maillol. At table Hofmannsthal was hopelessly confused. He ate nothing, said nothing and said his goodnights immediately. A while later I went and knocked on his door. He called me in – he was standing in his nightshirt, crying, and obviously in a state of nervous collapse. I told him I had come to put an end to the matter. He sobbed as he thanked me and asked me to forgive his behaviour. 'He had acted as he did because of his nervous condition as a result of his seasickness and the hot sun that morning; he knew that his behaviour had been unforgivable' and without a pause added 'was it really so terrible to look into the travel case of a travelling companion?' I said there was nothing to discuss; I had come only to tell him that I had <u>forgotten</u> the incident: that was all. He flung his arms around my neck.[66]

What was in Kessler's travel case? Almost certainly erotic homosexual literature or photographs. But by this stage the die had been cast: Hofmannsthal was to return early, leaving Kessler and Maillol to continue their Greek escapade together. The *Diary* records one last and significant conversation, and Kessler's summary judgement of an artist and man he had by now known for nearly a decade, and who had shown gratifying signs of depending on him for artistic guidance and practical help:

> He felt that he could never produce anything here, or at most only after he had lived his way into a much more intimate relationship with the landscape. But now he absolutely had to make a start on his work this spring. *Casanova* was all ready in his head; all it needed was a few untroubled days to get it all down on paper. He couldn't take any chances with this, etc.' I think that I have gradually come to realise that much of

---

[65] Easton, pp. 170–4.
[66] *Diary IV*, pp. 461–2.

Hofmannsthal's obvious moodiness, nervousness, excitability springs from an inner drama, from a struggle for productivity, from fear of a sudden attack of total impotence. In this I have to think of something that Simmel once told me about him.[67]

From his departure for Greece on 25 April 1908, Kessler was now to spend the next nine months away from Germany. He corresponded with Hofmannsthal periodically, from Paris and from his mother's house in Sainte Honorine, Normandy, but there were no face-to-face meetings until 25 January 1909, when Kessler went to Dresden for the première there of the Strauss–Hofmannsthal *Elektra*. The *Diary* records their first meeting since the disastrous attempted holiday in Greece in sober, factual terms:

> In Dresden Hofmannsthal came to fetch me before a morning meal in the Bellevue. I went to the Galerie with him, to meet his wife and the Schalks. He looks as if he is quite well again now. He looks healthy and makes a crisp impression. He and his wife sat down with me while I ate; Richard Strauss and his wife then joined us; Hermann Bahr as well.[68]

So in considering the Kessler–Hofmannsthal relationship to this point – a week before the two men sat down together to construct the scenario for *Der Rosenkavalier* – the aspects to emerge most clearly from the *Diary* and from their correspondence can be summarised as follows. Hofmannsthal was undoubtedly gratified and flattered by the attentions of Kessler, his patronage, his skill at networking and his encyclopaedic knowledge of Classical Greek as well as European theatre and literature. He had looked up to Kessler from nearly the start of their relationship and, increasingly, he had asked him for help and advice with his own writings – particularly his stage plays. He wanted to please Kessler – that is abundantly clear in some of the more sycophantic turns of phrase in his pre-1909 letters – and he wanted his approval. Whether he hoped for more tangible favours in the form of financial support and assistance is a moot point: the *Diary* entries sometimes hint that Hofmannsthal was casting around for offers, financial or otherwise from Kessler, but actual hard evidence is lacking. Above all, however, by 1909 Hofmannsthal was already in creative dialogue with Kessler about his own work in progress: they had worked on *Oedipus* together, on the Reinhardt production of *Lysistrata*, and Hofmannsthal had asked for help – lots of help – with *Semiramis*, which he had long had in mind for Strauss, and with the much more recent Casanova comedy (*Cristina's Homecoming*) on which Strauss was pressing him for an operatic treatment. All the evidence thus suggests that Hofmannsthal trusted Kessler's theatrical instincts and judgement, took constructive criticism

---

[67] *Diary IV*, p. 467. Sociologist and Berlin University professor Georg Simmel (1858–1915), a contact of Kessler: Simmel's best-known work is his 1900 essay on money, *Philosophie des Geldes* (*Philosophy of Money*). At this point in the *Diary* there is a half-page space, destined either for a photograph or a written insert. What Simmel actually told Kessler remains unrecorded.

[68] *Diary IV*, pp. 539–40.

from Kessler on his own earlier work, and was well disposed – almost eager – to work on something actively with his friend and mentor Kessler.

The converse assessment, Kessler's view of Hofmannsthal at this point, is more nuanced. Kessler was excited by Hofmannsthal's youthful talent for language, for lyrical expression and for poetic thought. He was less convinced of Hofmannsthal's skill as a dramatist. He enjoyed debating with Hofmannsthal, on aesthetics, on national literatures and their specific characteristics (especially French, English and German), but the more time he spent in Hofmannsthal's company, the more it was that certain attributes of Hofmannsthal's character seemed to irk him. He nonetheless wanted to be of service to Hofmannsthal, to see him published more widely and to help with the development of his career. Kessler felt absolutely confident about making structural criticisms of Hofmannsthal's stage plays and suggesting that he change them accordingly. He seems to have regarded himself as the teacher, not the pupil, in their relationship. At the same time – particularly after the episode in Greece, but more generally because of certain traits in Hofmannsthal that Kessler perceived as Jewish (as opposed to his own Aryan German background) – Kessler was aware of a gulf between them. He was thus not an

47 Hugo von Hofmannsthal in 1901

48 Harry Kessler in 1908 with one of his favourite dachshunds, Fip

unconditional fan of Hofmannsthal's talent, rather a well-disposed mentor with the intellectual, social and artistic background and awareness that could be used in order to help the promising writer do better.

This context is vital for a proper understanding of what actually went on during Hofmannsthal's visit to Kessler in Weimar in February 1909. The Hofmannsthal letter to Strauss, already quoted, makes it sound almost accidental that Hofmannsthal should have devised an original opera scenario while staying with Count Kessler, the implication being that Hofmannsthal took time away from his host, drafted the scenario quietly on his own, and then discussed the result with Kessler for the latter's approbation. A close look at the making of the scenario as it took shape shows, however, that it was anything but an accident that the work was devised on this particular visit to this particular host: without the latter, *Der Rosenkavalier* would not even have come into existence.

Committing thoughts to paper

How did it all begin? The evidence is now clear – the scenario for *Der Rosenkavalier* was first of all crafted in a series of day by day conversations between Kessler and Hofmannsthal, then written down either as they went along, or shortly afterwards between their creative sessions together. Kessler gave Hofmannsthal the initial idea and the stimulus, with his full description of *L'Ingénu libertin*, in the afternoon of 9 February 1909. Hofmannsthal then went to bed that evening with volume one of the novel on which *L'Ingénu libertin* is based, *Une Année* (which he borrowed from Kessler's library). He would hardly have had time to read the entire three-volume novel, but nor would he have needed to, for Kessler – from the programme notes to *L'Ingénu libertin*, quoted in Act One – is likely to have said that the episode at the heart of the opérette occupies no more than fifty or so pages of *Une Année*. Hofmannsthal would therefore have had time to read the relevant passage several times overnight and early the following morning.

In the afternoon of 10 February Hofmannsthal told Kessler that he would like to go ahead with an opera libretto for Strauss, by combining the *Faublas* episode with the character of Pourceaugnac.[69] This insertion of the title character from a Molière play fitted the dramatic construct of *L'Ingénu libertin* just as well, and perhaps made the borrowing less obvious: instead of two male dupes (Rosambert and the Marquis de Bay), neither of whom achieves the object of his amorous affection, a single Pourceaugnac figure, suffering the same fate, gave added colour and a slightly simpler line to the narrative. Hofmannsthal added that Pourceaugnac should become compromised as a result of a rendezvous with Faublas – a rendezvous (as Kessler must have told him) that the Marquis de Bay tries to arrange from the first time he encounters Faublas cross-dressed as a girl in *L'Ingénu libertin*. Kessler and Hofmannsthal then started work on their own new scenario immediately.

---

[69] *Monsieur de Pourceaugnac*, a 1669 comédie-ballet by Molière and Lully. A fuller consideration of this work comes later in this chapter.

From the *Diary* entries it is possible to reconstruct their working sessions, and approximate minimum durations, as follows:

9 Feb: 1 hour in the afternoon (Kessler's description of the Artus narrative).
10 Feb: 3 hours from tea to dinner (act order planned, varied and then finally determined).
11 Feb: 3 hours, in a morning session and an afternoon session (Act II).
12 Feb: 4 hours, all afternoon until dinner (Act III completed).
13 Feb: 2 hours' discussion on the train from Weimar to Berlin.
15 Feb: 2 hours in the morning, 2 hours in the afternoon (Acts I and II, in detail).

Kessler's concluding entry on 15 February is:

> At five o'clock we had completed the scenario, which is now worked out in intimate detail, situation by situation and practically gesture by gesture; all that it lacks are the words spoken by the characters as they act out the pantomime.[70]

The time both men had so far spent together on the scenario is thus around seventeen hours, spread over seven days, starting in Weimar and finishing at Reinhardt's house in Berlin. This is a world away from the impression given by Hofmannsthal to Strauss in the 11 February letter, with its reference to 'three quiet afternoons' and to 'Count Kessler, with whom I discussed it'. The *Diary* shows that even by that stage they had both been at work for seven hours together!

It is an accident of history that Kessler's *Diary* was lost to the world for 50 years and that a great deal of Strauss-Hofmannsthal scholarship took place before it was found again. But now that is has been found, it is perhaps permissible to draft an alternative version of Hofmannsthal's 11 February letter (which is still quoted in countless programme notes around the world for productions of *Der Rosenkavalier*) and to conjecture *the letter that might – and in the moral sense, should – have been written*:

> *Dear Dr. Strauss,*
>
> *As you well know, I have been fretting for some time over the operatic project that we might embark on as our first fully-fledged collaboration. You have made a number of proposals which do not really suit me and I am afraid that Casanova will not do, as I remain determined to see it mounted as a stage play first, before even considering adapting it as an opera libretto. I have told you this already, of course. But on the second day of my stay here in Weimar with Count Kessler, I asked him to describe the Terrasse opérette* Les Travaux de Hercule, *and this prompted him to tell me all about the much more promising* L'Ingénu libertin *by Terrasse and Artus. Do you know the piece? He saw it last year in Paris and both of us think that we could adapt it and turn it into something entirely original of our own, for you to set.*

---

[70] *Diary IV*, p. 563.

Act Three: Scene One – devising the scenario 137

> *We have spent most of the last three days devising the scenario together and talking of little else! We have bounced ideas off each other, for hours at a time, and the dramatic structure is now clear. From Kessler's full description of the Terrasse piece (which he seems to recall in every detail), I have taken two of the principal, older male characters and combined them into one comic dupe, Pourceaugnac (from Molière) – I can also add one or two comic episodes from that play. This will give us a scenario full of burlesque situations and characters, with lively action, pellucid almost like a pantomime. There will be two big parts, one for baritone and another for a graceful girl dressed up as a man, à la Farrar or Mary Garden. Period: the old Vienna under the Empress Maria Theresa.*
>
> *Kessler and I will travel together to Berlin on Saturday, and I shall come alone to you on Sunday and take you through the piece as we have devised it so far. Kessler is entirely content to remain in the background and wants neither acknowledgement nor any financial reward for the project. We have agreed that I shall write the libretto in Rodaun, sending it to him for his comments as we proceed, and that to all intents and purposes it will appear to the outside world as a work devised entirely by the two of us. We both know that we can rely on Kessler's utter discretion in this matter. I think you will be as excited as I am by the comic, dramatic and musical possibilities that this scenario will offer us…*

The above passage is pure fiction, of course, but every statement in it is based on fact and it reflects, accurately and straightforwardly, what actually transpired between Hofmannsthal and Kessler during those three frenetic days in Weimar. There are, moreover, both contemporary and subsequent corroborative accounts of the working method as described. The *Diary* for 12 February 1909 is clear and concise:

> In conversation the work done by Hofmannsthal and by me is so intertwined that it becomes impossible to separate out our respective contributions. One of us has an idea, a train of thought, the other criticises and as ideas pass to and fro, something quite different emerges; it is often the case that ten minutes later neither he nor I can say who actually thought up a given scene.[71]

In a letter to his sister Wilma on 18 February 1909, Kessler wrote:

> Entre temps Hofmannsthal and I had written, together, the scenario for Rich. Strauss's new opera; it took us only three days to write and although I am half party to it, I can say it is charming: […] We used to work about three or four hours a day, walking up and down, each of us giving une idée by turns, so that it is now quite impossible for either of us to say which is which, and who is the author of this part

---

[71] *Diary IV*, p. 560.

or of that. In three days we thus managed to set down the scenario *dans ses plus petits détails, jusqu'aux jeux de scène*, so that only the words are still missing.[72]

At the same time, Hofmannsthal was writing to his father. Two letters in quick succession, on 14 and 16 February 1909 respectively, confirm Kessler's accounts of the methodology and add detail. The first letter was written by Hofmannsthal on a Sunday morning, the day after he and Kessler had arrived in Berlin by train from Weimar. During this train journey they had continued discussion of the scenario that Hofmannsthal was to present to Strauss, with Kessler recording: 'Talked further about the *Faublas* with Hugo in the train,'[73] but on arrival on the Saturday night, after dinner at the Hotel Adlon, they split up. In the morning Hofmannsthal wrote to his father:

> Berlin, Sunday a.m. I need to stay here just a few more days, I have quite a lot to do. For I have just done the scenario for a charming opera in Weimar with Kessler, that I am going to present to Strauss this afternoon and which will possibly require several more discussions.[74]

After the afternoon meeting with Strauss, Hofmannsthal then rejoined Kessler, the latter subsequently recording:

> Afterwards went with the Hofmannsthals to the Schadow exhibition.[75] In the evening went with him and Musch to see Kainz in *Hamlet*.[76] A flat, deadly dull performance; Kainz merely a technician, without any spark of genius. Hofmannsthal said quite correctly that he was always alongside the character, never inside him.[77]

This entry makes no mention, however, of the outcome of Hofmannsthal's meeting with Strauss, nor of anything that was said on the subject. Once again, it was Hofmannsthal who made a contemporary record in the form of a second letter to his father, this time dated 16 February 1909:

> [...] Even more important is the fact that Strauss is absolutely delighted with the scenario that I completed with Kessler in Weimar (down to the smallest detail). He hopes to complete this three act lighthearted opera within one and a half years. Incidentally it is entirely possible that taking these two projects together I shall earn a quarter of a million Marks.

---

[72] Kessler to Wilma de Brion, m/s letter of 18 February 1909 in Manuscript Department, German Literature Archive, Marbach (HS.1971.0001).

[73] *Diary IV*, p. 561.

[74] Hugo von Hofmannsthal, *Briefe 1900–1909* (Vienna: Bermann-Fischer Verlag, 1937), letter 273.

[75] Johann Gottfried Schadow (1764–1850), sculptor, friend and correspondent of Johann Wolfgang von Goethe (1749–1832).

[76] Joseph Kainz (1858–1910) was a well-known Austrian actor who performed in many German theatres (Munich, Berlin, Weimar) and in Vienna. He performed in Hofmannsthal's early plays and Hofmannsthal subsequently wrote verses in memoriam for him.

[77] *Diary IV*, p. 562.

Act Three: Scene One – devising the scenario 139

> I am now going through the comedy [*Cristina's Homecoming*] scene by scene with Kessler, it has to be completely redone, with a comic figure as the bridegroom and omission of the awful scene with the chimney.[78]

The first full scenario of *Der Rosenkavalier* was thus the product of interaction, the original creative stimulus being supplied by Kessler, the reactive embellishment by Hofmannsthal, and as the process got under way, the roles often clearly being reversed. Towards the end of his life Hofmannsthal recalled (accurately but incompletely) just how the work, which had meanwhile made him a millionaire, came about, writing in his preface to a new and popular edition of *Der Rosenkavalier* a passage that has often been quoted subsequently under the title *Der Rosenkavalier – Zum Geleit*:

> As jovial as the piece is, so was its creation. The scenario really was born in conversation, in conversation with the friend to whom the book is dedicated (and dedicated in terms that indicate true collaboration), Count Harry Kessler.[79]

There was certainly conversation, but the writing of the scenario called for much more. On 10 February, according to Kessler, they started as follows:

> Morning. Faublas climbs out of the Marquise's bed. Pourceaugnac, a relative of the Marquise, arrives from the provinces for his engagement to Sophie, who is actually the girl that Faublas loves, and has himself announced to the Marquise. Faublas is quickly disguised as a chambermaid. Pourceaugnac enters and is received from her bed by the Marquise. Marquise's levée: hairdressers, lackeys, moneylenders etc (Hogarth's levée from 'Marriage à la Mode'). As it ends Pourceaugnac makes an assignation with Faublas, taking him for a girl.[80]

The individual elements here are very clear. Faublas, the Marquise and Sophie are three of our 'beginners' and, of course, from *L'Ingénu libertin*. Morning, with Faublas climbing out of the Marquise's bed is the start of Act III of that work. Pourceaugnac arriving from the provinces for his engagement to a young girl, in an arranged marriage, is from Molière, but also from *L'Ingénu libertin*. For as soon as the Comte de Rosambert meets up with Faublas in Act I, and tells him about the libertine adventure on which he hopes to embark, he also tells Faublas that he will shortly be engaged to the young girl Sophie, just out of her convent. The fact that Sophie is the very girl whom Faublas loves is once again *L'Ingénu libertin*, as is Faublas being disguised in women's clothes. The Hogarthian levée scene pays homage to 'Marriage à la Mode', although there is also the charming levée scene in Act III of *L'Ingénu libertin*, already described and involving the Marquise, her four

---

[78] This fuller version of the letter published by Bermann-Fischer Verlag in 1937 is in the forthcoming critical edition of Hofmannsthal's correspondence with his parents, to which advance electronic access was granted in the Hofmannsthal Archive at the Freies Deutsches Hochstift, Frankfurt am Main.
[79] *Zum Geleit*, pp. 2–3.
[80] *Diary IV*, p. 558.

maidservants and Faublas. The Pourceaugnac assignation with Faublas (taken for a girl) is based on the Marquis de Bay in *L'Ingénu libertin*, who tries throughout the opérette to make an assignation with Faublas (who, in a dress, calls himself not Mariandel, but Sophie du Portail).

> Act II at Sophie's house, in the hall. Love scene between Faublas and Sophie. Faublas fetches a male and a female 'intriguer' to spoil Pourceaugnac's plan. Pourceaugnac arrives; pays his respects to Sophie. Entry of P. with lots of luggage, retinue etc.[81]

Apart from the Faublas/Sophie relationship, which is the motif and main driver of the plot in *L'Ingénu libertin*, the other elements in this act come from *Monsieur de Pourceaugnac*. In the Molière, the male and female intriguers who spoil Pourceaugnac's plans are Sbrigani and Nérine: however there is no grand entrance with luggage and retinue, which seems to have been dreamt up by Kessler and Hofmannsthal purely as an opportunity for pantomime – perhaps (in Kessler's mind) inspired by the piles of onstage hampers and the torchlit procession that arrives in the boudoir of the Marquise de Bay at the start of Act II of the opérette.

> Act III. An inn, where Pourceaugnac has made his assignation with Faublas. At the crucial moment the intriguers usher in the vice squad to catch them. The intriguers also usher in a crowd of low life people whom they have dressed up as 'grands seigneurs'. Pourceaugnac, who believes that they are all nobles, is arrested and crushed.[82]

The lively street scene at carnival time, with an onstage inn, tables and chairs is Act I of *L'Ingénu libertin*. The arrival of the vice squad (*police des moeurs*), prompted by Rosambert, to catch Faublas in an illicit liaison with the Marquise is the finale of Act II of *L'Ingénu libertin*. The downfall of Pourceaugnac is a combination of the downfall of Rosambert in *L'Ingénu libertin*, who never has his mooted affair with the Marquise, and that of Pourceagnac in the Molière, who returns mightily relieved to Limoges. All the essential structural elements of *Der Rosenkavalier* are here assembled from a combination of two French stage works.

So far, so clear. But Hofmannsthal began to have reservations about the love triangle at the centre of the piece, suggesting to Kessler that it would be too gross to have Faublas simultaneously as the Marquise's lover and suitor to Sophie – would audiences accept that? He suggested making Faublas Sophie's cousin, the two falling in love as the piece developed. So in a decision that long had wide implications for *Der Rosenkavalier* scholarship, both Kessler and Hofmannsthal wrote out separately their own copies of a revised scenario (which I shall call 'the first variant'). This reversed the order of Acts I and II. Hofmannsthal's manuscript copy was found among his papers, after his death, by Willi Schuh, who used it as the basis for his 1951 article in the Swiss magazine *Trivium*, which was entitled *Die Entstehung des Rosenkavalier* ('The Creation of *Der Rosenkavalier*').[83] Kessler's

---

[81] *Diary IV*, p. 558.
[82] *Diary IV*, p. 558.
[83] *Trivium*, p. 69.

Act Three: Scene One – devising the scenario 141

copy was not found until the manuscript pages of his *Diary* were repatriated to Germany from the Mallorca bank thirty-three years later, in 1984.

Before looking in detail at the assumptions made and consequent wrong conclusions drawn by Schuh in 1951, although it must immediately be said that he corrected these and realised some of the importance of *L'Ingénu libertin* as an important source work for *Der Rosenkavalier* after publication of the Hofmannsthal–Kessler letters in 1968, the two versions of 'the first variant' (of 10 February 1909) should be compared side by side. The version found by Schuh is on the right-hand side:

Kessler	**Hofmannsthal**
Act I. Géronte's house. Sophie and Faublas. Sophie tells Faublas of her engagement and looks forward to marriage. Pourceaugnac arrives. Arrival of his baggage. Sophie aghast at her coarse future lord and master. Asks Faublas to free her.	I. Géronte's house. He is waiting for his son-in-law who comes from good country nobility. Sophie with the delightful Faublas and talks of marriage. She is surprised that this angers him. Arrival of Pourceaugnac and two elderly aunts, pets and extra-ordinary luggage (double bed). Conspirators are sent for. Marquise: rendezvous for the night with Faublas. He is not altogether delighted. Sophie begs for rescue. The conspirators.
Act II. Scene with the Marquise as before. Faublas gets out of bed, Pourceaugnac has been invited by the Marquise to the levée. He makes the assignation with Faublas. Scene 2: at Sophie's house. Faublas and Sophie. F. discovers his love for Sophie.	II. The Marquise's bedroom. Night of love. Morning. Gratitude. Pourceaugnac announced. Faublas so similar: of course, all noblemen's natural children. Hairdresser, servants etc all importune Pourceaugnac. While Marquise is having her hair done, Pourceaugnac invites the maid for supper. Pourceaugnac stingy (detailed discussion where supper is to be). Pourceaugnac departs. Conspirators arrive and say how it shall be done.
Act III as before; but I suggested there had to be some external reason why the father had to marry off Sophie so quickly. So Faublas would have to step forward (he is a Count, old nobility and rich); and Géronte, whom he is helping out of some dreadful embarrassment (what?) is delighted to bless the match immediately.	III. Room at an inn. Rehearsal of assistants. Supper. Faublas's boots under dress. Arrest. Géronte compromised in front of courtiers. Marquise enters. Géronte wants to go into the bridal chamber. Faublas appears *en travesti*. The Marquise confirms that he is a man.

The slight difference in emphasis between both men in the first variant is interesting: Kessler is concerned with logic and structure, the motivation behind the plot, whereas Hofmannsthal is already putting in more pictorial detail, the boots under the dress, Pourceaugnac's surprise at the facial similarity between the Faublas he has met in Act I and the chambermaid (Faublas disguised as Mariandel) in this version of Act II. Kessler had of course seen most of this onstage at the Bouffes Parisiens, so probably had no need to record it specifically: Hofmannsthal, who only had Kessler's oral account of *L'Ingénu libertin* to go on, was allowing his imagination to work and noting down details as he thought of them. However, this time it was Kessler who then objected to what the embryonic scenario had become: 'This scenario much weaker than the first one: less of a clear-cut, straight line, the need for a second scene in the second act and moreover, just as before, Pourceaugnac almost entirely passive.'[84] Evidently the two men then took a break from their labours, for the crucial reversion to the original act order and the accompanying changes that would solve Hofmannsthal's objections came to Kessler, on his own, as he thought further about the scenario whilst dressing for dinner. The 'second variant', being the definitive outline of the *Rosenkavalier* that we know today, is described thus in the *Diary*:

> As I got dressed the solution came to me, and I told it to Hofmannsthal in the carriage: namely Acts I and II in the original order. **Faublas does not yet know Sophie at all**, but is sent to her by the Marquise on Pourceaugnac's behalf, to announce P. to her. This is where the fun begins with 1) Faublas falling in love with Sophie, 2) Sophie meeting Pourceaugnac and loathing him on sight. The reason why Géronte absolutely has to have a husband for his daughter immediately must be the result of some base intrigue by Pourceaugnac himself. In addition Pourceaugnac must have been the one to introduce the intriguers, whom Faublas then bribes and makes use of them himself. These changes will turn Pourceaugnac from an almost passive figure into the main driving force of the work; he is the cause of all his own misfortune and he is even responsible for Sophie and Faublas getting to know each other, with Faublas going to her on his behalf at the Marquise's request. In addition, Faublas will come over in a better light in the theatre than if he were in one woman's bed while loving another, and then sparking off some dirty intrigue; all he does is to <u>exploit</u> Pourceaugnac's intrigues in order to eliminate the latter; which is much more ingenious. In this way Faublas and Pourceaugnac are not merely young and old, beauty and ugliness, bad and good behaviour but are also contrasts in stupidity and cleverness of spirit; the antithesis emerges very clearly. As in real life, stupidity is the driving force, but cleverness exploits this to its advantage. Moreover the line of the piece is very clear: Act I: love scene, Tableau (of the servants), maybe a ballet. Act II: Faublas in love. Tableau (Pourc's entry). Love scene. Act III: Clown scene (disguises for the 'grands seigneurs'), grotesque love scene between Pourc. and Faublas, who tries to animate Pourceaugnac more and more (Grace) Tableau (unmasking, entrance of the bogus nobility), Faublas's offer of service and love scene Sophie X Faublas. Hofmannsthal accepted all this immediately.[85]

---

[84] *Diary IV*, p. 559.
[85] *Diary IV*, pp. 559–60.

Act Three: Scene One – devising the scenario   143

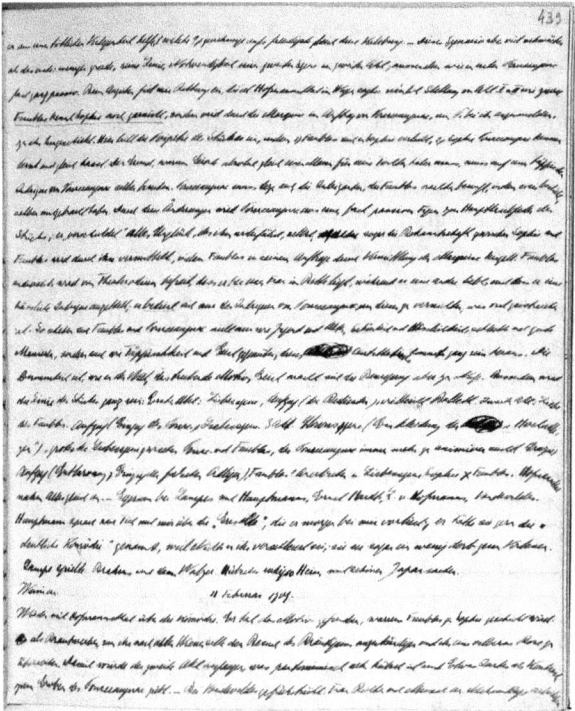

49 Diary entry 10 February 1909: the emphatic **X** inserted between the words Faublas and Sophie refers almost certainly to the Marquise, and thus to the trio that is the highlight of the final act (just as it was in *L'Ingénu libertin*)

Since Kessler wrote this almost immediately after the long and intensive working session that day with Hofmannsthal, there is no reason to doubt the essential accuracy of his account. It articulates, very precisely, Kessler's theatrical vision for the embryonic work, incorporating a number of striking elements that make this *Der Rosenkavalier* scenario much more the specific construction that it is today, and much less of a mere reworking of *L'Ingénu libertin* and of *Monsieur de Pourceaugnac*, to say nothing of the Beaumarchais/da Ponte/Mozart (*Le Nozze di Figaro*) antecedents that are also commonly ascribed to the piece.[86] The crucial change made by Kessler is to turn Faublas and Sophie into strangers to each other and to have Faublas sent to Sophie by the Marquise on Pourceaugnac's behalf. This is entirely original on Kessler's part. In *L'Ingénu libertin*, Faublas and Sophie are already young sweethearts in the back story, and only meet up again in Act III; similarly, neither in *L'Ingénu libertin* nor in *Monsieur de Pourceaugnac* is the young

---

[86] Edward J. Dent, *Opera* (Harmondsworth: Penguin Books, 1940), p. 133, for example: there are of course obvious similarities between Cherubino's activities (including cross-dressing as a servant girl) in Almaviva's palace, and those of Octavian: but Faublas is the proximate model.

hero (Faublas or Eraste) used as any sort of emissary to the young heroine in the piece. However, for all the dramaturgical reasons given by Kessler, the dynamic of the scenario in his version is completely altered: Pourceaugnac becomes the author of his own misfortune and (almost literally) drives the two young lovers into each other's arms. There is here of course a distinct parallel with the narrative line of *L'Ingénu libertin*: in this work it is Rosambert who makes Faublas put on women's clothes (Act I) to pique jealousy from the Marquise, and ends up discomfited at seeing the two, clearly having been in the Marquise's bed for the night, in Act III (and Kessler was to refer to this in a subsequent letter to Hofmannsthal). Yet given the joint decision to start *Der Rosenkavalier* with the Act III situation from *L'Ingénu libertin* (and with no hint that Octavian has ever needed to dress up as a girl in order to bed the Marschallin), Kessler's idea is inspired: it preserves the comedy inherent in Pourceaugnac mistaking a boy for a girl (and making an assignation with 'her') while introducing a wholly new element that was to lend itself to unforgettable stage music from Strauss: the *coup de foudre* of Faublas (Octavian) and Sophie's first meeting and falling instantly in love at the start of Act II of *Der Rosenkavalier*.

The assumptions made and incorrect conclusions drawn by Schuh when he first came across, and wrote about Hofmannsthal's version of 'the first variant' can be disregarded now, given the subsequent evidence that has emerged, but Schuh was such an authority on Strauss that his 1951 article had huge implications for the next twenty years of *Rosenkavalier* scholarship: it appeared definitive, and was consequently reproduced in many articles and programme notes. His main points were as follows. His first assumption was that Hofmannsthal went to see Kessler with 'the first variant' already written: in other words, Hofmannsthal already had a draft scenario for a Strauss opera in mind (although the sheet of paper in Hofmannsthal's handwriting appears to bear the date 10 II 09 in the top right-hand corner). As is now clear from all the evidence, Hofmannsthal arrived in Weimar with nothing definite at all in mind for Strauss, apart from the unfinished play text for *Cristina's Homecoming*, which he told Kessler he was on the point of abandoning. So Schuh's rhetorical questions posed in *Die Entstehung des Rosenkavalier* about the first variant were misconceived:

> Was this scenario intended to be set to music from the outset? It is an open question. If so, then the draft indicates an opera buffa, not a comedy that reaches the upper spheres of touching sentiment, of which the author once spoke with reference to the Marschallin. – There are lots of draft comedies by Hofmannsthal, and he only completed a small proportion of them.[87]

Schuh cannot of course be blamed for ignorance of what was later to emerge, firstly in the Hofmannsthal–Kessler correspondence and secondly in Kessler's *Diary* for the crucial years. His assessment of Hofmannsthal's capabilities and intentions at the time does appear flawed, however, in the light of all the evidence

---

[87] *Trivium*, p. 70.

Act Three: Scene One – devising the scenario 145

now available, and again betrays the critical tendency to judge Hofmannsthal's capabilities as a dramatic librettist with hindsight, and not with the dramatic and theatrical qualities he possessed in 1909:

> This work was however to grow extraordinarily, not only because it was designed to meet the expectations and hopes of the composer, but because lucky chance brought the poet to someone who knew how to return in conversation the ball that Hofmannsthal threw him when he narrated to him his little scenario. […] Hofmannsthal visited his friend in Weimar in February 1909 and – undoubtedly on the basis of a quick narration of the scenario already outlined – a conversation started on the planned comedy.[88]

Schuh's firm belief that Hofmannsthal was the initiator, Kessler merely the respondent, has found its way into many accounts of the creation of *Der Rosenkavalier* ever since.[89] It also seems to have influenced some of the subsequent German scholarship on the issue: after working with Schuh on the critical edition of the text of *Der Rosenkavalier*,[90] Dirk O. Hoffmann wrote slightly critically of Kessler, in terms of the relative importance of his input to *Der Rosenkavalier* in its final form.[91] This line of argument is also to be found in Jörg Schuster's introduction to Volume IV of the *Diary*.[92] Schuster argues that the charm and individual vision of Hofmannsthal's words, combined with the greater emphasis he gave to the character and psychological portrait of the Marschallin, all serve to diminish the legitimacy of any claim by Kessler to be co-author or co-creator of *Der Rosenkavalier*. Once again, this is retrospective judgement and seems to have been written without any real consideration of the theatrical qualities of *L'Ingénu libertin*. For *Der Rosenkavalier*, as a piece of music theatre, ended up as it did because it started from all the basic elements that went into its creation – the cast of characters, the scenario, the dramaturgy and the stage décor – and then, of course, the words – of a work that Strauss was to set to music. In addition, Kessler's *Diary* has a great deal more to say that is pertinent on this score. On 11 February for example:

> Discussed the comedy with Hofmannsthal again. He has thought of the motive for Faublas being sent to Sophie: as bridegroom's intermediary, to pre-announce a visit by the bridegroom according to the old Viennese custom and to hand her a silver

---

[88] *Trivium*, p. 70.
[89] Jefferson; Norman Del Mar, *Richard Strauss: a critical commentary on his life and works* (London: Barrie and Rockliff, 1962); Jakob Knaus, *Hofmannsthals Weg zur Oper 'Die Frau ohne Schatten'* (Berlin, New York: De Gruyter, 1971), Robert Mühlher, *Osterreichische Dichter seit Grillparzer* (Wien, Stuttgart: Wilhelm Braumüller, 1973), and many others.
[90] *Vol. XXIII*.
[91] Dirk Hoffmann, *Zu Harry Graf Kesslers Mitarbeit am Rosenkavalier* (Freiburg: Hofmannsthal-Blätter 21/22, 1979), pp. 153–60. This of course pre-dated rediscovery of the *Diary* for the crucial years.
[92] *Diary IV*, pp. 17–26.

rose. Act II would begin with this, which would be a very pretty pantomime and provide some tenderness in contrast to Pourceaugnac's crudeness.[93]

Kessler had been the one to devise the fact of Faublas being sent to Sophie by the Marquise on Pourceaugnac's behalf, so as to announce Pourceaugnac to her, and this had cut brilliantly through the Gordian knot of establishing relationships between the various characters and the dynamics of their stage actions. But the embellishment of this idea with a silver rose as visual token came from Hofmannsthal, with symbolism in mind, and this illustrates perfectly the productive theatrical interaction between both men. The working period in Weimar is then rounded off by a *Diary* entry that could be described as emblematic of Kessler's theatrical vision for the progression of Chevalier to Cavalier, of his acute perception how the finished opera might look and sound once Strauss had composed it. It follows straight on from Kessler's remark (quoted earlier) that after ten minutes back and forth in conversation with Hofmannsthal, it was often impossible to identify their respective contributions:

> [...] ten minutes later it is often impossible for him or for me to say who actually conceived the scene. **All that I claim for myself** is the final tableau, with the characters exiting one after the other in groups, rather ballet-like, until the two lovers are left alone and then exit, joking and holding torches, with just a few little negro boys left onstage; then moonlight. Music like Strauss writes, **which reaches such huge crescendos, seems to me perfect for an opera with this fading finale, as the light fades in parallel, until the stage is dark and lit only by moonlight**. Discussed Hauptmann with Hofmannsthal after dinner.[94]

This claim by Kessler to sole authorship of the finale to Act III concept, the gradual emptying of the stage, the final scene for the two lovers, the exoticism of the 'few little negro boys' (who became just one, 'ein kleiner Neger' in the final cast list) is just as significant theatrically as Kessler's decision to turn Faublas and Sophie into complete strangers to each other. For, once again, Kessler is departing here from the matrix of *L'Ingénu libertin*. What he had seen the previous year on the stage of the Bouffes Parisiens was an entirely conventional ending to the piece. As we already know, following the trio, in which the Marquise (not without a tear) relinquishes Faublas and he pairs off with Sophie, the happy couple are joined by the entire cast, who celebrate the announcement of their marriage – and the work ends with a bright, D major full chorus. This is the antithesis of the projected ending of *Der Rosenkavalier* – to which Kessler lays 'sole claim'. He, correctly, predicts that a quiet, elegant, balletic and tableau-like ending to the work, played against a long Straussian *decrescendo*, will be effective and original. That, in dramaturgical and structural terms, is almost exactly how *Der Rosenkavalier*

---

[93] *Diary IV*, p. 560.
[94] *Diary IV*, pp. 560–1 – my added emphasis.

turned out, and the subsequent stage directions (by Alfred Roller) for the final scene echo Kessler's vision almost exactly:

> One of the servants who has come in from [door] B with Faninal and the Marschallin, now takes from the small front table the candelabra which had been on the dining table and which is now the only source of light in the room, so as to light the way for those who exit. As a result, the room becomes (fairly) dark. From this moment on: moonlight through the oval window, hitting the left-hand side wall or [door] C, brightening imperceptibly and illuminating Octavian and Sophie.[95]

In terms of the visual, dramatic architecture of the piece, this is pure Kessler, the perfect accompaniment to the Straussian *decrescendo* that he also imagined at this point, nearly two years before its onstage realisation. There is, however, even earlier evidence of Kessler's enchantment with a very similar stage picture. On 15 April 1901 he had attended a performance of *Twelfth Night* at Her Majesty's Theatre, Haymarket, and had been very taken by its tragic-comic nature, by Shakespeare's ability to conjure up pure comedy from the tragedy of human emotions, stuttering relationships and the characters' inability to see things clearly through their disguises, noting:

> The meaning of the play was very much underlined by the masked procession at the end, with all the characters leaving the stage hand in hand like a sort of dance of death; finally the Fool is left on his own and delivers the epilogue with a high flute sound.[96]

It is thus quite possible, as Kessler thought back for theatrical examples of elegant endings to comedies of mistaken identity and of cross-dressing, that this production of *Twelfth Night* came to mind, and that he imagined the emptying stage as a similar final tableau, but this time with a Straussian orchestral accompaniment.

There is one further *Diary* entry that records Kessler's specific input to the scenario as it was developing at this stage. The two men had now moved to Berlin, Hofmannsthal had been to see Strauss on his own, had obtained his approval of the whole concept, and Max Reinhardt's dining room had now become their place of work. On 15 February Kessler wrote:

> Worked in detail with Hofmannsthal morning and afternoon in Reinhardt's dining room at *Unter den Zelten* on the 'Faublas' scenario, first and second act. I had noted down things for both these acts that H. accepted. For example the interplay between Pourceaugnac, the Marquise and Faublas in the first act, which rests on Faublas wanting to creep away as fast as possible while P., taking him for a girl, tries to keep him there. The Marquise, who notices P.'s infatuation and is amused by the jest, finally gets out a miniature of Faublas and draws P.'s attention to the likeness herself, adding that the chambermaid is a natural sister to her nephew Faublas; would P. find this young

---

[95] *Fassungen*, p. 179.
[96] *Diary III*, p. 402.

man suitable as his envoy? The Marquise's audacity provides the motive for F. to act as the bridegroom's messenger. In Act II, in place of the banquet, in order to get Pourc. and Géronte offstage and to leave Sophie and Faublas alone, notaries, who have to draw up the marriage contract with P. and G. and therefore go into a sideroom with them: if we had left the banquet, Faublas and Sophie would have had to attend. An added advantage is that the entry of the whole retinue in Act I, which H. thinks very important in visual terms, becomes part of the plot in that the Marquise admits them all in order to introduce P. to her notary, who is in the retinue. This means that Pourc. can give the notary his instructions in Act I while the Marquise is having her hair done on the right and a flautist is playing mellifluously. By five we had completed the scenario which has now been worked out in detail, situation by situation and almost gesture by gesture: all that is missing are the words that the characters speak as they act out the play. **I pressed literally for all the situations to be intensified in terms of the dramatic and the pantomime (visual) effects, whereas in Hofmannsthal's imagination they all tend to blend together in somewhat insipid fashion.**[97]

Kessler's reading of their respective attitudes and contributions to the theatrical aspect of the scenario finds a distinct echo in a letter sent to him by Hofmannsthal six months later, after work on the libretto itself was well under way. Saying that, uniquely among his friends, he could not write to Kessler and omit any mention his work, and asking Kessler never to chivvy him for details on exactly how the work of creation was progressing, Hofmannsthal added:

> Dear Harry, you won't misunderstand this, will you? It does not affect our relationship in any way, and neither does it affect your relationship with all the other stages of my work, which – conversely – I hope will become ever more intimate. For there is hardly a plan that enters my head, such as my latest modern social comedy, without me absolutely longing to discuss the plan with you. Likewise I am expecting from you some decisive advice on the *Sylvia* play, when you get round to it.[98]

However selective his memory, and however much Hofmannsthal began to feel that he was creating an original work of his own, as he sat and penned the *Rosenkavalier* libretto in Rodaun in 1909–10, he cannot have been unaware – as he referred back to the written scenario – of all the little details that had in fact been suggested by Kessler. In terms of the piece's visual and theatrical effects, the very first scene on which he worked was the revamped Act III Scene 1 of *L'Ingénu libertin*, Hofmannsthal's initial task being to put words into the mouths of two protagonists: Faublas and the Marquise (Octavian and the Marschallin) as they wake up in bed together. Even as he worked, and as the draft *Rosenkavalier* libretto began to take shape, he received constant reminders by letter from Kessler of the shape and visual outlines of the work that was to be shown onstage. As we know,

---

[97] *Diary IV*, pp. 562–3 – my added emphasis.
[98] Burger, p. 261.

Kessler had seen the Ballets Russes in *Le Pavillon d'Armide* in early June 1909: he promptly wrote to Hofmannsthal:

> For the costumes, the ones in *Le Pavillon d'Armide* by the Ballets Russes give me ideas: baroque (in this instance, old Viennese of course) with a hint of Beardsley, in order to emphasise the fantastical in the operetta. I think it would be good, once you have finished the text, if you were to *go into the smallest details* in your stage edition, because otherwise traditional *opera* direction is hopelessly unartistic everywhere. You have made a good start with Octavian and his footmen. But I think *later on, and systematically,* you should give directions for exact *colours* and *style* from start to finish. Best of all obviously would be direct *coloured illustrations* (standard professional ones) to be attached to the score, either by Roller (although he is heavy-handed) or by Stern (who is very talented), or by one of the Russians who has done the simply *wonderful* costumes and décor for the ballet here. The man who designed the *Pavillon d'Armide* would be the perfect choice, with his Beardsley-like imagination coupled with his ability to keep everything exactly in period. I don't dare think of Craig any more for this, obviously.[99]

Kessler was running ahead here, visualising the reworked *L'Ingénu libertin* in its completely new, Viennese setting and applying his artist's eye to details of exactly how the new creation would look. Hofmannsthal meanwhile was working out the 'great scenario' that he and Kessler had already devised, and incorporating as many of its effective features as possible into the text that he was already sending to Strauss. So, in terms of visual effects, the (repeated) joke with the likeness of Faublas to the chambermaid, the interplay between Pourceaugnac, the Marquise and Faublas in the first act, all this, once again, comes from *L'Ingénu libertin*, in which the Marquis de Bay makes constant reference to his expertise in physiognomy and his unfailing ability to 'read' people – while failing miserably to detect that the disguised and attractively feminine-looking Faublas is a young male. Out of exactly this construct springs Ochs, with his vague awareness that Mariandel and Octavian are suspiciously similar in appearance – explained away however by his assumption of their (common) noble natural parentage. Likewise Kessler's suggestion that the Marquise (Marschallin) should be audacious enough to get out a miniature of Faublas (Octavian) and to draw Pourceaugnac's (Ochs's) attention to the likeness: this is very much in character with the Marquise of Artus and Terrasse, who dominates the stage and takes all the key decisions that move the plot along. She it is, after all, who having had one night of lovemaking with Faublas gives her blessing to his reconciliation with Sophie and brings about the final dénouement:

[99] Burger, p. 241.

> The Marquise *very moved*
>
> I forgive you.
>
> *And to Sophie – spoken – while the orchestra softly murmurs the 'Colin Maillard' melody*
>
> You deserve him the most,
> So keep him, this child whom I adore.
>
> *And as a radiant Sophie is about to untie the knot in the scarf, the Marquise stops her*
>
> I should like to dry my eyes,
> Leave the blindfold on him, for a moment.[100]

The hint of melancholy, the elegant resignation of the Marschallin as she moves offstage leaving Octavian with Sophie, the emotion she feels as her lover abandons her for another, younger girl, all these elements are also present in this vignette from *L'Ingénu libertin*. The details correspond too: the Marquise refers to Faublas as *cet enfant*, the Marschallin to Octavian as *mein Bub*: the erotic mother figure/young person relationship is preserved. The argument attempted by some previous critics, that the French work is a mere light-hearted boulevard pot-boiler and that Hofmannsthal was to change its character out of all recognition, does not therefore really run. There is a great deal more of the Artus scenario, character development and colour in *Der Rosenkavalier* than has ever previously been admitted.

At the end of Act One, there was an attempt to recreate the performance of *L'Ingénu libertin* seen by Kessler on 18 January 1908. The effect it had on him provides plausible context for the clarity and force of his narration to Hofmannsthal on 9 February 1909, which triggered the collaboration that resulted in *Der Rosenkavalier*. Kessler had seen a work of literary quality, with music by one of the foremost exponents in the genre, with décor and costumes by craftsmen at the top of their game. There was clearly more than a frisson of eroticism to the scenario, and to its onstage execution, and the representation of French eighteenth-century *libertinage* certainly struck a chord not only with Kessler but also with a number of French critics.[101] Kessler's *Diary* entry for 18 January 1908, as noted already, had highlighted the leading actress, Arlette Dorgère; had contrasted libertinage and 'sentiment', Lovelace and Clarissa, Crébillon fils and Rousseau, and had evoked Heine as an author capable of unifying all these different elements.

If Kessler saw the eighteenth and nineteenth-century dialectic between *libertinage* and 'sentiment' or sensibility portrayed onstage in *L'Ingénu libertin*, he was situating the piece well within his own literary and dramatic vision and understanding, formed, as we have seen, through intense and constant exposure to a vast

---

[100] Artus, p. 159.
[101] Nozière in *Gil Blas* of 12 December 1908, for example.

range of works of French, English and German theatre and literature. He had read Richardson's *Clarissa* in 1906 and had been overwhelmed by it, writing on 23 June:

> Finished volume V of *Clarissa* with stupendous admiration. Balzac and Dostoevski are the only comparable authors: nobody who writes English epic novels, not even Fielding. The incredible novelty of his approach and the genius of its execution put Richardson in a class of his own.[102]

A month later, Kessler had finished Rousseau's *La Nouvelle Héloïse* and was making detailed comparisons between Rousseau and Richardson, between the lyrical realism of the former (leading through subjectivity to later impressionism) and the epic realism of the latter (leading through objectivity to *le document vécu*).[103] Kessler's conclusion was that the relationship between Rousseau and Richardson was akin to that of a photographic negative and positive. Kessler's subsequent thoughts, post *L'Ingénu libertin*, on the interdependence of Crébillon fils and Rousseau, of Lovelace and Clarissa, of *libertinage* and *sentiment*, are echoed rather strikingly in modern Crébillon fils scholarship:

> It has already been noted that the balance to be achieved between sensibility, that is *sentiment*, and *libertinage* is never decisive and varies throughout the period of the eighteenth century. [...] Sensibility, for the major novelists Prévost, Marivaux, Diderot and Rousseau, was reflected in the importance given to feeling, the study of feelings, reflection on the emotions and accentuating them to allow refined and detailed analysis. The novel of sensibility was popularised by Richardson in both England and France, followed by Jean-Jacques Rousseau, the foremost pre-Romantic novelist of the period, with the publication of *La Nouvelle Héloïse* (1761).[104]

The fact that Kessler saw two opposing poles in the source material of *L'Ingénu libertin* – the need to illuminate Faublas with Rousseau and Rousseau with Faublas – is eloquent also of his deeper understanding of what was going on: *La Nouvelle Héloïse* being a narrative of moral and emotional repair, the need for the heroine Julie to recover after her fall, meaning the loss of her virginity. Clarissa never recovers from her fall, and wills herself to death: Julie and Saint-Preux concentrate on the long period of time needed for recovery. It is telling also that Kessler saw a union of these opposites in Heine, a poet with the ability to combine, to embody even, a mixture of raw sensuality and dreamy sentimentality. Kessler had long been preoccupied with the differing strains that made up Romanticism, and, precisely of Heine had noted in the diary in 1903:

---

[102] *Diary IV*, p. 151.
[103] *Diary IV*, p. 163.
[104] Patrick Fein, *Crébillon fils, Les Egarements du Coeur et de l'esprit* (London: Grant & Cutler, 2000), p. 10.

The mixture is most easily separated in Heine. The sentimental is his Romanticism. His love of real life turns out to be a joke. Thus his joke is also what has remained and continues to be effective.[105]

So the 18 January performance of *L'Ingénu libertin* crystallised in Kessler's mind some of his previous thinking about *libertinage* and 'sentiment' in works of eighteenth-century French and English literature, and he saw a combination of these symbiotic elements in the work of the nineteenth-century German poet Heine. This sort of thinking, this desire to situate the character of Faublas among a gallery of pre-existing literary characters, was also exemplified in the Preface written by Hippolyte Fournier to a new edition of *Les Aventures du Chevalier Faublas* in 1884. Fournier wrote:

> Faublas is well situated, taking his place between the Lovelace of Richardson and the Cherubino of Beaumarchais: he is seductive sentimentality, giving the gracefulness of love to man's desire for pleasure, whereas Cherubino represents eclectic desire, dazzled to the point of blindness, not at all refined but simply greedy, and as brutal in his artful caresses as Lovelace's cold sensualism is corrupt.[106]

Richardson, Rousseau, Crébillon fils, Beaumarchais were all therefore authors whose creations were seen to impinge on the world created in novelistic form by Louvet de Couvray, and dramatised subsequently onstage – as outlined in Overture and Beginners – throughout the nineteenth century. Kessler was certainly aware of all these currents of thinking, and perhaps he saw too in Hofmannsthal a poet capable of expressing in German some of the subtleties that Artus may not quite have captured: in a prescient letter of 3 August 1909, when work on the libretto of *Der Rosenkavalier* was well under way, Kessler wrote:

> But joking apart, of course 'Quin-Quin'[107] will be much better than Artus's *Faublas*, **because it will be overlaid with poetic 'charme', the strange and individual nature of your vision**. This is what is declining especially among modern French authors, including Bernard and Becque, 'charme', the last one to have it was Musset. Somehow all these Parisians lack the fragrance, the soft down that sits on works created out of true poetic imagination. Their world is not the enchanted world of Balzac or Shakespeare. They interest me but I am never drawn to them, I never really long to see them. **So if you learn their métier, and where to go beyond it, this is what will make your comedy incommensurably better than theirs**. The person who has

---

[105] *Diary III*, p. 528.
[106] http://dbooks.bodleian.ox.ac.uk/books/PDFs/N10271587.pdf. This passage is on page xxiii of the separately printed preface, for which no other publication details are given.
[107] Octavian's nickname was one of several working titles for *Der Rosenkavalier*; the others were *Der Vetter vom Land*, and *Ochs von Lerchenau*, although *Mariandel, Die galanten Abenteuer des Barons von Lerchenau, Der Grobian in Liebesnot* and *Der Grobian im Liebesspiel* were also considered (Burger, pp. 264–9).

showed genius in learning from the French in this way is undoubtedly Ibsen: he provided the roast, they gave him the sauce.[108]

Kessler thus anticipated that Hofmannsthal would come up with a libretto that went beyond the formulaic, that added to the scenario that the two men had put together over their seventeen hours of joint endeavour. However, he saw Hofmannsthal's contribution precisely as this overlay, an addition and accretion of highly individual language and idiosyncratic lyric poetry, to the essentially sound and workmanlike dramatic structure that had been created. These were the terms in which he had high hopes of the collaboration that had started so promisingly.

---

[108] Burger, pp. 255–6 – my added emphasis.

Scene Two – characterisation and authorship

Who are the characters who fill and empty the stage every time a performance of *Der Rosenkavalier* is given? We have met them in outline, in Overture and Beginners, and their antecedents – both literary and occasionally real life – have often been addressed in *Rosenkavalier* scholarship in the past. But since the publication of the Kessler *Diary*, from 2004 onwards, nobody has aligned its revelations with a close reading of the Hofmannsthal–Kessler correspondence (published 1968) and the Hofmannsthal–Strauss letters (published 1926 onwards) – until now. But that is what has to be done to understand the creation of *Der Rosenkavalier* as a three-dimensional piece of music theatre.

Derivation of the opera's essential narrative and dramatic architecture from *L'Ingénu libertin* has already been established, but the work done subsequently by Kessler and Hofmannsthal – and, of course, by Strauss – was transformative, resulting in a new piece of music theatre that rapidly conquered the opera houses of the world. Versions of the carefully defined, prescriptive original production of *Der Rosenkavalier* opened in opera houses all over Germany and in Italy from 1911 onwards, were seen in London and in New York in 1913, although, interestingly, the opera did not receive its first performances in France until 23 March 1926, when it premièred at the Monte Carlo Opéra, followed by its première at the Paris Opéra on 10 February 1927. By this time – sixteen years after its Dresden première – any audience memories of the look of the stage settings, characters and costumes for *L'Ingénu libertin* had, presumably, long since faded. But the question that remains is what the full, accurate genesis of these *Rosenkavalier* characters really was, and how authorship of them came about; how they were imagined, visualised and then fashioned as individual characters on the stage.

The nature of authorship in general, and more particularly its definition, is a much-debated issue: as it involves Hofmannsthal, Kessler and Strauss, it needs to be considered. On Sunday 14 February 1909, having arrived in Berlin from Weimar the previous evening, Hofmannsthal narrated to Strauss the reworked version of *L'Ingénu libertin* that Kessler and he had devised, and invited him, in effect, to author the music for it. Strauss's acceptance of the proposition was more or less instantaneous: in *Zum Geleit* Hofmannsthal himself described it thus:

> [...] I travelled to Berlin without any notes, apart from the cast of characters scribbled on the back of a menu card, but in my mind I had a plot that could be narrated. The effect of this narration on Strauss is as memorable to me as if it had happened

yesterday. **The way he listened to me was truly productive. I could feel him allocating music as yet unborn to characters who had hardly been born**. Then he said: 'We'll do it'.[1]

50 Richard Strauss in 1910, the year in which he completed the score of *Der Rosenkavalier*

Hofmannsthal had travelled to Berlin in the same train carriage as Kessler and it is somewhat unlikely that he had no notes: as has been shown, he and Kessler had talked of little else during the preceding four days in Weimar, and during the two-hour journey from Weimar they had gone over the *Faublas* scenario in minute detail. Regardless of that, his narration of the scenario must have been as interesting and inspiring to Strauss on 14 February as Kessler's narration of *L'Ingénu libertin* to Hofmannsthal had been a few days previously. It is also interesting – if Hofmannsthal's retrospective account is broadly correct – that Strauss's musical response to the scenario, and to the characters who would figure in it, should have been so immediate and so intuitive. This suggests that Strauss began to have some

---

[1] *Zum Geleit*, p. 3 – my added emphasis.

feeling for the musical shape of the embryonic work purely on the basis of Hofmannsthal's oral description of its main features: in other words, before he had seen a single line of the libretto. As is well known, there were several subsequent examples of Strauss composing musical passages for *Der Rosenkavalier* and then asking Hofmannsthal to supply additional lines of text, the most famous being the final love duet between Octavian and Sophie in Act III.[2]

On this basis, the initial authorship of *Der Rosenkavalier* can thus reasonably be ascribed to the jointly conceived dramatic scenario, in which Kessler played as much of a role as Hofmannsthal (and was the driving force in the process of its construction), and to Strauss's immediate acceptance of that scenario as the next opera he would set to music. The question that then arises is the degree to which Hofmannsthal's words – once Strauss had said yes to the project – usurped joint authorship of the dramatic construct, the scenario, and became the factor that most inspired Strauss's music. In other words, who created *Der Rosenkavalier*? This is where theoretical definitions of authorship may come into play. In literature, Barthes famously refers to text as 'a multi-dimensional space in which a variety of writings, none of them original, blend and clash', and again as 'a tissue of quotations drawn from the innumerable centres of culture'.[3] This is apt: the texts of Hofmannsthal as literature, both coincidentally and objectively speaking, often fit that description. Branscombe expresses similar thoughts about certain aspects of Hofmannsthal's dramatic writings:

> From the conscious and admitted adaptations it is fascinating to turn to the hidden literary borrowings, more or less conscious memories of his passionate and voracious reading in several languages; antecedents of the most varied kind can be found for a vast number of tiny details in his writings. Yet these borrowings are so creative, his use of them so subtle, that the accusation that he was a kleptomaniac has only the most superficial application.[4]

Yet these textual, pointillist details added by Hofmannsthal are embellishments in the main: they create atmosphere and suggest back stories to characters who have already been authored in their essential dimensions by the scenario that has been constructed around them. The Marschallin's mention of going to eat with 'Uncle Greifenklau, who is old and lame' in Act I of *Der Rosenkavalier* is just one such example of pathos and colour being added by the text to the principal female character, who has already emerged in theatrical terms, the sentiment underlined even further by Strauss's music at this point. Authorship in literature, moreover, and the Barthes contention that 'the birth of the reader must be at the cost of the death of the author'[5] is not strictly or necessarily applicable to authorship for the

---

[2] Hamm./Osers, pp. 33–5 give three such examples.
[3] Barthes, p. 146.
[4] Peter Branscombe, 'Hugo von Hofmannsthal – Man of Letters', in *Der Rosenkavalier*, ed. Nicholas John (London: Calder Publications, 1981), pp. 33–6 (p. 35).
[5] Barthes, p. 148.

stage, where actors and actresses assume their roles, decide on their interpretation, and are then subject to designers, and costumiers, and above all to directors, for onstage incarnation of the character who performs the written text, their delivery of that text being no more than one element in their performance overall – and its reception. The lengthy (and ongoing) debate on authorship of the plays of Shakespeare is relevant to this contention: of modern Shakespeare scholars, Jonathan Bate has written most persuasively about the collaborative nature of what we refer to as 'Shakespeare', pointing out a fundamental misconception on the part of those who look for an alternative single author:

> The Romantic idea of authorship locates the essence of genius in the *scene of writing*. […] This conception of what it is to be a genius has the effect of investing talismanic power in *the author's original manuscript*. This in turn has the effect of removing Shakespeare from the playhouse – it was in the Romantic period that idealists began complaining that the plays were too great to be soiled by the stage.[6]

Bate goes on to develop more fully the notion of joint authorship of some of the plays of Shakespeare's time:

> Shakespeare's contribution to *Sir Thomas More* reveals a number of things about his working life. He was a man of the theatre. He did jobbing work, fulfilling particular commissions as well as creating plays of his own. He contributed to plays which had different scenes written by different dramatists. He revised other writers' work. […] Such a Shakespeare is utterly unlike the Romantic image of authorship in which the poet works alone in his study, is answerable only to his own inspiration, and cherishes his manuscripts.[7]

This then leads him to the following conclusion:

> For by 'Shakespeare' we mean not an individual, but a body of work, and that body was, I argued in part one, shaped by many individuals – by the dramatist's education and his precursors, by the actors of his company, by the audience without whom no play can be completed.[8]

In a subsequent book, and dealing with what he describes as *The Myth of Shakespeare's Retirement*, Bate goes into greater detail on Shakespeare's co-authors and collaborators, and the works (and parts of works) that they fashioned together.[9] With such examples in mind, it is at least arguable that the notion of Hofmannsthal crafting the libretto for *Der Rosenkavalier* all alone in his Rodaun study is akin to the Romantic image of authorship as quoted above, and that the *scene of writing* alluded to by Bate is but one component in the work of music theatre that was

---

[6] Bate, p. 82.
[7] Bate, p. 99.
[8] Bate, p. 185.
[9] Jonathan Bate, *Soul of the Age, The Life, Mind and World of William Shakespeare* (London: Penguin Books, 2009), pp. 359–63.

put together by Kessler, by Hofmannsthal and by Strauss: that the finished work, therefore, is more than a mere fusion of words and music, but rather a musico-dramatic experience in which the *unsaid*, or rather *unsung* (or as Kessler would have put it, the *pantomimic* and visual elements) play a crucial theatrical role.

To address this basic question of authorship of the whole piece, of the structure that surrounds and supports the characters, of the scenario according to which they act out their roles, we have to return to the evidence: this involves analysis of the main recorded exchanges on the topic, particularly between Kessler and Hofmannsthal; inclusion of some of the subsequent pronouncements by both men on the creation of *Der Rosenkavalier*; and assessment of critical comment on the issues raised by their collaboration, which has for the most part postdated publication of their correspondence and of Kessler's *Diary* (indeed, before publication of their correspondence, Kessler was merely known, if at all in this context, as the man in whose house Hofmannsthal was staying when he seemingly came up with the *Rosenkavalier* ideas).

The whole question of authorship was an issue that arose between both men, in acute form, in July 1910, and the exchanges that passed between them at that time show that each of them had a very different conception of the contribution made by the other, as will be seen. The broad issues raised, but not fully answered, are exemplified, however, by a comment on Kessler by Jürgen Haupt in 1970, shortly after the Hofmannsthal–Kessler correspondence first appeared:

> It would be unfair on him if – as Hofmannsthal did – one were to minimize or overlook the intellectual and creative side in this. It is precisely his artistic cooperation with Hofmannsthal in the years leading up to the Great War that provides proof of the original, artistic productive energy in Kessler. As we now know, ideas and important details in *Der Rosenkavalier* come from him, as well as motifs for *Cristina's Homecoming*.[10]

This is echoed, seventeen years later, by Gerhart Baumann, in his contribution to a collection of essays on Kessler as a pioneer of modernism. Baumann suggests:

> The initiatives, added passages, objections made in respect of *Cristina's Homecoming* or *Der Rosenkavalier* are worthy of a study all to themselves, they develop the possibilities inherent in creative criticism that extinguish the boundaries between the critic and the creator.[11]

Kessler as constructive critic and co-creator is perhaps a concept that is beginning to emerge. Likewise, more recently and more tentatively, Ilya Dürhammer considers Hofmannsthal's relationship to the female characters in his stage works:

---

[10] Jürgen Haupt, *Konstellationen Hugo von Hofmannsthals* (Salzburg: Residenz Verlag, 1970), p. 60.

[11] Gerhart Baumann, *Harry Graf Kessler: Ein Wegbereiter der Moderne*, ed. Gerhard Neumann and Gunter Schnitzler (Freiburg im Breisgau: Rombach, 1997), p. 15.

At this point we should once again recall Hofmannsthal's efforts to deal with the androgynous figure [...] – and Harry Graf Kessler, who played a major part in the conception both of *Der Rosenkavalier* and of the ballet *Josephs Legende*. It is worth considering in this respect the considerable degree to which the aesthetic of a homoerotic influenced Hofmannsthal's conception.[12]

Hofmannsthal himself did not really illuminate any of these issues by contributing, in 1927, a warm tribute to Kessler followed immediately by some remarks on the origins and authorship of *Der Rosenkavalier* that, like his famous (or infamous) letter to Strauss of 11 February 1909, do not tell the whole story. The tribute is repeated here for ease of reference: immediately thereafter he wrote:

> The scenario was really born out of conversation, in conversation with the friend to whom the book is dedicated (and dedicated with a formulation which points towards true collaboration), Count Harry Kessler. **The figures were there and moved around before us, even before we had names for them: the buffo, the old man, the young girl, the lady, the 'Cherubino'. They were types, waiting to be turned into individuals by the executive pen. The plot arose from the eternal ways these figures related to each other.**[13]

This may be how Hofmannsthal thought back on his work some eighteen years later, and chose to write about it, but it is entirely untrue and highly misleading on his part (intentionally?) to reduce the characters from *L'Ingénu libertin* to mere types without names, and to ignore its specific narrative. For the very first drafts of the scenario of *Der Rosenkavalier*, analysed above, show that all the characters bore the names that denoted their stage origins, as they were bound to – Faublas, the Marquise, Sophie and Pourceaugnac, the latter being the only name introduced by Hofmannsthal at that stage. Nor, strictly speaking, does the evidence support Hofmannsthal's contention that 'the plot arose from the eternal ways these figures related to each other'. As has been shown, the basic idea, the very concept of the comic opera that was to be written for Strauss, was Kessler's narration of all the elements he had taken from *L'Ingénu libertin*, plus Hofmannsthal's decision to combine these elements with 'the Pourceaugnac figure', followed by the initial seventeen hours of joint work, refashioning and recrafting the elements thus brought together. It would therefore, with today's evidence before us, be more accurate to change Hofmannsthal's formulation to something like: 'the plot arose from our joint deconstruction of the very specific ways Faublas, Sophie, Rosambert and the Marquise related to each other in *L'Ingénu libertin* and our refashioning of those elements, plus some new ones, and the order in which the narrative unfolds, into the *Rosenkavalier* scenario'. That might however have started hares running in 1927, and the first ever volume of correspondence between Strauss and Hofmannsthal

---

[12] Ilja Dürhammer, *Richard Strauss, Hugo von Hofmannsthal Frauenbilder*, ed. Ilja Dürhammer and Pia Janke (Vienna: Edition Praesens, 2001), p. 233.

[13] *Zum Geleit*, p. 3 – my added emphasis.

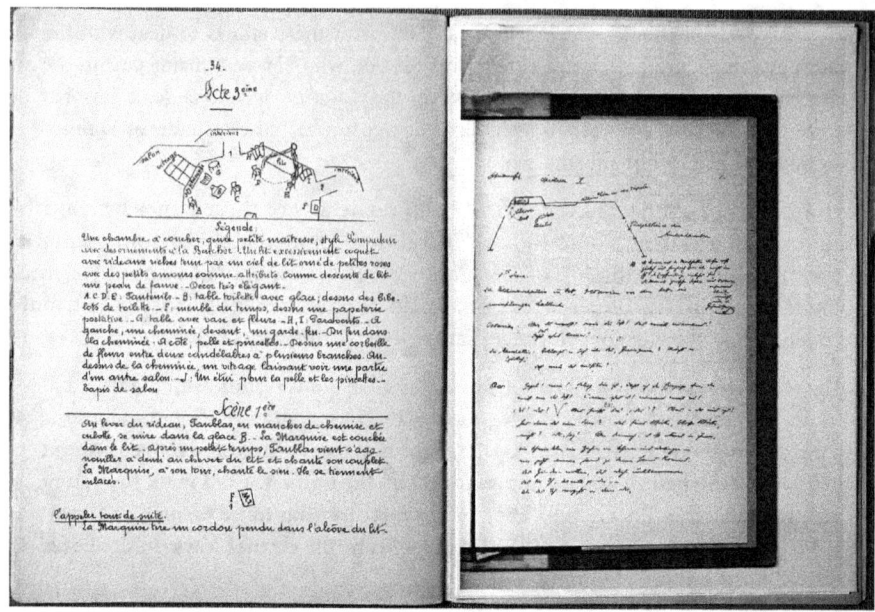

51 Hofmannsthal's preliminary sketch for Act One of *Der Rosenkavalier* can only have come from Kessler's detailed description of Act Three of *L'Ingénu libertin* – the correspondence of the stage layout is striking

had only recently been published,[14] thus awakening general public and critical interest in their collaborative methods: but that formulation, or something similar, is precisely what Kessler's *Diary* and the full Hofmannsthal–Kessler correspondence both show. It may well be, however, that as he was working on the characters so vividly and accurately described to him by Kessler, Hofmannsthal found it necessary for his own purposes to reduce them in his imagination to cipher figures, before recreating them in their *Rosenkavalier* incarnations. Hofmannsthal's letter to Kessler of 27 June 1909 rather suggests this: reflecting on the difficulty of creating real flesh and blood characters for the opening scene of the play *Cristina's Homecoming*, he remarked: 'This requires a completely different effort than **playing with types and typical situations in the operetta.**'[15]

None of this is to deny that Hofmannsthal's subsequent imaginative crafting of the language put into the mouths of each of these remodelled characters is anything other than poetic, idiosyncratic, nuanced and for much of the time profoundly original. It is a truism that precisely Hofmannsthal's multilingual text, High German and Austrian German for the most part but enriched with borrowings from Italian and French, and enlivened by dialect, by archaisms and by

---

[14] Richard Strauss, *Briefwechsel mit Hugo von Hofmannsthal*, ed. Dr Franz Strauss (Berlin: Paul Zsolnay Verlag, 1926).

[15] Burger, p. 247 – my added emphasis.

colloquialisms, in itself creates the new setting, half real and half imaginary (as Hofmannsthal himself described it) of Vienna in the time of Maria Theresa. Hofmannsthal is thus both author and writer of this milieu. This, too, is precisely what Kessler wanted and intended all along: his aim from the outset had been to free Hofmannsthal of the burden of plotting, motivation and dramatic structuring, thus leaving him to concentrate on what he was to do best of all: characterisation, by means of language, of the new roles in their new setting. There are many pointers to this very process in the Hofmannsthal–Kessler correspondence: it provides much of the evidence as to how one work of art was completely transformed into another.

A vital aspect to bear in mind in this context is that the guiding theatrical vision for the *Rosenkavalier* scenario, including many details of exactly how the work was to be performed onstage, came from the experience, already described, of a single performance of *L'Ingénu libertin*, seen by Kessler on 18 January 1908. The world created onstage by this work was undoubtedly attractive, visually pleasing, intriguing and effective. With its sumptuous, thought-through settings, and above all with its cast of characters, the stagecraft worked, in marked contrast to some of the previous stage adaptations of *Faublas*, as demonstrated in 'Overture' and 'Beginners'. However, although this is clearly what happened, Kessler's way of briefing and instructing Hofmannsthal on how all the characters in *L'Ingénu libertin* performed their roles, and related to one another dramatically, is the one factor in the equation that is hardly recorded; most likely because it was a major feature of the many hours of intensive conversation between both men that surrounded, but was not included in, the very first written scenario as recorded by Kessler in his *Diary*, the first variant, both in the *Diary* and on the Hofmannsthal paper found by Schuh, the reversion to the original scenario and act order and the many subsequent drafting revisions that followed.[16] Since specific evidence of the Kessler–Hofmannsthal conversations here is lacking, the most fruitful way of attempting to assess the origins and authorship of the performance aspects of *Der Rosenkavalier* is to analyse the characters and situations in their 'before and after' contexts, one by one.

Baron Ochs of Lerchenau

The generally accepted prototype of Baron Ochs is Monsieur de Pourceaugnac, the principal character in Molière's 1669 comédie-ballet (with music by Lully) of the same name. As soon as Kessler had narrated *L'Ingénu libertin* to Hofmannsthal, and the latter had subsequently read the relevant section of text in *Une Année*, the idea had come to Hofmannsthal of combining the narratives of the Pourceaugnac and Faublas characters, and of having the former compromised by means of an assignation with the latter.[17] The name Pourceaugnac thus figures in all the early

---

[16] See, in particular, *Vol. XXIII*, which details all the successive stages.
[17] *Diary IV*, p. 558.

draft scenarios, until its replacement by the name of Ochs in the second half of March 1909. Pourceaugnac is not, however, the only model for Ochs. Jefferson ranges more widely than some in his search for the origins of Pourceaugnac/Ochs:

> Hofmannsthal felt that the character of Ochs made *Der Rosenkavalier* more readily acceptable in England than in France, for there are a number of similarities between the Baron and several characters in the English drama: Falstaff himself, including Verdi's knight (although Falstaff is older); Sir Toby Belch in *Twelfth Night*; Sir Tunbelly Clumsey in Vanbrugh's *The Relapse* (1696); Bob Acres in Sheridan's *The Rivals* (1775); Tony Lumpkin in Goldsmith's *She Stoops to Conquer* (1773).[18]

The Falstaff of Verdi and Boito as a role model for Ochs was also in the minds of Kessler, Hofmannsthal and Strauss as the characterisation progressed – Strauss drew Hofmannsthal's specific attention to it for the scene with the wounded Ochs on the sofa at the end of Act II, in his letter of 13 August 1909.[19] To this list might also be added Squire Western in *Tom Jones* by Fielding, whom Kessler specifically mentioned to Hofmannsthal when he first suggested a thoroughgoing revision to Ochs's big aria in Act I. Kessler's suggestions for the sort of characterisation that might be applied to Ochs derived in equal measure from literature and fine art: 'Auerbachs Keller, Squire Western, Jordaens (not Giorgione), Jordaens [sic] Teniers strike the right note in this context.'[20] The bucolic student scenes set in Auerbachs Keller in Goethe's *Faust*, and the scenes of aristocratic and peasant merriment painted by Jacob Jordaens and by David Teniers the Younger were undoubtedly mentioned by Kessler as a visual and literary prompt to Hofmannsthal to make Ochs a more rounded, plausible, theatrical character and not – as the first draft of the aria had presaged – a mere mouthpiece for lyrical poetry. As Kessler went on to put it in his critique of the first draft, more colloquially: 'This aria by Ochs comes across to me as if Caliban were suddenly to start speaking like Ariel, or Bottom the Tailor like Titania.'[21]

The other elements of *Monsieur de Pourceaugnac* that Hofmannsthal incorporated in the *Rosenkavalier* scenario, but with changes, are these: a Parisian father (Oronte) deciding to marry off his daughter (Julie) to a rich provincial promising a dowry (Pourceaugnac, a lawyer from Limoges); a pair of intriguers (Sbrigani and Nérine) meddling in the affair and stage-managing the discomfiture of Pourceaugnac; the arrival onstage (prompted by the intriguers) of fake former wives of Pourceaugnac (Lucette, and Nérine in disguise) who produce fake children to taunt Pourceaugnac with cries of 'Mon papa! Mon papa!'; and the final flight of

---

[18] Jefferson, p. 14.
[19] Hamm./Osers, p. 47.
[20] Burger, p. 228.
[21] Burger, p. 228. Kessler had studied the works of Jacob Jordaens (1593–1678) and David Teniers the Younger (1610–90) as part of his projected *magnum opus* on art, originally entitled *History of European Colour since Giotto*, which he began to research seriously in 1906 (but never completed).

Pourceaugnac from Paris back to Limoges, bewildered and defeated at every turn, thus allowing Julie to marry Eraste, her intended all along.

The dramatic structure of *Monsieur de Pourceaugnac* is, however, completely different from that of *Der Rosenkavalier* and the characterisation of Pourceaugnac and of Ochs has next to nothing in common: they both come from the provinces, but that is about all. The outcome of *Monsieur de Pourceaugnac* – that parents will always fail if they try to prevent young love – is told in advance by the musical prologue, orchestrated and controlled onstage by Eraste: in the first and second scenes, Julie, Eraste, Nérine and Sbrigani describe comprehensively how Pourceaugnac will be dealt with once he dares to show his face in Paris.[22] When he does so, his role turns out to be that of a passive dupe. He is tricked and ridiculed at every turn by accomplices of Sbrigani pretending to be doctors, an apothecary, lawyers, officers – even by Eraste, who pretends to have spent time in Limoges and to know all of Pourceaugnac's friends and acquaintances there. What is more, Pourceaugnac is bemused by Paris from the moment of his arrival in the city – his first speech, to an offstage crowd, tells us so and it is his utter helplessness that allows Sbrigani to make a show of befriending him, in order to unleash a series of plots against him. As a character, therefore, Pourceaugnac is entirely reactive: his sin is his presumption, that a lawyer from Limoges could come to Paris to marry a smart young Parisienne, and his punishment is pre-ordained, with the entire cast of characters against him. Julie and Eraste, Sbrigani and Nérine, all work hand in glove from the outset to inflict successive humiliations on their hapless victim. Pourceaugnac does nothing except arrive, become bewildered, protest and depart. There is therefore a simple narrative, but no dramatic development in the piece.

As a character, moreover, Pourceaugnac is at the opposite end of the spectrum from Ochs. The latter's arrival onstage in the first act of *Der Rosenkavalier* is forceful and entirely self-assured: he arrives in Vienna with a large and rowdy retinue of servants and supporters. Ochs practically forces his way into the Marschallin's bedroom, brooking no interference from servants who try to hinder his passage (and creating, incidentally, both the initial frisson of fear that the noise offstage might be the Marschallin's husband returning home unexpectedly, and the motivation for Octavian to disguise himself as Mariandel, thus launching the sub-plot with the Ochs–Mariandel assignment almost immediately). From the moment of his arrival, Ochs is the driving force of the narrative, in the sense intended by Kessler: he is in Vienna with a purpose, he tries to see this purpose through, he is at the centre of the stage action for large sections of all three acts. The financial motive is also reversed: Pourceaugnac has a dowry of three or four thousand crowns (écus) on offer for the hand of Julie, whereas the straightened Ochs, with only his noble lineage on offer, is unashamedly after Faninal's substantial wealth. Ochs thus drives the narrative of *Der Rosenkavalier* and is the active, dynamic

---

[22] *Pourceaugnac*, pp. 446–7.

force within it; the narrative of *Monsieur de Pourceaugnac* involves its passive victim, Pourceaugnac, in one misfortune after another.

From this dramaturgical point of view, the character and behaviour of Ochs have far more in common with two of the male protagonists in *L'Ingénu libertin* – the Comte de Rosambert and the Marquis de Bay – than they have with Pourceaugnac. These features must therefore derive from Kessler's narration of the Artus scenario. To deal with the Marquis first: from the moment that he meets Faublas, cross-dressed as Mademoiselle du Portail, he starts to flirt with the beguiling creature before him and attempts to arrange an assignation. The similarity between this sub-plot and that of Ochs–Mariandel is striking. The Marquis de Bay is also a self-styled expert in physiognomy, and claims to recognise Faublas as the daughter of M. du Portail as soon as he learns the name.[23] The same construct is applied to Ochs in Act I of *Der Rosenkavalier* – when the Marschallin shows him the medallion of Count Octavian Rofrano, the man she has designated to become bearer of the silver rose for Ochs, the latter is struck by the facial similarity to Mariandel but draws entirely the wrong conclusions: she must be an out-of-wedlock sister to Octavian (and he chuckles over the naughtiness of it all). There is however one major difference between the Marquis de Bay and Ochs, in that the former remains unaware of his wife's infidelity throughout the piece, whereas Ochs finally becomes aware of the Marschallin's infidelity with Octavian, and is enjoined to forget all about it and leave Vienna.

Many of Ochs's strong, positive attributes, by contrast, are pre-echoed in the character of Rosambert. It is his forthcoming marriage with Sophie, to the dismay of Faublas, that is announced in Act I.[24] It is Rosambert who wants to have his quick affair with the Marquise de Bay before his wedding day, and who persuades Faublas to cross-dress as Mademoiselle du Portail: Rosambert's view that the business of marriage should not be allowed to mar the fun of his seduction of other women is thus exactly the attitude that Ochs exemplifies. It is therefore Rosambert who is the main driver of the narrative in *L'Ingénu libertin*, since his attempted use of a cross-dressed, jealousy-inspiring third party (Faublas) to achieve his affair with the Marquise results in nothing of the sort: Rosambert neither has his intended affair, nor does he marry Sophie. Here too is a parallel with Ochs: the latter's attempted use of a third party (Octavian) to prosecute his suit with Sophie merely drives the two into each other's arms: and his projected affair with Mariandel comes to nothing either. This is precisely what must have been in Kessler's mind on 10 February 1909 when he wrote: 'These changes will turn Pourceaugnac from an almost passive figure into the main driving force of the work; he is the cause of all his own misfortune [...].'[25]

In his narration of *L'Ingénu libertin*, Kessler clearly recounted in detail to Hofmannsthal the characteristics and plot functions of the Marquis de Bay and

[23] Artus, pp. 34–5.
[24] Artus, p. 25.
[25] *Diary IV*, p. 559.

of Rosambert. There is another distinct echo of the latter in a small passage of dialogue in Act II of *Der Rosenkavalier*, which adds to the perception that Hofmannsthal had this model at least partly in mind when characterising Ochs: as the latter is about to leave the stage to sign the marriage contract in the notary's presence, Ochs encourages Octavian to flirt with Sophie during his absence:

Baron (*eifrig*) Natürlich wird's belieben

(*im Vobeigehen zu Octavian, den er vertraulich anfasst*)

> Hab' nichts dawider
> Wenn du ihr möchtest Äugerl machen, Vetter,
> Jetzt oder künftighin,
> Ist noch ein rechter Rührnichtan.
> Betracht's als förderlich, je mehr sie dégourdiert wird.[26]

[Baron (eagerly) Of course I'm pleased to come!

(*as he passes, to Octavian, gripping him conspiratorially*)

> I've nothing against it
> Cousin, if you want to flirt with her,
> Now, or anytime in future,
> She's still a very prim little customer
> I regard it as a service, the more she's warmed up.]

In *L'Ingénu libertin*, Rosambert promises Faublas a little reward if the latter will aid him with his stratagem for seducing the Marquise de Bay. The reward will be an introduction to Sophie de Pontis, the day after she has married Rosambert:

Faublas (à part): Sophie!
Rosambert: Je pense que tu ne la connais pas, bien qu'elle soit ta parente. Elle n'est guère sortie de son couvent.
Faublas: Je ne la connais pas.
Rosambert: Tu lui feras la cour et elle te dégourdira. Nous en usons ainsi, entre gens du bel air.[27]

[Faublas (aside): Sophie!
Rosambert: I don't think you know her, even though you are related. She has only just left her convent.
Faublas: I don't know her.
Rosambert: You can make love to her and she will relax you a bit. This is the way we aristocrats behave.]

The placing of the unusual and somewhat titillating word 'dégourdieren' in

---

[26] Pahlen, p. 147. Of interest here is Hofmannsthal's use of the passive tense, with Sophie being the character to be 'dégourdiert' or 'warmed up'. Compare the Artus below.
[27] Artus, p. 25. Here it is Sophie who is doing the relaxing – the active party!

Ochs's mouth can only have come from Hofmannsthal's subsequent reading of the Artus libretto, although Kessler cannot have given a detailed account of the work that he had seen without sketching out the dramatic relationship between Rosambert and Faublas, and between the Marquis de Bay and Faublas, right from the outset; and Hofmannsthal's borrowing of the character traits and dramatic functions of both men, to create a vital, dramatically powerful Ochs, is a long way removed from the entirely passive, beaten before he starts, figure of Pourceaugnac. Strictly in performance terms, therefore, it is both more convincing and more rewarding to see many of the origins of Ochs of Lerchenau in *L'Ingénu libertin* rather than in *Monsieur de Pourceaugnac*. The derivation is now perfectly clear.

Valzacchi and Annina – the intriguers

Molière's play does however provide convincing surface prototypes for the intriguers Valzacchi and Annina, in the form of Sbrigani and Nérine. Yet once again there are some key dramaturgical differences. At the outset of *Monsieur de Pourceaugnac*, we are introduced to a quartet of characters who know each other, trust each other and who resolve to work together to destroy the importunate provincial Pourceaugnac and to dash any hopes he might entertain of marrying Julie. Eraste and Sbrigani may or may not be social equals, but Eraste refers to him in flattering terms throughout: Sbrigani is 'adroit' and 'subtle' and can be relied upon unequivocally (*Pourceaugnac*, p. 446). This is quite a different construct from Valzacchi and Annina, who simply turn up at the Marschallin's levée and seek their respective fortunes from there, offering their services to the highest bidder. The Marschallin rejects their offer of the latest scandal sheet, and clearly despises them and all that they stand for. So Valzacchi and Annina have a different dramatic, and somewhat extraneous function in *Der Rosenkavalier*: their onstage denunciation of Octavian and Sophie in Act II, and their summoning of the crowd of extras for the inn scene in the first half of Act III, to see Ochs ridiculed and denounced, are mechanical, plot devices, more akin to the ancient *deus ex machina* prototype than to the integrated, harmonious function of Sbrigani and Nérine as part of the plot against Pourceaugnac. There is no pair of intriguers in *L'Ingénu libertin*, nor is there any need, given the way its narrative unfolds, for this particular dramatic device.

There is however one scene that closely resembles the onstage imbroglio of the first half of Act III of *Der Rosenkavalier*, when Ochs is surprised during his attempted seduction of Mariandel and has to face, not only the crowd of fake extras and his supposed former wives and children, but the full force of the law in the form of a police commissioner and his constables who are duly summoned to the scene. This is in fact a combination of elements from *Monsieur de Pourceaugnac* and from *L'Ingénu libertin*. The climax of Act II of the latter sees the arrival of a large crowd at the Marquise de Bay's house, headed by a police commissioner (*police des moeurs*, or vice squad) with orders to search the house for Faublas, allegedly engaged in immoral behaviour.[28] This has been prompted by Rosambert, anxious to prevent Faublas from climbing between the sheets with the Marquise (he is too late). A full chorus sings of searching the house from top to bottom: 'from the attics to the cellars, let's search every cupboard, every basket' – the mood created is one of urgency and excitement, with the music at this point underpinning the dramatic certainty that someone, or something, will be found and revealed. In *L'Ingénu libertin* this dénouement comes when Sophie dons the Act I dress abandoned by Faublas, steps forward and claims to be him: she is led away for a night in prison.[29] In *Der Rosenkavalier* the Act III tumult ceases with the arrival of the Marschallin, and the dénouement follows from there. The 'stage moment' in each case is similar: a point of arrival, at a given moment, and a new departure. In this context, what happens to Valzacchi and to Annina is of no interest: having helped to move the plot along, they are simply discarded, along with the crowd of extras. By contrast Sbrigani, in *Monsieur de Pourceaugnac*, maintains his pivotal role and status right to the end, appearing alongside Eraste, Julie and Oronte in the very last scene before the final, celebratory masques.[30]

Faninal and Sophie – father and daughter

Géronte is a commonly used name for an old man, and the fact that Hofmannsthal used it for the father figure in the revised scenario of 10 February 1909 (the first variant) has led many commentators to search more widely in the works of Molière, and elsewhere, for the prototype of Faninal. Sure enough, Géronte is the father of Lucinde in *Le Médecin Malgré Lui* and another Géronte is the father of Hyacinte in *Les Fourberies de Scapin* (the Molière play to which Kessler specifically referred in his letter to Hofmannsthal of 3 August 1909). There is nothing specific to the father–daughter relationship in either play, however, that goes beyond the relationship between Oronte and Lucie in *Monsieur de Pourceaugnac* as a basic model for the rebellious Sophie, once she has met Ochs and been appalled by him, defying Faninal and saying that she will not obey his orders to marry. The spirited exchanges between Sophie and Faninal in Act II of *Der Rosenkavalier*, with their repetitions and parallel phrases[31] are precisely foreshadowed in *Monsieur de Pourceaugnac*, when Julie, knowing that Oronte has been set against Pourceaugnac already, pretends to be determined to marry him, thus increasing further Oronte's opposition to the match.[32] Hofmannsthal's borrowing from the structural and performance aspects of this particular scene in *Monsieur de Pourceaugnac* seems very clear. Might he have misremembered Oronte's name and unwittingly sent countless subsequent researchers down an irrelevant, old man Géronte trail?

[28] Artus, p. 148.
[29] Artus, p. 121.
[30] *Pourceaugnac*, p. 463.
[31] Pahlen, pp. 175–9.
[32] *Pourceaugnac*, pp. 457–8.

Sophie, viewed in isolation in performance terms, is an interesting case. Breaking away from all previous stage adaptations of Louvet de Couvray's novel, Artus makes her one of the principal characters in *L'Ingénu libertin*, brings her out of her convent and places her onstage, at the centre of the action, showing her to be quick-witted, resourceful, able to command (and outwit) her chaperones (Mademoiselle Sauce and La Jeunesse) and to rise to the climactic scene of the opérette, her sentimental duet with Faublas followed by the decisive trio in Act III. The role, moreover, gives the singer playing Sophie the chance for considerable comic by-play as a maladroit waiter at table during the 'getting to know you' scene in the Marquise de Bay's salon in Act II. By her sacrifice (a night in prison), the Sophie of *L'Ingénu libertin* proves herself to be the equal of her intended, Faublas, and she enjoys some spirited arguments with him in which she more than holds her own – particularly when Faublas tries to argue in Act III that a man's casual affair with a woman is of no real importance.[33]

In performance terms, the Sophie of *Der Rosenkavalier* is somewhat of a reversion to the more passive Sophie of Louvet de Couvray's original novel: she is the pretty, but ordinary, conventional young girl, obedient to her father's wishes in the matter of her arranged marriage, and without much original – or interesting – spark of her own: until she has met, and fallen in love with Octavian. Her existence in the confines of Faninal's house is loosely analogous to the existence of Louvet de Couvray's Sophie in her convent, and not at all to Artus's Sophie, who roams Paris freely and who seeks out her Faublas when she scents the danger of his imminent involvement with another woman. This *Rosenkavalier* Sophie, however, is entirely consistent with Kessler's theatrical vision for the piece. For if, as Kessler suggested when making the biggest single initial change to the Artus scenario, Sophie and Faublas do not know each other before the narrative starts, then she has to be located – not quite imprisoned – in the location in which Faublas can be sent off to find her: and that location, Faninal's house, has the added advantage (in visual, pantomimic terms, Kessler's strong point) of being eminently suitable for grand display. The only real sign of an original character shown by Hofmannsthal's Sophie occurs during her Act II argument with Faninal, when she threatens to defy him at every turn if he persists with the intended match with Ochs. As outlined above, this is a borrowing from Julie and Oronte.[34]

Octavian – the Cavalier

There is a rich stage history of females playing the parts of males, *en travesti*, both in the theatre and on the opera stage, but the legion of possible, theoretical generic predecessors to Octavian should not be allowed to obscure the simple fact that the character started life in the *Rosenkavalier* scenario as Faublas, and this is the character on whom he is most closely modelled in performative terms. Faublas

---

[33] Artus, pp. 146–7.
[34] Pourceaugnac, pp. 457–8.

is a mezzo-soprano in male attire who, in the course of *L'Ingénu libertin*, sings of his love for two females – so does Octavian. Faublas cross-dresses onstage and finds himself, in female attire, to be the object of unwelcome male attention from the Marquis de Bay – so does Octavian, from Baron Ochs. Faublas is discovered *nu et en chemise*[35] in the bedroom of the Marquise, after a night of passionate lovemaking – so is Octavian. Faublas, having tasted the delights of love with an older woman, falls for the younger girl (his own age) – so does Octavian. It should be remembered, incidentally, that the act order of Octavian's narrative is a mirror image of that of Faublas, with *L'Ingénu libertin* moving Faublas from public place to grand drawing room to bedroom, while *Der Rosenkavalier* moves Octavian from bedroom to grand drawing room to public place. The resolution of the narrative is, in each case, the same.

Hofmannsthal's letter to Strauss of 11 February 1909 had indicated clearly the sort of singer who would take one of the two big parts: 'a graceful girl dressed up as a man, à la Farrar or Mary Garden'.[36] Both Geraldine Farrar (1882–1967) and Mary Garden (1874–1967) were known to Kessler, who, having seen Jeanne Alba, a relatively new and inexperienced actress, take the part of Faublas, must have thought – along with some of the critics, as noted in Act One – that a big name would invest the role of Octavian with the star quality that it required. Kessler's opinion of Farrar varied: as noted earlier, he saw her debut at the Berlin Court Opera on 15 October 1901, singing Marguerite in Gounod's *Faust*, and praised her great all-round talent, then got to know her over lunch in December 1901 – making no further comment on her – and subsequently heard her sing privately, in the presence of Cosima Wagner, judging her performance as 'disastrous'.[37] Farrar's onstage allure, however, and her ability to inspire devotion among a growing army of female fans as well as male admirers, may well have been factors in the decision to include her name, as a prompt to Strauss of the sort of starring role that was envisaged by Kessler and by Hofmannsthal at that early stage.

The name of Mary Garden was an equally strong prompt to Strauss – she had, after all, studied the role of Salomé with him for the French version of the opera in Paris[38] and by 1907 she had become a strong and versatile performer in Paris. Kessler had seen her at the Opéra Comique on 8 May 1902, creating the role of Mélisande in Debussy's *Pelléas et Mélisande* under the baton of Messager: his *Diary* entry for that day is full of thoughts about the work, its dramaturgy and its

---

[35] Jean-Claude Bologne, *Histoire de la Pudeur* (Paris: Olivier Orban, 1986), p. 134. The sexual frisson provoked by a woman in male undergarments, allowing the shape of her body and legs to be seen onstage, was a hallmark of actresses such as Virginie Déjazet (1798–1875) and many others. The stage direction for Faublas at the start of Act III runs: 'Faublas, qui vient de sortir du lit, est dans sa petite culotte et chemisette de cavalier. Sa robe de nuit est sur un meuble.' [Faublas, who has just got out of bed, is in his underpants and cavalier's undershirt. His nightshirt is on a chest of drawers] (Artus, p. 125).
[36] Hamm./Osers, p. 27.
[37] *Diary III*, p. 457.
[38] Kennedy, p. 142.

restrained instrumentation, but says nothing about the performers.[39] Kessler must have seen her three times that month, for he records subsequent visits on 10 May and 15 May, but he merely notes the fact of his attendance. Nearly four years later, on 3 April 1906, Kessler saw Garden playing the lesbian role of Chrysis in Camille Erlanger's *Aphrodite*, again at the Opéra Comique, but his comment is enigmatic: 'Pretty dances: not much else.'[40] What else Garden might have brought to the role of Octavian was her experience of the title role in Jules Massenet's *Chérubin*, an opera recounting the subsequent adventures of the Cherubino of Beaumarchais and of Mozart, which premièred in Monte Carlo on 14 February 1905. Her ability to switch from seductive femininity onstage to trouser roles such as Chérubin (and, later in America, to play Jean – originally written for a tenor – in Massenet's *Le Jongleur de Notre Dame*, based on the Anatole France story) has led to judgements such as that by Terry Castle: 'Garden, who cultivated an air of sexual ambiguity quite brazenly [...]'[41] in respect of her performance skills.

The assumption can safely be made that Kessler, just as he wanted all along for Hofmannsthal to improve on the Artus libretto by applying 'poetic charm, the individual and rare qualities of your vision,'[42] wanted equally the mezzo who was to be cast as Octavian to be a striking actress-singer, someone with qualities akin to those already being displayed in the opera house by Garden and Farrar. Too late for it to have any bearing on the casting of *Der Rosenkavalier*, but still of aesthetic and theatrical interest in that context, Kessler did actually see onstage the female singer whom he described to Hofmannsthal as: 'the ideal Quinquin, the absolute ideal, such as we shall, alas, never see in *Der Rosenkavalier*'.[43] His description of an act he had seen at the third night of the newly opened London Palladium makes clear the Faublas (Octavian) he had been envisaging from the outset:

> This miracle is called Ella Shields, the most attractive, fresh little face, the slimmest, most boyish figure, apart from two budding little hints of breasts, her movements like a young, gracious schoolboy and a pretty, but not very strong soprano voice, which nevertheless filled the huge auditorium (5,000 seats): she cannot be more than nineteen or twenty. She sings and dances as a young gentleman in a tailcoat and as a lieutenant in uniform. I have seldom seen anything as charming and gracious, without a hint of saccharine or equivocal colouring. So, a perfect Quinquin is possible [...].[44]

Kessler was fooled by the stage appearance of American-born Ella Shields (later to achieve music hall immortality as Burlington Bertie from Bow) – she was in fact

---

[39] *Diary III*, p. 493.
[40] *Diary IV*, p. 112.
[41] Terry Castle, 'In Praise of Brigitte Fassbaender', in *En Travesti, Women, Gender Subversion, Opera*, ed. Corinne E. Blackmer and Patricia Juliana Smith (New York: Columbia University Press, 1995), pp. 20–58 (p. 27).
[42] Burger, p. 255.
[43] Burger, p. 317.
[44] Burger, pp. 317–18.

52 Ella Shields, photographed in London in 1910. American-born, she had come to London for the opening night of the London Palladium, where Kessler saw and imagined her as the ideal Octavian

31 when Kessler saw her that night. His description of her shows, however, that the Octavian he visualised was to be slim, androgynous, stylish and elegant – a far cry from the 'fat, contented mother of ten to fourteen breast-fed children, in bulging knee-breeches' that he dreaded seeing onstage as Octavian in Dresden or Berlin, as he went on to write in that same letter. Kessler's theatrical vision in 1910, honed by the hundreds of operas he had seen in the preceding decade, clearly encompassed the ideal as well as the predictable.

Concentration on Faublas as the immediate model for Octavian does not, of course, eliminate all thoughts of Mozart and Da Ponte's Cherubino as a more distant predecessor. Strauss wanted *Der Rosenkavalier* to be his Mozart opera, and he, Hofmannsthal and Kessler had all referred *en passant* to Cherubino in their correspondence during the *Rosenkavalier* gestation period. In March 1911, two months after *Der Rosenkavalier* had been launched in the opera houses of Europe, Hofmannsthal referred to the relationship between *Der Rosenkavalier* and *Le Nozze di Figaro* as: 'not [...] an imitation, but bearing a certain analogy'.[45] So authorship of Octavian must include certain elements of Cherubino that were also to be found in the stage incarnation of Faublas: both the latter share a spirited attitude and manner, attractive to the older woman with whom they may or may not become romantically entangled (Countess Almaviva and the Marquise de Bay); they also betray willingness to defy the male authority figure in their own pursuit of personal, including sexual, pleasure (Count Almaviva and Rosambert); and they both sing of frank, exuberant enjoyment of the opposite sex. Cherubino is, however, a vivid but minor figure in the narrative scheme of *Figaro*, portraying a young page who is attracted by every new woman he meets and thus indiscriminate in his feelings. Whatever happens, *Le Nozze di Figaro* will reach its narrative conclusion without him. Both Faublas and Octavian, on the other hand, are major figures in their respective narratives, and it is their specific decision, in both cases, to renounce the charms of the older woman in favour of the young, innocent Sophie (in Octavian's case, with a little prompting from the Marschallin), that resolves the main dramatic construct. As for the construct itself, one could go back much further than Da Ponte and Mozart: to take but one example, Shakespeare's *Twelfth Night*. Here, the young female character (Viola), dressed as a boy, is sent by Count Orsino as his love emissary to Olivia: the latter falls in love with the boy who appears before her, who is supposedly prosecuting his master's suit. Shakespeare's gender confusions were all the more entertaining, in that the young man who originally played Viola had to convey the femininity of her character (that exerts its attraction on Orsino) and the masculinity of her disguise (that makes Olivia fall for her). The operatic treatment in reverse, with a mezzo soprano or alto playing a male role but subsequently cross-dressing as a female character, is no more than yet another variation of a centuries-old theatrical device. It is thus both Faublas and Octavian who have ancient stage pedigrees.

The Marschallin – a Marquise by another name

The final main character in *Der Rosenkavalier* to be considered in terms of performance and authorship is Die Feldmarschallin Fürstin Werdenberg (Marie Theres'), called throughout the piece the Marschallin. Although she appears only in Act I, and in the second half of Act III, the Marschallin is a role that can make a huge impression on audiences and, by their own admission, on some notable singers who have performed her. In her reminiscences of the role, Lotte Lehmann wrote:

> It became one of my favourite roles, yes, I think even the one I loved most. It is a part in which one has to be an actress to be convincing. I don't believe that anyone can be

---

[45] Hamm./Osers, p. 76.

really successful if she is only a good singer and not at the same time a good actress. This role must be played with great subtlety and it takes a long time to make it really one's own. Only a fully mature mind can grasp the delicate feelings of this aging woman who says goodbye to love and to youth with a smile.[46]

Strauss himself, referring to the 'aging woman' in his 1942 reminiscences of the première of *Der Rosenkavalier*, had an important requirement:

> The Marschallin must be a young, beautiful lady aged thirty-two at most, who comes across to herself as an 'old lady' once, when comparing herself in a bad mood with the seventeen year old Octavian, but she is absolutely not David's Magdalena, who incidentally is often played too old. Octavian is neither the first nor the last lover of the beautiful Marschallin, who also must not play the end of her first act sentimentally or as a tragic farewell to life, but always with Viennese grace and lightness, with one eye moist and the other dry.[47]

53 Elizabeth Harwood as the Marschallin, Glyndebourne Festival Opera 1980 and 1982, described by Max Loppert as "a beautifully measured creation … a true Marschallin"

[46] Lotte Lehmann, *Memoirs of Rosenkavalier* (essay in sleevenote to RCA Victor LP boxed set LCT-6005 (2), pp. 7–10 (pp. 9–10).
[47] Richard Strauss, *Betrachtungen und Erinnerungen*, ed. Willi Schuh, 3rd edition (Zurich: Atlantis, 1981), pp. 237–8.

As with Octavian, *Le Nozze di Figaro* and this time its older woman character, Countess Almaviva, has generally been regarded as a prototype, if not *the* prototype, for the Marschallin.[48] Moreover, even though the name 'Marquise' figured in the very first scenarios for *Der Rosenkavalier*, for a long time very little consideration was given, in critical commentary on the work, to the actual features of the society lady described in Louvet de Couvray's novel – how she might be dramatised and portrayed onstage – since she was regarded merely as a literary figure, and not as a stage creature. In other words, before thought was given to the Marquise de Bay of *L'Ingénu libertin* as a possible precursor of the Marschallin, she seemed to have no obvious or immediate onstage predecessor. The role was thus assumed to be a more original stage creation from Hofmannsthal's pen than, it will be argued, was truly the case. Jörg Schuster echoed and summarised earlier commentators in this respect, when he wrote in the Introduction to *Diary IV*:

> As Hofmannsthal worked on the libretto, the balletic and pantomimic character based on the Molière *comédie-ballet*, which was in Kessler's mind, became less and less significant. In place of the ornamental dance-like elements [...] there arose a comedy for music with clearly differentiated lyrical and psychological elements. This tendency is expressed most clearly in the Marschallin, who is basically a newly-conceived figure compared with the initial scenario, and who feels herself to be a ageing woman, who finally renounces her young lover, Octavian.[49]

Kessler was in fact absolutely in agreement with the treatment that Hofmannsthal began to give to the role of the Marschallin as the character took shape in his head. Yet Schuster is right to point out, as Hoffmann and others have done before him, that the initial scenario makes no mention of the Marschallin coming to the fore, and leading off in the trio that was to form the musical climax of Act III. Kessler's own original *Diary* entry for the end of Act III merely recorded: 'Pourceaugnac, who believes that they are all nobles, is arrested and crushed.' Hofmannsthal, in the first variant, wrote: 'Fablas appears *en travesti*. The Marquise confirms that he is a man.' The clue to what might have been in Kessler's mind, at least, comes however from his final *Diary* entry for 10 February 1909, after the original act order had been restored following his decision to make Sophie and Faublas strangers to each other. The entry for the culmination of Act III reads: 'Faublas' offer of service and love scene Sophie X Faublas'.[50]

The question is precisely what the capital X signifies here. It could merely mean Sophie AND Faublas but a possible – and, in context, perfectly plausible – explanation is that Kessler merely wrote a capital X rather than specifying that the Marquise was also to figure here. The words 'love scene' (*Liebesszene*) would thus refer to the love triangle of Marschallin, Octavian and Sophie and its resolution into the Sophie–Octavian duet. For it is scarcely conceivable that Kessler and

---

[48] Jefferson, p. 13.
[49] *Diary IV*, p. 21.
[50] *Diary IV*, pp. 559–60.

54 Hugo von Hofmannsthal at work in his salon at Rodaun,
his house just outside Vienna

Hofmannsthal, deconstructing and rearranging all the major elements of *L'Ingénu libertin* as they had decided to do, would omit the highlight of that piece – its longest and most striking musical number – and dispose of the characters in some other way. Indeed, the Act III trio of *L'Ingénu libertin* could be said to be so striking and remarkable that Kessler and Hofmannsthal may have regarded it as wise counsel to make no specific written references to it as their work on *Der Rosenkavalier* progressed. The opérette and the opera were always going to end in this way, both men knew it and had agreed it, and there was therefore no need to write down any further detail. The detailed way of doing so, in libretto form, came to Hofmannsthal gradually as his work on Act III progressed, and he undoubtedly gave a deeper and more elaborate wistful dimension to the Marschallin, as he characterised her in words, than the Marquise of Artus can be said to possess. This, however, is partly because of the timelines of the respective narratives: in *L'Ingénu libertin* we see the start of the affair, the conquest by the Marquise of the youthful affections of Faublas and their resulting night of lovemaking. She therefore has to be characterised as beautiful, elegant, attractive and vibrant, and as a lady with enough presence of mind and social skill to conduct her affairs under the nose of her foppish husband and of Rosambert, the man with designs to make her his mistress! The Marschallin has all these qualities too, but we see her and Octavian at the end of their affair (it is never revealed exactly how long it has lasted), and this allows Hofmannsthal, with the Feldmarschall conveniently and always well away from Vienna, to develop different aspects of her character: the lonely woman behind the mask of an assured, elegant, all-commanding social presence.

However, in theatrical terms she is still basically the Marquise, the *maîtresse de l'heure* (to borrow Kessler's phrase), the central figure in the Act III dénouement. The claim, therefore, that she is 'a newly-conceived figure compared with the initial scenario' is simply not supported by the evidence, which now includes detailed knowledge of the role played by the Marquise in *L'Ingénu libertin*, and the striking performance given in that role by its first and only exponent, Arlette Dorgère.

Long-distance collaboration

The stage was set for the *Rosenkavalier* project in the brief but highly intense personal collaboration between Kessler and Hofmannsthal, between 9 and 22 February 1909. The period of time spent putting flesh on the bones, or inserting 'the words [that] are still missing' as Kessler had written to his sister, then ran from the moment that they parted company in Berlin and began to correspond. As close analysis will show, the thoughts and ideas exchanged by both men between late February 1909 and January 1911 are as important and revealing in considering the creation of *Der Rosenkavalier* as the thoughts and ideas exchanged between Hofmannsthal and Strauss during the same period. There can be no doubt, either, that Hofmannsthal and Kessler both thought from the outset that they were authoring the new work together: there is no other explanation for the intensive dramaturgical, textual and stage business exchanges they had by letter, Kessler coming up with a constant stream of suggestions as to how and why the characters would and should behave as they did, whenever Hofmannsthal sent him the emerging libretto, scene by scene (sometimes) and act by act. In total, Kessler sent 46 *Rosenkavalier* letters to Hofmannsthal, mostly long, detailed and full of constructive – and occasionally hard-hitting – criticism, and he received 38 letters from Hofmannsthal in return. (This compares with 37 letters from Hofmannsthal to Strauss in the same period, and 36 in return.[51]) The Strauss–Hofmannsthal correspondence over *Der Rosenkavalier* has long been regarded as providing detailed insight into the ways in which such an opera can be created. Reconsideration of the Hofmannsthal-Kessler correspondence on *Der Rosenkavalier* is similarly instructive, especially if it takes particular account of the relevant *Diary* entries and, above all, of the stage pictures and dramaturgy that were in Kessler's mind on the basis of his theatrical experience with *L'Ingénu libertin* at the Bouffes Parisiens.

'I am hard at work on the opera,' wrote Hofmannsthal to Kessler on 17 March 1909[52] and, a month later, 'You of course will get a copy [of the Act I libretto] simultaneously [with Strauss].'[53] Kessler received his copy on 17 May 1909 and wrote a three-page critique the same day: he found the language put by Hofmannsthal

---

[51] Klaus Dieter Schneider, 'Harry Graf Kesslers Einfluß auf die Gestaltung der Komödie für Musik "Der Rosenkavalier"'. Typed diss. (Celle, 1970), held by the Hofmannsthal Archive, Freies Deutsches Hochstift, Frankfurt am Main.
[52] Burger, p. 214.
[53] Burger, p. 218.

into Baron Ochs's mouth, particularly in his aria, much too poetical and out of character; he found the Marschallin's aria slightly too sad and sensitive (making her not sufficiently Voltairean as a character); and he suggested some new stage business whereby Octavian tries to leave the Marschallin's bedroom and Ochs keeps stopping him from making good his escape in Act One. This stage business can be seen in virtually every production of *Der Rosenkavalier* up to the present day. Kessler followed up the next day with an even longer letter, reinforcing and justifying all his reservations about the Ochs aria, revising his initial opinion of the Marschallin ('The Marschallin seems to me to be the most successful of the characters') and adding new ideas for the role of Octavian, to make him bolder, more manly, less effeminate: he also had praise for the introduction of the characters in the levée scene, for 'the little moor who brings in the chocolate' and he highlighted the generally amusing qualities of the whole act – 'up among the very best, stylistically, of your work'.[54] Kessler makes no further reference to the 'little moor' but his February 1909 visualisation of the concluding scene of the opera ('all that I claim for myself') had included, as we have seen, 'a few little negro boys' left onstage as the lights dimmed, the moonlight grew bright and a Straussian *diminuendo* ended the piece. This shows that this particular piece of visual stage imagery had been in Kessler's mind from the outset, all the more interesting in that there are no signs of any little negro or moorish pageboys in the surviving photographs of the production of *L'Ingénu libertin* – although, of course, precisely that construct – a handsome black servant and a boy slave in Moorish dress – figure in Plate Four, 'The Countess's Levée', in Hogarth's 'Marriage à-la-Mode', which Mary E. Gilbert (in particular) has analysed in great detail for its many visual and narrative correspondences with *Der Rosenkavalier*.[55] Kessler had mentioned this specific plate as part of the original scenario, in his *Diary* entry for 10 February 1909 and had long been an enthusiastic admirer of the narrative force and detailed observation to be found in Hogarth's pictures: his comments on the Hogarths in the Royal Academy Winter Exhibition of January 1908 are also pertinent: 'When you decrypt a Hogarth picture, you go from one idea to another, each of which is an exciting and significant and newly-projected shape; among modernist painters, the one who comes closest to him in this respect is Bonnard.'[56] Six years previously, while studying Hogarth's pictures intensively in London, Kessler had referred to him as 'the most significant painter in English art' and had added: 'However, in terms of detail he remains one of the great masters of all time, the greatest pure "painter" of the English race'.[57] The stage imagery to be found in Hogarth's scenes, which could be used for an onstage levée, thus must have added significantly to the visual impact on Kessler of the levée scene that he had seen in Act III of *L'Ingénu libertin*.

---

[54] Burger, pp. 227–30.
[55] Mary E. Gilbert, 'Painter and Poet: Hogarth's Marriage à-la-Mode and Hofmannsthal's *Der Rosenkavalier*', Modern Languages Review, 64 (1969), 818–27.
[56] *Diary IV*, p. 403.
[57] *Diary III*, pp. 558–9.

On 20 May 1909 Hofmannsthal accepted the stage business proposed by Kessler in his first letter, and explained his portrayal of the Marschallin and the language he had placed in the mouth of Ochs, saying of the former:

> If she has great, almost too great an appeal here, then that is correct, because as I only understood while working on this, she and Ochs, as opposite poles, are the main characters, Octavian and Sophie, the pair of lovers, are subsidiary. The polarity is between absolute coarseness, but not without a certain wit, and a noble,[58] mature personality: and this is how the Marschallin will end the piece: she will not be abandoned, but with a magisterial gesture she will command Octavian to go to Sophie. (I am not at all fond of the pair of lovers as the epicentre, Wagner-like; this was not quite so clear to us when we drafted the scenario.[59]

This may not have been quite so clear to Hofmannsthal when the scenario was drafted, but it is precisely what Kessler had seen onstage at the Bouffes Parisiens when the Marquise de Bay takes command at the end of the Act III trio, and as suggested in Act One, it made a marked impression on him. To recapitulate: at the cue *je vous pardonne* the stage directions in the *mise en scène* are:

> Sophie, still in the number three position, takes the blindfold off Faublas, who implores the Marquise. The latter, smiling, indicates Sophie to him. Faublas, turning sideways, holds out his arms to her. Sophie throws herself into them.[60]

These are very precise gestural indications, as if for a dumb show or pantomime, and Kessler cannot have failed to take them in when he saw them sung and acted. However, before he could make any reply to Hofmannsthal, a second letter arrived (also dated 20 May) with a warm reaction to Kessler's earlier words of praise: 'A thousand thanks for your second lovely letter. I am truly delighted that implementation of our joint scenario gives you pleasure, taken all in all' and Hofmannsthal went on to undertake a rethink of Ochs's aria ('If you feel this so strongly I am convinced that you must basically be right') and to reveal how much he was deriving from the entire exercise:

> Otherwise it will be for the Marschallin and the Baron to share the main interest between them: this is how I now see the accents in the mechanics of this little staging (**and incidentally I shall have learned quite a lot from it**).[61]

The tone of Hofmannsthal's letters to Kessler at this time often suggests that Hofmannsthal is writing not only for Kessler's pleasure but also for his approval. It indicates a voice of inexperience seeking ratification by someone with greater theatrical understanding and insight. Even the new features and developments that

---

[58] The German word here is 'vornehm', meaning superior, posh, refined, even aristocratic – I have used 'noble' for its allusive reference to nobility and to nobleness of character.
[59] Burger, p. 225.
[60] *mise en scène*, p. 40.
[61] Burger, p. 230 – my added emphasis.

Hofmannsthal was introducing as the libretto progressed were, however, within the parameters of the piece that the two men had discussed and envisioned together, and it will have come as no surprise to Kessler that Hofmannsthal now saw the Marschallin and Baron Ochs as the key figures. As suggested above, from the moment that Kessler had reverted to the original act order but had turned Faublas and Sophie into strangers to each other, he had hit upon the dramatic motivation and mainspring of the whole piece ('these changes will turn Pourceaugnac from an almost passive figure into the main driving force of the work; he is the cause of all his own misfortune and he is even responsible for Sophie and Faublas getting to know each other'). Nor can he ever have entertained any doubts about the key role to be played by the Marquise, or Marschallin, in her new incarnation, as the central, most important female character, particularly in the Act III dénouement. As the reception of *L'Ingénu libertin* has shown, Arlette Dorgère as the Marquise de Bay had been the undoubted star of the piece, rising in particular to the extended musical and dramatic highlight in the third act in which she takes charge of the situation, confronts Faublas with the decision he has to make – choose Sophie or me – and hands him over to the younger woman, with a tear in her eye but with magisterial dignity, once Faublas has finally confessed his true feelings. Kessler's reply to Hofmannsthal's second letter of 20 May reflected this precisely:

> I am very interested by what you say about the Marschallin. The character as such is completely plausible: I am just fascinated to know how you will place her at the right distance from the audience in the third act. By the way, I can name a contemporary of hers who was very like her, Jeanne d'Albert de Luynes, Comtesse de Verrue, a wonderful friend of the Regent, who wrote her own epitaph with the following words: *Here, in profound peace/This voluptuous lady died/Who, to make absolutely certain/Enjoyed her paradise in this world.* I can imagine the Marschallin too being the author of these words.[62]

Adding a further plea for Octavian to be made a more vivid, headstrong character so as to bring out more contrast between the mezzo in male attire and the mezzo cross-dressed as Mariandel, Kessler finished the *Rosenkavalier* section of this letter with a revealing sentence in answer to Hofmannsthal's admission on how much he had now learned: 'I am delighted that this little comedy has proved to be useful in general for you, I hope it is merely the start of a series.' It does not demand deep analysis to detect a master/pupil tone in Kessler's words (a tone that Hofmannsthal was subsequently to find somewhat wearisome, as his letter of 27

---

[62] Burger, p. 233. Whether or not Kessler remembered this at the time of his letter to Hofmannsthal, a very similar quote had been sent in a note from Bernhard von Bülow to Kessler's mother in 1878 after she had rebuffed his amorous advances: 'I see that I was wrong and you are not like the witty lady who placed this epitaph on her gravestone *Here lies a lady who enjoyed her paradise on earth, uncertain of the one beyond the grave* (CW, I, p. 78). It is at least possible that Kessler had seen certain features of his beautiful, thespian mother in the Marquise of Arlette Dorgère and was now seeing them in the emerging character of the Marschallin.

January 1910 to his wife Gerty clearly indicated),[63] and to conclude that he saw the authorial relationship between them – at this stage – as if it were proceeding according to plan.

Hofmannsthal's next letter, a week later, admitted the force of Kessler's objections to the lyrical poetry that had been placed in the mouth of Baron Ochs ('I am eternally grateful to you for your sharp and lively critique'), added that the aria had now been rewritten, and he then addressed – for the first time in their *Rosenkavalier* correspondence – the question of Strauss's musical style. The reservations that Hofmannsthal expressed were that Strauss would simply ladle a symphonic outpouring over the narrative dialogue in the libretto ('he pours an – unnecessary – symphony over it like sauce over a roast') unless forced into musical depiction of each of the characters ('through the arias I force him into characterising the main figures by means of their melodic lines – not just through the orchestra – and this is the only way an organic opera can come about').[64] Hofmannsthal went on to plead for Kessler to approve the rewritten Ochs passages, confirmed that he had already enlivened the role of Octavian and ended:

> Act II is on its way to you by registered letter in the same post. Please give me your critique. As I have said, it has not yielded as much as I and III. The ending is (maybe?) a little quiet. **But, just like everything else, it is sticking to the great scenario. I am still very happy about your participation.**[65]

These few words from Hofmannsthal are almost as if he were trying to forestall the criticism from Kessler that he knew – or felt strongly – would be forthcoming, in particular his insistence that he was sticking to their joint scenario. But Kessler replied positively and constructively five days later. He now praised the Ochs aria as having exactly the right tone, or value.[66] He suggested a number of ways in which Ochs's words could be accompanied by mime or gesture and he asked Hofmannsthal to have a word with Strauss, so that the music would clearly differentiate such moments, 'by becoming *piano* and *detached* from the overall flow, maybe by different orchestration or a new motif or something'. Kessler went on to say:

> Another passage where the music can add greatly to the comedy is on p. 24, 4 lines from the bottom, the lines *Dear Sir* which Ochs will have to sing fortissimo *all puffed up like a turkey*. The music must have all these accents *within itself*, this is what makes Wagner so dramatic, the fact that the accents, the *mimic* ones, are so heavily underlined musically that no singer can ever miss them.[67]

---

[63] Referring to Kessler's many (justified) suggestions for improving Act III of *Cristina's Homecoming*, Hofmannsthal wrote sarcastically: 'Before going to bed I usually find a letter from Kessler with suggestions on how the last act of the comedy really ought to be done, or something equally pleasant' (*Diary IV*, p. 18).
[64] Burger, p. 234.
[65] Burger, p. 235 – my added emphasis.
[66] Once again, Kessler uses the French word 'valeur'.
[67] Burger, p. 236.

Act Three: Scene Two – characterisation and authorship

Kessler's letter of 5 June 1909 is his longest in his *Rosenkavalier* correspondence with Hofmannsthal. It contains a detailed critique of Act II, with unqualified praise for the first 7 pages – the arrival of the Rosenkavalier and his meeting with Sophie ('what is most important of all, it is musical through and through, i.e. devised for music') – and with suggested minor changes to the libretto on pages 7, 9, 10, 11, 13, 15, 16, 24, 26 and 27; some of Kessler's objections being to the language placed in the mouth of Sophie, and some being dramaturgical in nature, in particular to make clearer the motivation for the Italian intriguers Valzacchi and Annina to change sides from Ochs to Octavian. (In general, Hofmannsthal rejected Kessler's linguistic suggestions or merely changed words here and there, but accepted his dramaturgical, plot and narrative points.) It went on to say:

> I am not very happy about the ending to the act either. As it is, we have *three quiet* act endings. I think that this one should be loud and *buffo*-like, as a contrast to the quiet and contemplative endings to Acts I and III.[68]

Kessler then signed off by expressing delight that Hofmannsthal was writing the piece 'so quickly and easily, since it offers me the best possible proof that you are in good health and mentally alert'.[69]

This letter from Kessler of 5 June (which he described as 'endless' in a follow-up letter the very next day) illustrates perfectly the need to superimpose the Hofmannsthal–Kessler correspondence on the Hofmannsthal–Strauss correspondence – and on the Kessler *Diary*. For Kessler's precise points were taken up by Hofmannsthal, as if they were his own original thoughts, in his letter to Strauss of 12 June. Extracting and reordering the essential points reveals the following:

Kessler **to Hofmannsthal, 5 June**	**Hofmannsthal to Strauss, 12 June**
Nuances of expression must be marked in this aria [by Ochs] so that the music brings out the characterisation and emphasises it.	When you enter once more into the detail of composition, further appropriate and characteristic shades may suggest themselves to you for this aria [by Ochs].
There must always be a haystack nearby (at this point Ochs cups his hand over his mouth and leans conspiratorially towards the ear of the Marschallin).	The line 'there must always be a haystack nearby' can never conceivably be acted or sung in any but a sentimental manner. Ochs must whisper it to the Marschallin as a stupid and yet sly piece of coarse familiarity, with his hand half covering his mouth;
As it is, we have *three quiet* act endings. I think that this one should be loud and *buffo*-like. [...] At the same time, more pantomimic, more ballet-like.	Three 'quiet' curtains are impossible; they might even endanger the whole effect. [...] This gives us an energetic, grotesque, ballet-like curtain for the Act...

---

[68] Burger, p. 238.
[69] Burger, p. 239.

This is the only way of properly justifying Annina and Valzacchi switching from Ochs to Octavian, the fact being that Ochs is *miserly* and *does not pay them*.	I know already how to do it: Annina demands a tip for bringing her message, the miserly Ochs refuses her…
I would prefer to see Valzacchi brought on as well, with a *buffo*-like balletic quarrel between both of them and Ochs, who puffs himself up and calls in his retinue..	…Valzacchi comes to support her, the Baron calls in his retinue and makes them beat up and throw out the Italians, while he himself smugly watches and hums his little song.
The music must have all these accents *within itself,* this is what makes Wagner so dramatic, the fact that the accents, the *mimic* ones, are so heavily underlined that no singer can ever miss them.[70]	Here the music must force the singers to act with unfailing authenticity, as Wagner's operas so happily contrive to do. […] Wagner differentiates such things in declamation with marvellous nicety.[71]

In addition to writing to Strauss on 12 June with the points outlined above, Hofmannsthal also wrote to Kessler the same day. 'You are absolutely right about the act ending, I shall look for a *buffo*-like finale.' This was followed by an extraordinary outburst against Strauss:

> Three quiet act endings will not do! If only I had a more refined, more artistic composer. Everything he says, everything he wants, his every tendency I find really rather disgusting.[72]

It was Strauss however, going further than Kessler had done and reordering the draft Act II much more radically, who was to solve the dramaturgical problems that had already been identified, when he intervened decisively a month later. His letter of 7 July 1909 was a masterly combination of the reassuring ('Well then, up to the Baron's entrance everything is fine') and the devastating ('But I feel that, as it now stands, I can't do anything with the second act. It's too much on one level. I must have a great dramatic construction if I want to keep myself interested for so long in a particular setting').[73] Meanwhile the dialogue between Hofmannsthal and Kessler had continued. On 26 June 1909 Hofmannsthal wrote to Kessler:

> I shall be very brief and business-like, with no apologies, since the 'business' is a happy turn of events that has brought us together, an amusing, friendly plaything that binds us. Turning to Quinquin, Act II. I have done the burlesque ending in rhyming verse, with a balletic punch-up as the finale. It is rather strange that I did not end it like this from the outset, it must have been a combination of absent-mindedness and semi-mindless adherence to the scenario that had already been settled.[74]

The correspondence between both men now began to embrace, in much more

---

[70] Burger, pp. 235–40.
[71] Hamm./Osers, pp. 34–5.
[72] Burger, p. 244.
[73] Hamm./Osers, pp. 37–9.
[74] Burger, p. 247.

detail, the play that Hofmannsthal was attempting to write simultaneously with *Der Rosenkavalier*. Analysis of the letters exchanged on the dramaturgy of *Cristina's Homecoming* shows, just as clearly as those concerning *Der Rosenkavalier*, how much Hofmannsthal was looking for, and how much he depended on his friend Kessler for guidance with plot, dramatic structure and overall theatrical style. Kessler's letter of 7 July 1909 illustrates perfectly the way opera and play were being interwoven in both men's thoughts:

> [...] I have found the time to read through the scenes in your play carefully several times. But I find it impossible to criticize anything *in particular*; for my objections concern the style of the *whole*, which seems to me somewhat broad and conventional, even a bit old-fashioned Viennese. I do not know whether today's theatregoing public will have the patience for this sort of scene painting. Especially because there is a *second* aspect; the fact that the events, the life conjured up in such detail that has to be absorbed, is somewhat external to a stage comedy. People enjoy this in opera or in farce, when everything happens simply because puppet strings are being pulled skillfully; but in my view people want something more in a stage comedy.[75]

Having then made a number of (quite drastic) dramaturgical suggestions for simplifying and decluttering the stage in *Cristina's Homecoming*, Kessler finished his letter with a further tribute to the quality of Hofmannsthal's work on *Der Rosenkavalier*: 'In this respect, in my view, *Quinquin* represents major progress as a work of art, as a piece *that works*.' Coming from Kessler, whose tongue could be sharp and malicious about the many failures and fiascos he had experienced as a spectator in European theatres, this practical affirmation of the writing that had been done so far must have been very welcome to Hofmannsthal: Kessler knew that *L'Ingénu libertin* had worked in theatrical terms, and if he were seeing an equally effective new construct emerging from Hofmannsthal's pen, the chances of a successful outcome onstage must have seemed quite high.

Indeed, Hofmannsthal's reaction to this criticism was almost ecstatic: 'a thousand thanks' and 'your letter is precious to me, especially just now when I am assembling, working on, *contextualizing* the comedy'. And, once again reflecting on how much he was learning (implicitly from Kessler as part of this whole learning process), Hofmannsthal continued:

> The short, concise sentence you wrote on the atmosphere of the comedy is among the best of many good things that you have said or written to me. It is good that *Quinquin* is better; it needs to be, and the converse would be depressing. You have *to make progress* year by year in these matters. And the fact is that I have only been trying to assimilate and appropriate the métier of stage comedy for precisely the last two years.[76]

Kessler accepted these kind words from Hofmannsthal graciously, in a letter in

---

[75] Burger, p. 250.
[76] Burger, p. 251.

reply of 27 July 1909, but suggested that the author should not restrict himself to French authors and dramatists as his role models:

> As for the *atmosphere* that is to be created from *within*, i.e. from within the main characters, it seems to me that in this respect you should not take the French as your model but rather Shakespeare, Kleist, Ibsen, Hauptmann. The French always *cloak things* with intellect, something *moral*, and thus no longer purely sensory and artistic.[77]

In the midst of these exchanges on both works, Hofmannsthal reported the following day that he had now obtained the libretto of *L'Ingénu libertin*. He had clearly had time to read it, and to make comparisons with the *Rosenkavalier* draft libretto as it now stood, for he said:

> I have also obtained the libretto of the Faublas operetta, which gave us our impetus in those first hours in Weimar, and I find it very delightful. It is by Louis Artus. If my effort *as a whole* turns out just as good, and then has a little extra something, then I shall be very content.[78]

Hofmannsthal did not mention in this letter that he had also obtained from Paris a copy of the stage comedy by Artus, *Coeur de Moineau (Heart of a Sparrow)*, which had been a huge hit at the Théâtre de l'Athénée in 1905 (see Act One). *Heart of a Sparrow* is a light, drawing room comedy about a man who finds all women irresistible: a reading of this text will have given Hofmannsthal further insights into Artus's stage writing style. Purely coincidentally, there is an offstage aria by an Italian tenor at the end of Act II of the play, which enchants the two onstage protagonists as they sit on their onstage balcony and look out over the bay, listening to a sentimental Italian song wafting over the evening air. Did this prompt a thought in Hofmannsthal's mind for the *Rosenkavalier* levée scene?

In the spirit of fully fledged collaboration, embarked on in Weimar in February 1909, continued in Berlin later that month and pursued in correspondence thereafter, Kessler now absorbed and commented on the implications of Strauss's drastic revision of Act II. In a letter of 3 August 1909 he wrote:

> Strauss is undoubtedly right: the act is so much better, excellent even! I also love the *spooky face* motif that presages Act III. It is really very funny, all the more as it provides much deeper motivation for Lerchenau's aversion, which he doesn't realize (but the audience does), through the *manliness* of socalled Mariandel. I only see one obstacle to avoid, a departure from the balletic and ornamental in the duet, the scene with the bandages etc. I think these motifs have to be *accentuated* in rhythmical fashion, by repetition, parallel figures etc., like in Molière's little plays (Fourberies

---

[77] Burger, p. 252.
[78] Burger, p. 253.

de Scapin, e.g. the scene where the sack gets beaten etc.)[79] Nothing incites more laughter than comical situations in stylized performance. – Incidentally, I think that we three, you, Strauss and I, could deliver a regular little Sardou.[80] But, joking aside, of course Quinquin will be much better than Artus's Faublas, because the additional factor will be poetic *charm*, the individual and rare qualities of your vision.[81]

Once again, this is a very clear statement by Kessler of what it was he thought he was doing: providing Hofmannsthal with a structure, a vehicle, on the basis of which Hofmannsthal's poetic language could take wing. This particular letter, after some further strictures on the inadequacies of modern French writers ('the last one to have had charm was Musset'), finishes with some gloomy remarks on the sad fates of a number of personal friends in recent years ('suicide, grief, long and painful illness and death') and makes an enjoinder:

> Life, at least in certain areas, is a very dangerous and fragile affair. This is why we need a lot of humour **and a lot of good comedy, which Mr. v. H. will have to write for us**.[82]

In the summer of 1909 Kessler was travelling in France: his letters reached Hofmannsthal from Aix-en-Provence, Marseille, Arles, Avignon and, finally, from his mother's house at Sainte Honorine in Normandy. In every letter he had something to say about *Der Rosenkavalier* (and in most of them, something about *Cristina's Homecoming*). On 8 August 1909 Kessler wrote:

> I am imagining your tone in this direction. I am filled with great expectations thinking about this change of style in Quinquin and the stage comedy. [...] Every time I think of the very comical change that Strauss's brainwave has brought about, I am filled with delight. It is very good to be able to show Lerchenau's cowardice in Act II already, since Act III is so firmly built on that. He will surely start by trying to avoid the duel with Quinquin? In *fatherly* fashion, which cowardly old rogues like him love to do. At all events, I am impatient to see this duel scene.[83]

A week later, Hofmannsthal attempted to moderate Kessler's 'great expectations', writing on 15 August:

> I should like to say something: you are not expecting, are you, in the second act of the operetta a complete implementation of the *figures* from Molière comedies (parallelism, repetition etc.) any more than the first act has them. I have not adopted this

---

[79] In Act III Scene 2 of *Les Fourberies de Scapin*, Scapin hides Géronte in a sack, assumes a number of different threatening voices and beats the sack repeatedly, until Géronte realises what is happening and chases Scapin offstage.

[80] Victorien Sardou (1831–1908) was renowned as an author of well-made plays and had enjoyed great success with *Madame Sans-Gêne* (1893), co-written with Emile Moreau. The latter's son, Philippe Moreau, was the conductor of *L'Ingénu libertin*.

[81] Burger, p. 255.

[82] Burger, p. 256 – my added emphasis.

[83] Burger, p. 257.

tone, but a more nuanced one, with more realism – think of the flow of the first act. Nonetheless, the second act contains even more of the same controlled playing as the first. Strauss seems to be very happy with the new version and given his sound instinct, I can be certain that the main lines are right. Among the many advantages of the new version is that Faninal has become a really amusing character (previously he was just a stop-gap). Those to whom I have shown the finished work were very sorry that the Marschallin, who had become very endearing, does not appear in II. Since she really is the nicest character, I shall now have to do everything to ensure in III that she enjoys all the advantages of a dominating and at the same time moving situation, so that to the audience she becomes a main character or almost *the* main character.[84]

Nothing in what Hofmannsthal said here can have come as any real surprise to Kessler. He had seen the portrayal of the Marquise de Bay onstage and can have been in no doubt, in the third act of *L'Ingénu libertin*, just how she came to dominate proceedings in an equivalent and equally effective stage situation. He answered the points made by Hofmannsthal, both on the second and third acts, in a letter of 22 August, sent from Paris:

Obviously I never expected that the second act of the comedy[85] would be that stylized. But I am delighted that the balletic side will also come in here, because this mixture of reality and ballet-like acts was one of the considerations that launched the whole idea. [...] I also felt immediately that the Marschallin is a very specially moving figure. I find it absolutely appropriate to the natural gravitas of the characters if she comes to the fore in the third act. The whole course of the plot also provides her with the decisive role at a certain point: at that moment she naturally becomes *master of the hour*, or rather, *mistress*, and it is lovely if this moment then becomes, through its scope and brilliance, the supreme value[86] in the whole piece.[87]

The 'scope and brilliance' of the Marschallin's appearance in Act III of *Der Rosenkavalier*, her dismissal of Ochs from the stage, her launch of the trio with the words '*Hab' mir's gelobt...*' have indeed become, for many operagoers the world over, the 'supreme value in the whole piece', just as Kessler wrote, although this has as much, if not more, to do with Strauss's melodic invention at this point and with his brilliance in stretching a poignant moment into the realms of successive chromatic harmonies that illustrate perfectly the conflicting emotions being revealed by the characters onstage. Once again, one is reminded of the comment by Robert de Flers in respect of *L'Ingénu libertin*, when he wrote: 'The trio in the last act is the very best in opéra-comique, and of the utmost delicacy' (see Act One): in a different convention, Terrasse also excelled at the culminating moment

---

[84] Burger, pp. 258–9.
[85] Kessler uses the word 'Komödie' here, but the context makes it clear that he is thinking of, and meaning to refer to *Der Rosenkavalier*.
[86] *Valeur*, once again.
[87] Burger, pp. 259–60.

Act Three: Scene Two – characterisation and authorship 187

55 The first ever *Rosenkavalier* trio onstage – Minnie Nast as Sophie,
Eva von der Osten as Octavian and Margarethe Siems as the Marschallin
(Dresden, 26 January 1911)

56 The trio at Glyndebourne Festival Opera later in 1982:
Rachel Yakar as the Marschallin, Felicity Lott as Octavian, Deborah Rees as Sophie
in a production designed by Erté

of his *conte galant*. Kessler is the binding link between *L'Ingénu libertin* and *Der Rosenkavalier*, the only one of the team of three who saw both works onstage. And as Kessler's letter shows, the Marschallin came out under Hofmannsthal's pen exactly as she was destined to, and as the whole course of the plot indicated she would, on the basis of the character of the Marquise de Bay and of her central role in the resolution of *L'Ingénu libertin*. This cannot have come about by chance, and although Hofmannsthal's subsequent reading of the Artus libretto may have given him some additional ideas, the basic construct that had been agreed in February 1909 between Hofmannsthal and Kessler was the one to emerge.

From late August 1909, with the libretto taking detailed shape around the architecture of the piece, and with Strauss now articulating regular demands of his own for insertions and amendments to scenes he had already composed, in letters dated 9, 13 and 15 August 1909 for example,[88] the intensity of exchanges between Kessler and Hofmannsthal on all the constituent elements of *Der Rosenkavalier* began to abate, although comments and observations on what was being created still came back and forth. With his letter of 28 August 1909, Kessler sent to Hofmannsthal a number of books, designed to help him to develop his theatrical style and understanding: a volume of plays by Tristan Bernard that had just appeared ('very light reading but with lovely insights, for browsing in bed') and a selection of plays by Jean-François Regnard[89] ('these plays seemed to me to have an extraordinary similarity in style and colour with Quinquin, much more so than Molière') as well as: 'All in all the scenic invention (the pantomime) in Regnard seems to me almost more modern and clever than in Molière; whereas the human side, the characters, are incomparably weaker.'[90] Hofmannsthal replied to this letter on 10 September by saying that he was not that sure about Regnard, but preceding his comments, somewhat introspectively, with a fulsome personal tribute to Kessler and a frank admission that their relationship had now reached a point where he could never write [a letter to Kessler] without mentioning his own work – adding that this made Kessler unique, not even his own parents having enjoyed this status – but that his personal creative process was such that Kessler was never to interrogate him on exactly how things were going, 'whether this piece has been completed, that one started'; yet that he hoped, for all other stages of his productive output, that their relationship would become ever closer: 'Likewise I am expecting decisive advice from you on the Sylvia play, in due course.'[91] There are complex messages here which Kessler, possibly with the excitement of how matters had been progressing with *Der Rosenkavalier* and *Cristina's Homecoming*, may have failed to pick up: viewed dispassionately, and with the benefit of hindsight, Hofmannsthal was acknowledging the unique and creative role that Kessler had started to play,

---

[88] Hamm./Osers, pp. 46–8.
[89] Jean-François Regnard (1655°1709) was the author of *Le Joueur*, *Les Folies Amoureuses* and *Le Retour Imprévu*, among other plays.
[90] Burger, pp. 260–1.
[91] Burger, p. 261.

as dramatic adviser, confidant and sounding board, while drawing a line in the creative process that Kessler was not to cross. In the earlier letters there are no more than hints or indications of an ultimate severance of dependency, but the more of the *Rosenkavalier* libretto that Hofmannsthal – working simultaneously with Kessler and with Strauss – managed to complete, the more his personal possessiveness began to show. Within a year the dispute that arose between them over authorship of *Der Rosenkavalier* was to revisit this territory.

Between September and December 1909 Hofmannsthal and Kessler swapped ideas on possible titles for *Der Rosenkavalier*. Hofmannsthal and Strauss rejected *Quinquin* as a title because of its onomatopoeic associations with French farces such as *To-To* and *Rip-Rip* and Hofmannsthal asked Kessler what he thought of *Der Rosencavalier*. Kessler replied from Paris with a string of suggestions: *Der Grobian in Liebesnot, Der Grobian im Liebesspiel*, then *Die galanten Abenteuer des Barons von Lerchenau* (or *Baron von Ochs*).[92] On 18 December 1909 Hofmannsthal wrote 'I am quite firmly for *Ochs von Lerchenau*, which places the *buffo* centre stage.' In this, Hofmannsthal was reflecting Strauss's preference: as the Strauss–Hofmannsthal correspondence shows, Strauss remained in favour of *Ochs* as the title until mid-1910: 'Title? I'm still in favour of *Ochs*!'[93] But most of the main dramaturgical exchanges between Kessler and Hofmannsthal on *Der Rosenkavalier* had now taken place, and their correspondence began to embrace other theatrical projects, including the scenario for Hofmannsthal's social comedy *Der Schwierige (The Difficult Man)* and the imminent first production (by Max Reinhardt) of *Cristina's Homecoming* in Berlin. With this in mind, and with all that had passed between them since work on *Der Rosenkavalier* and on *Cristina's Homecoming* had begun in earnest in Weimar the preceding February, Hofmannsthal paid Kessler a compliment in his letter of 9 January 1910:

> I am very pleased by all that you have to say about these people. Thus does the theatre as a métier bring forth wonderful people here and there. Purely personally, Reinhardt is becoming more and more precious to me. **His and your existence are the factors that keep me in the theatre and are the means by which I shall in the end produce something adequate and lasting for the theatre.**[94]

There is no evidence, elsewhere in Hofmannsthal's correspondence, of him regarding any other friend quite in this light, although he never seems to have considered Kessler to be among his three closest personal friends; that accolade being bestowed on his own father, on Eberhard von Bodenhausen and on Richard Beer-Hofmann.[95] True, moreover, to his earlier stricture that he would always

---

[92] Burger, p. 266. Grobian indicates a coarse fellow, and Liebesnot/Liebesspiel a complicated love situation. Possible titles at this stage all made reference to Ochs.
[93] Hamm./Osers, p. 55.
[94] Burger, p. 272 – my added emphasis.
[95] Hugo von Hofmannsthal, Richard Beer-Hofmann, *Briefwechsel* (Frankfurt am Main: S. Fischer Verlag, 1972), p. vii.

be critical of Hofmannsthal's literary output where he found it to be at fault, Kessler (in a letter of 25 January 1910) did not shy away from criticism of *Cristina's Homecoming* even as Reinhardt began his initial rehearsals of the piece. He praised the magisterial beginning, the exposition, but found much wrong with the third act, and concluded:

> These are two lovely and powerful situations [in the final act] and they make me sorry that you have not been able to ask Reinhardt for more time, so as to perfect and finalise the third act. As I have said, I do not think the piece will fail, and it does contain so many lovely things that it would undoubtedly be a pity not to have it performed.[96]

Yet by 28 January, in a letter expressing uncertainty as to whether or not he would be able to attend the imminent première of *Cristina's Homecoming*, Kessler's reservations about the third act had hardened:

> All in all I do regret that the piece is going to be performed with the third act as it is. I have strong reservations that are increasing rather than diminishing. I find (this is a detail, but an important one) that Florindo's arrival just five minutes after Cristina has said 'yes' is a very old and stale theatrical device! Nor am I happy about the motivation for this return; it is right outside the piece, an afterthought of a mechanism, impossible to foresee on the basis of the original stagecraft.[97]

As with Kessler's dramaturgical criticisms and suggestions for *Der Rosenkavalier*, Hofmannsthal responded promptly to these critical remarks on Florindo and Cristina in the third act, writing on 1 February:

> In respect of Act III, I have retouched lots and lots of things, including some of the mimic indications, which should be very effective, and I have made big textual changes. The end of the first engagement scene between Cristina and Tomaso will remain more *in suspenso* and all the free accents of emerging tenderness have been saved for the final scene between the two of them. This is also when she calls him 'dearest one' for the first time. Both Reinhardt and I think that anything *more* in the Florindo scene in this piece is inconceivable, likewise any other, less discreet direction of this scene.[98]

Hofmannsthal had therefore clearly taken Kessler's criticisms on board and had discussed them with Reinhardt, whose judgement he respected (and in quoting Reinhardt, he was perhaps seeking to minimise Kessler's role and the force of his criticisms). In retrospect, for this first production they were too little and too late anyway. Kessler does not mention the première of *Cristina's Homecoming* in his *Diary*, but on 12 February 1910 he wrote to his sister Wilma:

---

[96] Burger, p. 275.
[97] Burger, p. 279.
[98] Burger, pp. 281–2.

Hofmannsthal's piece went as I had predicted; a great success for the first two acts, utterly destroyed and made useless by the complete failure of the third; the net result of course is a failure [...].[99]

Der Rosenkavalier was still never far from either man's thoughts, however. On 25 January 1910 Kessler met Thadée Natanson[100] in Paris by chance, and told him of the project: the outcome was a long and enthusiastic letter to Hofmannsthal suggesting that Natanson and Kessler should translate the libretto into French and then negotiate its rapid appearance on the Parisian stage, avoiding the Opéra Comique and entrusting the work instead to Director Franck, of the Gymnase and Théâtre Apollo, with a specially assembled orchestra and conductor and a continuous long run of performances immediately after the Dresden première.[101] The answer from Hofmannsthal was a resounding 'no', both because the translation rights had already been ceded to the publishers but equally because, in Hofmannsthal's view, Kessler was underestimating the 'dreadful, dispiriting, dismal task' of matching French words to Strauss's score. The promptness with which Hofmannsthal turned down the suggestion does however rather betray a reluctance on his part to give Kessler free rein – in French, which in Kessler's case was as good as his German and English – with his own artfully and skilfully constructed German libretto. Kessler took the refusal in his stride – 'A pity, it would have been amusing' – and moved on. More importantly, Hofmannsthal was now turning to the third act of *Der Rosenkavalier*, and wrote to Kessler on 8 March 1910:

> I am very well and hard at work, starting with III of the opera. It is not easy to get rid of the Baron and to resolve simultaneously the definitive situation between the 3 lovers (it has to be *simultaneous*, not sequential) but it is a delightful task. I hope to finish the act in 6–10 days.[102]

It took, inevitably, slightly longer, even though the mechanism for simultaneous resolution of the Marschallin/Octavian/Sophie relationship must have been perfectly clear to Kessler (and to Hofmannsthal) from the outset: the matrix for this, in Act III of *L'Ingénu libertin*, is the trio between the Marquise, Faublas and Sophie, which confronts Faublas with his moment of decision, and which resolves the love triangle in Sophie's favour. If, moreover, Hofmannsthal was merely referring to the difficulty of getting Baron Ochs offstage quickly and decisively so that the trio could get under way, he also had an elegant and ready-made example in the Artus libretto: immediately before the final chorus, the Marquise dismisses Faublas, suggesting that he marry Sophie in the country and keep out of Paris for

---

[99] Burger, p. 537.
[100] Thadée Natanson and his brothers moved in the same artistic circles in Paris as Kessler, their mutual friends including Misia Sert (Thadée's first wife), Pierre Bonnard, Edouard Vuillard and other members of the Nabis: *La Revue Blanche* was published by the Natansons until its closure in 1903. Thadée was also a playwright and was influential in the Parisian theatre world.
[101] Burger, pp. 275–6.
[102] Burger, p. 283.

57 The trio at Scottish Opera in 1971: Elizabeth Harwood as Sophie, Janet Baker as Octavian and Helga Dernesch as the Marschallin.

58 Triangular relationships abound in *Der Rosenkavalier*: Octavian courts Sophie as the household intriguers listen in (Act Two: Elizabeth Harwood as Sophie, Janet Baker as Octavian)

Act Three: Scene Two – characterisation and authorship 193

a time, for reasons of discretion, and bids farewell to the Comte de Rosambert. In agreeing to go, the latter suggests he might enjoy some 'compensations' in return for his silence, but the Marquise turns him down and says she has vowed to behave properly from now on.[103] Hofmannsthal in effect recreates the same moment when Baron Ochs, realising that Mariandel and Octavian are one and the same, and that Octavian has been having an affair with the Marschallin, wonders aloud what he should think of the whole 'qui-pro-quo': the Marschallin, fixing him with a long and steady gaze, reminds him that he is a gentleman and tells him that he should think nothing at all about it. The dramatic complicity thus created between the Marquise–Rosambert and the Marschallin–Ochs, and their respective partings, is identical at this point.[104]

His 'delightful task' resolved, on 27 March 1910 Hofmannsthal reported that he was only missing the last five to six minutes of the opera, but further exchanges by letter were mostly on general matters of theatrical interest to both men, including a dramatic and theatrical *credo* from Kessler in a long letter that was clearly intended to stimulate Hofmannsthal's thinking about his own qualities as a dramatist. Kessler had been to see a Berlin production of *Tantris der Narr (Tantris the Fool)* by Ernst Hardt, a dramatic treatment of the Tristan legend that had shared the 1908 Schiller Prize.[105] Kessler's intended message to Hofmannsthal emerges clearly from his account of the piece (emphasis in original):

> In my view, *Tantris* has far greater qualities than you realize simply by reading it. Hardt is undoubtedly a *born dramatist*, such as we simply have not had since Schiller and Wagner (I am totally disregarding here poetic and literary qualities). The 'values' in every situation, from the first to the last, are as completely correct as those in a picture by a 'born artist'; or to put it another way, *all the tensions are in the right places*, absolutely right in terms of intensity, elasticity and tempo in the way they relate to all the other tensions in the piece, they all come together as a single organism, a quality that you can judge entirely as you wish in general aesthetic terms, just like the design of a chair or a cupboard; but this is the fundamental quality of a true dramatist, without which all his poetry and onstage characterization is as ineffective as a lovely ornament on a chair that you cannot sit on. I now find that Hardt has this quality, as stated, to a degree that you could almost label genius [...].[106]

Kessler's reference to poetry and ornamentation betrayed perhaps an undercurrent in his thinking about Hofmannsthal that had been present almost from

---

[103] Artus, p. 164.
[104] As Ochs wonders aloud what he should think of the love affair that has just become apparent to him, the resolution is as follows. Marschallin *(mit einem langen Blick)*: Er ist, mein' ich, ein Kavalier? *(dann mit grosser Sicherheit)*: Da wird Er sich halt gar nichts denken. Das ist's, was ich von Ihm erwart. [You are, I think, a gentleman? *(then, very confidently)*: So you will think nothing of it at all. That is what I expect from you] (Pahlen, pp. 245–7).
[105] Ernst Hardt was the pen name of Ernst Stockhardt (1876–1947), dramatist and theatre manager, and an acquaintance of Kessler from 1907 onwards.
[106] Burger, p. 287.

the start of their relationship: his fear that Hofmannsthal might end up as no more than a 'tea party poet and boudoir philosopher'. However, as often happened in their correspondence, Kessler followed up his letter on Hardt as a born dramatist with more encouraging words for Hofmannsthal, comparing him favourably with Tristan Bernard, whose play *Le Costaud des Epinettes (The Local Tough Guy)* Kessler had just seen:

> However the main charm is in the individual *colouring*, which is brought about by mixing up different types from completely different milieux. Talking to a theatre director or banker even a thief or a pimp becomes quite romantic. The highly-coloured atmosphere that is created in this way is what makes Bernard's plays so charming. But actually he has *little* poetry and so he substitutes sentimentality for the places that poetry would have been needed; like most of the French, actually. This is where you would be vastly superior to him, because you could cloak similar subjects, playing across several different worlds, in true poetry.[107]

Their correspondence went on to cover several other projects, including a revised and much-abridged version of *Cristina's Homecoming* that was to travel to Budapest before its first appearance in Vienna, at the Theater an der Wien (in late May). Then, however, on 5 July 1910, Hofmannsthal sent Kessler a letter that was to cause a serious rupture in the personal and professional relationship between them that had been building over the previous decade. The exchanges that followed go to the heart of what their collaboration had been all about.

---

[107] Burger, p. 290.

Epilogue

Two views of the authorship of *Der Rosenkavalier*

This is what Hofmannsthal wrote to Kessler:

> My dear, as you liked the comedy for music, maybe more than it deserves, I should like to dedicate it to you, if I may. (Obviously the book edition, not the purely commercial libretto). I had this idea of denoting you simply with your initials, as the *hidden helper*. But perhaps your full name is more correct – but then without any attribution.[1]

These two words *hidden helper*, in Hofmannsthal's letter to Kessler of 5 July 1910, reached the latter while he was exercising with his regiment, the 3rd Guard Lancers, in Potsdam. Kessler makes no mention of its receipt in his *Diary*, nor does he record anything other than militaria in occasional entries (which are sparse in this period anyway) until 10 August, when he said farewell with regret to the squadron he had been leading. It was not until 21 August 1910 – almost seven weeks later – that Kessler replied to Hofmannsthal, from Paris, as follows:

> As for the *Rosenkavalier* dedication, very many thanks for your kind thought. I actually thought we had agreed, in accordance with your wishes, that my part in it should not be mentioned officially; and I would still be happy if this is so. On the other hand, and I have to say this, even though I am very unhappy saying it to you of all people, I find the dedication as you have formulated it *not agreeable*: I mean the word 'helper'. You and Borchardt and I are 'helpers' with Schröder's Homer, or if you like, I with *Cristina*; i.e. we help to finalise and polish a work that has basically been produced already by an author, by means of good advice and greater or lesser *corrections*. [...] In the *Rosenkavalier* case however, the very concept and the implementation of the pantomime, the essentials, i.e. the *substance* of the piece come partly from me and partly from you. If subsequently you have taken this outline and built an airy and charming poetic structure on top of it, this no more reduces me to the status of a mere 'helper' than it reduces you to a 'helper' of Strauss, who has decorated your poetry with music. In the absolutely normal, common sense of the term, all three of us are *collaborators*,[2] and this is the only term I would permit to be used in the dedication, if any. To repeat, I am perfectly happy with *nothing at all*: but if there has

---

[1] Burger, p. 296.
[2] 'Mitarbeiter' in German.

to be a dedication to me, it has to be to me as a *collaborator,* such as: to the unknown collaborator H.K. I *very much* agree with the use of mere initials: I like that.[3]

As with Hofmannsthal's letter to Kessler of 10 September 1909, there are mixed messages here, with Kessler seeking to define his role in the collaboration very precisely, while assuring Hofmannsthal that he would still be perfectly happy not to be mentioned at all. Tellingly, Kessler also (in relation to the 'agreement' between them that he should not be mentioned), immediately used the phrase 'in accordance with your wishes'. The nature of this agreement and the reasons for Hofmannsthal to wish that Kessler's name be kept out are not recorded in their correspondence, nor in Kessler's *Diary*, but will be examined below in the context of Kessler's subsequent exchanges with their mutual friend Eberhard von Bodenhausen, nearly two years later.

Hofmannsthal replied almost immediately, on 25 August 1910, with a long letter of apology for any hurt feelings he might inadvertently have caused, and with justification for the terms in which he had thought up the suggested dedication, saying that he did not like the word collaborator ('Mit-arbeiter') because of its ugly, composite nature. He added that co-creator ('Mit-schöpfer') might have been nicer, but pretentious in respect of his own person. Hofmannsthal then continued:

> My collaborator in constructing a scenario might have been Schnitzler, or Rudi Schroeder, or Andrian. But I wonder, when such a scenario were there, whether I would have found the desire, the inner compulsion to overcome a certain aversion and scepticism over my ability to make real characters out of the sketchy figures who have to perform their little dance – unless, as here, such a precious imponderable had been added in the form of your wonderfully friendly yet always forceful participation in the implementation, your criticism that was so warm for the successful parts and so sharp for the parts that were wrong. Where the scenario left me cold occasionally – the thought of your participation made me buckle down – the certainty of your constructive criticism stiffened my resolve, even against myself. I found myself with the pleasant task of saying all this to you, to Strauss, to our mutual friends. The dedication was supposed to summarise it all once again. [...] Your role in the Homer by Schroeder is different, and seems to me to be as valuable as the share you have in the creation of the operetta, however incommensurable such intellectual contributions are: neither of these two works would have been created without you.[4]

The whole tone of Hofmannsthal's letter is rather anguished, and he gets the date of Kessler's letter wrong. His salutation and sign-off also indicate his state of mind: his letter starts 'My dear Kessler' and ends 'Sincerely, Your Hugo Hofmannsthal', a reversion to the more formal mode of address that had been abandoned in their correspondence from 1905 onwards. Two points of particular interest in this letter are these: firstly, his admission how hard he had found it to motivate himself to

---

[3] Burger, pp. 297–8.
[4] Burger, pp. 298–9.

complete the work of transforming the scenario into the finished work of art that was the *Rosenkavalier* libretto, and secondly, the admission that he had talked about Kessler's role 'to Strauss, to our mutual friends'. Hofmannsthal does not of course reveal the terms in which he talked about Kessler's participation, and the written evidence suggests that he rather played it down, but this admission at least makes clear that Strauss was aware, through Hofmannsthal, of Kessler's active involvement. This is further confirmed, although the entry is tantalisingly short on detail, by a look back to Kessler's *Diary* for 21 February 1910:

> In the afternoon to the Richard Strauss's with the Hofmannsthals, where we had tea, and Strauss played us the duel scene, the letter scene and the finale from the second act of the opera. Mrs Strauss danced and sang to the waltz with her skirts hitched up.[5]

This glimpse of Kessler, Hofmannsthal and Strauss all together in Berlin,[6] listening to the emerging *Rosenkavalier* score with Strauss at the piano, nearly a year before its première in the opera house, is the only recorded example of the three 'collaborators' at work: according to the *Diary*, the last time Kessler had spoken to Strauss (on his own) had been in Dresden on 27 January 1909, after a performance of *Salome* the previous evening. This entry merely records: 'In the morning, before departure, I spoke to Richard Strauss again for a moment.' Whatever their topic of conversation might have been, this was just two weeks before Kessler and Hofmannsthal were to meet up in Weimar, develop their 'full and entirely original scenario' together, and embark by train for Berlin, in order for Hofmannsthal to go to Strauss with an oral, extempore outline of their characters and plot, in order to see if he were interested.

Eighteen months later, after all the work they had done together, both Hofmannsthal and Kessler now reviewed their *Rosenkavalier* collaboration in a series of difficult, pained letters that ran into the autumn. On 27 August Kessler wrote to Hofmannsthal, explaining that he had thought it better to speak openly and honestly right from the start ('I have often kept quiet about feelings, but I have discovered that suppressed emotions grow stronger, not weaker, with time'), and adding in conciliatory fashion that as things had blown up between them, he was now happy to accept Hofmannsthal's original dedication. Hofmannsthal replied on 6 September, putting the blame on Craig for the uneasiness that had arisen between them. Kessler had been trying since April 1910 to get Craig to do the scenery, costumes and lighting for the planned Reinhardt production of *Oedipus the King* in the Musikfesthalle, Munich, but Hofmannsthal – horrified by Craig's financial demands – had resisted the idea.[7] Hofmannsthal's letter ended with a PS:

---

[5] *Diary IV*, p. 590.
[6] Strauss was in Berlin to conduct *Elektra*, which Kessler attended that evening with the Hofmannsthals, and all had supper at the Kaiserhof afterwards (*Diary IV*, p. 590).
[7] Hofmannsthal's campaign against Craig's involvement was successful: the première on 25 September 1910 had scenery by Franz Geiger and costumes by Ernst Stern (Newman, p. 68).

In the meanwhile, more by thinking about it myself than as a result of your letter, I have so got to like the word 'collaborator' that I earnestly ask you to be allowed to use this word instead of the other one, because it characterizes the actual relationship in the nicest and most rightful way.[8]

Kessler replied on 14 September, saying that he was happy with either of the two suggested formulations, admitting that Hofmannsthal's handling of the Craig affair had influenced his reaction to the suggested dedication, and wishing *Der Rosenkavalier* ('what a terrible title', he added) every success. Kessler wrote again on 23 September to express his condolences on the death of Kainz and to revert to the more businesslike tone of previous *Rosenkavalier* correspondence:

Alongside this sad news I have read the happy report that Strauss has again come to terms with Seebach, and that S. has even agreed to Roller's scenery and costumes; since I know how much these mean to you, I am delighted on both counts for you. This reminds me that I have not even read the end of your libretto, so I would be very happy if you could send this to me when convenient.[9]

There was then a long silence on Hofmannsthal's part, a period of over a month, before he sent Kessler the saddest, most depressed letter in their entire correspondence to date. Full of dramatic statements – 'in these weeks it seemed to me quite impossible ever to see you again or ever to enter your house again' – the letter drew the conclusion, *inter alia*, that true friendship can never have existed between both men. Once again, displacement activity is evident, Hofmannsthal going to some lengths to explain and justify his attitude and activity in respect of the disagreements that had arisen between Reinhardt's team and Craig (rather than addressing directly the question of Kessler's real role in the creation of *Der Rosenkavalier*), and the letter ends with a cry for help:

Your great temperament is matched only by your good sense, your fairmindedness and your sense of humour. All you have to do is read over my letters of May, June and August to realize how totally I am in tune with you. But I cannot get over this simply by being in tune with you. So, please, help me.[10]

Kessler replied to this letter promptly but without providing that much help, in the sense that Hofmannsthal had requested. He spelled out in greater detail just how hurt he had been by the outcome of the Craig–Reinhardt project and, moreover, by Hofmannsthal's apparent indifference to a project that had meant so much to him, Kessler, personally. Ignoring whether or not they had ever been true friends, Kessler nevertheless suggested that they had a very special productive relationship and expressed this hope: 'It has been, and is, and I hope will be, a joint

---

[8] Burger, p. 302.
[9] Burger, p. 303.
[10] Burger, p. 305.

effort, with both of us increasing the strengths that lie within us by our mutual sympathy.'

Hofmannsthal's reply to this letter, again prompt, did not move on, as Kessler had invited him to do, but went instead into further detail about Craig's behaviour and disproportionate financial demands, telling Kessler how angry this had made him and how he was now 'endlessly sad' over the behaviour of a third party, who had perhaps turned Kessler against him: Hofmannsthal also expressed his opinion that correspondence on the topic was driving them further apart, and that face-to-face discussion might be the only way to resolve matters. This letter, dated 9 November 1910, crossed with one from Kessler dated 10 November and prompted the latter to send a follow-up letter in reply the following day. The first assured Hofmannsthal of the very special place he had in Kessler's affections, which is why Kessler had devoted ten years of his life in promoting Hofmannsthal in every possible way and why he expected more in return from Hofmannsthal than he might, for example, expect from other friends and acquaintances, while repeating the essential message:

> But as for the dedication, even under normal circumstances the wording that you selected would not have pleased me because, in the way that I understood it initially, it offended my objective feeling of things and, if you like, my self-esteem. I might however have kept quiet about it, if our relationship had not already been under such strain that I wanted to avoid any further impediment, coûte que coûte.[11]

The second letter stressed even more strongly that Kessler now wished to put the entire episode behind them, and it provided a pithy yet elegant summary of where matters now stood:

> Really, my dear, there is so little warmth in this world, there are so few people for whose being one feels involuntary sympathy, and it is even rarer that such an elective affinity can form the basis in practice for a human relationship; we have now known each other for half a lifetime, we know approximately what we expect of each other and what we can give to each other; should we risk all of this simply because we have each, unintentionally, hurt each other in the heat of the moment, at a time when perhaps we were both particularly sensitive and prickly because of other things?[12]

Hofmannsthal's reply, dated 15 November, was gracious: 'I thank you from the heart for the lovely, beneficial words in your latest letter,' and responsive, at last, to the root cause of their disagreement:

> What is always necessary is to try and see things from the other's point of view. It is then perhaps possible for me to understand full well how you were able to – or

---

[11] Burger, p. 311.
[12] Burger, p. 313.

had to – transfer the justifiable disgruntlement you were feeling to the other highly delicate and intimate matter of your contribution to the dramatic work in progress.[13]

The correspondence over the suggested dedication had now run on for nineteen weeks, from 5 July to 15 November 1910. The end result was a new and definitive formulation by Hofmannsthal: 'I dedicate this comedy to Count Harry Kessler, to whose collaboration it owes so much.' As mentioned earlier in this chapter, Hofmannsthal referred back to this wording when, in 1927, he wrote the Preface to a new edition of *Der Rosenkavalier* and said that the formulation of this dedication pointed towards true collaboration with his friend, Count Harry Kessler. The latter's feelings had, however, long since been expressed in a letter to his sister, written just after the Dresden première of *Der Rosenkavalier*:

> As for Hofmannsthal, I think he has gone as far in trying to be just to me as his nature (which is not generous) will allow him; but I don't think it very likely I shall ever collaborate with him again; and certainly not on these terms.[14]

There is an oddity in this protracted quarrel, however, that has only emerged after a recent study by Burkhard Stenzel of the books lost from Kessler's former library in Weimar. When Kessler left Germany in 1933 he took no steps to protect his assets there, and gradually all his possessions were looted, destroyed or sold to pay current bills. But quite a large number of the books once in Kessler's library have now been located, and are in the process of being catalogued and stored at the Anna Amalia Library in Weimar. And in the copy of *Cristina's Homecoming* presented to Kessler by Hofmannsthal in 1910, the manuscript dedication runs:

> To my collaborator Harry Kessler, in friendship. Hofmannsthal, Weimar, 10 February 1910.[15]

Semantics aside, the question that is thus posed, and still not answered unequivocally even after a hundred years of *Rosenkavalier* performance history and scholarship, is whether or not Hofmannsthal took as much from Kessler – in terms of the dramatic architecture of the piece, the unfolding of the narrative, the stage characterisation of the principal figures, all key characteristics of authorship – as the latter clearly thought he did. This is no longer a simple issue of whether or not Kessler bears major responsibility for the initial scenario of *Der Rosenkavalier* – quite clearly, he does – but rather the degree to which Kessler's theatrical vision

---

[13] Burger, p. 314.
[14] Letter from Harry Kessler to Wilma dated 3 February 1911: in DLA (Manuscript department), HS.1971.0001
[15] Burkhard Stenzel, *Widmungen Hugo von Hofmannsthals. Einblicke in Werke der ehemaligen Weimarer Bibliothek von Harry Graf Kessler*, in *Mitteldeutsches Jahrbuch für Kultur und Geschichte* (Dössel: Verlag Janos Stekovics, 2009), pp. 101–14 (p. 109). The German is: 'Harry Kessler dem Mitarbeiter in Freundschaft.' If Hofmannsthal thought of Kessler as his 'Mitarbeiter' for *Cristina*, it is illogical that he should have gone to such lengths to avoid using the same word for *Der Rosenkavalier*.

Act Three: Epilogue 201

for a reworked, improved *L'Ingénu libertin* in its new guise actually corresponds to the *Comedy for Music* that bears the names of Hofmannsthal and Strauss. Before attempting to answer that question, some of the subsequent pronouncements of both Hofmannsthal and Kessler, relevant to their respective views of the authorship of the piece, need to be included.

Hofmannsthal saw in the New Year of 1910–11 at Schloss Neubeuern in Upper Bavaria, at a gathering hosted by Julie von Wendelstadt and her sister-in-law (and Hofmannsthal's close friend) Ottonie von Degenfeld: his stay lasted from 28 December 1910 to 9 January 1911 (the *Rosenkavalier* première in Dresden then being a mere seventeen days away).[16] Other members of the house party included Eberhard von Bodenhausen, who made an entry in his own diary for 1 January 1911: 'Long walk with Hugo in the afternoon, he told me about the Kessler business over the *Rosenkavalier* dedication.'[17] Exactly what Hofmannsthal told him is not recorded, but he evidently reverted to the same theme over a year later, as can be inferred from a meeting in Paris between Bodenhausen and Kessler on 24 March 1912: this time there is a more detailed record by Kessler of what was said:

> I told Bodenhausen how embarrassed I was about Hofmannsthal's behaviour in the ballet project; particularly so soon after he had treated me in such a cavalier fashion over *Der Rosenkavalier*. This provoked Bodenhausen into replying that he did not understand what I could accuse H. of in the *Rosenkavalier* business; he had learned from Hofmannsthal a few weeks ago in Berlin what my part had been in *Der Rosenkavalier*, and he did not think he had treated me badly. So I asked how H. had described my part. Bodenhausen: Hofmannsthal had told him that I had 're-arranged a scene' here and there. To this I replied that H. was quite simply an infamous liar if he claimed that: my part in the invention and scenario of *Der Rosenkavalier* was just as great, if not greater than his. Bodenhausen was clearly very shaken by my detailed objections and rejoinders and advised me not to take the matter tragically but rather to treat it as pathological on Hofmannsthal's part […].[18]

Kessler's decision, however, was to think things over and to write a long, detailed letter to Bodenhausen the same day. This letter, written under the shock of having just learned how Hofmannsthal was describing to close, mutual friends the extent of Kessler's alleged contribution to *Der Rosenkavalier*, and written moreover to Bodenhausen – a man whose opinion Kessler had valued extremely highly, ever since their joint membership of the editorial board of *Pan* at the turn of the century – can be taken as Kessler's considered view of what he had done, and of how he had done it:

> Paris, 24.III.1912. My dear friend, in order to avoid any misunderstanding, I would like to set down **in writing** my main objections to Hofmannsthal's version as told

---

[16] http://www.navigare.de/hofmannsthal/Neubeuern.html.
[17] Simon, p. 182.
[18] *Diary IV*, p. 802.

to you of my part in *Rosenkavalier*. Forget any talk of mere redrafting, correcting or advice, for the fact is I was half responsible **for the very theme of the work**, in other words the idea of the cross-dressing and the figure of Quinquin, the actual Rosenkavalier. Moreover from the very outset the **entire content** of the piece (except for the added duel scene, and the scandal scene in Act III, that were added by **Strauss**, not by Hofmannsthal) was **created jointly** by Hofmannsthal and by me, **in ongoing work act by act and situation by situation**. Work on this took place in my house in Weimar and went on for several days (three or maybe four), with each of us taking what had been decided so far and adding our own ideas for the scene being developed, so that **our joint creative efforts** were discussed thoroughly in order to determine a final version that Hofmannsthal wrote down. In this way the final version was made up of **at least as many ideas and creative concepts on my part** as it was on Hofmannsthal's. At the time **Hofmannsthal thought exactly the same too**; for he often said that authors like Flers and Caillavet undoubtedly collaborated in the way we were doing; for the first time he could now see how plays could be co-written in this way: and neither of us could now say (then say) which bit came from him and which from the other. For a time Hofmannsthal continued to believe this; for he said so, **in all seriousness**, and repeated it, and **not** as a mere politesse in the later conversation I mentioned. Basically the later conversation was this: in my study in Weimar H said to me that in view of my role in *Rosenkavalier*, I really ought to be credited as co-author of the work on the title page. But I was completely unknown as a dramatist; for a major work like this a new name had its dangers, might even perplex Strauss; and given that so much was riding on this for him, Hofmannsthal (financially and in other ways), he would be grateful to me if I would renounce my right on this occasion. This was absolutely not some kind of politesse on Hofmannsthal's part; it was a serious, businesslike conversation, as evidenced by its length and by the whole tone that Hofmannsthal adopted. I agreed immediately not to be named, whereupon Hofmannsthal added somewhat vaguely that maybe my co-authorship or the part that I had played could be announced **later**; (i.e. once the **success** of the piece could no longer be adversely affected by this). And I would never have raised all this again, if H had not tried to **misrepresent** to the general public my contribution when he thought of dedicating the work to me as his 'helper'. I refused to sanction this clear misrepresentation of our working relationship, and that was the origin of our subsequent disagreements. Those are the basic facts of the matter in our conversation this morning.[19]

It is immediately apparent that, for the purposes of his argument, Kessler omitted one very salient fact: that the cross-dressing and the figure of Quinquin, the actual Rosenkavalier, was not strictly speaking his invention, but rather a creative borrowing from the Bouffes Parisiens opérette that he had seen a year previously. Yet that should not take away the force of his main argument: the contents of this entire chapter refute any notion that all Kessler did was to 're-arrange a scene

---

[19] Simon, pp. 92–4.

here and there'. Likewise, the letter seems to have convinced Bodenhausen to some degree, for Kessler records a further conversation the following day, 25 March 1912:

> Bodenhausen came to me early and discussed Hofmannsthal. I asked him to do nothing, since H. and I really are too close to each other for a third party to be able to act as intermediary. Bodenhausen agreed: he said H. virtually <u>loves</u> me. Maybe, but this is a peculiar form of love![20]

In considering everything that Kessler had said, and subsequently written, to him, Bodenhausen may even have thought back to the last time that he had seen *Der Rosenkavalier* onstage, a few months previously. For in an enthusiastic letter to Hofmannsthal written on 19 November 1911, Bodenhausen had said: 'Your mastery of the stagecraft seems to me to be in a different league to anything that I have seen [from you] before.'[21] It undoubtedly was, with the single possible exception of *Elektra* (play and opera), but the scale of the two works, and size of cast, is very different, and *Der Rosenkavalier* had by then launched Hofmannsthal into European and world prominence as an original and highly successful opera librettist. The huge improvement on his earlier stage works was being noted.

The only other recorded allusion by Hofmannsthal to Kessler's work on *Der Rosenkavalier* came two years later, at a time of heightened tensions between both men over the creation of the ballet *Josephs Legende*. In a letter of 2 June 1914 to Strauss, and in an attempt to distance himself from the criticism that the introductory essay to *Josephs Legende* had started to attract, Hofmannsthal wrote:

> [...] I was distressed to think of you without any acceptable work: the Russians wanted a ballet from you, and so I drafted this one and brought in Kessler since he had been present at these discussions anyway (and because he had assisted me with the drafting of the *Rosenkavalier* scenario, pleasantly and skilfully, though perhaps he tends rather to over-estimate the importance of his help).[22]

Hofmannsthal may have had his particular reasons for his choice of words but, once again, referred to assistance from Kessler in terms that indicate (at the very least) that the driving force for the scenario came from the librettist, who availed himself of a little help from his friend. To Strauss it may not have mattered that much, or at all, precisely how the amusing scenario and subsequent libretto came about (and he had certainly been aware of some involvement by Kessler right from the outset, and during the creative process – as shown by the *Diary* entry for 21 February 1910, quoted above), but to posterity it is both of interest and importance to pay proportionate tribute to the creators of the work. Kessler moreover, as the

---

[20] *Diary IV*, p. 802.
[21] Hugo von Hofmannsthal, Eberhard von Bodenhausen, *Briefe der Freundschaft* (Berlin: Eugen Diederichs Verlag, 1953), p. 133.
[22] Hamm./Osers, p. 198. The Hammelmann translation here is of the original German 'die Wichtigkeit welches Dienstes er vielleicht ziemlich überschätzt', which might better be rendered as: 'the importance of which service he perhaps somewhat over-estimates'. It is a biting comment.

continuation of his letter of 24 March 1912 to Bodenhausen clearly shows, was at pains to keep matters in proportion:

> You were surprised that I embarked on this way of collaborating with Hofmannsthal at all and did not prefer to write plays or ballets on my own. This is explained by a very clear realisation of the limits of Hofmannsthal's poetic gifts and of mine. Hofmannsthal simply does not have precisely what I do have as a dramatic author and vice versa. Hofmannsthal has no talent for constructing things, and he has only a limited talent for developing and ordering dramatically pre-existing material; this is why, except for purely lyrical dramas, he has always taken existing scenarios. But if there is an effective scenario, he can make it come wonderfully alive in lyrical terms, breathing life into the characters and situations by use of the lyrical. This is precisely the talent that I lack; I cannot make the characters speak in voices that belong to them (the great gift of a lyricist) but I can, much more clearly and securely than Hofmannsthal, invent and order a dramatic plot. This means that I shall never write a play on my own that is alive in the way that I believe necessary; but what I had thought was that I would write plays together with Hofmannsthal, which would have been dramatically secure and effective in a way that Hofmannsthal will never achieve on his own. I believe that this is evidenced by *Rosenkavalier* and by much in the first two acts of *Cristina*, although these were only the beginning.[23]

If one takes, and analyses Kessler's letter to Bodenhausen as a whole, particularly in the light of some of Kessler's *Diary* entries, a consistent theme emerges. The entries for 15 and 18 February 1909 are instructive. On 15 February Kessler recorded: 'Hofmannsthal said the following about *Faublas*: making a scenario in this way with someone else gives him the same sense of security as taking the scenario from someone else's play.' On 18 February Kessler wrote (referring this time to their ongoing collaboration over *Cristina's Homecoming*):

> H. said that the huge service this way of working gave him was the fact that it forced him to reflect on things. Hitherto he had never been able to reflect on his work; he had always worked in purely visionary fashion; as a result, the detail had often got in the way of the main subject, and the shaping of his pieces had lacked assurance.[24]

This reported gratitude on Hofmannsthal's part for Kessler's provision of security, or assurance, in their joint endeavours gives credence to Kessler's main claims in the letter to Bodenhausen: namely that Hofmannsthal understood as a result of his sessions with Kessler in Weimar and then in Berlin how Robert de Flers and Gaston de Caillavet could have collaborated, successfully, on their works for the stage, and that he and Kessler were now engaged in a very similar creative process. These thoughts on Hofmannsthal's part are dated – both from the *Diary* and from the context of Kessler's letter to Bodenhausen – to February 1909, a time when both men were in Berlin and were presumably feeling exuberant that they had drafted

[23] Simon, p. 94.
[24] *Diary IV*, p. 565.

a viable scenario and that Strauss had accepted it. The letter goes on, however: 'Basically the **later** conversation was this: **in my study in Weimar H. said to me** that in view of my role in *Rosenkavalier*, I really ought to be credited as co-author of the work on the title page.' If this conversation was indeed later, and if it took place in Kessler's study in Weimar, then its timing can only have been between 23 and 28 February 1910 – a whole year later – for Kessler had spent all of the rest of 1909 travelling, mainly in France, and had not met up with Hofmannsthal at all. The *Diary* entry for 23 February 1910 is consistent with this interpretation, running as follows:

> Travelled to Weimar with the Hofmannsthals in the afternoon. In the evening Hofmannsthal said to me, in respect of the theatre, that he thought of himself like a young man who had boasted that he could ride horses and who had then been mounted on a very demanding steed; once up in the saddle he was surprised that he could sort of manage, and not fall off; but he still felt that the slightest wrong move would inevitably lead to an accident. Now, after *Cristina*, he felt that he <u>could</u> ride. Even *Elektra* had merely been a sleepwalking successful exercise.[25]

This stay with Kessler lasted nine days, the first few days being spent on elaboration of the scenario for Hofmannsthal's much later social comedy *The Difficult Man* (completed in 1919, first performed in Munich and in Berlin in 1921). There is, however, one *Rosenkavalier* entry, dated 'February 1910' but attributed by Burger to 1 March: 'In the evening, at home, Hofmannsthal read aloud *Der Rosenkavalier*.'[26] The *Diary* makes no mention of those who attended the reading but Burger lists them as the families Nostitz, Van de Velde, Forster-Nietzsche and Von Hofmann, adding that Rilke was present as well, the reading being of the third act which Hofmannsthal achieved 'with great comic success'.[27] This context – nine days with Kessler in Weimar, further collaboration with him on a dramatic scenario, a *Rosenkavalier* reading to an invited audience of close friends – makes it likely to the point of near certainty that Hofmannsthal seized this particular moment to ask his friend and mentor to remain in the background of the fast-emerging *Der Rosenkavalier*, to practise reticence and discretion, and to come out of the shadows – possibly – later on. What rings particularly true, in addition in Kessler's letter to Bodenhausen, is the reported admission by Hofmannsthal that 'so much was riding on this for him, financially and in other ways', for by February 1910 the first two acts had largely been completed, with much of the third act under way, and the promising, potentially lucrative dimensions of what had already been achieved were increasingly clear both to Strauss and to Hofmannsthal.

---

[25] *Diary IV*, p. 591.
[26] *Diary IV*, p. 592.
[27] Burger, p. 537.

Authorship – a summary view

The genesis and authorship of the characters in *Der Rosenkavalier* has become clearer following publication of the prolific correspondence between Hofmannsthal and Kessler and of the Kessler *Diary*. No longer can the correspondence between Strauss and Hofmannsthal be regarded as a stand-alone authority on the genesis of the opera. Apart from these three invaluable sources, no *Rosenkavalier* letters from Strauss to Kessler nor from Kessler to Strauss appear to exist. Strauss undoubtedly realised that Kessler was in some way behind the sudden burst of creativity on Hofmannsthal's part – given that the rapid and fluent emergence of the scenario, and the libretto for Act I, and the stream of ideas for the work as a whole, were all in complete contrast to Hofmannsthal's stone-walling on any question of an original opera libretto ever since Strauss had first asked him to consider writing something new for him in March 1906 – but even so, he seems to have been content to accept what was coming his way, and not to enquire further. This is in character for Strauss.

59 Harry Kessler in later life. His relationship with Hofmannsthal, although partially restored for their later ballet scenario *Josephs Legende* (1914), never really recovered from their disagreement over authorship of *Der Rosenkavalier*

A line of argument could be developed that Hofmannsthal had begun to exploit Kessler's ideas, and to use him rather cynically, intending all along to drop him, from the moment he wrote the letter to Strauss of 11 February 1909 outlining his 'new and entirely original scenario'. This would be consistent with his reference to the 'delight of Count Kessler', and 'with whom I discussed it'. It would also be consistent with Hofmannsthal going alone to see Strauss in Berlin on 14 February, obtaining his agreement, and only then rejoining Kessler for the Schadow exhibition and for the theatre that evening: a deliberate attempt to keep Kessler out of the picture. But there is too much else in the multi-faceted relationship between Hofmannsthal and Kessler in the 1900–10 period, too many positives in their interaction, to support the notion that Hofmannsthal acted so cynically, and so cold-heartedly, and with such selfish purpose, just as Kessler had come up with such promising ingredients for Hofmannsthal's first real operatic collaboration with Strauss. It seems more likely that Hofmannsthal, having been stimulated and inspired from the outset by Kessler's keen sense of the operatic possibilities in a reworked and augmented *L'Ingénu libertin*, genuinely began to think as his work in Rodaun progressed that the language of his libretto, and the esoteric onstage Vienna of his imagination as it emerged in the course of 1909 and 1910, were sufficiently original and important so as to change the underlying parameters of the collaboration to which he had initially subscribed. He lacked the interpersonal skills however, or the psychological understanding of Kessler, to make this proposition in a way that the latter could ever accept.

An associated question is why it was, almost from the outset, that Kessler had ever agreed to be so self-effacing: to act in the background as Hofmannsthal's collaborator and ideas man, to provide a dramatic architecture for the piece that (in Kessler's view) Hofmannsthal would have been incapable of providing by himself, and to devote so much time, energy and passion to the project without seeking any public recognition of his role. No reader of Kessler's letters to Hofmannsthal from May 1909 onwards can fail to be struck by the energy, the flood of ideas, the detailed and reasoned critiques that came from Kessler's pen in response to each new section of the draft libretto that he read. However, what Kessler wanted – clearly wanted at that stage – was for Hofmannsthal to enjoy sole credit for the piece, to make a major name for himself, and to earn a substantial sum of money from the project (Kessler in 1909 had no need of any additional wealth and probably thought that he would never need to earn more money in his lifetime). It is thus a reasonable assertion that Kessler's theatrical vision for the new piece was intended all along as a gift to Hofmannsthal, a gift moreover that although behind the scenes on this occasion, might have led to a fuller, more overt theatrical association between the two men in due course. This is perhaps the sense in which Kessler's mention to Bodenhausen of his collaborative work on *Cristina's Homecoming* and *Der Rosenkavalier* – 'although these were only the beginning' – should be understood.

Creating *Der Rosenkavalier*
– a retrospective

In examining the creative process leading from Chevalier to Cavalier in such intimate detail, certain dangers have not entirely been avoided. Where has Richard Strauss been throughout? How was the music created that has given so much joy to opera lovers for eleven decades, and counting? As I said at the outset, this book has not been yet another attempt to analyse the words and music of the opera nor

60 Richard Strauss in 1910, in the garden of his villa at Garmisch-Partenkirchen

61 Strauss in 1911, after the enormous, Europe-wide success of *Der Rosenkavalier*

62 The villa at Garmisch-Partenkirchen. Strauss wrote the 'Recognition scene' in *Elektra* shortly after moving in (June 1908) but *Der Rosenkavalier* was the first full opera he composed here

to assess the relationship between them. But in looking back at the creative process, the established canon of *Rosenkavalier* critical assessment ought to be held up briefly against the new findings that give such creative prominence to *L'Ingénu libertin* and to Kessler, if only to tie the various threads together.

The compositional timelines are well-known and relatively easy to summarise. After Kessler and Hofmannsthal had travelled together by train from Weimar to Berlin, and Hofmannsthal had put the *Rosenkavalier* proposition to Strauss at their meeting on Sunday 14 February 1909, librettist and composer went their separate ways. Hofmannsthal returned to Rodaun: Strauss had just moved into his newly built villa in Garmisch Partenkirchen, his customary practice being to compose in the spring and summer months, then to conduct (and to orchestrate what he had composed) during the winter. Having been enthused by the *Rosenkavalier* scenario, Strauss urged Hofmannsthal to send him text to set as quickly as possible – the first scenes arrived in April and the whole of Act I on 3 May. Strauss composed the 'rough sketch' for this act in 18 days and began to urge Hofmannsthal to supply Acts II and III. Act II was subjected to a radical revision in July 1909, but Strauss had composed its music (with the more boisterous ending, and the Baron Ochs waltz refrain as the curtain song) by September. There was then the agreed winter gap, during which Strauss completed the autograph full score for Act I (December 1909) and for Act II (April 1910).

By July 1910 Hofmannsthal had sent Act III to Strauss and it was composed virtually on receipt: by September 1910 Strauss had completed the autograph full score for this act and thus for the whole opera. The speed at which he worked is remarkable: for as Joseph Jones has pointed out, the musical composition of *Der Rosenkavalier* basically went through four successive stages.[1] Firstly, as Strauss read and absorbed each section of the emerging libretto, he annotated musical motifs, key signatures, melodic fragments in the margins of the text. Secondly, he transferred these musical motifs and developed them in a pocket-sized sketchbook (all of Strauss's extant sketchbooks are now held by the Richard Strauss Institute at Garmisch Partenkirchen and can be consulted – they offer fascinating insights into his melodic world). Thirdly, Strauss then produced a short score or *Particell*, with the vocal parts harmonised over a two-stave accompaniment. Fourthly, and finally, he wrote the autograph full score. These processes of course overlapped: indeed, it was a feature of Strauss's method for him to compose ahead while awaiting receipt of the next section of libretto. And as *Der Rosenkavalier* evolved, Strauss sometimes had to call on Hofmannsthal to supply extra lines of text, purely to complement a musical passage that he had already composed and wished to retain. The final duet in Act III between Octavian and Sophie is but one well-known example of the words being added subsequently to already existing music.

This creative process between Hofmannsthal and Strauss – the interaction of words and music – took place through the medium of relatively formal, relatively brief and factual letters. These letters have customarily been used to document and analyse the creation of *Der Rosenkavalier*, but as we have seen, they ignore (apart from the vital intervention by Strauss over the reordering of Act II) the third, theatrical dimension that was going on simultaneously between Hofmannsthal and Kessler. Hofmannsthal only met Strauss in person twice between launch of the project and the opera's first night – once in June 1909, when Hofmannsthal visited Garmisch and Strauss played Act I on the piano to him, and once in February 1910, when Strauss played Act II on the piano to Hofmannsthal and Kessler in Berlin (and Pauline sang 'with her skirts hitched up'). The fiery, passionate creative exchanges that Hofmannsthal was having with Kessler throughout the *Rosenkavalier* period, both by letter and (less frequently) in person, are nowhere to be found in the written exchanges between Hofmannsthal and Strauss. And, as already pointed out, there are more Hofmannsthal–Kessler letters relating to *Der Rosenkavalier* than Hofmannsthal–Strauss letters in the same period.

Strauss liked to work on his own, to compose in secret as has sometimes been claimed. He liked to read the emerging libretto, digest it, think about it for as long

---

[1] Joseph Jones, *Der Rosenkavalier: Genesis, Modelling and New Aesthetic Paths* (Ann Arbor: ProQuest, 2009).

as possible – and then set it to music. The days of spirited discussion, suggestions, ideas and counter-proposals to the creative ideas that Kessler and Hofmannsthal enjoyed in Weimar followed by Berlin (between 9 and 22 February 1909) would probably not have appealed to Strauss. Yet without them, he would have had neither characters nor theatrical situations to set to music. Act Three has illuminated the lengths to which Kessler and Hofmannsthal subsequently went in trying to quantify and evaluate the respective contribution each had made to the theatre of *Der Rosenkavalier*. But even had he known of their interpersonal dramas at the time, it is unlikely that Strauss would have been that concerned: he needed text to set, and as long as he received it, all was well. Did Strauss know at the time just how much Kessler had contributed behind the scenes? There is only one allusory hint that he might have: 'You're da Ponte and Scribe rolled into one,' Strauss wrote to Hofmannsthal on 21 April 1909. Was he hinting that he knew both men were hard at work on the project, with Kessler (and his extensive Paris associations, known to Strauss) being referred to as Scribe?

Compartmentalised, three-way affairs can have their dangers. There are several examples of Hofmannsthal writing both to Strauss and to Kessler on the same day. On 12 June 1909, for example, he wrote to Strauss:

> My dear Doctor, Everything you played to me from the first act of the opera is most beautiful and has given me great and lasting pleasure.[2]

But his letter the very same day to Kessler ran:

> Strauss is just such a fabulously unrefined man. He has a ghastly tendency for the trivial, kitschy in him. All the little changes and extra lines he asks me for go in this direction. For example, I had exactly the same mimicry in mind as you suggest for Ochs's aria. He has him booming it all out prestissimo, so lacking in nuances that the changes to the words count for nothing, the music bearing so little correlation with the words [...] He won't kill it dead, but it will be as far removed from Beardsley as a Bavarian cow is from dancing the minuet![3]

The tone in each discreet set of correspondence is therefore very different. The creative exchanges between Kessler and Hofmannsthal give a strong impression of complicity between two writers entirely on the same wavelength, intimate friends who understood each other well. Those between Hofmannsthal and Strauss are on a very different plane. Hofmannsthal even wrote towards the end of the same 12 June letter to Kessler:

> If only I had a more refined, more artistic composer. Everything he says, he wants, the tendency he has, disgusts me quite strongly.[4]

It is good for opera history, one might say, that Hofmannsthal placed each letter

---

[2] Hamm./Osers, p. 34.
[3] Burger, p. 242.
[4] Burger, p. 244.

in its rightful envelope that June 1909 day! And Hofmannsthal's deeper reservations, that Strauss had not set his words with sufficient care and feeling, were to go on emerging in years to come, each time he attended a new production of *Der Rosenkavalier* and heard its effect in the theatre. Indeed, as early as March 1911 he was writing to Strauss:

> [...] *Rosenkavalier* – which as a fusion of word and music satisfies me *greatly* but not *wholly* [...].[5]

Apart from Hofmannsthal and Strauss, did others know of Kessler's involvement in or association with the *Rosenkavalier* project? He was a prominent guest at the première (although a late-running train caused him to miss Act I – he saw it again a couple of nights later) and he was given VIP treatment at the post-performance party and supper. So plenty of people saw him in the company of Strauss, of Hofmannsthal and of Max Reinhardt, who had played such a vital role in pulling the whole production together. However, nothing emerged in the critical reception of the piece to suggest anything other than a straightforward – and amazingly successful – collaboration between Hofmannsthal as librettist and Strauss as composer. But as the work began to gain its national and international prominence throughout 1911 and into 1912, rumours clearly began to spread in certain theatrical and literary circles that something was not quite right after all with the authorship of the piece. Some form of plagiarism was hinted at, suggesting that Hofmannsthal was not being entirely straight or honest about the circumstances of the work's creation. On 6 August 1912 Moritz Heimann, writer, critic and publisher's reader (for Fischer Verlag) wrote the following urgent words of warning to Hofmannsthal's publisher, and his own employer, Samuel Fischer:

> You ought to inform him of this unsettling cloud hanging over him! He is one of your authors, an unusual man, which one of us doesn't have foibles that we forgive all the time! He must be given the chance to defend himself against the blow that is threatening him.[6]

What exactly was the unsettling cloud, and what was the threatened 'blow'? A fuller version of Heimann's letter, included in an anthology of correspondence between Samuel and Hedwig Fischer and their authors, makes matters clearer:

> But your letter, which has just arrived today, forces me to write to you. The Kessler story is terrible! However it turns out, it is still terrible. I cannot yet believe it as it is being reported, because even something innocent can be tarnished via Blei and Holländer. But there will be something in it, and enough to cause trouble. Accusations of this sort have been common in literature; justified and unjustified. I do not believe that a single line in Hofmannsthal's name will have been written by Kessler: but there will be ideas, thoughts, inventions, H. will have taken these from his friend

---

[5] Hamm./Osers, pp. 76–7.
[6] *Cat. 43*, p. 266.

as unscrupulously (and justifiably despite everything!) just as he has always taken things from everything that he has read and from everything that he has heard from others. – I do not understand Kessler at all. Why is he coming out with this revelation now, why is he telling Reinhardt and his man Holländer? How could he go into their relationship like this? Or is it not simply the case in civil law that if an engagement is broken off, you can ask for your presents to be returned? It is a complete mystery.[7]

Over the last hundred years, those scholars who have examined the Heimann notion that 'there will be something in it' have concluded, with various degrees of nuance, that Kessler must have been wrong in claiming privately as great a share as he clearly did of the authorship of *Der Rosenkavalier*, and that he had misjudged, given Hofmannsthal's achievement with the libretto, the importance of his own contribution. Yet none of those scholars had enjoyed access to the *Diary*, to the Hofmannsthal–Kessler correspondence or to *L'Ingénu libertin*. So Kessler's private claims, even if voiced to only a few of his extensive circle of friends and acquaintances, were undoubtedly what were seized on by such inveterate gossips as Franz Blei, the Austrian writer, critic and translator, and by Felix Holländer, critic and dramaturg to Reinhardt. And Reinhardt himself, who knew Kessler well and who had played such a decisive part in the success of the *Rosenkavalier* première, may well have confirmed privately to friends just how much of the theatricality of *Der Rosenkavalier* had been inspired by Kessler. The rumours were obviously unnerving to friends and supporters of Hofmannsthal such as Heimann, but their precise slant and extent are undocumented to this day, and the outgoing letter from Samuel Fischer to Heimann, which seems to have prompted the latter's immediate and alarmed reply, is not included in the volume of correspondence quoted above. From today's perspective, the most likely trigger for Kessler to have made his revelations (whatever they were) to Reinhardt and to Holländer is the 24 March 1912 meeting and subsequent written exchanges he had had with Bodenhausen in Paris (analysed in Act Three). But even today there are still echoes to be found of something being not quite right, or clear, or settled, over the gestation of *Der Rosenkavalier*, in unlikely quarters. The collected papers of Edward Gordon Craig at the Bibliothèque Nationale de France (BNF) include his personal copy of the 1912 Fürstner edition of *The Rose Bearer* by Richard Strauss. Across the middle of the title page, underneath the words: 'The Rose-Bearer (Der Rosenkavalier), Comedy for Music in three Acts by Hugo von Hofmannsthal (English version by Alfred Kalisch), Music by Richard Strauss, Op. 59', is an annotation, in pencil, in Craig's own handwriting (emphasis in original): 'I had <u>understood</u> that Harry Ct Kessler had written the text.'[8] Kessler had obviously been talking to Craig as the *Rosenkavalier* project was taking shape.

---

[7] Samuel Fischer, Hedwig Fischer, *Briefwechsel mit Autoren*, ed. Dierk Rodewald and Corinna Fiedler (Frankfurt am Main: S. Fischer Verlag, 1989), pp. 335–6.

[8] EGC 16* 1010.

A Retrospective

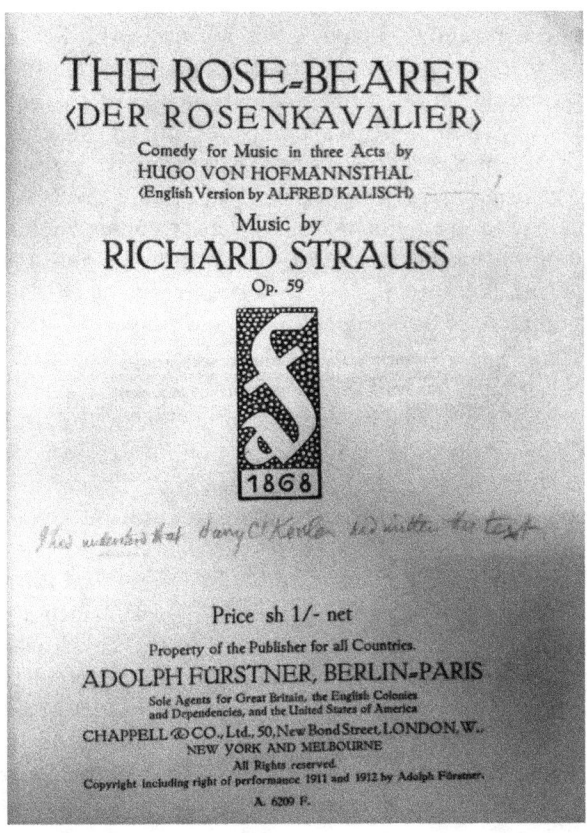

63 Edward Gordon Craig's copy of the *Rose Bearer* libretto. His pencilled annotation indicates regret or puzzlement that Kessler had received no recognition for his role in creating *Der Rosenkavalier*

If the theatricality, and dramatic characterisation of *Der Rosenkavalier* owes so much to the Kessler–Hofmannsthal reworking of *L'Ingénu libertin*, the musical treatment of the piece certainly does not. Strauss's *Rosenkavalier* music is in a completely different idiom from that of Terrasse: through-composed, symphonic, requiring a huge and opulent-sounding modern symphony orchestra, as opposed to the smaller, elegant eighteenth-century sound devised by Terrasse for a number opérette. Strauss was not in Paris anyway between 11 December 1907 and 2 February 1908, and cannot therefore have seen the Terrasse piece. The only putative subsequent connection is slim: Strauss visited Paris to conduct the *Concerts Colonne* Orchestra in late February 1908, where the young man who had conducted *L'Ingénu libertin* with such distinction, Philippe Moreau, was already at work (he later became the orchestra's assistant conductor). Might Moreau have mentioned to Strauss his recent triumph at the Bouffes Parisiens and told him about the piece? It is possible, but the music Strauss went on to compose for *Der Rosenkavalier*, inspired by the scenario and emerging libretto for that work, owes little or nothing to the period charm and concision of Terrasse's score.

Nevertheless, considered as a three-dimensional creation, a piece of music theatre with words by Hofmannsthal and music by Strauss, it is hard in the light of all the evidence to deny Kessler a place as one of the work's authors. Much of his input was derivative (from *L'Ingénu libertin*) but, equally, much was original and inspired: the new relationship that Kessler created between Faublas and Sophie, the amalgamation of Rosambert and the Marquis de Bay into the character of Pourceaugnac/Ochs, the dispatch by Ochs of Faublas to be his love emissary to Sophie, the pantomime of the Sophie–Faublas meeting at the start of Act II, the final scene of Act III, as well as countless small details of stagecraft and dramatic characterisation throughout. And these moments in the opera inspired Strauss to write some of his finest, most effective music for the piece. The Act III trio for the three principal female characters is not original on Kessler's part, for it performs exactly the same function – resolution of the love triangle – for Artus as for Hofmannsthal, but it remains a key element that Kessler brought to the *Rosenkavalier* table in Weimar.

The overall conclusion must therefore be that Kessler's theatrical vision for a reworked, adapted, improved *L'Ingénu libertin* is very largely reflected in the *Comedy for Music* that bears the names of Hofmannsthal and Strauss, much more so than has been admitted hitherto, and that his creative interaction with Hofmannsthal was a key determinant of the lasting success that *Der Rosenkavalier* has enjoyed. The road from Chevalier to Cavalier was mapped largely by Kessler: the world of twentieth-century opera, and the Strauss–Hofmannsthal partnership that went on to develop, would not and could not have been the same without him.

Bibliography

Primary sources

d'Abancourt, Willemain, *Le Chevalier de Faublas* (Paris: Chez Brunet, Librairie, 1789)
Artus, Louis, *L'Ingénu Libertin* (Paris: Librairie Théâtrale, 1908)
Artus, Louis and Claude Terrasse, *L'Ingénu libertin ou La Marquise et le Marmiton – Mise en scène* (Paris: Société d'Editions Musicales, 1907)
——*L'Ingénu libertin*, programme book dated 10 December 1907 (Paris: Landais and Legay, 1907)
Craig, Edward Gordon, *The Art of the Theatre* (Edinburgh and London: Foulis, 1905)
——*Die Kunst des Theaters*, ed. and trans. Maurice Magnus with an introduction by Harry Graf Kessler (Berlin and Leipzig: Seeman, 1905)
Dupeuty, Charles, Léon-Lévy Brunswick and Victor Lhérie, *Faublas* (Paris: J.N. Barba, Delloye, Bezou, 1836)
Hofmannsthal, Hugo von, *Operndichtungen I, Kritische Ausgabe, Vol. XXIII*, ed. Dirk Hoffmann and Willi Schuh (Frankfurt am Main: Fischer Verlag, 1986)
——*Ballette, Pantomimen, Filmszenarien, Kritische Ausgabe, Band XXVII*, ed. Gisela Bärbel Schmid and Klaus-Dieter Krabiel (Frankfurt am Main: Fischer Verlag, 2006)
—— *Gesammelte Werke*, ed. Bernd Schoeller and Rudolf Hirsch, 10 vols (Frankfurt am Main: Fischer Taschenbuch Verlag, 1979)
——*Der Rosenkavalier* (Berlin: Adolph Fürstner, 1911)
——*Der Rosenkavalier von Richard Strauss, Musik für Alle Vol. 1, Nr. 246*, ed. W. Hirschberg (Berlin: Ullstein, 1927)
——*Buch der Freunde* (Leipzig: Insel Verlag, 1929)
Jarry, Alfred, *Oeuvres complètes en trois volumes*, ed. Arrivé and others (Paris: Pléiade, 1972–88)
Jarry, Alfred and Claude Terrasse, *Ubu roi* (Paris: Editions Mercure de France, 1897)
Kessler, Harry Graf, *Das Tagebuch 1880–1937*, 9 vols (Stuttgart: Cotta, 2004–)
——*Gesichter und Zeiten – Erinnerungen: Erster Band 'Völker und Vaterländer'* (Berlin: S. Fischer Verlag, 1935)
——*Souvenirs d'un Européen I: de Bismarck à Nietzsche, traduit de l'Allemand par Blaise Briod* (Paris: Librairie Plon, 1936)
——*Gesammelte Schriften in drei Bändern*, 3 vols (Frankfurt am Main: Fischer Taschenbuchverlag, 1988)
—— *Tagebücher 1918–1937*, ed. Wolfgang Pfeiffer-Belli (Frankfurt am Main: Insel Verlag, 1961)
——*The Diaries of a Cosmopolitan 1918–1937*, trans. and ed. Charles Kessler (London: Weidenfeld & Nicolson, 1971)
——*Das Tagebuch 1880–1911 und 1916–1937, Rohtranskription* (Marbach: CD-ROM for subscribers to the 9 volumes of diaries still in course of publication (Stuttgart: Cotta, 2006)

Kessler, Harry Graf and Hugo von Hofmannsthal, *Josephs Legende* (Berlin, Paris: Adolph Fürstner, 1914)
——*The Legend of Joseph*, trans. Alfred Kalisch (Berlin and Paris: Fürstner, 1914)
Louvet de Couvray, Jean-Baptiste, *Les Aventures du Chevalier de Faublas* (Brussels: Librairie Universelle de Rozez, 1881)
Molière, *Oeuvres Complètes* (Oxford: Oxford University Press, 1900)
Strauss, Richard, *Betrachtungen und Erinnerungen*, ed. Willi Schuh (Zurich: Atlantis Verlag, 1949)
——*Der Rosenkavalier, Study Score* (Vienna: Verlag Dr. Richard Strauss GmbH & Co. KG, 1996)
——*Josephs Legende, Two piano score, arr. Otto Singer* (London: Boosey & Hawkes Ltd, 1943)
Terrasse, Claude, *La Marquise et le Marmiton ou L'Ingénu libertin* (Eschig, undated, private copy of manuscript full orchestral score)
——*La Marquise et le Marmiton ou L'Ingénu libertin*, Vocal Score (Paris: Société d'Editions Musicales, 1907)
——*L'Oeuvre de Jacques Offenbach* in *Musica* (1908), reprinted in *Ecrits non musicaux* (Paris: Editions du Fourneau, Collection 'La Marguerite', no. 4, 1997)

Primary sources – Correspondence

Bodenhausen, Eberhard von and Harry Graf Kessler, *Ein Briefwechsel 1894–1918*, ed. Hans-Ulrich Simon (Marbach am Neckar: Marbacher Schriften, 1978)
Hofmannsthal, Hugo von, *Briefe 1900–1909* (Vienna: Bermann-Fischer Verlag, 1937)
Hofmannsthal, Hugo von and Eberhard von Bodenhausen, *Briefe der Freundschaft*, ed. Dora Freifrau von Bodenhausen (Berlin: Eugen Diederichs Verlag, 1953)
Hofmannsthal, Hugo von and Harry Graf Kessler, *Briefwechsel 1898–1929*, ed. Hilde Burger (Frankfurt am Main: Insel Verlag, 1968)
Strauss, Richard, *Briefwechsel mit Hugo von Hofmannsthal*, ed. Dr Franz Strauss (Berlin: Paul Zsolnay Verlag, 1926)
Strauss, Richard and Hugo von Hofmannsthal, *The correspondence between Richard Strauss and Hugo von Hofmannsthal*, ed. Hanns Hammelmann and Ewald Osers (London: Collins, 1961)
Strauss, Richard and Hugo von Hofmannsthal, *Richard Strauss–Hugo von Hofmannsthal: Briefwechsel*, ed. Willi Schuh (Zürich: Atlantis, 1964)
Strauss, Richard and Willi Schuh, *Richard Strauss: Briefwechsel mit Willi Schuh* (Zurich: Atlantis Verlag, 1969)

Secondary sources

Abbate, Carolyn, *Unsung Voices* (Princeton: Princeton University Press, 1991)
Abbate, Carolyn and Roger Parker, *A History of Opera* (London: Allen Lane, 2012)
Alewyn, Richard, *Über Hugo von Hofmannsthal* (Göttingen: Vandenhoek and Ruprecht, 1958)
Allen, Charles, *Soldier Sahibs* (London: John Murray, 2000)
Applegate, Celia, and Pamela Potter, eds, *Music and German National Identity* (Chicago: University of Chicago Press, 2002)
Arlaud, Sylvie, 'Hugo von Hofmannsthal's Return to Molière 1909–23: The Conditions of Reception', *Austrian Studies*, 13, 1 (1 October 2005), 55–76

Artus, Louis, *Coeur de Moineau* (Paris: Librairie Théâtrale, 1905)
—— *La Plus Belle Histoire d'Amour Du Monde* (Paris: Editions Denoel, 1945)
—— *La Maison du Sage* (Paris: Emile-Paul Frères, 1920)
Ashley, Tim, *Richard Strauss* (London: Phaidon Press, 1999)
Aubry, Raoul, 'Soirée Parisienne', *Gil Blas*, 12 December 1907, 3–4
Austin, Gerhard, *Phänomenologie der Gebärde bei Hugo von Hofmannsthal* (Heidelberg: Winter, 1981)
Bablet, Denis, *The Theatre of Edward Gordon Craig*, trans. Daphne Woodward (London: Eyre Methuen, 1966)
Barker, Harley Granville, *Plays by Harley Granville Barker*, ed. Dennis Kennedy (Cambridge: Cambridge University Press, 1987)
Barthes, Roland, 'Death of The Author' (1968), in *Image – Music – Text*, essays selected and trans. Stephen Heath (London: Fontana Press, 1977)
Barzantny, Tamara, *Harry Graf Kessler und das Theater* (Köln: Böhlau Verlag, 2002)
Bate, Jonathan, *The Genius of Shakespeare* (London: Picador, 1997)
—— *Soul of the Age, The Life, Mind and World of William Shakespeare* (London: Penguin Books, 2009)
Beck-Mannagetta, Christian, *Der Ochs von Lerchenau: eine historische Betrachtung zum 'Rosenkavalier'* (Vienna: Edition Praesens, 2003)
Bellin, Klaus, *Das Weimar des Harry Graf Kessler* (Berlin: A-B Fischer, 2013)
Bennett, Benjamin, *Hugo von Hofmannsthal. The Theatres of Consciousness* (Cambridge: Cambridge University Press, 1988)
Benois, Alexandre, *Reminiscences of the Russian Ballet*, trans. Mary Britnieva (London: Putnam, 1941)
Bentley, Eric, *The Theory of the Modern Stage* (London: Penguin Modern Classics, 2008)
Bergerat, Emile, *Faublas malgré lui* (Paris: Librairie Ollendorf, 1903)
Bitterli, Urs, 'Harry Graf Kessler: Aussenseiter in vielen Rollen', *Schweizer Monatshefte für Politik, Wirtschaft, Kultur*, 76 (1996), 32–3
Blackmer, Corinne E. and Patricia Juliana Smith, eds, *En Travesti, Women, Gender Subversion, Opera* (New York: Columbia University Press, 1995)
Blay, Philippe, 'Un théâtre français, tout à fait français, ou un débat fin de siècle sur l'Opéra Comique', *Revue de musicologie*, 87, 1 (2001), 105–44
Blom, Philipp, *The Vertigo Years: Change and Culture in the West, 1900–1914* (London: Weidenfeld & Nicolson, 2008)
Bologne, Jean-Claude, *Histoire de la Pudeur* (Paris: Olivier Orban, 1986)
Bottenberg, Joanna, *Shared Creation: Words and Music in the Hofmannsthal–Strauss Operas* (Frankfurt: Peter Lang, 1996)
—— 'The Hofmannsthal–Strauss Collaboration', in *A Companion to the Works of Hugo von Hofmannsthal*, ed. Thomas A. Kovach (Rochester, NY: Camden House, 2002), pp. 117–38
Boyden, Matthew, *Richard Strauss* (London: Weidenfeld & Nicolson, 1999)
Branscombe, Peter, 'Hugo von Hofmannsthal – Man of Letters', in *Der Rosenkavalier*, ed. Nicholas John (London: Calder Publications, 1981), pp. 33–6
Brayshaw, Teresa and Noel Witts, *The Twentieth Century Performance Reader*, 3rd Edition (London and New York: Routledge, 2014)
Brindejont-Offenbach, J., 'Cinquante ans de l'opérette française', in *Cinquante ans de musique française* (Paris: Rohozinski, 1925), pp. 199–322
Brissac, Anne de Cossé, *La comtesse Greffulhe* (Paris: Perrin, 1991)
Brosche, Günter, *Richard Strauss: Werk und Leben* (Vienna: Edition Steinbauer, 2008)

Brotchie, Alistair, *Alfred Jarry, A Pataphysical Life* (Cambridge, MA: MIT Press, 2011)
Bruford, W.H., *Culture and Society in Classical Weimar, 1775-1806* (Cambridge: Cambridge University Press, 1961)
Bruyas, Florian, *Histoire de l'Opérette en France* (Lyon: Emmanuel Vitte, 1974)
Bruyr, José, *L'Opérette* (Paris: Presses Universitaires de France, 1974)
Buckle, Richard, *Diaghilev* (New York: Atheneum, 1979)
Budden, Julian, *The Operas of Verdi*, 3 vols (Oxford: Oxford University Press, 2002)
Burger, Hilde, 'Trois visages d'un ingénu ou Les chevaliers sans et avec rose (Louvet de Couvray, Louis Artus et Hofmannsthal)', *Australian Universities Language and Literature Association Proceedings and Papers of the Congress*, 14 (1972), 140-1
Cain, Georges, *Anciens Théâtres de Paris* (Paris: Eugène Fasquelle, 1906)
Canitzgesellschaft, *Harry Graf Kessler, Eine Spurensuche mit der Canitzgesellschaft*, ed. Canitzgesellschaft (Berlin: Köthen, 2008)
Cannon, Robert, *Opera* (Cambridge: Cambridge University Press, 2012)
Cathé, Philippe, *Claude Terrasse* (Paris: L'Hexaèdre, 2004)
——'Claude Terrasse (1867-1923), Thèse de Nouveau Régime' (Paris-IV, 2001)
Caughie, John, ed., *Theories of Authorship* (London: Routledge, 1981)
Charlton, David, ed., *The Cambridge Companion to Grand Opera* (Cambridge: Cambridge University Press, 2003)
Chauveau, Philippe, *Les Théâtres Parisiens Disparus* (Paris: Editions de l'Amandier, 1999)
Christiansen, Rupert, *Prima Donna: A History* (Harmondsworth: Penguin, 1984)
Cohen, H. Robert, *Cent ans de mise en scène lyrique en France (environ 1830-1930): Catalogue descriptif des livrets de mise en scène, des libretti annotés et des partitions annotés dans la Bibl. De l'Association de la Régie Théâtrale (Paris)* (New York: Pendragon Press, 1986)
Courtès, Noémie, 'Les Jardins d'Armide – du topos classique au mythe moderne', in *Les mythologies du jardin de l'antiquité à la fin du XIXe siècle*, ed. Gérard Peylet (Bordeaux: Presses Universitaires de Bordeaux, 2004), pp. 101-14
Crébillon, Claude Prosper Jolyot de, *Oeuvres* (Paris: Editions François Bourin, 1992)
Crittenden, Camille, *Johann Strauss and Vienna: Operetta and the Politics of Popular Culture* (Cambridge: Cambridge University Press, 2000)
Cryle, Peter, *Geometry in the Boudoir: Configurations of the French Erotic Narrative* (Ithaca and London: Cornell University Press, 1994)
Dehmel, Richard, *Ausgewählte Briefe. Vols 1 and 2: 1883-1902* (Berlin: S. Fischer, 1923)
Del Mar, Norman, *Richard Strauss – a critical commentary on his life and works* (London: Barrie and Rockliff, 1962)
Denis, Maurice, *Journal, Vol. 2: 1905-1920* (Paris: La Colombe, 1957)
Dent, Edward J., *Opera* (Harmondsworth: Penguin Books Ltd, 1940)
Diet, Edmond, 'L'Ingénu libertin', *Comoedia*, 12 December 1907, 1
Drummond, John, *Speaking of Diaghilev* (London: Faber & Faber, 1997)
Dubois, Claude, ed., *Dictionnaire Encyclopédique Larousse* (Paris: Librairie Larousse, 1979)
Dufresne, Claude, *Histoire de l'Opérette des Origines à nos Jours* (Paris: Fernand Nathan, 1981)
Dürhammer, Ilja and Pia Janke, eds, *Richard Strauss, Hugo von Hofmannsthal Frauenbilder* (Vienna: Edition Praesens, 2001)
Duteutre, Benoît, *L'Opérette en France* (Paris: Editions du Seuil, 1997)

Easton, Laird, 'The Red Count: The Life and Times of Harry Kessler' (Ph.D diss., Stanford University, 1991)
——*The Red Count – the Life and Times of Harry Kessler* (Berkeley: University of California Press, 2002)
——*Der Rote Graf: Harry Graf Kessler und seine Zeit* (Stuttgart: Klett-Cotta, 2005)
——*Journey to the Abyss, The Diaries of Count Harry Kessler 1880–1918* (New York: Alfred A. Knopf, 2011)
Edelmann, Bernd, 'Das Lever im I. Akte des *Rosenkavalier*: Szene und Musik', in *Richard Strauss und das Musiktheater: Bericht über die Internationale Fachkonferenz in Bochum, 14–17 November 2001*, ed. Julia Liebscher (Berlin: Henschel Verlag, 2005), pp. 245–62
Emmerson, Charles, *1913: The World before the Great War* (London: The Bodley Head, 2013)
Everist, Mark, 'Jacques Offenbach – The Music of the Past and the Image of the Present', in *Music, Theater and Cultural Transfer, Paris 1830–1914*, ed. Annegret Fauser and Mark Everist (Chicago: University of Chicago Press, 2009), pp. 72–98
Exner, Richard, 'Hugo von Hofmannsthal, Harry Graf Kessler, Briefwechsel 1898–1929', *Books Abroad*, 43.3 (1969), 417
Fein, Patrick, *Crébillon fils, Les Egarements du Coeur et de l'esprit* (London: Grant & Cutler Ltd, 2000)
Fell, Jill, *Alfred Jarry* (London: Reaktion Books, 2010)
Fiedler, Leonhard Maria, *Max Reinhardt und Molière: Text – und Bilddokumentation* (Salzburg: O. Müller, 1972)
——*Hugo von Hofmannsthals Molière-Bearbeitungen* (Darmstadt: Agora, 1974)
Fischer, Samuel and Hedwig Fischer, *Briefwechsel mit Autoren*, ed. Dierk Rodewald and Corinna Fiedler (Frankfurt am Main: S. Fischer Verlag, 1989)
Foucart, Claude, *D'un monde à l'autre. La correspondance André Gide–Harry Graf Kessler (1903–1933)* (Lyon: Centre d'Etudes gidiennes, Université de Lyon II, 1985)
Fournier, Hippolyte, *Louvet et le roman de Faublas* (Paris: Librairie des Bibliophiles, 1884)
Fournier, Jean-Claude, 'Claude Terrasse', *Opérette*, 47 (April 1983), 24–7
Fulcher, Jane F., *French Cultural Politics and Music: From the Dreyfus Affair to the First World War* (New York: Oxford University Press, 1999)
Gainham, Sarah, 'In the Twenties', *Encounter*, XXIX, 1 (July 1967), 7–17
Garafola, Lynn, *Diaghilev's Ballets Russes* (New York: Oxford University Press, 1989)
Garafola, Lynn and Nancy Van Norman Baer, eds, *The Ballets Russes and its World* (New Haven and London: Yale University Press, 1999)
Gerigk, Horst-Jürgen, 'Literarische Vergänglichkeit: Notizen zu Oscar Wilde's "Bildnis des Dorian Gray" und Hugo von Hofmannsthals "Rosenkavalier" mit Rücksicht auf Johann Peter Hebels "Unverhofftes Wiedersehen"', in *Bilderwelten als Vergegenwärtigung und Verrätselung der Welt: Literatur und Kunst um die Jahrhundertwende*, ed. Volker Kapp, Helmuth Kiesel and Klaus Lubbers (Berlin: Duncker und Humblot, 1997), pp. 139–44
Gide, Andre, *Journals. 1889–1949* (New York: Penguin, 1967)
Gilbert, Mary, 'Painter and Poet: Hogarth's *Marriage à la Mode* and Hofmannsthal's *Der Rosenkavalier*', *Modern Language Review*, 64 (1969), 818–27
Gilliam, Bryan, *The Life of Richard Strauss* (Cambridge: Cambridge University Press, 1999)
Gilliam, Bryan, ed., *Richard Strauss and his World* (Princeton: Princeton University Press, 1992)
——*Richard Strauss: New Perspectives on the Composer and his Work* (Durham and London: Duke University Press, 1992)

Goncourt, Edmond et Jules de, *La Femme au Dix-huitième Siècle* (Paris: Librairie de Firmin Didot Frères et Cie, 1862)
Gourret, Jean, *Histoire de l'Opéra Comique* (Paris: Editions Albatros, 1983)
Grout, Donald Jay, *A Short History of Opera* (New York and London: Columbia University Press, 1947)
Grupp, Peter, *Harry Graf Kessler 1868–1937: Eine Biographie* (München: C.H. Beck, 1995)
Hamburger, Michael, *Hofmannsthal: Three Essays* (Princeton: Princeton University Press, 1972)
Hartmann, Rudolf, *Richard Strauss: The Staging of His Operas and Ballets* (Oxford: Phaidon, 1982)
Hartnoll, Phyllis, ed., *The Oxford Companion to the Theatre, Fourth Edition* (Oxford: Oxford University Press, 1983)
Haupt, Jürgen, *Konstellationen Hugo von Hofmannsthals* (Salzburg: Residenz Verlag, 1970)
Hauptmann, Gerhart, *Sämtliche Werke*, 6 vols (Berlin: Ullstein Verlag, 1996)
Heine, Heinrich, *Gesammelte Werke*, 5 vols (Berlin and Weimar: Aufbau Verlag, 1974)
Heinemann, Michael, Matthias Herrmann and Stefan Weiss, eds, *Richard Strauss: Essays zu Leben und Werk* (Laaber: Laaber-Verlag, 2002)
Heisler Jr, Wayne, *The Ballet Collaborations of Richard Strauss* (Rochester, NY: University of Rochester Press, 2009)
Heldt, Gerhard, *Der Rosenkavalier* (Berlin-Lichterfelde: Robert Lienau, 1981)
Hirsch, Rudolf, 'Hofmannsthal und Frankreich. Zwei Beträge', *Etudes Germaniques*, 29, 2 (1974), 145–53
—— 'Hugo von Hofmannsthal und das Ballett. Zwei unbekannte Entwürfe für das Russische Ballett und Zeugnisse zur Entstehung der Josephslegende', *Neue Zürcher Zeitung und schweizerisches Handelsblatt, Fernausgabe,* 202. Jg., Nr. 17, 23 January 1981
—— *Ein Brief des Lord Chandos* in *Beiträge zum Verständnis Hugo von Hofmannsthals* (Frankfurt am Main: S. Fischer Verlag, 1995), pp. 45–52
Hoffmann, Dirk, 'Zu Harry Graf Kesslers Mitarbeit am *Rosenkavalier*', in *Hofmannsthal-Blätter*, 21/22 (1979), 153–60
Hoffmann, Dirk and Ingeborg Haase, 'Der Rosenkavalier: das Ergebnis einer schöpferischen Zusammenarbeit', *Richard Strauss Blätter 15* (Vienna: Internationale Richard Strauss Gesellschaft, 1986), 1–20
Hofmannsthal, Hugo von, *Buch der Freunde* (Leipzig: Insel Verlag, 1929)
—— *Briefe an Marie Herzfeld*, ed. Horst Weber (Heidelberg: Lothar Stiehm Verlag, 1967)
—— *Andreas*, trans. Marie D. Hottinger (London: Pushkin Press, 1998)
Hofmannsthal, Hugo von and Leopold von Andrian, *Briefwechsel*, ed. Walter Perl (Frankfurt am Main: S. Fischer Verlag, 1968)
Hofmannsthal, Hugo von and Edgar Karg von Bebenburg, *Briefwechsel*, ed. Mary Gilbert (Frankfurt am Main: S. Fischer Verlag, 1966)
Hofmannsthal, Hugo von and Richard Beer-Hofmann, *Briefwechsel*, ed. Eugene Weber (Frankfurt am Main: S. Fischer Verlag, 1972)
Hofmannsthal, Hugo von and Rudolf Borchardt, *Briefwechsel*, ed. Marie-Luise Borchardt and Herbert Steiner (Frankfurt am Main: S. Fischer Verlag, 1954)
Hofmannsthal, Hugo von and Rudolf Pannwitz, *Briefwechsel 1907–1926*, ed. Gerhard Schuster (Frankfurt am Main: S. Fischer Verlag, 1993)
Höhn, Gerhard, *Heine Handbuch* (Stuttgart, Weimar: Verlag J.B. Metzler, 1997)
Hyman, Timothy, *Bonnard* (London: Thames & Hudson, 1998)

Ibsen, Henrik, *Four Major Plays*, trans. James McFarlane and Jens Arup (Oxford: Oxford World's Classics, 1998)
Illies, Florian, *1913 Der Sommer des Jahrhunderts* (Frankfurt am Main: S. Fischer, 2012)
Jacobshagen, Arnold, 'Staging at the Opéra-Comique in Nineteenth-Century Paris: Auber's *Fra Diavolo* and the *livrets de mise en scène*', *Cambridge Opera Journal*, 13, 3 (2001), 239-60
Jahn, Bernhard, 'Übergang und Gabe als Dimension der Zeit im "Rosenkavalier" von Hofmannsthal und Strauss', *Deutsche Vierteljahrsschrift für Literaturwissenschaft und Geistesgeschichte*, 3 (1999), 419-56
Jefferson, Alan, *Richard Strauss – Der Rosenkavalier* (Cambridge: Cambridge University Press, 1985)
Join-Diéterle, Catherine, *Les décors de scène de l'Opéra de Paris à l'époque Romantique* (Paris: Picard, 1988)
Jones, Joseph E., *Der Rosenkavalier: Genesis, Modelling and New Aesthetic Paths* (Ann Arbor: ProQuest, 2009)
Kahan, Sylvia, *Music's Modern Muse: A Life of Winnaretta Singer, Princesse de Polignac* (Rochester, NY: University of Rochester Press, 2003)
Kappacher, Walter, *Der Fliegenpalast* (St Pölten-Salzburg: Residenz Verlag, 2009)
Kendrick, M. Gregory, 'Tending the Garden: The Kessler-Bodenhausen Circle and the Cultural Policies of Imperial Germany' (diss., University of California, Los Angeles, 1995)
Kennedy, Michael, '*Rosenkavalier* and the Third Man', *Welsh National Opera on Tour programme* (1990)
——*Richard Strauss* (New York: Schirmer, 1996)
——*Richard Strauss – Man, Musician, Enigma* (Cambridge: Cambridge University Press, 1999)
Kerman, Joseph, *Opera as Drama* (New York: Random House, 1956)
Knaus, Jakob, *Hofmannsthals Weg zur Oper 'Die Frau ohne Schatten'* (Berlin, New York: De Gruyter, 1971)
Kohler, Stephan, 'Musikdrama ohne Worte – zur Entstehungsgeschichte der Josephs Legende', in *Josephs Legende: Programmheft der Bayerischen Staatsoper* (München: Bayerische Staatsoper, 1980), pp. 12-29
Kolb, Annette, 'Harry Graf Kessler', *Mass und Wert*, 4 (1938), 630-1
König, Christoph, *Hofmannsthal. Ein moderner Dichter unter den Philologen* (Marbach: Wallstein Verlag, 2003)
Krakauer, Siegfried, *Jacques Offenbach und das Paris seiner Zeit* (Frankfurt am Main: Suhrkamp, 1994)
Krause, Ernst, *Richard Strauss – the Man and his Work*, trans. John Coombs (London: Collet's, 1964)
Krüger, Karl-Joachim, *Hugo von Hofmannsthal und Richard Strauss* (Berlin: Junker und Dünnhaupt, 1935)
Lacy, Robin Thurlow, *A Biographical Dictionary of Scenographers* (New York: Greenwood Press, 1990)
Lamothe, Peter, 'The Music of *Ubu roi*: Terrasse's Parallel World of Absurdity', chapter in 'Theater Music in France, 1864-1914' (diss., University of North Carolina, Chapel Hill, 2008)
Landolfi, Andrea, 'L'aiutante segreto, Kessler, Hofmannsthal e il *Rosenkavalier*', *Studi Germanici, nuova serie*, 30/31 (1992-3), 361-74

—'Harry Kessler e la nascita del *Rosenkavalier*', in *Der Rosenkavalier di Richard Strauss, Festival del Maggio Musicale Fiorentino*, 75 edizione (2012), 262–73

Ledout, Annie, 'Le théâtre des Bouffes-Parisiens, historique et programmes, 1855–1880' (Ph.D. diss., Université de Paris IV, 2001)

Legrand, Raphaelle and Nicole Wild, *Regards sur l'Opéra Comique: trois siècles de vie théâtrale* (Paris: Editions du CNRS, 2002)

Lehmann, Lotte, *Five Operas and Richard Strauss* (New York: Macmillan, 1964)

—*Memoirs of Rosenkavalier* (essay in sleevenote to RCA Victor LP boxed set LCT-6005 (2))

Leibnitz, Thomas, *Richard Strauss: 100 Jahre Rosenkavalier* (Vienna: Österreichische Nationalbibliothek, 2010)

Lockspeiser, Edward, *Debussy: His Life and Mind*, 2 vols (Cambridge: Cambridge University Press, 1978)

Lomagne, B. de, 'Les Premières', *Le Soir*, 12 December 1907, 3

Mahler, Alma, *Gustav Mahler: Memories and Letters*, trans. Basil Creighton, ed. Donald Mitchell and Knud Martner (London: Cardinal, 1990)

Mahler, Gustav and Richard Strauss, *Correspondence 1888–1911*, ed. Herta Blaukopf and trans. Edmund Jephcott (Chicago: University of Chicago Press, 1984)

Maître Friand, 'Chez Madame la Comtesse de Kessler', *The Table*, 28 January 1888, requoted in *Kataloge*, 43, p. 21

Mango, Lorenzo, 'The Manuscripts of *The Art of the Theatre* by Edward Gordon Craig', in *Acting Archives Essays, Supplement*, 7 April 2011

Mann, Golo, *Erinnerungen und Gedanken: Eine Jugend in Deutschland* (Frankfurt am Main: S. Fischer, 1986)

Mann, Thomas, *Joseph und seine Brüder*, 4 vols (Frankfurt am Main: S. Fischer Verlag, 2007)

—*Lotte in Weimar* (Frankfurt am Main: S. Fischer Verlag, 1990)

Mann, William, *Richard Strauss – a critical study of the operas* (London: Cassell, 1964)

Mazouer, Charles, *Molière et ses comédies-ballets* (Paris: Honoré Champion, 2006)

Messmer, Franzpeter, *Kritiken zu den Uraufführungen der Bühenwerke von Richard Strauss* (Pfaffenhofen: W. Ludwig Verlag, 1989)

Meyer, Mathias, ed., *Rudolf Hirsch: Beiträge zum Verständnis Hugo von Hofmannsthals* (Frankfurt: S. Fischer Verlag, 1995)

Miller-Degenfeld, Marie-Therèse, *The Poet and the Countess: Hugo von Hofmannsthal's Correspondence with Countess Ottonie Degenfeld*, trans. Eric Barcel (Rochester, NY: Camden House, 2000)

Millington, Barry, *Richard Wagner: The Sorcerer of Bayreuth* (London: Thames & Hudson, 2012)

Morel, Jean-Paul, 'Claude Terrasse et Erik Satie', *Magazine Littéraire*, 368 (2000), 35–8

Mühlher, Robert, 'Hugo von Hofmannsthal: Die Komödie für Musik *Der Rosenkavalier*', in *Oesterreichische Dichter seit Grillparzer: Gesammelte Aufsätze* (Wien, Stuttgart: Wilhelm Braumüller, 1973), pp. 321–8

Nabokov, Nicolas, *Bagazh: Memoirs of a Russian Cosmopolitan* (New York: Atheneum, 1975)

Neumann, Gerhard and Gunter Schnitzler, eds, *Harry Graf Kessler: Ein Wegbereiter der Moderne* (Freiburg im Breisgau: Rombach, 1997)

Newman, L. M., *The Correspondence of Edward Gordon Craig and Count Harry Kessler*, ed. L.M. Newman (London: W.S. Maney and Son Ltd, 1995)

Nostitz, Helene von, *Aus dem alten Europa* (Frankfurt am Main: Insel Verlag, 1979)

Nozière, Fernand, 'Le Théâtre', *Gil Blas*, 12 December 1907, 3

Osborne, Charles, *The Complete Operas of Richard Strauss* (London: Michael O'Mara Books, 1988)
——*The Complete Operas of Strauss: A Critical Guide* (London: Victor Gollancz, 1992)
Osborne, Harold, ed., *The Oxford Companion to Art* (Oxford: Oxford University Press, 1970)
Pahlen, Kurt, 'Zur Geschichte der Oper "Der Rosenkavalier"', in *Der Rosenkavalier, Textbuch, Einführung und Kommentar*, ed. Kurt Pahlen (Mainz–München: Piper–Schott, 1980), pp. 288–360
Päpke, Corinna, ed., *Hommage à Harry Graf Kessler* (Berlin: Bröhan Museum, 2007)
Paris Opéra library, Palais Garnier: Microfilmed record entitled *Bouffes Parisiens*, réserve pièce no. 39
Patureau, Frédérique, *Le Palais Garnier dans la société parisienne, 1875–1914* (Liège: Pierre Mardaga, 1991)
Perry, Gill, *The First Actresses – Nell Gwyn to Sarah Siddons* (London: National Portrait Gallery, 2011)
Phillips, John, *The Marquis de Sade, A Very Short Introduction* (Oxford: Oxford University Press, 2005)
Poppenberg, Felix, *Literarisches Echo*, 14 (1911), 1254–9
Prost-Romand, Cécile, 'La Légende de Joseph', *Revue de Littérature Comparée*, I (1989), 77–83
Proust, Marcel, *Remembrance of Things Past*, trans. Scott Moncrief and Terence Kilmartin (London: The Folio Society, 2000)
Puffett, Derrick, *Richard Strauss: Elektra* (Cambridge: Cambridge University Press, 1989)
Renner, Ursula and Gisela Bärbel Schmid, eds, *Hugo von Hofmannsthal, Freundschaften und Begegnungen mit deutschen Zeitgenossen* (Würzburg: Königshausen & Neumann, 1991)
Renucci, Françoise Salvan, *Ein Ganzes von Text und Musik – Hugo von Hofmannsthal und Richard Strauss* (Tutzing: Hans Schneider, 2001)
Révoil, Fanély, 'Claude Terrasse, compositeur de la Belle Epoque', *Les Annales*, 176 (June 1965), 22–34
Richardson, Samuel, *Clarissa* (London: Penguin Books, 1985)
Richter, Thomas, 'Die Bibliothek Harry Graf Kesslers. Möglichkeiten und Grenzen einer Rekonstruktion', in *Bibliotheken und Sammlungen im Exil*, ed. Claus-Dieter Krohn and Lutz Winckler (München: et+k, 2011), pp. 42–68
Riethmüller, Albrecht, 'Komödie für Musik nach Wagner: Der Rosenkavalier', in *Hofmannsthal Jahrbuch zur Europäischen Moderne 4/1996*, ed. Gerhard Neumann and others (Freiburg: Rombach Verlag, 1997), pp. 277–96
Robichez, Jacques, *Le symbolisme au théâtre: Lugné-Poe et les débuts de l'Oeuvre* (Paris: L'Arche, 1957)
Rösch, Ewald, 'Komödie und Berliner Kritik. Zu Hofmannsthal's Lustspielen *Cristinas Heimreise* und *Der Schwierige*', in *Hugo von Hofmannsthal: Freundschaften und Begegnungen mit deutschen Zeitgenossen*, ed. Ursula Renner and G. Bärbl Schmid (Würzburg: Königshausen & Neumann, 1991), pp. 163–90
Rothe, Friedrich, *Harry Graf Kessler* (München: Siedler Verlag, 2008)
Rothenstein, William, *Men and Memories, Vol. 2: 1900–1922* (London: Faber & Faber, 1932)
Sadie, Stanley, ed., *The New Grove Dictionary of Music and Musicians, Second Edition*, 29 vols (Oxford: Oxford University Press, 2001)
Sammons, Jeffrey L., *Hugo von Hofmannsthal, the Elusive Poet* (New Haven and London: Yale University Press, 1969)

Schlögel, Karl, 'Das Jahrhundertprotokoll: Harry Graf Kesslers Tagebuch 1880-1937', *Merkur: deutsche Zeitschrift für europäisches Denken*, 58 (2004), 557-68

Schlötterer, Reinhold, ed., *Musik und Theater im 'Rosenkavalier' von Richard Strauss* (Vienna: Österreichischen Akademie der Wissenschaften, 1985)

Schneider, Klaus Dieter, 'Harry Graf Kesslers Einfluß auf die Gestaltung der Komödie für Musik "Der Rosenkavalier"' (diss., Celle, 1970)

Schneider, Louis, 'L'Ingénu libertin', *Comoedia*, 12 December 1907, 1-2

Scholes, Percy A., *The Oxford Companion to Music, Tenth Edition*, ed. John Owen Ward (Oxford: Oxford University Press, 1970)

Schuh, Willi, ed., *Der Rosenkavalier, Fassungen, Filmszenarium, Briefe* (Frankfurt am Main: S. Fischer Verlag, 1971)

—— 'Hofmannsthal, Kessler und die Josephslegende', *Hofmannsthal Blätter*, 27 (1983), 48-55

—— *Hugo von Hofmannsthal und Richard Strauss* (Munich: Carl Hanser Verlag, 1964)

—— *Richard Strauss: A Chronicle of the Early Years 1864-1898*, trans. Mary Whittall (New York: Cambridge University Press, 1982)

—— *Die Entstehung des Rosenkavalier* (Zurich: Atlantis Verlag, *Trivium* Year IX, Vol. 2, 1951), 65-91

—— *Umgang mit Musik* (Zurich/Freiburg: Atlantis Verlag, 1970)

Schuster, Gerhard and Margot Pehle, eds, *Harry Graf Kessler, Tagebuch eines Weltmannes, Eine Ausstellung des Deutschen Literaturarchivs im Schiller-Nationalmuseum Marbach am Neckar* (Marbach: Marbacher Kataloge, 43, 1988)

—— 'Auf den Spuren von Harry Graf Kesslers Nachlass', *Sinn und Form*, 2 (2008), 278-84

Shattuck, Roger, *The Banquet Years* (New York: Vintage Books, 1967)

Sheehy, Helen, *Eleonora Duse: A Biography* (New York: Alfred A. Knopf, 2003)

Sherard, Robert Harborough, *Twenty Years in Paris* (London: Hutchinson & Co., 1905)

Signorelli, Olga, *Eleonora Duse*, trans. Isabel Quigly (London: Thames & Hudson, 1959)

Smith, Patrick, *The Tenth Muse, A historical study of the opera libretto* (London: Victor Gollancz, 1971)

Soubies, Albert, *Histoire du Théâtre-Lyrique* (Paris: Librairie Fischbacher, 1894)

—— *Le Théâtre Italien de 1801 à 1913* (Paris: Librairie Fischbacher, 1913)

Souvestre, Pierre, 'L'Ingénu libertin', *Comoedia*, 12 December 1907, 2

St Denis, Ruth, *An Unfinished Life: An Autobiography* (New York: Harper & Brothers, 1939)

Stenzel, Burkhard, *Harry Graf Kessler: Ein Leben Zwischen Kultur und Politik* (Köln: Böhlau, 1995)

—— 'Gerhart Hauptmann und Harry Graf Kessler', *Euphorion* (Heidelberg: Universitatsverlag, Winter 102.4 (2008), 413-49

—— *Widmungen Hugo von Hofmannsthals. Einblicke in Werke der ehemaligen Weimarer Bibliothek von Harry Graf Kessler*, in *Mitteldeutsches Jahrbuch für Kultur und Geschichte* (Dössel: Verlag Janos Stekovics, 2009), pp. 101-14

Stewart, Robert Sussman, ed., *Richard Strauss, Der Rosenkavalier* (London: Michael Joseph, 1982)

Stillinger, Jack, *Multiple Authorship and the Myth of Solitary Genius* (New York: Oxford University Press, 1991)

Stoullig, Edmond, *Les Annales du Théâtre et de la Musique 1907* (Paris: G. Charpentier, 1908)

Sutcliffe, Tom, *The Faber Book of Opera* (London: Faber & Faber, 2000)

Sutherland, Millicent Duchess of, *Six Weeks at the War* (Chicago: A.C. McClurg, 1915)

Thelen, Albert Vigoleis, *The Island of Second Sight; being the Applied Recollections of Vigoleis*, trans. Donald O. White (Cambridge: Galileo Publishers, 2010)

———*Meine Heimat bin ich selbst, Briefe 1929–1953* (Köln: Dumont, 2010)
Traubner, Richard, *Operetta – A Theatrical History* (New York: Routledge, 2003)
Trenner, Franz, ed., *Richard Strauss: Dokumente Seines Lebens und Schaffens* (München: C.H. Beck Verlag, 1954)
———*Richard Strauss Chronik zu Leben und Werk* (Vienna: R. Strauss Verlag, 2003)
Trillat, Joseph, 'Le Mois', *Bulletin français de la Société Internationale de la Musique* (January 1908), pp. 82–3
Uglow, Jenny, *Hogarth A Life and a World* (London: Faber & Faber, 1997)
Van de Velde, Henri, *Récit de ma Vie*, ed. Anne van Loo and Fabrice van de Kerckhove (Brussels: Versa Flammarion, 1995)
Vogel, Juliane, 'Schattenland des ungelebten Lebens. Zur Kunst des Prologs bei Hugo von Hofmannsthal', *Hofmannsthal Jahrbuch I* (1993), 165–81
Vogel, Juliane, ed., *Hugo von Hofmannsthal Operndichtungen* (Salzburg: Residenz Verlag, 1994)
Walter, Michael, *Richard Strauss und seine Zeit: Grosse Komponisten und ihre Zeit* (Laaber: Laaber Verlag, 2000)
Warrack, John and Ewan West, *The Oxford Dictionary of Opera* (Oxford: Oxford University Press, 1992)
Weber, Horst, *Hugo von Hofmannsthal Bibliographie des Schrifttums 1892 bis 1963* (Berlin: de Gruyter, 1966)
———*Hugo von Hofmannsthal Bibliographie Werke Briefe Gespräche Übersetzungen Vertonungen* (Berlin, New York: de Gruyter, 1972)
Wedekind, Frank, *Gesammelte Werke*, 6 vols (München und Leipzig: Georg Müller, 1912–14)
Weisstein, Ulrich, '(Pariser) Farce oder wienerische Maskerade? Die französischen Quellen des *Rosenkavalier*', in *Hofmannsthal-Forschungen*, 9, ed. Wolfram Mauser (Freiburg im Breslau, 1987), 75–102
Wild, Nicole, *Dictionnaire des théâtres parisiens au XIX siècle: Les théâtres et la musique* (Paris: Aux Amateurs de Livres, 1989)
Wilhelm, Kurt, *Richard Strauss Persönlich: Eine Bildbiographie* (Munich: Kindler, 1984)
———*Richard Strauss: An Intimate Portrait* (London: Thames & Hudson, 1989)
Wolff, Stéphane, *Un demi-siècle d'opéra-comique* (Paris: André Bonne, 1953)
Yon, Jean-Claude, 'La création du Théâtre des Bouffes-Parisiens (1855–1862), ou La difficile naissance de l'opérette', *Revue d'histoire moderne et contemporaine*, 39 (1992), 575–600
Youmans, Charles, ed., *The Cambridge Companion to Richard Strauss* (Cambridge: Cambridge University Press, 2010)
Zeller, Bernhard, *Harry Graf Kessler, Zeuge und Chronist seiner Epoche* (Mainz: Akademie der Wissenschaften und der Literatur, 1989)
———'Aus unbekannten Tagebüchern Harry Graf Kesslers', in *Jahrbuch der deutschen Schillergesellschaft*, 31 (1987), 3–34
Zimmermann, Hans, ed., *100 Jahre Cranach Presse* (Berlin: Otto Meissners Verlag, 2013)

Index of Works

A Doll's House (Ibsen) 85
Aphrodite (Erlanger) 170
Arabella (Strauss) 115
As You Like It (Shakespeare) 88
Aux Temps des Croisades (Terrasse) 31

Capriccio (Strauss) 3
Casanova (Hofmannsthal) 132, 133, 136
Chandos Brief (Hofmannsthal) 121
Chérubin (Massenet) 170
Chonchette (Terrasse) 31
Clarissa (Richardson) 151
Clématite (Artus) 38
Coeur de Moineau (Artus) 38, 41, 184
Collected Works (Hofmannsthal) 115
Comus (Milton) 104
Cristinas Heimreise (Hofmannsthal) 114,
    131, 133, 139, 144, 158, 183, 185, 188,
    189, 190, 194, 195, 200, 205, 207
Cyrano de Bergerac (Rostand) 62

Dantons Tod (Büchner) 118
Das gerettete Venedig (Hofmannsthal) 105
Das Rheingold (Wagner) 89
Der Abenteurer und die Sängerin
    (Hofmannsthal) 124
Der Biberpelz (Hauptmann) 97
Der Kammersänger (Wedekind) 101
Der Marquis von Keith (Wedekind) 101
Der Rosenkavalier (Strauss) x, xii, 1, 2, 3, 4,
    5, 7, 8, 9, 10, 11, 12, 21, 23, 42, 44, 47,
    49, 51, 54, 58, 64, 67, 69, 75, 91, 94,
    95, 96, 97, 100, 104, 105, 107, 109,
    110, 112, 160, 173, 187, 192, 202, 203,
    205, 215, 216, Plate 3, Plate 11, Plate
    12, Plate 13, Plate 15
  devising the scenario 113–53
  characterisation and authorship 154–94
  quarrel between Hofmannsthal and
    Kessler over authorship 195–201

  summary of genesis and
    authorship 206–7
  Strauss compositional timelines
    for 209–12
  early rumours of Kessler's
    involvement 213–4
Der Schwierige (Hofmannsthal) 189
Der Triumph der Zeit
    (Hofmannsthal) 117
Die Entstehung des Rosenkavalier
    (Schuh) 140
Die Frau im Fenster (Hofmannsthal) 123
Die Hochzeit der Sobeide
    (Hofmannsthal) 124, 131
Die Meistersinger von Nürnberg
    (Wagner) 91, 121
Die Walküre (Wagner) 90, 92
Die Weber (Hauptmann) 96, 97, 98
Die Zauberflöte (Mozart) 91

Einsame Menschen (Hauptmann) 93
Elektra (Hofmannsthal) 108, 117, 121, 129
Elektra (Strauss) 115, 118, 119
Erdgeist (Wedekind) 101

Fanny Hill (Cleland) 7
Faublas (Dupeuty/Brunswick/
    Lhérie) 14–17
Faublas (Cadol/Duval) 18
Faust (Goethe) 162
Faust (Gounod) 169
Fin des Amours du Chevalier de Faublas
    (Louvet de Couvray) 7
Florian Geyer (Hauptmann) 96, 98
Fortunio (Messager) 23, 52
Friedensfest (Hauptmann) 100

Geneviève de Brabant (Offenbach) 36
Götterdämmerung (Wagner) 90
Griechischer Frühling (Hauptmann) 99

Index of Works

Hamlet (Shakespeare) 138
Hanneles Himmelfahrt (Hauptmann) 97
Henry V (Shakespeare) 105
Hue and Cry after Cupid (Jonson) 104
Hunger (Craig) 106

Jedermann (Hofmannsthal) 127
Joseph in Egypt (Méhul) 91–2
Josephs Legende (Strauss) xii, 91, 96, 159, 203

L'Après-midi d'un faune (Debussy) 33
L'Ingénu libertin (Terrasse/Artus) 1, 2, 4, 5, 8, 10, 12, 16, 19, 26, 40, 46, 48, 51, 56, 61, 63, 64, 66, 68, 110, 113, 114, 126, 131, 135, 136, 146, 148, 149, 150, 151, 152, 154, 155, 159, 177, 179, 183, 184, 186, 188, 191, 201, 207, 210, 214, 215, 216, Plate 2, Plate 6, Plate 7
   creation, performance and treatment by author and composer 21–71
   Kessler's use of for the *Rosenkavalier* scenario 139–44
   prototype characters for *Der Rosenkavalier* 161–76
La Basoche (Messager) 27
La belle Hélène (Offenbach) 36, 82
La Botte secrète (Terrasse) 31
La Duchesse Potiphar (Artus) 38
La Fille de Madame Angot (Lecocq) 27
La Maison du Fou (Artus) 39
La Maison du Sage (Artus) 39
La Marquise et le Marmiton see *L'Ingénu libertin*
La Mascotte (Audran) 27, 89
La Nouvelle Héloise (Rousseau) 151
La Petite Femme de Loth (Terrasse) 29, 35
La Ponelle (Artus) 38, 41
La Puce à l'Oreille (Feydeau) 22
L'Ecole des Filles (L'Ange/Millot) 7
Le Chemineau (Leroux) 23
Le Chevalier de Faublas (Willemain d'Abancourt) 13–14
Le Costaud des Epinettes (Bernard) 194
Le Jongleur de Notre Dame (Massenet) 170
Le Marriage de Figaro (Beaumarchais) 119
Le Médecin Malgré Lui (Molière) 167

Le Nozze di Figaro (Mozart) 4, 61, 91, 143, 171–2, 174
Le Pavillon d'Armide (Fokine/Benois) 46–7, 149
Le Sire de Vergy (Terrasse) 28, 35, 36–8, 52
Le Vin de ta Vigne (Artus) 39
Les Amours de Faublas (Lockroy/Lhérie) 17
Les Braconniers (Offenbach) 18
Les Cloches de Corneville (Planquette) 27
Les Fourberies de Scapin (Molière) 167, 184–5
Les Jardins d'Armide 45–6, 47, 60
Les Liaisons dangereuses (Nozière after Choderlos de Laclos) 50
Les Mousquetaires au Couvent (Varney) 27
Les P'tites Michu (Messager) 27
Les Travaux d'Hercule (Terrasse) 25, 35–6, 52, 55, 114, 136
Léocadie (Auber) 16
Light (Das Licht) (Hellmesberger) 91–2
Lysistrata (Hofmannsthal) 130–1, 133

Madame sans Gêne (Sardou) 55
Moloch (Schillings) 118
Monsieur Beaucaire (Messager) 27
Monsieur de la Palisse (Terrasse) 28, 52
Monsieur de Pourceaugnac (Molière) 4, 135, 140, 143, 146, 161, 162, 163, 166, 167
Much Ado About Nothing (Shakespeare) 104, 105
Musotte (Maupassant) 85
Mutter Erde (Halbe) 93

Oedipus (Hofmannsthal) 101, 105, 130, 133, 197

Parsifal (Wagner) 89, 91
Patience (Gilbert & Sullivan) 89
Pelléas et Mélisande (Debussy) 169

Rosmersholm (Ibsen) 98

Salome (Strauss) 117, 118, 121, 197
Salome (Wilde) 101
Semiramis (Hofmannsthal) 117, 118, 127
She Stoops to Conquer (Goldsmith) 162
Siegfried (Wagner) 90

Sir Thomas More (Shakespeare and others) 157
Six Semaines de la Vie du Chevalier de Faublas (Louvet de Couvray) 7
Soldier Sahibs (Allen) 80

Tannhäuser (Wagner) 89, 91
Tantris der Narr (Hardt) 193
Tartuffe (Molière) 118
Terzinen (Hofmannsthal) 123
The Art of the Theatre (Craig) 105
The Birth of Tragedy (Nietzsche) 92
The Clouds (Aristophanes) 88
The Faithful Shepherdess (Fletcher) 104
The Libertine (anthology) 8
The Masque of London 105
The Masque of Love 105
The Merchant of Venice (Shakespeare) 88, 103
The Merry Widow (Lehár) 30
The Merry Wives of Windsor (Shakespeare) 88
The Red Count (Easton) 73, 132
The Relapse (Vanbrugh) 162
The Rivals (Sheridan) 162
The Shepherd's Song (Hauptmann) 124
The Vertigo Years (Blom) 74
The Vikings (Ibsen) 104, 105
Thérèse philosophe (Anon) 8
Thermidor (Sardou) 118
Tom Jones (Fielding) 162
Tristan und Isolde (Wagner) 89
Twelfth Night (Shakespeare) 103, 147, 162, 172

Ubu roi (Jarry) 28, 33–4, 35, 41
Und Pippa tanzt (Hauptmann) 99, 100
Une Année de la Vie du Chevalier de Faublas (Louvet de Couvray) 7, 8, 11, 12, 23, 42, 44, 62, 71, 115, 135, 161
Une Aventure de Faublas (Sauvage/Lecouturier) 14

Venice Preserved (Otway) 105
Vénus dans le Cloître (Abbé du Prat) 8
Vive la France! (Terrasse) 35

Zum Geleit (Hofmannsthal) 154

Index

References to illustrations in **bold**

Adam, Alphonse 27
Alba, Jeanne ('Jane') 1, 54, 55, 57, 169, Plate 2
Albert, Mary 18
Allen, Charles 80
Andrian-Werburg, Leopold von 196
Ange, Jean L' 7
Ansorge, Conrad 95
Antoine, André 100
Appia, Adolphe 108
Archives Nationales, Paris, St. Denis 83
Aristophanes 88
Artus, Louis 1, **5**, 12, 19, **26**, 37, **39**, 41, 42, 44, 51, 136, 150, 152, 164, 165, 170, 175, 184, 185, 188, 191, 216
  Artus and Terrasse create *L'Ingénu libertin* 23–7
  Artus as critic collaborator 38–9
  treatment by Artus of Louvet de Couvray 45–50
  characterisation by Artus of Sophie 167–8
Auber, Daniel François Esprit 16, 27
Aubry, Raoul 52
Auden, Wystan Hugh xii
Audran, Edmond 27, 28, 89
Auffmordt merchant and banking family of Hamburg 78
Avril, Paul **9, 10, 11, 16,**

Bach, Johann Sebastian 59
Bahr, Hermann 133
Baker, Janet **192**
Ballets Russes, Les 47, 100, 149
Balzac, Honoré de 151–2
Barker, Elisabeth 80
Barthes, Roland 156
Barzantny, Tamara 75, 103
Basset, Serge (real name Paul Ribon) 41–2

Bate, Jonathan 157
Baudouin, Pierre-Antoine 48, 67, **67**, **68**, 69, 70
Baumann, Gerhart 158
Bay, Marquis de (Alexandre, Maître de Bay) 45
Beardsley, Aubrey 149, 212
Beaumarchais, Pierre Augustin Caron de 8, 143, 152, 170
Beecham, Sir Thomas xii
Beer-Hofmann, Richard 189
Beethoven, Ludwig van 29
Becque, Henry François 152
Benois, Alexandre 46
Bernard, Tristan 29, 34, 35, 114, 152, 188, 194
Bernhardt, Sarah 85
Beust, Count Friedrich Ferdinand von 78
Bierbaum, Otto Julius 96
Bismarck, Countess Marie von **79**
Bismarck, Count Otto von **79**, 98
Blei, Franz 213, 214
Bleichröder, Gerson von 129
Blom, Philippe 74
Blosse Lynch, Alice Harriet (see also Kessler, Countess Alice) 74, **82**, **84**, **86**, 93
  as society hostess 75–8
  has private theatre built 75–6, **76**
  family background and upbringing 79–81
  rumoured affair with Kaiser Wilhelm I 81–4
  as singer and actress and influence on Kessler 87–8
Blosse Lynch, Caroline Jane Mary 81
Blosse Lynch, Henry 80–1
Blosse Lynch, Quested Finnis 81
Blosse Lynch, Rose 81
Blosse Lynch, Stephen 80

Blosse Lynch, Thomas Kerr 80–1
Bode, (Arnold) Wilhelm von 96
Bodenhausen, Eberhard von 73, 96, 98,
    122, 123, 189, 196, 201, 207, 214
  meeting with Kessler in Paris 201
  receives *Rosenkavalier* letter from
    Kessler 201–3
  learns of respective artistic roles in *Der
    Rosenkavalier* 204–5
Boito, Arrigo 115, 162
Bonaparte, Princess Pierre 77
Bonaparte, Roland 77
Bonnard, Andrée 31
Bonnard, Charles 31–2
Bonnard, Pierre xii, 26, 31–3, **32**, 35, 110,
    177, Plate 4, Plate 5
Borchardt, Rudolf 195
Boucher, François 68
Bourget, Paul 124
Brahm, Otto 105, 123, 131
Branscombe, Peter 156
Brieux, Mlle 57
Brigands, Les (music theatre company) 31
Brunswick, Léon-Lévy 14, **15**, 17
Bruyas, Florian 55
Büchner, Georg 118
Burger, Hilde 126, 205
Byron, Lord 88

Cadol, Edouard 18
Caillavet, Gaston de 23, 29, 35–8, **35**, 39,
    202, 204
Cambon, Charles 22
Cantacuzène, Princess Elsa 123
Carpézat, Eugène-Louis 21
Castle, Terry 170
Cathé, Philippe 30, 33
Cecil, Hotel (London) Plate 8
Channon, Sir Henry 'Chips' 4
Chesney, Sir Francis 80
Clary, Mlle 18
Clermont Tonnerre, Comte de 50
Coizeau, Jean 54
Conder, Charles 27
Courtès, Noémie 46
Craig, Edward Gordon 75, 88, 100, 102,
    108, 110, 149, 197, 198, 199, 214, **215**
  relationship with Kessler 104–7

Cranach Press, Weimar (Kessler's
    publishing house) 73
Crébillon fils, Claude Prosper Jolyot de 8,
    27, 71, 131,
  on the balance between *libertinage* and
    sentiment 150–2
Crowe, Lucy Plate 15
Cunard, Lady Maud ('Emerald') xii

Debussy, Claude 30, 32, 37, 169
Degenfeld, Ottonie 122, 201
Dehmel, Richard 5, 95, 96, 97, 99, 116, 122,
    124
Déjazet, Virginie 54
Denis, Maurice 32, 110
Dernesch, Helga **192**
Deval, Abel 25, 38, 40–2, 57
Diaghilev, Serge xii, 91, 96, 105
Dickens, Charles 88
Diderot, Denis 8, 151
Diet, Edmond 55
Dieudonné, Robert 54
Divonne, Andrée 54, 57
Doche, Alexandre 16, 17
Doche, Joseph Denis 14, 17
Donizetti, Gaetono 87
Dostoevski, Fyodor 151
Dorgère, Arlette 1, 22, 27, 37, 52, **53**, 54, 57,
    150, 176, 179, Plate 7
Douai, Emile 14
Drault, Jean 52, 54
Dressel Restaurant (Berlin) 97
Dreyfus, Alfred 35
Dukas, Paul 30
Dumas, Alexandre 101
Dungern, Otto von 95
Dupeuty, Charles 14, **15**
Dürhammer, Ilya 158
Duscha 310
Duse, Eleonore 85
Duteutre, Benoît 30, 36
Duval, Georges 18
Dvorak, Antonin 46

East India Company 80, 81
Easton, Laird 73, 74, 81, 85, 98, 132
Eden Musée of New York 78
Emmanuel, Maurice 37

Emmerson, Charles 74
Erlanger, Camille 170
Erté **187**
Esterhazy, Prince Paul (and his orchestra) 78
Euphrates and Tigris Steam Navigation Company 80

Farrar, Geraldine 121, 137, 169, 170
Fauré, Gabriel 30
Feydeau, Georges 22, **22**
Fielding, Henry 151, 162
Fischer, Hedwig 213
Fischer, Samuel 81, 213, 214
Flaischlein, Cesar 123
Flers, Robert de 23, 29, **35**, 35–8, 39, 52, 186, 202, 204
Fletcher, John 104
Förster-Nietzsche, Elisabeth 94, 205
Fokine, Michael 46
Fortuny, Mariano 108
Fournier, Hippolyte 152
Franc-Nohain (Maurice Etienne Legrand) 29, 34, 35
France, Anatole 170
Franck, Alphonse 191
Friedrichshagen Group, Berlin 97
Fuller, Loie 106
Fürstner, Adolph (publisher) 214, **215**

Garden, Mary 121, 137, 169, 170
Gaugin, Paul 32
Gide, André 96
Gigout, Eugène 31
Gilbert, Mary 177
Gilliam, Bryan 115
Gluck, Christoph Willibald von 46
Gobemouche, Léonard (Willemain d'Abancourt, François-Jean) 13
Goethe, Johann Wolfgang von 93, 98, 162
Goldsmith, Oliver 162
Gorki, Maxim 101
Gounod, Charles 32, 34, 169
Grand Hotel (Paris) 26
Granier, Jeanne 54
Grapperon, Philippe 31
Grupp, Peter 74, 92

Hading, Jane 77
Hahn, Reynaldo 30
Halbe, Max 93, 97
Hamsun, Knut 97
Hardt, Ernst 193, 194
Harrach, Ferdinand and Helene von 95
Harry Graf Kessler Gesellschaft e.V. (Kessler Society) 74
Hart brothers (*Friedrichshagen Group, Berlin*) 97
Harwood, Elizabeth 173, **192**
Hasti 57
Haupt, Jürgen 158
Hauptmann, Gerhart 93, 95, 96, 102, 106, 109, 110, 124, 127, 146, 184, Plate 9
  relationship with Kessler 97–101
Hauptmann, Margarete 99
Haydn, Joseph 46
Heimann, Moritz 213, 214
Heine, Heinrich 27, 71, 150, 151, 152
Heinrich XIV, Prince of Reuss 84
Heller, Max 41, 42
Hervé, (Florimond Roger) 25
Heyse, Paul von 124
Hoffmann, Dirk 145, 174
Hofmann, Ludwig von 99, 205
Hofmannsthal, Gerty 128, 180
Hofmannsthal, Hugo von x, 2, 3, 4, 12, 21, 23, 27, 42, 43, 49, 56, 65, 69, 71, 73, 88, 92, 93, 94, 96, 97, 101, 102, 104, 105, 106, **107**, **122**, **134**, **160**, **175**, 202–16
  meets and gets to know Kessler 107–110
  considers *Casanova* as opera material for Strauss 113–4
  relationship with Strauss 115–21
  relationship with Kessler by 1909 122–6
  creative exchanges with Kessler 127–31
  trip to Greece with Kessler and Maillol 131–3
  devising the *Rosenkavalier* scenario with Kessler 135–53
  characterisation in and authorship of *Der Rosenkavalier* 154–94
  quarrel with Kessler over dedication and authorship 195–201
Hogarth, William 4, 100, 113, 139, 177, Plate 14

Index

Holländer, Felix 213, 214
Holz, Arno 97

Ibsen, Henrik 85, 98, 104, 153, 184
Illies, Florian 74
Indy, Vincent d' 30
Isokowski, Soile Plate 15

Jarry, Alfred 28, 29, **34**, 35, 38
   first librettist for Terrasse with *Ubu roi* 33–4
Jefferson, Alan 162
John, Augustus 110
Jones, Joseph 211
Jonson, Ben 104
Jordaens, Jacob 162

Kainz, Joseph 100, 113, 124, 138, 198
Kalisch, Alfred 214
Kerst, Léon 38
Kessler, Adolf Wilhelm 74, **79**, 81,
   marriage to Alice Blosse Lynch 81, 83
   as society host in Paris 75–8, 85
   as successful banker and entrepreneur 78
   unusually fast ennoblement 84
Kessler, Countess Alice Harriet (née Blosse Lynch) 74, **76**, **79**, **82**, **84**, **86**
   object of her son's admiration 81–2, 87
   elicits warm tribute from Maupassant 85
   particular theatrical talent 87–8
   urges Kessler to write drama 93
Kessler, Count Harry Clément Ulrich x, **xi**, xii, 2, 3, 12, 23, 25, 32, 43, 46, 47, 48, 56, 57, **76**, 85, **90**, 95, 96, 113, 118, 121, **134**, 154, 155, 156, 158, 159, **160**, 162, 163, 164, 165, 168, 169, 174, 175, **206**, 210, 211, 212, 213, **215**, Plate 1, Plate 10,
   importance of his diary 4–5
   sees *L'Ingénu libertin* 21
   absorbs all its performative elements 58–71
   birth and early years 73–9
   rumours over his parentage 81–3
   early exposure to theatre and theatrical thought 86–94
   relationship with Gerhart Hauptmann 97–101
   relationship with Frank Wedekind 101–2
   relationship with Max Reinhardt 102–4
   relationship with Edward Gordon Craig 104–7
   getting to know Hofmannsthal 107–10
   recounts *L'Ingénu libertin* to Hofmannsthal 114–5
   introduces Hofmannsthal to Strauss 116
   the Kessler-Hofmannsthal relationship by 1909 122–35
   devising together the *Rosenkavalier* scenario 135–53
   Kessler's guiding theatrical vision for the scenario 160–1
   Kessler's vision of Ella Shields as Octavian 170–1
   long-distance collaboration between Kessler and Hofmannsthal 176–94
   quarrel with Hofmannsthal over dedication and authorship 195–201
   meeting with Bodenhausen in Paris and subsequent exchanges 201–5
   assessment of Kessler's role in authorship 206–7
   Kessler's theatrical input to *Der Rosenkavalier* 214–6
Kessler, Wilhelma Karoline Louis Alice, later Marquise de Brion 84, 86, 137, 190, 200
Kessler family addresses
   3 Rue de Luxembourg (later: Rue Cambon) 75
   89 Boulevard Malesherbes 75
   30 Cours la Reine 75, 77, 85
   19 Boulevard Montmorency 75, 85, **86**
   Sainte Honorine, Normandy 133, 185
Kinnersley, see Sneyd-Kynnersley H.W. 89
Kleist, Heinrich von 184
Klinger, Max 95
Koch, Sophie Plate 15
Koning, M. (director of *Le Gymnase*) 77

Laclos, Choderlos de 8

Lalande, Nérisaie de 85
Lamothe, Peter 33
Landolff (Maison Landolff), costumiers 22
Lavastre, Antoine 22
Lavastre, Jean-Baptiste 22
Lecocq, Charles 25, 27, 28, 30, 55
Lehár, Franz 30
Lehmann, Lilli 90
Lehmann, Lotte 172–3
Leroux, Emile 55
Leroux, Xavier 23, 54
Lesseps, Ferdinand de 76, 77
Levithan, Josh xii
Lhérie, Victor 14, **15**
Liebermann, Max 95, 96, 110
Liliencron, Detlev von 95
Loiseau-Roussea, Paul **24**
Lomagne, B. de 52
Loppert, Max **173**
Loris (pseudonym of Hugo von
 Hofmannsthal) 123
Lott, Felicity **187**
Louvet de Couvray, Jean-Baptiste 6, 7, 9,
 10, 12, 14, 19, 42–3, 44, 45, 152, 168,
 174
 triptych of Faublas novels 7
 characters in *Une Année* 8–12
 schematic of Louvet's narrative 49–50
Lugné-Poe, Aurélien 33
Luigini, Alexandre 18, 19
Luigini, Pauline 18
Lully, Jean-Baptiste 46, 161
Luynes, Jeanne d'Albert de, Comtesse de
 Verrue 179
Lynch of Galway 79–80
Lynch, Sir Henry 80
Lynch (later Blosse Lynch), Sir Robert 80
Lynch-Blosse baronetcy 80
Lynch Brothers (shipping company) 80

Maeterlinck, Maurice 106
Maillol, Aristide xii, 32, 96, 110
 ill-fated trip to Greece with Kessler and
  Hofmannsthal 131–2
Magnard, François 76, 77
Mancardi (silk merchants) 31
Manet, Edouard xii
Mann, Golo 83

Marivaux, Pierre 8, 52, 151
Marlowe, Christopher 129
Massenet, Jules 170
Maupassant, Guy de 85
Méhul, Etienne-Nicolas 91
Meier-Graefe, Julius 96
Mendès, Catulle 50
Mesmacker, Pierre 18
Messager, André 23, 27, 28, 30, 52, 169
Meyer, Milo de 22, **22**, 54, 57, **63**
Millot, Michel 7
Milton, John 104
Mirambeau, Christophe 58, **61**
Molière, Jean-Baptiste 4, 135, 137, 139, 140,
 161, 166, 167, 174, 184–5, 188
 Hofmannsthal mentions
  Pourceaugnac 135
 Monsieur de Pourceaugnac – similarities
  and differences 161–6
Monet, Claude xii
Montchénu-Lavirotte, Jane de **53**
Monzies, Louis **9, 10, 11, 16,**
Moreau, Philippe 22, 54, 55, 59, 215
Mors, Louis 41
Mozart, Wolfgang Amadeus 4, 31, 42, 91,
 92, 98, 115, 121, 143, 170, 171, 172
 Le Nozze di Figaro as prototype for *Der
  Rosenkavalier* 171–2, 174
Munch, Edvard xii, 96, 110, Plate 1, Plate 10
Music Schools
 Conservatoire de Lyon 18, 27, 31
 Conservatoire de Paris 54, 78, 83
 Ecole Niedermeyer 27, 30, 31
Musset, Alfred de 4, 152, 185

Nabis, Les (group of artists) 31–2
Nast, Minnie **187**
Natanson, Alexandre 32
Natanson, Thadée 32, 191
Newman, Lindsay 75
Nicolson, Sir Harold 4
Nietzsche, Friedrich 94, 95, 96
Nijinsky, Vaslav 46, 96, 100
Nostitz, Alfred von 91, 205
Nostitz, Helene von 122, 205
Novelli, Ernete 85
Nozière, Fernand (Weyl, Fernand) 39, 50,
 51, 54

Offenbach, Jacques 1, 18, 25, 27, 28, 29, 31, 37, 40, 55, 58, 82–3
Orlik, Emil Plate 9
Osten, Eva von der **187**
Otway, Thomas 105

Pahlen, Kurt 115
Pan, influential arts journal 98–9, 116, 123, 124, 201
Partry House, co. Mayo, home of the Blosse Lynch family 81
Pepys, Samuel 8
Petit, Jeanne 1, 54, Plate 6
Philip V, King of Spain 45
Piccini, Alexandre 17
Places mentioned in the text
   in England
      Ascot 88
      Belstead (Suffolk) 80
      London xii, 78, 89, 92, 93, 96, 103, 104, 113, 154, 177
   in France
      Aix en Provence 185
      Amiens 93
      Arbresle 31
      Arcachon 32, 33
      Arles 185
      Avignon 37, 185
      Cabourg 41
      Deauville 41
      Limoges 140, 162, 163
      Maisons Laffitte 50
      Marseille 185
      Paris xii, 1, 7, 18, 21, 27, 32, 36, 37, 38, 44, 56, 75, 78, 81, 83, 89, 92, 96, 105, 113, 116, 131, 133, 163, 168, 169, 186, 189, 191, 195, 201, 212, 214, 215
   in Germany
      Bad Ems 81, 82
      Bavaria 78
      Bayreuth 90, 91, 92
      Berlin xii, 74, 84, 89, 90, 91, 93, 95, 96, 99, 102, 105, 108, 113, 115, 116, 117, 123, 124, 125, 126, 129, 136, 137, 138, 147, 154, 155, 171, 176, 184, 193, 197, 204, 205, 207, 210, 211, 212
      Bonn 88, 94
      Cologne 91, 92
      Dresden x, 3, 23, 104, 118, 133, 154, 171, **187**, 191, 197, 200, 201
      Garmisch-Partenkirchen 210, 211
      Hamburg 75, 78, 88, 89, 91, 92, 95
      Leipzig 88, 90, 91, 92, 94, 95, 99
      Munich 92, 197, 205
      Naumburg 96
      Potsdam 91, 95, 195
      Weimar xii, 95, 96, 99, 104, 105, 107, 108, 109, 114, 115, 126, 129, 135, 136, 137, 138, 144, 145, 146, 154, 155, 184, 189, 197, 200, 202, 204, 205, 210, 212, 216
   Elsewhere
      Ballinrobe, co. Mayo, Ireland 80
      Budapest 194
      Delphi 132
      Linz 79
      Mallorca 96, 126, 141
      Milan 4, 58
      New York 78, 154
      Oslo (Christiana) 85
      Palestine 39
      Rodaun 137, 148, **175**, 207, 210
      Shanghai 92
      St Gallen 83
      St Maurice River 78
      St Petersburg 46
      Tokyo 92
      Vienna 161, 163, 164, **175**, 183, 194, 207
Planquette, Robert 27
Plon, Librairie (publishers) 81
Ponte, Lorenzo Da 115, 119, 121, 143, 171, 172, 212
Prévost, Abbé 151
Przybyszewski, Stanislaw 96, 97

Raphael 91
Rathenau, Walther 101
Reboux, Paul 50
Rees, Deborah **187**
Reinhardt, Max 95, 96, 100, 101, 105, 110, 130, 133, 136, 147, 189, 190, 197, 198
   relationship with Kessler 102–4
   as real director of *Der Rosenkavalier* 213–4
   aware of Kessler's role and status 214

Regnard, Jean-François 188
Renoir, Pierre-Auguste (Auguste) xii
Revue Blanche, La 32
Richardson, Samuel 71, 151, 152
Richemond, Jean 25, 38, 40, 41, 42, 57
Richepin, Jean 23
Richter, Hans 90
Richter, Giacomo Gustav ('Musch') 95, 103, 138
Rilke, Rainer Maria 96, 205
Ripon, Lady Constance Gladys xii
Rittner, Rudolf 99
Rodin, Auguste xii, 85, 96, 110
Roller, Alfred **112**, 147, 149, 198, Plate 3, Plate 11, Plate 12, Plate 13
Rose, Peter Plate 15
Rossini, Giacomo 46, 87
Rostand, Edmond 62
Rothe, Friedrich 74, 84
Rothenstein, Will 104, 110
Rousseau, Jean-Jacques 8, 27, 71, 150, 151, 152
Roussel, Ker-Xavier 32
Rubinstein, Ida 96

Sade, Marquis de 8
Salten, Felix **107**
Salvini, Tommaso 85
Samson, Charles 41
Sardou, Victorien 55, 118, 185
Sassoon, Siegfried xii
Schäfer, Wilhelm 116
Schalck, Franz 133
Scheerbart, Paul 116
Schiller, Friedrich 193
Schillings, Max von 118
Schlippenbach, Sascha 95
Schloss Neubeuern (Bavaria, Germany) 201
Schneider, Hortense ('La Sneyder') 82–3
Schnitzler, Arthur 196
Schröder, Rudolf Alexander 103, 195, 196
Schuh, Willi 116, 144, 145, 161
   discovers what he believes to be the original scenario for *Der Rosenkavalier* 140–1
Schuster, Jörg 145, 174
Schwabach, Paul Hermann von 129
Scott, Sir Walter 88

Scribe, Eugène 16, 212
Seebach, Count 198
Serusier, Paul 32
Seurat, Georges xii
Shakespeare, William 4, 88, 93, 99, 101, 103, 147, 152, 157, 172, 184
Shaw, George Bernard xii, 101
Sherard, Robert Harborough 77
Sheridan, Richard Brinsley 162
Shields, Ella 170–1, **171**
Siems, Margarethe **187**
Silvestre, Victor 41
Simon, Heinrich (publisher) 81
Simon, Joseph-Philippe ('Lockroy') 17
Sitwell, Osbert xii
Sneyd-Kynnersley, the Rev. and Mrs W.H. 89
Sophocles 117, 120
Springer, Anton 94
St Denis, Ruth 99, 100
Stenzel, Burkhard 74, 97, 200
Stoullig, Edmond 18, 39
Stern, Charles 149
Strauss, Johann 27
Strauss, Pauline 116, 133, 197, 211
Strauss, Richard x, xii, 2, **2**, 3, 4, 12, 21, 23, 42, 49, 56, 67, 71, 96, 99, 113, 114, **120**, 122, 126, 131, 133, 135, 136, 137, 138, 144, 145, 149, 154, **155**, 156, 158, 159, 162, 169, 171, 176, 177, 180, 185, 186, 188, 189, 195, 196, 197, 198, 201, 202, 203, 205, 206, 207, **209**, 214, **215**, 216
   early relationship with Hofmannsthal 115–7
   presses Hofmannsthal to write comedy 117–8
   difficulties with *Elektra* 118–9
   first news of *Der Rosenkavalier* idea 121
   fading finale to *Der Rosenkavalier* as envisaged by Kessler 146–7
   requirements for the ideal Marschallin 173
   Strauss-Hofmannsthal and Kessler-Hofmannsthal correspondence compared 181–2
   Compositional process and timelines for *Der Rosenkavalier* 209–13

Strindberg, August 97
Sucher, Rosa 90
Sutherland, Millicent Duchess of xii

Taillefer (*Théâtre Cluny*) 18
Taylor, Caroline Anne 80
Taylor, Harriet 80
Taylor, Colonel Robert 80
Taylor, Rose 80
Teniers, David the Younger 162
Terrasse, Andrée (née Bonnard) 31, 32, **32**, 33, Plate 5
Terrasse, Claude 1, **5**, 12, 18, 19, 24, 25, **26**, **28**, **32**, 33, 34, **35**, **36**, 41, 49, 51, 52, 54, 55, **56**, 136, 137, 186, 215, 216, Plate 4, Plate 5
   popular success with *L'Ingénu libertin* 21–3
   who was Claude Terrasse? 27–31
   meets Bonnard and joins the Nabis 31–2
   succès de scandale with Jarry's *Ubu roi* 33–4
   popular and commercial success with de Flers and de Caillavet 35–8
   scoring and musical treatment of *L'Ingénu libertin* 59–71
Terry, Ellen 104
Theatres and Opera Houses
   Theatres and Opera Houses in England (London)
     Garrick Theatre 103
     Her Majesty's Theatre, Haymarket 147
     Imperial Theatre 104
     London Palladium 170
     Savoy Theatre 89
     Strand Theatre 89
   Theatres and Opera Houses in France (Paris)
     Comédie Française 92
     Opéra Comique 18, 23, 52, 92, 169, 170, 191
     Opéra Nationale de Paris 39, 41, 92, 154
     Théâtre Apollo 191
     Théâtre de l'Athenée 38, 184
     Théâtre des Bouffes Parisiens 1, 21, 23, **24**, 25, **26**, 27, 35, 38, 39, **40**, 41, 42, 47, 50, 55, 57, 58, **59**, **60**, 83, 89, 92, 113, 142, 146, 176, 178, 202, 215
     Théâtre du Chatelet 23, 92
     Théâtre Cluny 18, 19, 38
     Théâtre de la Gaîté 23
     Théâtre du Gymnase 14, 76, 191
     Théâtre des Mathurins 35
     Théâtre de Monsieur 13
     Théâtre de l'Odéon 92
     Théâtre de l'Oeuvre 28, 33
     Théâtre du Palais Royal 38
     Théâtre des Pantins 35
     Théâtre de la Porte St Martin 17, 23
     Théâtre des Variétés 22, 36
     Théâtre du Vaudeville 14, 38
   Theatres and Opera Houses in France (elsewhere)
     Grand Théâtre de Lyon 31
     Opéra de Monte Carlo 154, 170
   Theatres and Opera Houses in Germany (Berlin)
     Berliner Theater 92
     Deutsches Theater 92, 98, 102, 103, 117, 123
     Freie Bühne 92, 97, 123
     Kleines Theater 102
     Kroll Opera 92
     Lessing Theater 92
     Neues Theater 92, 102
     Opera 92, 169
   Theatres and Opera Houses elsewhere
     Metropolitan Opera, New York 92
     Musikfesthalle, Munich 197
     Theater an der Wien, Vienna 194
Toller, Georg 104
Töpfers Hotel (Berlin) 118
Toulouse-Lautrec, Henri de 32
Tuileries Palace (Paris) 13

Universal (France) 58, **61**

Valloton, Félix 32
Vanbrugh, John 162
Varney, Louis 27
Velde, Henri van de xii, 102, 127, 205

Verdi, Guiseppe 42, 87, 115, 162
Vogel, Juliane 51
Vollard, Ambroise 26
Vuillard, Edouard 32

Wagner, Cosima 169
Wagner, Richard 89, 91, 92, 98, 106, 121, 130, 178, 180, 193
Watteau, Jean-Antoine 62
Wedekind, Frank 100
   Relationship with Kessler 101–2
Wendelstadt, Julie von 201
Wilde, Oscar 77, 101

Wilhelm I, King of Prussia, later Emperor of Germany 81, 83, 84, **84**
Wilhelm Ernst, Grand-Duke of Weimar 95, 99, 109
Wille, Bruno 97
Willemain d'Abancourt, François-Jean (Léonard Gobemouche) 13
Wundt, Wilhelm 94

Yacco, Sada 106
Yakar, Rachel **187**

Zacconi, Ermete 99

www.ingramcontent.com/pod-product-compliance
Lightning Source LLC
Chambersburg PA
CBHW051608230426
43668CB00013B/2028